Math 54

An Incremental Development

Second Edition

Math 54

An Incremental Development

Second Edition

Stephen Hake

John Saxon

Saxon Publishers, Inc.

Math 54: An Incremental Development
Second Edition

Copyright 2001 by Stephen Hake and John Saxon

Printed in the United States of America.

ISBN: 1-56577-033-1

Production Supervisor: David Pond

Production Coordinator: Joan Coleman

Graphic Artists: Matthew Arrington,
John Chitwood, Roger Hall, and
Timothy Maltz

Manufacturing Code: 08S0600

Printed on recycled paper.

Reaching us via the Internet

WWW: http://www.saxonpub.com

E-mail: info@saxonpub.com

Saxon Publishers, Inc.
2450 John Saxon Blvd.
Norman, OK 73071

Contents

Preface

To The Student

We study mathematics because it is an important part of our daily lives. Our school schedule, our trip to the store, the preparation of our meals, and many of the games we play all involve mathematics. Most of the word problems you will see in this book are drawn from our daily experiences.

Mathematics is even more important in the adult world. In fact, your personal future in the adult world may depend in part upon the mathematics you have learned. This book was written with the hope that more students will learn mathematics and learn it well. For this to happen, you must use this book properly. As you work through the pages of this book, you will find similar problems presented over and over again. **Solving these problems day after day is the secret to success.**

Each lesson begins with practice of basic number facts and mental math. These exercises will improve your speed, your accuracy, and your ability to do math "in your head." The accompanying pattern and problem-solving activities will give you practice using strategies that can help you solve more complicated problems. Near the end of the lesson is a set of practice problems that focus on the topic of the lesson. Following each lesson is a problem set that reviews the skills you are learning day by day. **Work every problem in every practice set and in every problem set. Do not skip problems. With honest effort you will experience success and true learning which will stay with you and serve you well in the future.**

Acknowledgments

We thank Shirley McQuade Davis for her ideas on teaching word problem thinking patterns.

Stephen Hake
Temple City, California

John Saxon
Norman, Oklahoma

Review of Addition •
Missing Addends, Part 1

Review of addition

When we count the dots on the top faces of a pair of number cubes (dice), we are adding. Addition is combining two groups into one group.

$$4 \quad + \quad 3 \quad = \quad 7$$

The numbers that are added are called **addends**. The answer is called the **sum**. The expression $4 + 3 = 7$ is a **number sentence**. A number sentence is a complete sentence that uses numbers and symbols instead of words. Here we show two ways to add 4 and 3.

4	addend	3	addend
+ 3	addend	+ 4	addend
7	sum	7	sum

Notice that if the order of the addends is changed, the sum remains the same. This is true for any two numbers. **When we add two numbers, either number may be first.**

$$4 + 3 = 7 \qquad 3 + 4 = 7$$

---

†For instructions on how to use the boxed activities, please consult the preface.

When adding three numbers, the numbers may be added in any order. Here we show six ways to add 4, 3, and 5. Each way the answer is 12.

$$
\begin{array}{cccccc}
4 & 4 & 3 & 3 & 5 & 5 \\
3 & 5 & 4 & 5 & 4 & 3 \\
+\ 5 & +\ 3 & +\ 5 & +\ 4 & +\ 3 & +\ 4 \\
\hline
12 & 12 & 12 & 12 & 12 & 12
\end{array}
$$

When we add zero to a number, the number is not changed.

$$4 + 0 = 4 \qquad 9 + 0 = 9 \qquad 0 + 7 = 7$$

Missing addends, part 1   If we know the sum and one addend, we can figure out the missing addend. Can you figure out the missing addend in this number sentence?

$$2 \quad + \quad ? \quad = \quad 7$$

Since we know that $2 + 5 = 7$, the missing addend is 5. Some of the problems in this book will have an addend missing. We will use a letter to represent the missing number. When an addend is missing and the sum is given, the problem is to find the missing addend.

Example   (a)
$$
\begin{array}{r}
4 \\
+\ N \\
\hline
7
\end{array}
$$

(b) $B + 6 = 10$

(c) Write a number sentence for this picture.

Solution   (a) The letter N stands for a missing addend. Since $4 + 3 = 7$, the letter N stands for the number **3**.

(b) This time the letter B is used to stand for the missing addend. Since $4 + 6 = 10$, the letter B stands for the number **4**.

(c) A number sentence for the picture is **$4 + 5 = 9$**. The number sentence **$5 + 4 = 9$** is also correct.

Practice Add:

    a. 5 + 6   **b.** 6 + 5   **c.** 8 + 0

    d. 4 + 8 + 6   **e.** 4 + 5 + 6

    Find the missing addend:

    f. $7 + N = 10$ **g.** $A + 8 = 12$

Problem set 1 Find either the sum or the missing addend:

1. $\begin{array}{r} 5 \\ + 7 \\ \hline \end{array}$	**2.** $\begin{array}{r} 6 \\ + 3 \\ \hline \end{array}$	**3.** $\begin{array}{r} 9 \\ + 4 \\ \hline \end{array}$	**4.** $\begin{array}{r} 8 \\ + 2 \\ \hline \end{array}$
5. $\begin{array}{r} 4 \\ + N \\ \hline 11 \end{array}$	**6.** $\begin{array}{r} W \\ + 5 \\ \hline 8 \end{array}$	**7.** $\begin{array}{r} 6 \\ + P \\ \hline 15 \end{array}$	**8.** $\begin{array}{r} Q \\ + 8 \\ \hline 8 \end{array}$

9. 3 + 4 + 5   **10.** 4 + 4 + 4

11. $6 + R = 10$ **12.** $X + 5 = 6$

13. $\begin{array}{r} 5 \\ 5 \\ + 5 \\ \hline \end{array}$	**14.** $\begin{array}{r} 8 \\ 0 \\ + 7 \\ \hline \end{array}$	**15.** $\begin{array}{r} 6 \\ 5 \\ + 4 \\ \hline \end{array}$	**16.** $\begin{array}{r} 9 \\ 9 \\ + 9 \\ \hline \end{array}$
17. $\begin{array}{r} M \\ + 9 \\ \hline 10 \end{array}$	**18.** $\begin{array}{r} 9 \\ + F \\ \hline 12 \end{array}$	**19.** $\begin{array}{r} Z \\ + 5 \\ \hline 12 \end{array}$	**20.** $\begin{array}{r} 0 \\ + N \\ \hline 3 \end{array}$

21. 3 + 2 + 5 + 4 + 6

22. 2 + 2 + 2 + 2 + 2 + 2 + 2

Write a number sentence for each picture:

23.   **24.**

25. Show six ways to add 2, 3, and 4.

LESSON 2

Missing Addends, Part 2

Facts Practice: 100 Addition Facts (Test A in Test Masters)

Mental Math: Add ten to a number.

   a. 40 + 10   **b.** 26 + 10   **c.** 39 + 10
   d. 7 + 10   **e.** 10 + 9   **f.** 10 + 63

Patterns: Have the class count by fives from 5 to 100 while the teacher or a student lists the numbers on the board. Which digits appear as final digits? Which numbers in the list are numbers we say when we count by twos from 2 to 100?

Derek rolled a number cube three times. This picture shows the top face of the cube after the first two rolls.

The total number of dots on all three rolls was 12. Can you draw a picture of Derek's third roll?

We will write a number sentence for this problem. The first two numbers are 5 and 3. We do not know the number of the third roll, so we will use a letter. We know that the total is 12.

$$5 + 3 + T = 12$$

To find the missing addend, we first add 5 and 3, which is 8. Then we think, "Eight plus what number equals twelve?" Since 8 plus 4 equals 12, the third roll was ⬚.

Example   Find the missing number:

(a)   6
         N
      + 5
      ⎯⎯⎯
        17

(b) 4 + 3 + 2 + B + 6 = 20

Solution   (a) We add 6 and 5, which makes 11. We think, "Eleven plus what number equals seventeen?" Since 11 plus 6 equals 17, the missing number is **6.**

(b) First we add 4, 3, 2, and 6, which equals 15. Since 15 plus 5 is 20, the missing number is **5.**

Practice   Find the missing number:

a. $8 + A + 2 = 17$ **b.** $B + 6 + 5 = 12$

c. $4 + C + 2 + 3 + 5 = 20$

Problem set 2   Find either the sum or the missing addend:

†1. (1)
$$\begin{array}{r} 5 \\ + 6 \\ \hline \end{array}$$

2. (1)
$$\begin{array}{r} 4 \\ + 7 \\ \hline \end{array}$$

3. (1)
$$\begin{array}{r} 9 \\ + N \\ \hline 13 \end{array}$$

4. (1)
$$\begin{array}{r} 7 \\ + 8 \\ \hline \end{array}$$

5. (1)
$$\begin{array}{r} P \\ + 6 \\ \hline 13 \end{array}$$

6. (2)
$$\begin{array}{r} 5 \\ 2 \\ + W \\ \hline 12 \end{array}$$

7. (1)
$$\begin{array}{r} 4 \\ 8 \\ + 5 \\ \hline \end{array}$$

8. (1)
$$\begin{array}{r} 9 \\ 3 \\ + 7 \\ \hline \end{array}$$

9. (2)
$$\begin{array}{r} 8 \\ B \\ + 3 \\ \hline 16 \end{array}$$

10. (1)
$$\begin{array}{r} 9 \\ 7 \\ + 3 \\ \hline \end{array}$$

11. (1)
$$\begin{array}{r} 2 \\ 9 \\ + 6 \\ \hline \end{array}$$

12. (1)
$$\begin{array}{r} 3 \\ 8 \\ + 2 \\ \hline \end{array}$$

13. (1)
$$\begin{array}{r} 9 \\ 5 \\ + 3 \\ \hline \end{array}$$

14. (2)
$$\begin{array}{r} 2 \\ M \\ + 4 \\ \hline 9 \end{array}$$

15. (2)
$$\begin{array}{r} 5 \\ 3 \\ + Q \\ \hline 9 \end{array}$$

16. (2)
$$\begin{array}{r} 2 \\ 3 \\ + R \\ \hline 7 \end{array}$$

17. (2)
$$\begin{array}{r} 5 \\ 3 \\ + T \\ \hline 10 \end{array}$$

18. (1)
$$\begin{array}{r} 8 \\ 4 \\ + 6 \\ \hline \end{array}$$

19. (2)
$$\begin{array}{r} 2 \\ X \\ + 7 \\ \hline 11 \end{array}$$

20. (1)
$$\begin{array}{r} 5 \\ 2 \\ + 6 \\ \hline \end{array}$$

21. (2) $5 + 8 + 2 + 7 + X + 3 = 30$

22. (2) $9 + 3 + 11 + 2 + 1 + N + 4 = 38$

---

†The italicized numbers within parentheses underneath each problem number are called *lesson reference numbers*. These numbers refer to the lesson(s) in which the major concept of that particular problem is introduced. If additional assistance is needed, reference should be made to the discussion, examples, practice, or problem set of that lesson.

Write a number sentence for each picture:

23.
(1)

24.
(1)

25.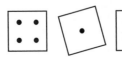
(1)

LESSON
3

Sequences

Facts Practice: 100 Addition Facts (Test A in Test Masters)

Mental Math: Add ten, twenty, or thirty to a number.

a.	20	**b.**	23	**c.**	43	**d.**	24	**e.**	50	**f.**	10
	+ 20		+ 20		+ 10		+ 30		+ 30		+ 65

g. One less than 24 is 23. What number is one less than 36? one less than 43? one less than 65?

Vocabulary: Copy these two patterns on a piece of paper. In each of the six boxes write either "addend" or "sum."

Counting is a math skill we learn early in life. Counting by ones, we say "One, two, three, four, five, …."

$$1, 2, 3, 4, 5, …$$

These numbers are called **counting numbers.** The counting numbers continue without end. We often count by a number other than one.

Counting by twos: 2, 4, 6, 8, 10, …

Counting by fives: 5, 10, 15, 20, 25, …

These are examples of counting patterns. A counting pattern is a **sequence.** The three dots mean that the sequence continues without end. A counting sequence may count up or count down. We may study a sequence to discover a rule for the sequence. Then we can find more numbers in the sequence.

Example 1 Find the next three numbers in this sequence:

10, 20, 30, 40, _____, _____, _____, ...

Solution The pattern is "Count up by tens." Counting this way, we find that the next three numbers are **50, 60,** and **70.**

Example 2 Find the missing number in this sequence:

30, 27, 24, 21, _____, 15, ...

Solution It looks like the rule is "Count down by threes." If we count down three from 21, we find that the next number in the sequence is **18.** We see that 15 is three less than 18, so 18 fits the pattern.

Practice Write the next three numbers in each sequence:

a. 10, 9, 8, 7, _____, _____, _____, ...

b. 3, 6, 9, 12, _____, _____, _____, ...

Find the missing number in each sequence:

c. 80, 70, _____, 50, ...   **d.** 8, _____, 16, 20, 24, ...

Problem set 3 Find either the sum or the missing addend:

1.
(1)
$$\begin{array}{r} 9 \\ 5 \\ 3 \\ + 9 \\ \hline \end{array}$$

2.
(1)
$$\begin{array}{r} 4 \\ 2 \\ 4 \\ + 5 \\ \hline \end{array}$$

3.
(1)
$$\begin{array}{r} 9 \\ 1 \\ 2 \\ + 7 \\ \hline \end{array}$$

4.
(2)
$$\begin{array}{r} 8 \\ 3 \\ + N \\ \hline 15 \end{array}$$

5.
(2)
$$\begin{array}{r} 5 \\ M \\ + 4 \\ \hline 12 \end{array}$$

6.
(2)
$$\begin{array}{r} 8 \\ 2 \\ + W \\ \hline 16 \end{array}$$

Write the next number in each sequence:

7. 10, 20, 30, _____, …
(3)

8. 22, 21, 20, _____, …
(3)

9. 40, 35, 30, 25, _____, …
(3)

10. 70, 80, 90, _____, …
(3)

Write the next three numbers in each sequence:

11. 6, 12, 18, _____, _____, _____, …
(3)

12. 3, 6, 9, _____, _____, _____, …
(3)

13. 4, 8, 12, _____, _____, _____, …
(3)

14. 45, 36, 27, _____, _____, _____, …
(3)

Find the missing number in each sequence:

15. 8, 12, _____, 20, …
(3)

16. 12, 18, _____, 30, …
(3)

17. 30, 25, _____, 15, …
(3)

18. 6, 9, _____, 15, …
(3)

19. How many small rectangles are
(3) shown? Count by twos.

20. How many X's are shown? Count
(3) by fours.

```
XX  XX  XX
XX  XX  XX

XX  XX  XX
XX  XX  XX
```

21. Write a number sentence for this picture.
(1)

22. (1)	**23.** (1)	**24.** (1)	**25.** (1)
4	9	8	2
8	5	4	9
7	7	7	7
5	8	2	5
+ 2	+ 3	+ 3	+ 4

LESSON 4

Digits

To write numbers we use digits. **Digits are the numerals 0, 1, 2, 3, 4, 5, 6, 7, 8, and 9.** The number 356 has three digits, and the last digit is 6. The number 67,896,094 has eight digits, and the last digit is 4.

Example 1 The number 64,000 has how many digits?

Solution The number 64,000 has **five digits.**

Example 2 What is the last digit of 2001?

Solution The last digit of 2001 is **1.**

Practice How many digits are in each number?

    a. 18   **b.** 5280   **c.** 8,403,227,189

What is the last digit in each number?

    d. 19   **e.** 5281   **f.** 8,403,190

Problem set 4

Write the next three numbers in each sequence:

1. 5, 10, 15, 20, _____, _____, _____, …
(3)

2. 7, 14, 21, 28, _____, _____, _____, …
(3)

3. 8, 16, 24, 32, _____, _____, _____, …
(3)

4. 4, 8, 12, 16, _____, _____, _____, …
(3)

Find the missing number in each sequence:

5. 90, _____, 70, 60, …
(3)

6. 10, 8, _____, 4, …
(3)

7. 6, _____, 12, 15, …
(3)

8. 50, 45, _____, 35, …
(3)

9. 45, 54, _____, 72, …
(3)

10. 16, _____, 32, 40, …
(3)

11. How many digits are in each number?
(4)
  (a) 593   (b) 180   (c) 186,527,394

12. What is the last digit in each number?
(4)
  (a) 3427   (b) 460   (c) 437,269

Find either the sum or the missing addend:

13.   4   **14.**   9   **15.**   7   **16.**   8   **17.**   9
(1)   3   (1)   3   (2) N (2) A (2)   8
        + 5   + 8   + 6   + 7   + D
        ___   ___   ____   ____   ____
                                          15   19   19

18. Write a number sentence for this
(1)   picture.

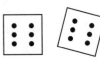

19. How many cents are in 4 nickels?
(3)   Count by fives.

5¢   5¢

5¢   5¢

20. How many X's are in this pattern? Count by threes.
(3)

X X X X X X X X X X
X X X X X X X X X X
X X X X X X X X X X

21. (1)	**22.** (1)	**23.** (1)	**24.** (1)
2	5	9	8
7	2	8	7
3	3	7	2
5	8	4	5
+ 4	+ 2	+ 3	+ 7

25. $5 + 4 + 3 + 2 + 1 + N = 20$
(2)

LESSON 5

Place Value

Facts Practice: 100 Addition Facts (Test A in Test Masters)

Mental Math: Add a number ending in zero to another number.

a.	**b.**	**c.**	**d.**	**e.**
24	36	50	33	40
+ 60	+ 10	+ 42	+ 30	+ 50

f. What number is one less than 28? 87? 54?

Patterns: Copy this design of ten circles on your paper. In each circle, write a counting number from 1 to 10 that continues the pattern (1, skip, skip, 2, skip, skip, 3, ...).

To help us with the idea of place value, we will use pictures to show different amounts of money. We will use $100 bills, $10 bills, and $1 bills.

Example 1   How much money is shown by this diagram?

Solution   Since there are 2 hundreds, 4 tens, and 3 ones, the amount of money shown is **$243.**

Example 2   Use play money or draw a diagram to show how to make $324 using $100 bills, $10 bills, and $1 bills.

Solution   To show $324, we draw 3 hundreds, 2 tens, and 4 ones.

3 hundreds   2 tens   4 ones

Places are named by the value of the place. Three-digit numbers like 324 occupy three different places.

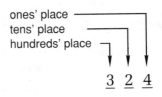

ones' place
tens' place
hundreds' place

3 2 4

Example 3   The digit 7 is in what place in 753?

Solution   The 7 is in the third place from the right, which shows the number of hundreds. So the 7 is in the **hundreds' place.**

Practice   a. Use play money or draw a diagram to show $231 using $100 bills, $10 bills, and $1 bills.

b. The digit 6 is in what place in each of these numbers?
(1) 16   (2) 65   (3) 623

c. Use three digits to write a number equal to 5 hundreds, 2 tens, and 3 ones.

Problem set 5 Find either the sum or the missing addend:

1.
(1)
$$\begin{array}{r} 4 \\ + N \\ \hline 12 \end{array}$$

2.
(1)
$$\begin{array}{r} 4 \\ 5 \\ + 3 \\ \hline \end{array}$$

3.
(1)
$$\begin{array}{r} 13 \\ + Y \\ \hline 19 \end{array}$$

4.
(1)
$$\begin{array}{r} 7 \\ + S \\ \hline 14 \end{array}$$

5.
(2)
$$\begin{array}{r} 3 \\ N \\ + 2 \\ \hline 11 \end{array}$$

6.
(2)
$$\begin{array}{r} 1 \\ M \\ + 5 \\ \hline 10 \end{array}$$

7.
(2)
$$\begin{array}{r} D \\ 2 \\ + 7 \\ \hline 18 \end{array}$$

8.
(2)
$$\begin{array}{r} 3 \\ N \\ + 2 \\ \hline 9 \end{array}$$

9. $4 + N + 5 = 12$
(2)

10. $N + 2 + 3 = 8$
(2)

Write the next three numbers in each sequence:

11. 9, 12, 15, _____, _____, _____, ...
(3)

12. 30, 24, 18, _____, _____, _____, ...
(3)

13. 12, 16, 20, _____, _____, _____, ...
(3)

14. 35, 28, 21, _____, _____, _____, ...
(3)

15. How many digits are in each number?
(4)
    (a) 37,432   (b) 5,934,286   (c) 453,000

16. What is the last digit in each number?
(4)
    (a) 734   (b) 347   (c) 473

17. Draw a picture to show $342.
(5)

18. How much money is shown by this picture?
(5)

Find the missing number in each sequence:

19. 24, _____, 36, 42, ...
(3)

20. 36, 32, _____, 24, ...
(3)

21. How many ears are on 10 rabbits? Count by twos.
(3)

22. The digit 6 is in what place in 365?
(5)

23. Write a number sentence for this
(1)   picture.

Find the missing addend:

24. $2 + 5 + 3 + 2 + 3 + 1 + N = 20$
(2)

25. $4 + B + 3 + 2 + 5 + 4 + 1 = 25$
(2)

LESSON 6

Ordinal Numbers • Months of the Year

Facts Practice: 100 Addition Facts (Test A in Test Masters)

Mental Math: Nine is one less than ten. When adding 9 to a number, we may mentally add 10 and then think of the number that is one less than that number. For 23 + 9 we may think: 23 + 10 is 33, and one less than 33 is 32.

a. 33	**b.** 33	**c.** 46	**d.** 46	**e.** 65	**f.** 65
+ 10	+ 9	+ 10	+ 9	+ 10	+ 9

Problem Solving: Tom has a total of ten coins in his left and right pockets. He has **some coins** (at least two) in each pocket. Make a table that lists the possible number of coins in each pocket.

Ordinal numbers If we count the number of children in a line, we say, "One, two, three, four, …." These numbers tell us how many children we have counted. To tell our place in a line, we use words like *first*, *second*, *third*, and *fourth*. Numbers that tell position or order are called **ordinal numbers.**

Example 1 There are ten children in the lunch line. John is fourth in line. How many children are in front of John? How many children are behind him?

Solution   A diagram may help us understand the problem. We begin by drawing a diagram and labeling the information given to us.

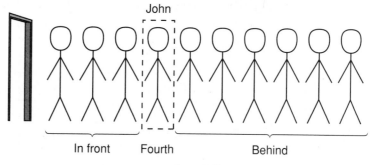

Lunch line

Since John is fourth in line, we see that there are **three children in front of him.** The rest of the children are behind John. From the diagram, we see that there are **six children behind him.**

Many times ordinal numbers are abbreviated. The abbreviation consists of a counting number and the letters *st*, *nd*, *rd*, or *th*. Here we show some abbreviations.

first	1st	sixth	6th	eleventh	11th
second	2nd	seventh	7th	twelfth	12th
third	3rd	eighth	8th	thirteenth	13th
fourth	4th	ninth	9th	twentieth	20th
fifth	5th	tenth	10th	twenty-first	21st

Example 2   Andy is 13th in line. Carl is 3rd in line. How many students are between Carl and Andy?

Solution   Begin by drawing a diagram.

From the diagram we see that there are **nine students between Carl and Andy.**

Months of the year We use ordinal numbers to name the months of the year and the days of each month. This table lists the twelve months of the year in order. A common year is 365 days long. A leap year is 366 days long. The extra day in a leap year is added to February.

ORDER	MONTH	DAYS
First	January	31
Second	February	28 or 29
Third	March	31
Fourth	April	30
Fifth	May	31
Sixth	June	30
Seventh	July	31
Eighth	August	31
Ninth	September	30
Tenth	October	31
Eleventh	November	30
Twelfth	December	31

Robert was born on the second day of June in 1988. Robert writes his birth date in month/day/year form this way.

6/2/1988

The "6" stands for the sixth month, which is June.

Example 3 Jenny wrote her birth date as 7/8/89. (a) In what month was Jenny born? (b) In what year was she born?

Solution (a) In the United States we usually write the number of the month first. The first number Jenny wrote was 7. She was born in the seventh month, which is **July.**

(b) Years are often abbreviated using only the last two digits of the year, when confusion is unlikely. We assume that Jenny was born in **1989.**

Practice a. John was third in line and Tom was eighth. How many people were between them?

b. Write your birth date in month/day/year form.

Problem set Find the missing addend:

6

1. 2   **2.** 1   **3.** 3   **4.** 1
(2)   6   (2)   Y   (2)   Z   (2)   N
    + X   + 7   + 5   + 6
    15   14   12   13

5. 2   **6.** 2   **7.** R   **8.** 3
(2)   5   (1)   + A   (1)   + 5   (1)   + T
    + W   7   11   5
    10

9. 2 + N + 3 + 7 = 16
(2)

10. What month is the eighth month of the year?
(6)

Write the next three numbers in each sequence:

11. 12, 15, 18, _____, _____, _____, ...
(3)

12. 16, 20, 24, _____, _____, _____, ...
(3)

13. 28, 35, 42, _____, _____, _____, ...
(3)

Find the missing number in each sequence:

14. 30, _____, 42, 48   **15.** 30, _____, 40, 45
(3)   (3)

16. Draw a picture to show $432.
(5)

17. Write a number sentence for this picture.
(1)

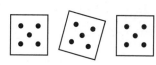

18. The digit 8 is in what place in 845?
(5)

19. Use three digits to write the number that equals 2
(5)   hundreds plus 3 tens plus 5 ones.

20. If the pattern is continued, what will be the next
(3)   number circled?

1, 2, ③, 4, 5, ⑥, 7, 8, ⑨, 10, ...

21. Seven boys have how many elbows? Count by twos.
(3)

22. (1)	**23.** (1)	**24.** (1)	**25.** (1)
5	5	9	8
8	7	7	7
4	3	6	3
7	8	5	5
4	4	4	4
+ 3	+ 2	+ 2	+ 9

LESSON 7

Review of Subtraction • Fact Families

Facts Practice: 100 Addition Facts (Test A in Test Masters)

Mental Math: Add one less than ten to a number.

   a. 28 + 9   **b.** 44 + 9   **c.** 87 + 9

Review:

   d. 63 + 20   **e.** 46 + 50   **f.** 38 + 30

Patterns: The months of the year repeat. Twelve months after January is January of the next year. Twenty-four months after January is January again. What month is twenty-five months after January? On Valentine's Day, Nathan's sister was 22 months old. In what month was Nathan's sister born?

Review of subtraction

We remember that when we add, we combine two groups into one group.

4   +   2   =   6

When we subtract, we separate a group into two groups. To take away two from six, we subtract.

6   −   2   =   4

When we subtract one number from another number, the answer is called the **difference.** If we subtract two from six, the difference is four.

$$
\begin{array}{r}
6 \\
-\ 2 \\
\hline
4
\end{array}\ \text{difference}
$$

We can check a subtraction problem by adding the two bottom numbers. **The sum of the two bottom numbers must equal the top number.** A good habit to develop is to "subtract down" to find the answer; then "add up" to check the answer.

SUBTRACT DOWN:		ADD UP:
Six minus two equals four.	$\begin{array}{r} 6 \\ -\ 2 \\ \hline 4 \end{array}$	Four plus two equals six.

In the practice and problem sets for the rest of the book, all subtraction problems should be checked by adding.

Fact families The three numbers 2, 4, and 6 form an addition and subtraction fact family. A *fact family* is a group of three numbers that may be arranged to form four facts.

$$
\begin{array}{cccc}
2 & 4 & 6 & 6 \\
+\ 4 & +\ 2 & -\ 2 & -\ 4 \\
\hline
6 & 6 & 4 & 2
\end{array}
$$

Recognizing addition and subtraction fact families can help us learn the facts.

Example The numbers 3, 5, and 8 are an addition and subtraction fact family. Write two addition facts and two subtraction facts using these three numbers.

Solution
$$
\begin{array}{cccc}
\mathbf{3} & \mathbf{5} & \mathbf{8} & \mathbf{8} \\
+\ \mathbf{5} & +\ \mathbf{3} & -\ \mathbf{3} & -\ \mathbf{5} \\
\hline
\mathbf{8} & \mathbf{8} & \mathbf{5} & \mathbf{3}
\end{array}
$$

Practice Subtract. Check by "adding up."

a.	**b.**	**c.**	**d.**	**e.**
$\begin{array}{r} 14 \\ -\ 8 \\ \hline \end{array}$	$\begin{array}{r} 9 \\ -\ 3 \\ \hline \end{array}$	$\begin{array}{r} 15 \\ -\ 7 \\ \hline \end{array}$	$\begin{array}{r} 11 \\ -\ 4 \\ \hline \end{array}$	$\begin{array}{r} 12 \\ -\ 5 \\ \hline \end{array}$

f. The numbers 5, 6, and 11 form a fact family. Write two addition facts and two subtraction facts using these three numbers.

Problem set

7

1.
(7)
$$\begin{array}{r} 14 \\ - \ 5 \\ \hline \end{array}$$

2.
(7)
$$\begin{array}{r} 15 \\ - \ 8 \\ \hline \end{array}$$

3.
(7)
$$\begin{array}{r} 9 \\ - \ 4 \\ \hline \end{array}$$

4.
(7)
$$\begin{array}{r} 11 \\ - \ 7 \\ \hline \end{array}$$

5.
(7)
$$\begin{array}{r} 12 \\ - \ 8 \\ \hline \end{array}$$

6.
(7)
$$\begin{array}{r} 11 \\ - \ 6 \\ \hline \end{array}$$

7.
(7)
$$\begin{array}{r} 15 \\ - \ 7 \\ \hline \end{array}$$

8.
(7)
$$\begin{array}{r} 9 \\ - \ 6 \\ \hline \end{array}$$

9.
(7)
$$\begin{array}{r} 13 \\ - \ 5 \\ \hline \end{array}$$

10.
(7)
$$\begin{array}{r} 12 \\ - \ 6 \\ \hline \end{array}$$

11.
(1)
$$\begin{array}{r} 8 \\ + \ N \\ \hline 17 \end{array}$$

12.
(1)
$$\begin{array}{r} A \\ + \ 8 \\ \hline 14 \end{array}$$

13. $3 + W = 11$
(1)

14. $1 + 4 + M = 13$
(2)

15. The numbers 4, 6, and 10 are a fact family. Write two
(7) addition facts and two subtraction facts using these three numbers.

Write the next three numbers in each sequence:

16. 16, 18, 20, _____, _____, _____, ⋯
(3)

17. 21, 28, 35, _____, _____, _____, ⋯
(3)

18. 20, 24, 28, _____, _____, _____, ⋯
(3)

19. How many days are in the tenth month of the year?
(6)

20. Draw a picture to show $326.
(5)

21. The digit 6 is in what place in 456?
(5)

Find the missing addend:

22. $2 + N + 4 = 13$
(2)

23. $A + 3 + 5 = 16$
(2)

24. $4 + 7 + 8 + 6 + 4 + W = 30$
(2)

25. $1 + 2 + 3 + M + 5 + 6 = 20$
(2)

**LESSON
8**

Writing Numbers Through 999

Facts Practice: 100 Subtraction Facts (Test B in Test Masters)

Mental Math: Add one less than ten to a number.

  a. 56 + 9   **b.** 63 + 9   **c.** 48 + 9

Review:

  d. 74 + 20   **e.** 60 + 30   **f.** 49 + 40

Problem Solving: Tom has a total of ten coins in his left and right pockets. He has some coins in each pocket. He has more coins in his right pocket than in his left pocket. Make a table that lists the possible number of coins in each pocket.

Whole numbers are the counting numbers and zero.

$$0, 1, 2, 3, 4, 5, \ldots$$

To write the names of whole numbers through 999 (nine hundred ninety-nine), we need to know the following words and how to put them together:

0	zero	10	ten	20	twenty
1	one	11	eleven	30	thirty
2	two	12	twelve	40	forty
3	three	13	thirteen	50	fifty
4	four	14	fourteen	60	sixty
5	five	15	fifteen	70	seventy
6	six	16	sixteen	80	eighty
7	seven	17	seventeen	90	ninety
8	eight	18	eighteen	100	one hundred
9	nine	19	nineteen		

You may look at this chart when you are asked to write the names of numbers in the problem sets.

The names of two-digit numbers greater than 20 that do not end with zero are written with a hyphen.

Example 1   Use words to write the number 44.

Solution   We use a hyphen and write **"Forty-four."** Notice that "forty" is spelled without a "u."

To write three-digit numbers, we first write the number of hundreds and then we write the rest of the number. **We do not use the word "and" when writing whole numbers.**

Example 2   Use words to write the number 313.

Solution   First we write the number of hundreds. Then we write the rest of the number: **three hundred thirteen.** (*Note*: We do **not** write three hundred *and* thirteen.)

Example 3   Use words to write the number 705.

Solution   First we write the number of hundreds. Then we write the rest of the number: **seven hundred five.**

Example 4   Use digits to write the number six hundred eight.

Solution   Six hundred eight means six hundreds and eight ones. There are no tens, so we write a zero in the tens' place: **608.**

Practice   Use words to write each number:

a. 0   **b.** 81

c. 99   **d.** 515

e. 444   **f.** 909

Use digits to write each number:

g. Nineteen   **h.** Ninety-one

i. Five hundred twenty-four

j. Eight hundred sixty

Problem set 8

Find the missing addend:

1.
(2)
$\begin{array}{r} 2 \\ 3 \\ + N \\ \hline 13 \end{array}$

2.
(2)
$\begin{array}{r} 3 \\ N \\ + 6 \\ \hline 14 \end{array}$

3.
(2)
$\begin{array}{r} 5 \\ N \\ + 2 \\ \hline 11 \end{array}$

4.
(2)
$\begin{array}{r} 2 \\ 6 \\ + N \\ \hline 15 \end{array}$

Subtract. Check by adding.

5.
(7)
$\begin{array}{r} 13 \\ - 5 \\ \hline \end{array}$

6.
(7)
$\begin{array}{r} 16 \\ - 8 \\ \hline \end{array}$

7.
(7)
$\begin{array}{r} 13 \\ - 7 \\ \hline \end{array}$

8.
(7)
$\begin{array}{r} 12 \\ - 8 \\ \hline \end{array}$

Use digits to write each number:

9. Two hundred fourteen
(8)

10. Five hundred thirty-two
(8)

Use words to write each number:

11. 301
(8)

12. 320
(8)

13. 312
(8)

14. Write a number sentence for this picture.
(1)

Write the next three numbers in each sequence:

15. 12, 18, 24, _____, _____, _____, ...
(3)

16. 15, 18, 21, _____, _____, _____, ...
(3)

Find the missing number in each sequence:

17. 35, 42, _____, 56, ...
(3)

18. 40, _____, 56, 64, ...
(3)

19. How much money is shown by this picture?
(5)

20. The numbers 7, 8, and 15 are a fact family. Write two
(7) addition facts and two subtraction facts using these
three numbers.

21. Brad was twelfth in line. His sister was sixth in line.
(6) How many people were between Brad and his sister?

22. Six nickels is equal to how many cents? Count by
(3) fives.

23. 4 + 7 + 8 + 5 + 4   **24.** 2 + 3 + 5 + 8 + 5
(1)   (1)

25. 5 + 8 + 6 + 4 + 3 + 7 + 2
(1)

LESSON 9

Adding Money

Facts Practice: 100 Subtraction Facts (Test B in Test Masters)

Mental Math: Nineteen is one less than 20. When adding 19
to a number, we may think of adding one less
than 20 to the number.

a.   36   b.   36   c.   47   d.   47   e.   24   f.   24
+ 20   + 19   + 20   + 19   + 20   + 19

Patterns: The days of the week repeat. Seven days before
Saturday was Saturday, and seven days after
Saturday is Saturday again. What day is ten days
after Saturday? What day was ten days before
Saturday? What day is seventy days after Saturday?

*Donna had $24. On her birthday she was given
$15. Then how much money did Donna have?*

We use $10 bills and $1 bills to add $15 to $24. The total is 3 tens and 9 ones, which is $39.

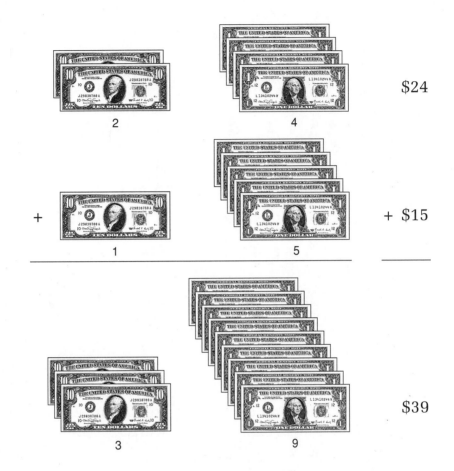

We may add $24 and $15 by acting out the addition with money, by mental math, or with pencil and paper. Using pencil and paper, we add the digits in the ones' place, and then the digits in the tens' place. Remember to include the dollar sign in the answer.

Add ones
Add tens

$24
+ $15
$39

Practice   **a.** $53 + $26   **b.** $14 + $75   **c.** $36 + $42

d. $27 + $51   **e.** $15 + $21   **f.** $32 + $23

Problem set 9

Use digits to write each number:

1. Three hundred forty-three
(8)

2. Three hundred seven
(8)

3. Use words to write 592.
(8)

4.
(2)
```
   2
   4
 + N
 ___
  12
```

5.
(2)
```
   1
   R
 + 6
 ___
  10
```

6.
(2)
```
   1
   T
 + 7
 ___
  14
```

7.
(2)
```
   2
   6
 + N
 ___
  13
```

8.
(9)
```
  $25
+ $14
_____
```

9.
(9)
```
  $85
+ $14
_____
```

10.
(9)
```
  $22
+ $16
_____
```

11.
(9)
```
  $40
+ $38
_____
```

12.
(7)
```
  13
 - 9
 ___
```

13.
(7)
```
  17
 - 5
 ___
```

14.
(7)
```
  17
 - 8
 ___
```

15.
(7)
```
  14
 - 6
 ___
```

16. Draw a picture to show the addition of $23 and $42.
(9)

17. How many days are in four weeks? Count by sevens.
(3)

18. Sarah was born on the fifth day of August in 1987.
(6)   Write her birth date in month/day/year form.

Write the next three numbers in each sequence:

19. 12, 15, 18, _____, _____, _____, ...
(3)

20. 28, 35, 42, _____, _____, _____, ...
(3)

21.
(1)
```
  5
  8
  7
  6
  4
+ 3
___
```

22.
(1)
```
  9
  7
  6
  4
  8
+ 7
___
```

23.
(1)
```
  2
  5
  7
  3
  5
+ 4
___
```

24.
(1)
```
  9
  3
  8
  4
  7
+ 6
___
```

25.
(1)
```
  4
  8
  7
  4
  5
+ 6
___
```

LESSON
10

Adding with Regrouping

Facts Practice: 100 Addition Facts (Test A in Test Masters)

Mental Math: Add 9 or 19 to a number.

    a. 28 + 9   **b.** 36 + 19   **c.** 43 + 9

    d. 25 + 19   **e.** 56 + 9   **f.** 45 + 19

Problem Solving: Tom has a total of ten coins in his left and right pockets. He has four more coins in his right pocket than in his left pocket. How many coins does Tom have in each pocket?

After her birthday, Donna had $39. Later she earned $14 more. Then how much money did Donna have?

We use $10 bills and $1 bills to add $14 to $39. The total is 4 tens and 13 ones, which is $53.

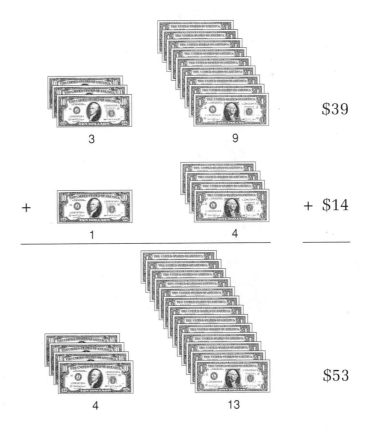

$39

3   9

+   1   4   + $14

4   13 $53

We can see the total easily if we exchange 10 of the ones for another $10 bill.

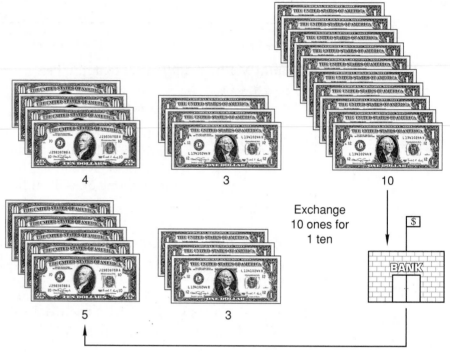

4   3   10

5   3

Exchange
10 ones for
1 ten

BANK

Now we see 5 tens and 3 ones, which is $53.

Using pencil and paper to add $14 to $39, we add the ones and get $13.

Add ones

$$\begin{array}{r} \$3\ 9 \\ +\ \$1\ 4 \\ \hline \textcircled{13} \end{array}$$

⟵ 1 ten and 3 ones

Since 13 ones is the same as 1 ten and 3 ones, we write just the 3 in the ones' place. We will add the 1 ten to the other tens. We show this by writing a 1 either above the column of tens or below the column of tens. Then we add the tens.

Add ones
Add tens

1 above ⟶ 1
$$\begin{array}{r} \$39 \\ +\ \$14 \\ \hline \$53 \end{array}$$

Add ones
Add tens

$$\begin{array}{r} \$39 \\ +\ \$14 \\ \hline \ \ \ \ \ \ 1 \\ \$53 \end{array}$$

1 below ⟶

Practice

a. $\begin{array}{r} \$36 \\ + \$29 \\ \hline \end{array}$ b. $\begin{array}{r} 47 \\ + \ 8 \\ \hline \end{array}$ c. $\begin{array}{r} \$57 \\ + \$13 \\ \hline \end{array}$

d. 68 + 24   e. $59 + $8   f. 46 + 25

Problem set 10

Use digits to write each number:

1. Six hundred thirteen   **2.** Nine hundred one
(8)   (8)

3. Use words to write 941.
(8)

4. $\begin{array}{r} 2 \\ 4 \\ + F \\ \hline 11 \end{array}$ **5.** $\begin{array}{r} 5 \\ G \\ + 2 \\ \hline 13 \end{array}$ **6.** $\begin{array}{r} H \\ 4 \\ + 7 \\ \hline 15 \end{array}$ **7.** $\begin{array}{r} 2 \\ 7 \\ + N \\ \hline 16 \end{array}$
(2)   (2)   (2)   (2)

8. $\begin{array}{r} 33 \\ + \ 8 \\ \hline \end{array}$ **9.** $\begin{array}{r} \$47 \\ + \$18 \\ \hline \end{array}$ **10.** $\begin{array}{r} 27 \\ + 69 \\ \hline \end{array}$ **11.** $\begin{array}{r} \$49 \\ + \$25 \\ \hline \end{array}$
(10)   (10)   (10)   (10)

12. $\begin{array}{r} 17 \\ - \ 8 \\ \hline \end{array}$ **13.** $\begin{array}{r} 12 \\ - \ 6 \\ \hline \end{array}$ **14.** $\begin{array}{r} 9 \\ - 7 \\ \hline \end{array}$ **15.** $\begin{array}{r} 13 \\ - \ 6 \\ \hline \end{array}$
(7)   (7)   (7)   (7)

16. What is the name for the answer when we add?
(1)

17. What is the name for the answer when we subtract?
(7)

18. Which month is two months after the twelfth month?
(6)

Write the next three numbers in each sequence:

19. 30, 36, 42, _____, _____, _____, ...
(3)

20. 28, 35, 42, _____, _____, _____, ...
(3)

21. What digit is in the hundreds' place in 843?
(5)

22. 28 + 6   **23.** $47 + $28   **24.** 35 + 27
(10)   (10)   (10)

25. 4 + 5 + 7 + 8 + 4 + 6 + 3
(1)

LESSON
11

Even Numbers • Odd Numbers

Facts Practice: 100 Subtraction Facts (Test B in Test Masters)

Mental Math: Review.

a. 20 + 60	**b.** 75 + 9	**c.** 45 + 30
d. 56 + 19	**e.** 47 + 40	**f.** 34 + 19

Problem Solving: Have each student write the counting numbers from 1 through 20 on a sheet of paper while the numbers are also written on the board. Then draw a line through every number on the list that we say when we count by twos from 2 to 20: 1, 2̸, 3, 4̸, 5, 6̸, 7, ... Say the numbers that remain. What are the final digits? Continue this sequence of numbers from 21 to 39.

Even numbers   The numbers we say when we count by twos are **even numbers.** Notice that every even number ends with either 2, 4, 6, 8, or 0.

$$2, 4, 6, 8, 10, 12, 14, 16, 18, 20, 22, 24, 26, \ldots$$

The list of even numbers goes on and on. We do not begin with zero when we count by twos. However, the number 0 is an even number.

Example 1   Which one of these numbers is an even number?

$$463 \qquad 285 \qquad 456$$

Solution   We can tell if a number is even by looking at the last digit. **A number is an even number if the last digit is even.** The last digits of these numbers are 3, 5, and 6. Of these, the only even digit is 6, so the even number is **456.**

Odd numbers   If a whole number is not an even number, then it is an **odd number.** We can make a list of odd numbers by beginning with the number 1. Then we add two to get the next odd number, add two more to get the next odd number, and so on. The sequence of odd numbers is

$$1, 3, 5, 7, 9, 11, \ldots$$

An even number of objects can be separated into two equal groups. Six is an even number. Here we show six dots separated into two equal groups.

If we try to separate an odd number of objects into two equal groups, there will be one extra object. Five is an odd number. Five dots will not separate into two equal groups because one dot is left over.

Example 2 There were the same number of boys and girls in the classroom. Which of these numbers could be the number of children in the classroom?

A. 25   B. 26   C. 27

Solution An even number of children can be divided into two equal groups. Since there are an equal number of boys and girls, there must be an even number of children in the classroom. The only even number among the choices is **B. 26.**

Example 3 List the five odd three-digit numbers that have a 7 in the hundreds' place and a 5 in the tens' place.

Solution The first two digits are 7 and 5.

$$\underline{7} \quad \underline{5} \quad \underline{}$$

The last digit can be either 1, 3, 5, 7, or 9. So the five numbers are

751, 753, 755, 757, and **759**

Practice Write "even" or "odd" for each number:

      a. 563   **b.** 328

      c. 99   **d.** 0

      e. List the five even three-digit numbers that have a 6 in the hundreds' place and a 3 in the tens' place.

Problem set 11

1. Use digits to write five hundred forty-two.
(8)

2. Use digits to write six hundred nineteen.
(8)

3. The numbers 4, 7, and 11 are a fact family. Write two addition facts and two subtraction facts using these three numbers.
(7)

Use words to write each number:

4. 903   **5.** 746
(8)   (8)

6. List the five odd three-digit numbers that have a 5 in the hundreds' place and a 0 in the tens' place.
(11)

7.
(2)
$$\begin{array}{r} 4 \\ N \\ +\ 3 \\ \hline 14 \end{array}$$

8.
(2)
$$\begin{array}{r} P \\ 4 \\ +\ 2 \\ \hline 13 \end{array}$$

9.
(2)
$$\begin{array}{r} 5 \\ Q \\ +\ 7 \\ \hline 14 \end{array}$$

10.
(2)
$$\begin{array}{r} R \\ 3 \\ +\ 2 \\ \hline 11 \end{array}$$

11.
(7)
$$\begin{array}{r} 15 \\ -\ 7 \\ \hline \end{array}$$

12.
(7)
$$\begin{array}{r} 14 \\ -\ 7 \\ \hline \end{array}$$

13.
(7)
$$\begin{array}{r} 17 \\ -\ 8 \\ \hline \end{array}$$

14.
(7)
$$\begin{array}{r} 11 \\ -\ 6 \\ \hline \end{array}$$

15.
(10)
$$\begin{array}{r} \$25 \\ +\ \$38 \\ \hline \end{array}$$

16.
(10)
$$\begin{array}{r} \$19 \\ +\ \$34 \\ \hline \end{array}$$

17.
(10)
$$\begin{array}{r} 42 \\ +\ 8 \\ \hline \end{array}$$

18.
(10)
$$\begin{array}{r} 17 \\ +\ 49 \\ \hline \end{array}$$

Write the next three numbers in each sequence:

19. 18, 21, 24, _____, _____, _____, ...
(3)

20. 18, 24, 30, _____, _____, _____, ...
(3)

21. Write a number sentence for this picture.
(1)

22. (1)	2 3 5 7 8 4 + 5	**23.** (1)	9 4 7 8 6 5 + 3	**24.** (1)	9 2 4 8 7 6 + 2	**25.** (1)	4 7 4 6 5 2 + 3

LESSON 12

"Some and Some More" Problems, Part 1

Facts Practice: 100 Addition Facts (Test A in Test Masters)

Mental Math: Add a number ending in 9 to another number.

a. 28 + 30	**b.** 28 + 29	**c.** 37 + 50	**d.** 37 + 49	**e.** 56 + 40	**f.** 56 + 39

Patterns: The math books were stacked neatly on the shelf in two piles. Marla glanced at the shelf and knew instantly that there were an even number of books. How did she know?

Many word problems tell a story. Some stories are about **putting things together.** Look at this story.

John had 5 marbles. He bought 7 more marbles. Now John has 12 marbles.

There is a pattern to this story. John had **some** marbles. Then he bought **some more** marbles. When he put the marbles together, he found out the **total** number of marbles. We will call these problems **"some and some more"** problems. In this book we will often use the letters SSM to stand for "some and some more."

PATTERN	PROBLEM	
Some	5 marbles	
+ Some more	+ 7 marbles	
Total	12 marbles	← Largest number

The "some and some more" pattern is an addition pattern. **We remember that the bottom number in an addition pattern is the largest number.** A "some and some more" pattern is shown in the box below. There are six lines and a plus sign. Three of the lines are for numbers. Three of the lines are for words. All the words are the same.

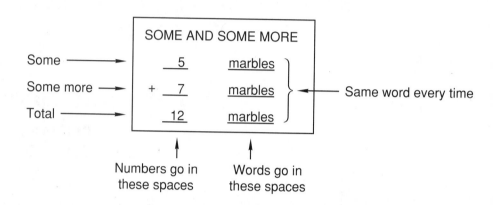

Example 1 Mickey saw 15 rabbits. Then he saw 7 more rabbits. How many rabbits did he see in all?

Solution This problem has the idea of some and some more. To practice the pattern, we draw six lines and a plus sign.

Some

Some more   + _____   _____

Total

Next, we write "rabbits" in the three spaces on the right.

Some   _____   rabbits

Some more + _____   rabbits

Total   _____   rabbits

Now we put in the numbers. In the beginning there were 15 rabbits. Then Mickey saw 7 more rabbits.

Some   15   rabbits

Some more +   7   rabbits

Total N rabbits

Now we must find the missing number. We add 15 and 7 to find the total number.

Some		15	rabbits
Some more	+	7	rabbits
Total		22	rabbits

Mickey saw **22 rabbits** in all.

Example 2 Joan found 5 beans on the floor, 3 beans behind the stove, and 6 beans in the cupboard. How many beans did she find in all?

Solution This problem puts beans together. There are 5 beans, 3 beans, and 6 beans to put together. This is a "some, and some more, and some more" problem.

Some		5	beans
Some more		3	beans
Some more	+	6	beans
Total		N	beans

If we add 5 beans and 3 beans and 6 beans, we find the total is 14 beans. She found **14 beans** in all.

Practice Draw the lines and a plus sign to make the "some and some more" pattern for each problem. Then work the problem.

a. Diane ran 5 laps in the morning. She ran 8 laps in the afternoon. How many laps did she run in all?

b. Nathan found 3 pencils on the table, 5 pencils behind his desk, and 11 pencils under his bed. Altogether, how many pencils did Nathan find?

Problem set 12

1. James had 17 balls. Then his brother gave him 8 more
(12) balls. How many balls does James have now? Draw a "some and some more" pattern.

2. Samantha saw rabbits in the field. She saw 5 rabbits in
(12) the east field. She saw 3 rabbits in the west field. She saw 4 rabbits in the north field. How many rabbits did Samantha see in all? Draw a SSM pattern.

3. Use digits to write seven hundred fourteen.
(8)

4. Use digits to write three hundred forty-seven.
(8)

Use words to write each number:

5. 706   **6.** 532
(8)   *(8)*

7. List five even three-digit numbers that have a 5 in the
(11) tens' place and a 7 in the hundreds' place.

8.   4   **9.**   *B*   **10.**   9   **11.**   5
(2)   *N*   *(2)*   7   *(2)*   *N*   *(2)*   2
       $+ \ 6$ $+ \ 4$ $+ \ 3$ $+ \ C$
       $\overline{15}$ $\overline{16}$ $\overline{12}$ $\overline{13}$

12.   14   **13.**   18   **14.**   17   **15.**   12
(7) $- \ 7$ *(7)* $- \ 9$ *(7)* $- \ 5$ *(7)* $- \ 6$

16.   \$27   **17.**   \$35   **18.**   28   **19.**   15
(10) $+ \ \$16$ *(10)* $+ \ \$38$ *(10)* $+ \ 9$ *(10)* $+ \ 8$

20. Name the month that is just before the seventh month.
(6)

Write the next three numbers in each sequence:

21. 14, 21, 28, _____, _____, _____, ···
(3)

22. 24, 32, 40, _____, _____, _____, ···
(3)

23. 4 + 3 + 7 + 8 + 5 + 6 + 4
(1)

24. 2 + 5 + 8 + 7 + 4 + 8 + 2
(1)

25. 9 + 3 + 2 + 4 + 6 + 5 + 7
(1)

LESSON
13

Number Lines

Facts Practice: 100 Addition Facts (Test A in Test Masters)

Mental Math: Add a number ending in 9 to another number.

a. 52 + 29   **b.** 63 + 9   **c.** 14 + 39
d. 26 + 49   **e.** 57 + 19   **f.** 32 + 59

Patterns: This "hundred number chart" lists the whole numbers from 1 to 100. We have shaded the squares on this chart that contain even numbers. On another chart, shade the squares that contain the numbers we say when we count by threes from 3 to 99.

1	2	3	4	5	6	7	8	9	10
11	12	13	14	15	16	17	18	19	20
21	22	23	24	25	26	27	28	29	30
31	32	33	34	35	36	37	38	39	40
41	42	43	44	45	46	47	48	49	50
51	52	53	54	55	56	57	58	59	60
61	62	63	64	65	66	67	68	69	70
71	72	73	74	75	76	77	78	79	80
81	82	83	84	85	86	87	88	89	90
91	92	93	94	95	96	97	98	99	100

(Hundreds chart is available in Test Masters.)

A line continues without end. When we "draw a line" with a pencil, we are actually drawing a **line segment.** A line segment is part of a line.

Line segment

To illustrate a line, we draw an arrowhead at each end of the line segment. The arrowheads show that the line continues.

Line

To make a number line, we begin by drawing a line. Next, we put tick marks on the line, keeping the distance between the marks the same.

Then we label the marks with numbers. On some number lines, every mark is numbered. On other number lines, only some of the marks are numbered. A number on a number line tells us how far the mark is from zero.

Example 1 The arrow is pointing to what number on this number line?

Solution If we count by ones from zero, our count matches the numbers given on the number line. So we know that the distance from one tick mark to the next tick mark is one.

We find that the arrow is pointing to **7.**

On some number lines, the distance from one tick mark to the next is not one. We may need to count by twos or by fives or by tens or by some other number to find the distance between tick marks.

Example 2 The arrow is pointing to what number on this number line?

Solution If we count by ones from tick mark to tick mark, our count does not match the numbers given on the number line. We try counting by twos and find that our count does match the number line. So the distance from one tick mark to the next tick mark on this number line is two. The arrow is pointing to a mark on the number line that is one mark after 4 and one mark before 8. The number that is two more than 4 and two less than 8 is **6.**

Example 3 The arrow is pointing to what number on this number line?

Solution Zero is not shown on this number line, so we will start our count at 40. Counting by ones from tick mark to tick mark does not fit the pattern. Neither does counting by twos. Counting by fives does fit the pattern. The arrow is pointing to **55.**

Practice The arrow is pointing to what number on each number line below?

a.

b.

c.

d.

Problem set   **1.** Sandra saw 4 horses at the fair. Then she saw 13
13   (12) horses on a farm. How many horses did Sandra see in
all? Draw a SSM pattern.

2. Mickey saw 14 gnomes in the forest and 23 gnomes in
(12) the valley. How many gnomes did Mickey see in all?
Draw a SSM pattern.

3. Use digits to write six hundred forty-two.
(8)

4. Use digits to write three hundred twelve.
(8)

5. Use words to write 713.
(8)

6. List the five odd three-digit numbers that have a 5 in
(11) the hundreds' place and a 7 in the tens' place.

7. To what number is the arrow pointing?
(13)

8. All the books were put into two equal stacks. Was the
(11) number of books an odd number or an even number?

9. (2)	**10.** (2)	**11.** (2)	**12.** (2)
5	N	7	M
B	5	A	2
+ 7	+ 3	+ 4	+ 8
18	15	12	14

13. (7)	**14.** (7)	**15.** (7)	**16.** (7)
12	14	12	13
− 3	− 7	− 8	− 6

17. (10)	**18.** (10)	**19.** (10)	**20.** (10)
74	93	28	28
+ 18	+ 39	+ 45	+ 47

Write the next three numbers in each sequence:

21. 12, 15, 18, _____, _____, _____, ...
(3)

22. 30, 36, 42, _____, _____, _____, ...
(3)

23. The numbers 5, 9, and 14 are a fact family. Write two
(7) addition facts and two subtraction facts using these
three numbers.

24.   4
(1)
            3
            5
            8
            7
            6
          + 2
         _____

25.   4
(1)
            3
            6
            7
            8
            4
          + 3
         _____

LESSON 14

Missing Numbers in Subtraction

Facts Practice: 100 Addition Facts (Test A in Test Masters)

Mental Math: Review.
   a. 30 + 60   **b.** 74 + 19   **c.** 46 + 9
   d. 63 + 29   **e.** 42 + 50   **f.** 16 + 39

Problem Solving: There were more than 20 math books on the
shelf but fewer than 30. Todd arranged the
books into two equal piles, and then he
rearranged the books into three equal piles.
Use these clues to figure out how many
math books were on the shelf.

Since Lesson 1 we have practiced finding missing
numbers in addition problems. In this lesson we will
practice finding missing numbers in subtraction problems.

Remember that we "subtract down" to find the bottom number and "add up" to find the top number.

Subtract Down:		**Add Up:**
Nine minus six equals three.	$\begin{array}{r} 9 \\ -\ 6 \\ \hline 3 \end{array}$	Three plus six equals nine.

We may use either "subtracting down" or "adding up" to find a missing number in a subtraction problem.

Example 1 Find the missing number:
$$\begin{array}{r} 14 \\ -\ N \\ \hline 6 \end{array}$$

Solution We may either "subtract down" or "add up." Which way seems easier?

Subtract Down:		**Add Up:**
Fourteen minus what number equals six?	$\begin{array}{r} 14 \\ -\ N \\ \hline 6 \end{array}$	Six plus what number equals fourteen?

Often it is easier to find a missing number in a subtraction problem by "adding up." If we add 8 to 6, we get 14. So the missing number is **8.** We can check our answer by subtracting.

$$\begin{array}{r} 14 \\ -\ 8 \\ \hline 6 \end{array} \quad \text{check}$$

Since $14 - 8 = 6$, we know our answer is correct.

Example 2 Find the missing number:
$$\begin{array}{r} B \\ -\ 5 \\ \hline 7 \end{array}$$

Solution Try both "subtracting down" and "adding up."

Subtract Down:		**Add Up:**
What number minus five equals seven?	$\begin{array}{r} B \\ -\ 5 \\ \hline 7 \end{array}$	Seven plus five equals what number?

Since 7 plus 5 is 12, the missing number must be 12. We rewrite the original problem using 12 to check the answer.

$$
\begin{array}{r}
12 \\
-\ 5 \\
\hline
7 \quad \text{check}
\end{array}
$$

The answer checks. The missing number is **12.**

Practice   Find each missing digit. Check your answer.

a.	**b.**	**c.**	**d.**
14	*N*	9	*N*
− *N*	− 5	− *N*	− 7
6	2	2	5

Problem set 14

1. Jimmy found forty-two acorns in the forest. Then he
   (12) found thirty-seven acorns in his backyard. How many acorns did he find in all? Draw a SSM pattern.

2. At first thirty-five fairies were flying about. Later,
   (12) twenty-seven more fairies began to fly about. In all, how many fairies were flying about? Draw a SSM pattern.

3. Use digits to write the number seven hundred fifteen.
   (8)

4. Use words to write 603.
   (8)

5. Nathan was born on the seventh day of June in 1990.
   (6) Write his birth date in month/day/year form.

6. Write the largest three-digit number that has a 6 in the
   (5) ones' place and a 4 in the tens' place.

7. To what number is the arrow pointing?
   (13)

8. 5
(2)   N
        + 6
       _____
        15

9. A
(2)   2
      + 5
     _____
      15

10. 7
(2)   2
       + N
      _____
       15

11. 4
(2)   A
       + 2
      _____
       15

12. N
(14)   − 6
      _____
        8

13. 16
(7)   − 8
      _____

14. 14
(7)   − 7
      _____

15. 12
(14)   − A
      _____
        7

16. B
(14)   − 6
      _____
        6

17. 13
(14)   − C
      _____
        8

18. $48
(10) + $16
     _____

19. $37
(10) + $14
     _____

Write the next three numbers in each sequence:

20. 28, 35, 42, _____, _____, _____, ···
(3)

21. 18, 21, 24, _____, _____, _____, ···
(3)

22. How many cents is nine nickels? Count by fives.
(3)

23. 2
(1)   3
         5
         7
         4
         8
       + 2
      _____

24. 2
(1)   5
         7
         3
         5
         8
       + 4
      _____

25. 7
(1)   3
         8
         5
         4
         3
       + 2
      _____

Comparing Numbers

Facts Practice: 100 Addition Facts (Test A in Test Masters)

Mental Math: Add a number ending in two zeros to another number.

 a. 300 + 400   **b.** 600 + 300   **c.** 250 + 300

Review:

 d. 63 + 29   **e.** 54 + 19   **f.** 28 + 49

Patterns: Shade the squares on a hundred number chart that contain the numbers we say when we count by fours from 4 to 100. Which of the shaded squares also contain even numbers?

When we compare two numbers, we decide whether one number is greater than, equal to, or less than another number.

Three **is equal to** three.

Three **is less than** four.

Four **is greater than** three.

The three sentences above compare two numbers. We may use digits and symbols to write the same sentences. We use the **equal sign** to show that two numbers are equal.

3 = 3   is read   "Three is equal to three."

We use the **greater than/less than** symbol to show the comparison for two numbers that are not equal.

> <

The pointed end points to the smaller number. We read from left to right. If the pointed end comes first, we say "less than."

3 < 4   is read   "Three is less than four."

If the open end comes first, we say "greater than."

4 > 3   is read   "Four is greater than three."

Example 1   Use digits and a comparison symbol to write "Five is greater than four."

Solution   The pointed end must point to the smaller number.

5 > 4

Example 2   Compare the following numbers by replacing the circle with the proper comparison symbol:

12 ◯ 21

Solution   We use the greater than/less than symbol. Since 12 is less than 21, we let the pointed end point to 12.

12 < 21

We read this by saying "Twelve is less than twenty-one."

Example 3   Which of these numbers is the greatest?

123   231   213

Solution   All of these numbers have the same digits, but their values are different because the place values are different. The greatest (largest) of these three numbers is **231.**

Example 4   Arrange these numbers in order from the least to the greatest:

640   406   ,   460

Solution   The least (smallest) is 406. The greatest is 640. Arranging the numbers in order, we write:

406   460   640

Practice   Write each statement using digits and a comparison symbol:

a. Thirteen is less than thirty.

b. Forty is greater than fourteen.

Replace each circle with the proper symbol:

   c. 432 ◯ 324   **d.** 212 ◯ 221   **e.** 316 ◯ 316

   f. Arrange the numbers 132, 123, and 213 in order from the least to the greatest.

Problem set 15

1. Forty-two students had red hair. Thirty-seven students did not have red hair. How many students were there in all? Draw a SSM pattern.
(12)

2. Seventeen brave students rode the loop-o-plane at the fair. Forty-seven others just watched. How many students were there altogether? Draw a SSM pattern.
(12)

3. Use digits to write the number six hundred forty-two.
(8)

4. Use words to write the number 502.
(8)

5. Use digits and a comparison symbol to write "Fourteen is greater than seven."
(15)

6. Compare: 16 ◯ 12
(15)

7. To what number is the arrow pointing?
(13)

8.   4
(2)
     N
  $+\ 5$
  $\overline{13}$

9. N
(2)
     6
  $+\ 2$
  $\overline{9}$

10.   5
(2)
     2
  $+\ P$
  $\overline{14}$

11.   3
(2)
     5
  $+\ K$
  $\overline{16}$

12. C
(14)
  $-\ 5$
  $\overline{7}$

13.   17
(7)
  $-\ 9$

14.   12
(7)
  $-\ 6$

15.   9
(14)
  $-\ A$
  $\overline{4}$

16.   37
(10)
  $+\ 28$

17.   36
(9)
  $+\ 40$

18.   \$68
(10)
  $+\ \$27$

19.   \$49
(10)
  $+\ \$24$

Write the next three numbers in each sequence:

20. 18, 27, 36, ____, ____, ____, ···
(3)

21. 32, 40, 48, ____, ____, ____, ···
(3)

22. 20, 24, 28, ____, ____, ____, ···
(3)

23. Todd wrote his birth date as 9/10/85. Rewrite Todd's
(6) birth date naming the month he was born and writing
     the full year.

24. The numbers 7, 8, and 15 are a fact family. Write two
(7) addition facts and two subtraction facts using these
     three numbers.

25. 2 + 5 + 7 + 6 + 5 + 4
(1)

LESSON 16

Adding Three-Digit Numbers

Facts Practice: 100 Addition Facts (Test A in Test Masters)

Mental Math: Add a number ending in two zeros to another
number.

  a. 400 + 500   **b.** 600 + 320   **c.** 254 + 100

Review:

  d. 64 + 29   **e.** 39 + 25   **f.** 19 + 27

Patterns: Copy this design of ten circles on
your paper, following the same
pattern as in Lesson 5. Then,
outside each circle, write the sum of
the numbers in that circle and in
the two circles next to that circle.
For example, the number outside of
circle 1 should be 13.

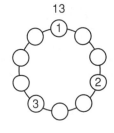

---

*Andrea had $675. When Denise landed on
Andrea's property, Denise paid Andrea $175 rent.
Then how much money did Andrea have?*

We will use bills to add $175 to $675. The sum is 7 hundreds, 14 tens, and 10 ones.

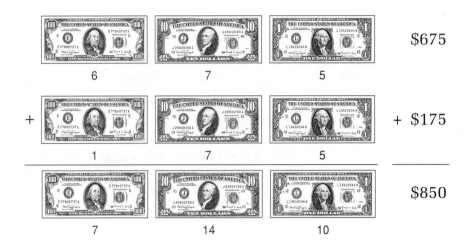

If we exchange 10 ones for 1 ten and 10 tens for 1 hundred, we will have 8 hundreds, 5 tens, and no ones, which is $850.

Using pencil and paper, we add the ones and regroup, add the tens and regroup, and then add the hundreds.

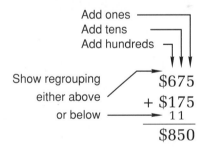

Example Add:
$$\begin{array}{r} 456 \\ + 374 \\ \hline \end{array}$$

Solution We begin by adding the digits in the ones' column. Then we move one column at a time to the left, writing the first digit of two-digit answers either above or below the next place column. The sum is **830.**

$$\begin{array}{r} 11 \\ 456 \\ + 374 \\ \hline 830 \end{array}$$

Practice   **a.** $579
                      + $186

b.   408
       + 243

c. $498
       + $89

d. $458 + $336   **e.** 56 + 569

Problem set   **1.** Seventy-seven students ran in circles and waved their
16   (12) arms. Nineteen students watched in amazement. How
                   many students were there in all? Draw a SSM
                   pattern.

2. The king counted seventy-five birds on the way to the
(12) fair. The queen counted thirty-eight birds on the way
     home. How many birds did the king and queen count
     in all? Draw a SSM pattern.

3. Use words to write the number 913.
(8)

4. Use digits to write the number seven hundred forty-
(8) three.

5. Use digits and a comparison symbol to write
(15) "Seventy-five is less than ninety-eight."

6. Compare: 413 ◯ 314
(15)

7. The numbers 7, 9, and 16 are a fact family. Write two
(7) addition facts and two subtraction facts using these
    three numbers.

8. To what number is the arrow pointing?
(13)

9. $475   **10.** $714   **11.**   743   **12.**   576
(16)   + $332   (16)   + $226   (16)   + 187   (16)   + 228

13.   8   **14.**   4   **15.**   9   **16.**   N
(2)   5   (2)   N   (2)   A   (2)   3
        + K   + 6   + 6   + 7
        ___   ___   ___   ___
         17   15   17   16

17. $\begin{array}{r} 8 \\ -\ N \\ \hline 2 \end{array}$
(14)

18. $\begin{array}{r} 17 \\ -\ 8 \\ \hline \end{array}$
(7)

19. $\begin{array}{r} 13 \\ -\ 7 \\ \hline \end{array}$
(7)

20. $\begin{array}{r} N \\ -\ 8 \\ \hline 7 \end{array}$
(14)

21. $\begin{array}{r} 14 \\ -\ N \\ \hline 6 \end{array}$
(14)

22. $\begin{array}{r} 16 \\ -\ A \\ \hline 9 \end{array}$
(14)

23. $\begin{array}{r} N \\ -\ 9 \\ \hline 7 \end{array}$
(14)

24. $\begin{array}{r} \$49 \\ +\ \$76 \\ \hline \end{array}$
(10)

25. Write the next three numbers in this sequence:
(3)

28, 35, 42, _____, _____, _____, ...

LESSON
17

"Some and Some More" Problems, Part 2

Facts Practice: 100 Subtraction Facts (Test B in Test Masters)

Mental Math: Add three numbers.
  a. 30 + 40 + 20 **b.** 300 + 400 + 200 **c.** 3 + 4 + 2

Review:
  d. 36 + 19   **e.** 39 + 27   **f.** 44 + 29

Patterns: The multiples of 5 are 5, 10, 15, 20, and so on. Shade the squares on a hundred number chart that contain a multiple of 5. Which of the shaded squares also contain even numbers?

We have been working problems that have a "some and some more" thinking pattern. In the problems we have worked so far, both the "some" number and the "some more" number were given. We add these numbers to find the total. If we have 5 marbles and get 7 more marbles, we will have 12 marbles in all.

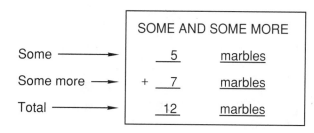

To review, we look at this thinking pattern carefully. The largest number is the total number. The largest number is at the bottom of the pattern.

Sometimes a "some and some more" problem gives us the total number and one other number. Then we must find the missing number. These problems are just like addition problems that have a missing addend.

Example 1 Walter had 8 marbles. Then Sam gave him some more marbles. He has 17 marbles now. How many marbles did Sam give him?

Solution **If we can recognize the pattern, we can solve the problem.** Walter had some marbles. Then he received some more marbles. This problem has a "some and some more" pattern. We know the "some" number. We know the total number. We put these numbers in the pattern. In a "some and some more" pattern, the bottom number is the largest number. **The sum of the two addends must equal the bottom number.**

Some	8	marbles
Some more	+ N	marbles
Total	17	marbles

We see that this time one of the addends is missing. One way to find the missing number is to ask an addition question.

"Eight plus what number equals seventeen?"
$$\begin{array}{r} 8 \\ + N \\ \hline 17 \end{array}$$

Another way is to ask a subtraction question.

"Seventeen minus eight equals what number?"
$$\begin{array}{r} 17 \\ - 8 \\ \hline N \end{array}$$

Both answers are **9 marbles.**

The key to the problem is recognizing the pattern. Then finding the answer is easy!

Example 2   Jamie had some pies. Then Frank gave her 5 more pies. Now she has 12 pies. How many pies did Jamie have at first?

Solution   This is a "some and some more" story problem. We fill in the pattern.

$$
\begin{array}{lrl}
\text{Some} & \underline{N} & \text{pies} \\
\text{Some more} & +\underline{5} & \text{pies} \\
\text{Total} & \underline{12} & \text{pies}
\end{array}
$$

Finding the answer is easy now. We can find the missing number by asking an addition question or by asking a subtraction question.

"Five added to what number equals twelve?"   (7)

"Twelve minus five equals what number?"   (7)

At first Jamie had **7 pies.**

Practice   Draw the lines to make a "some and some more" pattern for each problem. Then work the problem.

  a. Lucille had 4 marigolds. Jim gave her some more marigolds. Now she has 17 marigolds. How many marigolds did Jim give Lucille?

  b. Sid had some agates. Then he found 8 more agates. Now he has 15 agates. How many agates did he have at first?

Problem set 17

1. There were 11 towheads in the hall. There were 32
(12) towheads in the room. How many towheads were there in all? Draw a SSM pattern.

2. Christy saw 8 birds in the backyard. Then she saw
(17) some more birds in the front yard. She saw 17 birds in all. How many birds did she see in the front yard? Draw a SSM pattern.

3. Think of any even number and think of any odd
(11) number. Then add the numbers. Is the sum even or odd? Try another even number and another odd number. Is the sum even or odd?

4. Use words to write the number 904.
(8)

5. Use digits to write five hundred eleven.
(8)

6. Compare: 906 ◯ 609
(15)

7. 6 + 5 + N + 3 + 2 + 1 = 20
(2)

8. To what number is the arrow pointing?
(13)

9. $693
(16) + $148

10. $108
(16) + $699

11.   524
(16) + 219

12.   416
(16) + 328

13. N
(14) − 2
   5

14.   4
(1) + A
   8

15.   7
(1) + P
  13

16.   5
(14) − K
   1

17.   12
(14) − P
   7

18.   15
(14) − X
   9

19.   4
(2) N
 + 6
  15

20. C
(2)   5
 + 7
  15

21. How many sides are on seven triangles? Count by
(3) threes.

22. Write a number sentence for this picture.
(1)

23. What month is two months after the eleventh month?
(6)

24. The numbers 6, 7, and 13 are a fact family. Write two
(7) addition facts and two subtraction facts using these
three numbers.

25. Write the next three numbers in this sequence:
(3)
       42, 35, 28, _____, _____, _____, ...

LESSON
18

Subtracting Without Regrouping • Missing Two-Digit Addends

Facts Practice: 100 Subtraction Facts (Test B in Test Masters)

Mental Math: Add three numbers.
  a. 200 + 300 + 400 **b.** 240 + 200 + 100 **c.** 36 + 20 + 9
Review:
  d. 45 + 10 + 29   **e.** 56 + 20 + 19   **f.** 24 + 39 + 10

Patterns: Design a pattern of numbered circles like those in Lessons 5 and 16 using seven circles instead of ten. Describe the pattern to a classmate or write a description.

Subtracting without regrouping

By carefully looking at the numbers in a subtraction problem, we can see if regrouping is necessary. Regrouping is necessary if the ones' digit of the bottom number is greater than the ones' digit of the top number. Which of these two subtractions can be done without regrouping?

$$\begin{array}{r} \$54 \\ -\ \$23 \\ \hline \end{array} \qquad \begin{array}{r} \$53 \\ -\ \$24 \\ \hline \end{array}$$

The subtraction in the left-hand example can be done without regrouping because the bottom ones' digit, 3, is less than the top ones' digit, 4. However, to subtract the numbers in the right-hand example, regrouping is necessary because the 4 is greater than the 3.

$$\begin{array}{r} \$54 \\ -\ \$23 \\ \hline \$31 \end{array} \qquad \begin{array}{r} \$53 \\ -\ \$24 \\ \hline ? \end{array}$$

In this lesson, we will practice subtracting when regrouping is not necessary.

Example 1   Subtract 123 from 365.

Solution   Order matters when we subtract. We begin with 365 and subtract 123. When we subtract three-digit numbers with pencil and paper, we subtract the ones first. Then we subtract the tens. Then we subtract the hundreds.

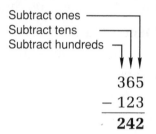

$$\begin{array}{r} 365 \\ -\ 123 \\ \hline \mathbf{242} \end{array}$$

Example 2   Subtract thirty-two from eighty-five.

Solution   We write the numbers using digits. We show two forms.

$$\begin{array}{r} 85 \\ -\ 32 \\ \hline \mathbf{53} \end{array} \qquad 85 - 32 = \mathbf{53}$$

Missing two-digit addends   The missing addend in this problem has two digits. We can find the missing addend one digit at a time.

Tens' column ⌐⌐ Ones' column

Five plus what   56   Six plus what
number is nine?   + __   number is eight?
Answer: 4   98   Answer: 2

The missing digits are 4 and 2. So the missing addend is 42.

Example 3
$$\begin{array}{r} 36 \\ +\ W \\ \hline 87 \end{array}$$

Solution   The letter W stands for a two-digit number. We find the missing digit in the ones' place, and then the missing digit in the tens' place.

$$\begin{array}{r} W \\ +\ 36 \\ \hline 87 \end{array}$$
One plus six is seven.
Five plus three is eight.

The missing addend is **51**.

Practice   **a.** $485 - 242$ **b.** $\$56 - \$33$

c. Subtract 53 from 97.

d. Subtract twenty-three from fifty-four.

e.   24   **f.** M
     $+\ Q$ $+\ 31$
     ───   ───
      65   67

Problem set 18

1. Forty-two red surfboards were on the first wave.
$^{(12)}$ Seventeen red surfboards were on the second wave. How many red surfboards were on the first two waves? Draw a SSM pattern.

2. Mindy saw four green grasshoppers in the first hour.
$^{(17)}$ In the second hour she saw some more green grasshoppers. She saw eleven green grasshoppers in all. How many green grasshoppers did she see in the second hour? Draw a SSM pattern.

3. Use the digits 1, 2, and 3 once each to name an even
$^{(11)}$ number less than 200.

4. Use words to write the number 915.
$^{(8)}$

5. Subtract seven hundred thirteen from eight hundred
$^{(18)}$ twenty-four.

6. Compare: 704 $\bigcirc$ 407
$^{(15)}$

7. What is the total number of days in the first two
$^{(6)}$ months of a common year?

8. To what number is the arrow pointing?
$^{(13)}$

9. $\$346$ **10.**   499   **11.** $\$421$ **12.**   506
$^{(16)}$ $+\ \$298$ $^{(16)}$ $+\ 275$ $^{(16)}$ $+\ \$389$ $^{(16)}$ $+\ 210$

13. $\$438$
(18) $\underline{-\ \$206}$

14. $\quad17$
(14) $\underline{-\ A}$
$\qquad9$

15. $\qquad7$
(1) $\underline{+\ B}$
$\qquad14$

16. $\qquad5$
(14) $\underline{-\ C}$
$\qquad2$

17. $\qquad8$
(1) $\underline{+\ D}$
$\qquad15$

18. $\quad15$
(14) $\underline{-\ K}$
$\qquad9$

19. $\qquad3$
(2) $\qquad N$
$\underline{+\ 2}$
$\qquad13$

20. $\quad476$
(18) $\underline{-\ 252}$

21. $\quad47$
(18) $\underline{-\ 16}$

22. $\quad28$
(18) $\underline{-\ 13}$

23. $\quad75$
(18) $\underline{+\ T}$
$\qquad87$

24. $\quad24$
(18) $\underline{+\ E}$
$\qquad67$

25. Write the next three numbers in this sequence:
(3)

$$81, 72, 63, \underline{\qquad}, \underline{\qquad}, \underline{\qquad}, \ldots$$

LESSON 19

Subtracting Two-Digit Numbers with Regrouping

Facts Practice: 100 Subtraction Facts (Test B in Test Masters)

Mental Math: Review.

    a. 250 + 300 + 100 **b.** 20 + 36 + 19   **c.** 76 + 9 + 9
    d. 64 + 9 + 10   **e.** 27 + 19 + 20   **f.** 427 + 200

Patterns: On this hundred number chart we began circling the multiples of three. We drew an "X" on the multiples of four. The number 12 has both a circle and an X. On another chart, finish the pattern. Then shade the boxes that have numbers with both a circle and an X.

1	2	③	✗	5	⑥	7	✗	⑨	10
11	⊗	13	14	⑮	✗	17	⑱	19	✗
21	22	23	24	25	26	27	28	29	30
31	32	33	34	35	36	37	38	39	40
41	42	43	44	45	46	47	48	49	50
51	52	53	54	55	56	57	58	59	60
61	62	63	64	65	66	67	68	69	70
71	72	73	74	75	76	77	78	79	80
81	82	83	84	85	86	87	88	89	90
91	92	93	94	95	96	97	98	99	100

Roberto had $53. He spent $24 to buy a jacket. Then how much money did Roberto have?

We will use pictures of bills to help us understand this problem.

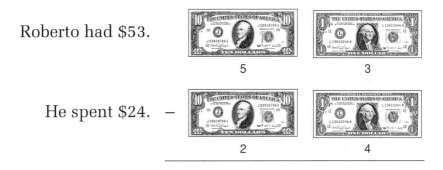

Roberto had $53.

He spent $24. −

Then he had ...

This picture shows that Roberto had 5 tens and 3 ones and that he needs to take from that 2 tens and 4 ones. We see that Roberto has enough tens but not enough ones. To get more ones, Roberto needs to trade 1 ten for 10 ones.

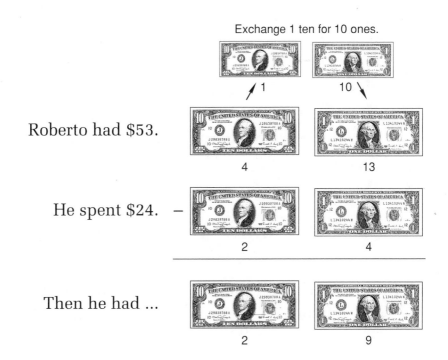

Exchange 1 ten for 10 ones.

Roberto had $53.

He spent $24. −

Then he had ...

After trading 1 ten for 10 ones, Roberto has 4 tens and 13 ones. Then he could take 2 tens and 4 ones from his money to pay for the jacket. That leaves him with 2 tens and 9 ones, which is $29.

Trading 1 ten for 10 ones is an example of **regrouping** or **exchanging** or **borrowing**. We often need to regroup when we subtract using pencil and paper.

Example   Find the difference: 56 − 29

Solution   We write the first number on top and see that we need to regroup.

$$\begin{array}{r} 56 \\ -\ 29 \\ \hline ? \end{array}$$

We understand that 56 means 50 and 6 and that 29 means 20 and 9. Since 6 is less than 9, we need to regroup before we subtract. We take 10 from 50 and add that 10 to the 6.

Take 10 from 50, leaving 40.

Add 10 to 6, making 16.

$$\begin{array}{r} \overset{40}{5\!\!\!/0} \text{ and } \overset{1}{6} \\ -\ 20 \text{ and } 9 \\ \hline 20 \text{ and } 7 \end{array}$$

This makes 56 into 40 and 16, which is still equal to 56. Now we subtract and get 20 and 7, which is **27.** This is how we usually show the regrouping.

$$\begin{array}{r} \overset{4}{5\!\!\!/}\,\overset{1}{6} \\ -\ 2\ 9 \\ \hline 2\ 7 \end{array}$$

Practice   Use bills or draw pictures to show these subtractions:

a. $53 − $29   b. $56 − $27

Use pencil and paper to find each difference:

c. 63 − 36   d. 40 − 13

Problem set 19

1. Jimmy found six hundred eighteen acorns under one tree. He found one hundred seventeen acorns under another tree. How many acorns did Jimmy find in all? Draw a SSM pattern.
(12)

2. On the first day Richard the Lion-Hearted had sixteen knights. On the second day some more knights came. Then he had seventy-six knights. How many knights came on the second day? Draw a SSM pattern.
(17)

3. Use the digits 3, 6, and 7 once each to write an even number less than 400.
(11)

4. Use words to write the number 605.
(8)

5. The smallest odd two-digit number is 11. What is the smallest even two-digit number?
(11)

6. Compare: 75 ◯ 57
(15)

7. Subtract 245 from 375.
(18)

8. To what number is the arrow pointing?
(13)

9. $426
(16) + $298

10. $278
(16) + $456

11. 721
(16) + 189

12. 409
(16) + 198

13. D
(1) + 7
——
  12

14. 18
(14) − A
——
   9

15. 8
(1) + B
——
 12

16. C
(14) − 4
——
  1

17. $456
(18) − $120

18. $54
(19) − $27

19. 46
(19) − 28

20. 35
(19) − 16

21. What is the total number of days in the last two months of the year?
(6)

22. The numbers 5, 6, and 11 are a fact family. Write four
(7) addition/subtraction facts using these three numbers.

23. 3 + 6 + 7 + 5 + 4 + 8
(1)

Write the next three numbers in each sequence:

24. 81, 72, 63, _____, _____, _____, ...
(3)

25. 14, 21, 28, _____, _____, _____, ...
(3)

LESSON 20

Expanded Form • More on Missing Numbers in Subtraction

Facts Practice: 100 Addition Facts (Test A in Test Masters)

Mental Math: Add a number ending in two zeros to a two-digit number.

a. 27 + 100   b. 63 + 200
c. 28 + 20 + 300   d. 36 + 9 + 200
e. 45 + 19 + 100   f. 48 + 29 + 300
g. What number should be added to each of these numbers for the total to be 10: 2, 5, 6, 3, 1?

Problem Solving: Bob had four coins in his pocket totaling 25¢. What coins did Bob have in his pocket?

Expanded form The number 365 means

3 hundreds and 6 tens and 5 ones

We can write this as

300 + 60 + 5

This is the expanded form of 365.

Example 1 Write 275 in expanded form.

Solution **200 + 70 + 5**

Example 2   Write 407 in expanded form.

Solution   There are no tens. We write

$$400 + 7$$

More on missing numbers in subtraction   We have found missing numbers in subtraction problems by "subtracting down" or "adding up." We can use these methods when subtracting numbers with one, two, or more digits.

SUBTRACTING DOWN:

$$\begin{array}{r} 56 \\ - \ W \\ \hline 14 \end{array}$$

We ask ourselves:

"Six minus what number is four?"

"Five minus what number is one?"

We find that the missing number is 42.

ADDING UP:

$$\begin{array}{r} N \\ - \ 56 \\ \hline 23 \end{array}$$

We add up:

"Three plus six is nine."

"Two plus five is seven."

The missing number is 79.

In this lesson we will practice another method for finding missing numbers in subtraction problems. Look for a pattern in each pair of subtraction facts shown here.

$$\begin{array}{rr} 12 & 12 \\ - \ 5 & - \ 7 \\ \hline 7 & 5 \end{array} \qquad \begin{array}{rr} 15 & 15 \\ - \ 6 & - \ 9 \\ \hline 9 & 6 \end{array} \qquad \begin{array}{rr} 23 & 23 \\ - \ 11 & - \ 12 \\ \hline 12 & 11 \end{array}$$

Notice that in each subtraction fact two numbers can be reversed. We may use this pattern to help us find missing numbers in subtraction problems.

Example 3   Find the missing number:

$$\begin{array}{r} 64 \\ - \ W \\ \hline 36 \end{array}$$

Solution   We will reverse the two lower numbers.

$$\begin{array}{r} 64 \\ - \ W \\ \hline 36 \end{array} \qquad\qquad \begin{array}{r} 64 \\ - \ 36 \\ \hline W \end{array}$$

Then we will subtract to find the missing number.

$$\overset{5}{\cancel{6}}\overset{1}{4}$$
$$-\ 3\ 6$$
$$\overline{\ \ 2\ 8}$$

We find that the missing number is **28.** Now we check 28 in the original problem.

64	$\overset{5}{\cancel{6}}\overset{1}{4}$	Sixty-four minus 28 is 36.
$-\ W$	$-\ 2\ 8$	The answer checks.
$\overline{36}$	$\overline{3\ 6}$	The missing number is 28.

Practice   Write each of these numbers in expanded form:

    a. 86   **b.** 325   **c.** 507

Find the missing numbers:

d. 36	**e.** 41	**f.** 50
$-\ P$	$-\ Q$	$-\ T$
$\overline{\ \ 19}$	$\overline{\ \ 24}$	$\overline{\ \ 17}$

**Problem set
20**

1. Twenty-three horses grazed in the pasture. The rest of
(17) the horses were in the corral. If there were eighty-nine
horses in all, how many horses were in the corral?
Draw a SSM pattern.

2. Three hundred seventy-five students stood silently in
(12) the hall. The other one hundred seven students in the
hall were shouting and jumping up and down.
Altogether, how many students were in the hall? Draw
a SSM pattern.

3. Use the digits 1, 2, and 8 once each to write an odd
(11) number less than 300.

4. Write 782 in expanded form.
(20)

5. The largest odd three-digit number is 999. What is the
(11) smallest three-digit even number?

6. Compare: 918 ◯ 819
(15)

7. How many days are in 6 weeks? Count by sevens.
(3)

8. To what number is the arrow pointing?
(13)

| | 300 | 400 | 500 |

9. $\$576$
(16) $+ \$128$

10. $\$243$
(16) $+ \$578$

11. 186
(16) $+ 285$

12. 329
(16) $+ 186$

13. D
(18) $+ 12$
      $\overline{17}$

14. 17
(14) $- A$
      $\overline{9}$

15. 8
(1) $+ B$
      $\overline{14}$

16. C
(14) $- 7$
      $\overline{2}$

17. 25
(19) $- 19$

18. 42
(19) $- 28$

19. 46
(19) $- 18$

20. 42
(19) $- 16$

21. 68
(20) $- D$
      $\overline{34}$

22. B
(20) $- 34$
      $\overline{15}$

23. 62
(20) $- H$
      $\overline{28}$

24. L
(20) $- 46$
      $\overline{36}$

25. Write the next three numbers in this sequence:
(3)
      16, 20, 24, _____, _____, _____, ...

LESSON
21

Adding Columns of Numbers

Sometimes the sum of the digits in the ones' column is a number greater than 19. When this happens, we bring a group of 2 tens or 3 tens or more to the tens' column.

Example 1 Add: 28 + 16 + 39 + 29

Solution We write the numbers in a column and add the ones. The sum is 32, which is 3 tens and 2 ones. We write the 3 tens either above or below the tens' column and finish adding.

$$
\begin{array}{ccc}
\text{3 above} & \text{or} & \text{3 below} \\
\begin{array}{r}
{\scriptstyle 3} \\
28 \\
16 \\
39 \\
+\ 29 \\
\hline
\mathbf{112}
\end{array}
& &
\begin{array}{r}
28 \\
16 \\
39 \\
+\ 29 \\
{\scriptstyle 3} \\
\hline
\mathbf{112}
\end{array}
\end{array}
$$

Example 2 Add: 227 + 88 + 6

Solution We line up the last digits of the numbers. Then we add the digits in the ones' column and get 21.

$$
\begin{array}{r}
227 \\
88 \\
+\ \ \ 6 \\
\hline
\textcircled{21}
\end{array}
$$

The number 21 is 2 tens plus 1 one. We record the 1 in the ones' column and write the 2 in the tens' column, and then we add the tens. The sum is 12 tens.

$$
\begin{array}{r}
\overset{2}{227} \\
88 \\
+\quad 6 \\
\hline
\textcircled{12}1
\end{array}
$$

We record a 2 in the tens' place and write the 1, which is 1 hundred, in the next column. Then we add in the hundreds' column.

$$
\begin{array}{r}
\overset{1\,2}{227} \\
88 \\
+\quad 6 \\
\hline
\mathbf{321}
\end{array}
$$

Practice

a.
$$
\begin{array}{r}
47 \\
29 \\
46 \\
+\ 95 \\
\hline
\end{array}
$$

b.
$$
\begin{array}{r}
28 \\
47 \\
+\ 65 \\
\hline
\end{array}
$$

c.
$$
\begin{array}{r}
38 \\
22 \\
31 \\
+\ 46 \\
\hline
\end{array}
$$

d.
$$
\begin{array}{r}
438 \\
76 \\
+\ \ 5 \\
\hline
\end{array}
$$

e. 15 + 24 + 11 + 25 + 36

Problem set 21

1. (17) One doctor put in twenty-four stitches. A second doctor put in some more stitches. There were seventy-five stitches in all. How many stitches did the second doctor put in? Draw a SSM pattern.

2. (12) Four hundred seven roses were in front. Three hundred sixty-two roses were behind. How many roses were there in all? Draw a SSM pattern.

3. (11) Use the digits 9, 2, and 8 once each to write an even number less than 300.

4. (20,8) Write 813 in expanded form. Then use words to write the number.

5. The largest two-digit even number is 98. What is the
(11) smallest two-digit odd number?

6. To what number is the arrow pointing?
(13)

7. 294
(21)   312
     +   5

8. $189
(16) + $298

9. $378
(16) + $496

10.   109
(16)   + 486

11.   14
(21)   28
       35
       16
     + 227

12.   14
(14)   − A
        7

13.   8
(1)   + B
       14

14.   C
(14)   − 13
        5

15.   11
(14)   − D
        9

16.   E
(14)   − 5
        8

17.   38
(19)   − 29

18.   57
(19)   − 38

19.   34
(18)   + B
       86

20.   48
(20)   − O
       25

21.   D
(20)   − 46
       15

22.   Y
(20)   − 15
       17

Write the next three numbers in each sequence:

23. 48, 44, 40, _____, _____, _____, ...
(3)

24. 12, 15, 18, _____, _____, _____, ...
(3)

25. The numbers 6, 9, and 15 are a fact family. Write four
(7) addition/subtraction facts using these three numbers.

**LESSON
22**

Reading Scales

Facts Practice: 100 Subtraction Facts (Test B in Test Masters)

Mental Math: Add tens and then ones. For example, 32 + 43
is 70 and 5, which is 75.

a. 32	**b.** 56	**c.** 45	**d.** 67	**e.** 41	**f.** 64
+ 41	+ 42	+ 24	+ 22	+ 53	+ 31

g. What number should be added to each of these numbers
for the total to be 10: 3, 8, 1, 5, 4?

Problem Solving: Sam had five coins in his pocket totaling
less than 50 cents. He didn't have any
pennies, but he did have a quarter. What
coins did Sam have in his pocket?

A **scale** is a type of number line often used for measuring. Scales are found on rulers, gauges, thermometers, speedometers, and many other instruments. The trick to reading a scale is to determine the distance between the marks on the scale. Then we can find the values of all the marks on the scale.

We use a thermometer to measure temperature. Temperature is usually measured in degrees Fahrenheit (abbreviated °F) or in degrees Celsius (abbreviated °C). On a Fahrenheit thermometer, tick marks are often two degrees apart.

Example 1 What temperature is shown on this Fahrenheit thermometer?

Solution There are five spaces between 50° and 60° on this scale, so each space cannot equal one degree. If we try counting by twos, we find our count matches the scale. We count up by twos from 50° and find that the temperature is **54°F.**

Example 2   This speedometer shows speed in miles per hour (mph). The speedometer shows that the car is going how fast?

Solution   By trying different counts on the scale, we find that each space equals five. If we count up by fives from 40, we see that the pointer points to 55. The car is going **55 mph.**

Practice   What number is indicated on each of these scales?

a.

b.

Problem set 22

1. The first flower had twenty-four petals. The second flower had more petals. There were fifty-six petals in all. How many petals did the second flower have? Draw a SSM pattern.
   (17)

2. Four hundred seventy-two soldiers strutted proudly in front. Two hundred seven soldiers walked sadly behind them. How many soldiers were there in all? Draw a SSM pattern.
   (12)

3. Use the digits 2, 5, and 7 once each to write an even number that is greater than 700.
   (11)

4. The tens' digit is 4. The ones' digit is 9. The number is
(5) between 200 and 300. What is the number?

5. Which of these numbers is an odd number that is
(11) greater than 750?

A. 846   B. 864   C. 903   D. 309

6. To what number is the arrow pointing?
(13)

7. $392	8. $439	9. 774	10. 389
(16) + $278	(16) + $339	(16) + 174	(16) + 398

11. 13
(21)   25
          46
          25
       + 29

12.   18
(20)   − A
          12

13.   8
(1)   + B
          16

14.   C
(14)   − 5
          3

15. 62
(19) − 48

16. 82
(19) − 58

17. 28
(21)   36
        57
     + 47

18. 35
(20) − Y
       14

19. 45
(18) + P
       55

20. 75
(20) − L
       47

21.   C
(20)   − 47
          35

22.   E
(18)   + 15
          37

23. Write 498 in expanded form.
(20)

24. Compare: 423 ◯ 432
(15)

25. 4 + 7 + 3 + 5 + 2 + 3 + 2 + 7 + 8
(1)

LESSON 23

Reading Time from a Clock

Facts Practice: 100 Subtraction Facts (Test B in Test Masters)

Mental Math: Review.

  a. 44 + 32   **b.** 57 + 20
  c. 57 + 19   **d.** 32 + 43 + 100
  e. 58 + 31 + 200   **f.** 56 + 29 + 100
  g. What number should be added to each of these numbers
      for the total to be 10: 7, 2, 9, 5, 6?

Patterns: The multiples of seven are 7, 14, 21, and so on. On
        a hundred number chart, shade the squares that
        contain a multiple of seven. Which of the shaded
        squares contain an even number that is a multiple
        of five?

The scale on a clock is actually two number lines in one.
One number line marks hours and is usually numbered.
The other number line marks minutes and usually is not
numbered. We have numbered the minute number line
outside this clock. Notice that each big mark is five
minutes. So counting by fives can help us find the number
of minutes before or after the hour.

To tell time, we read the location of the short hand on the
hour number line and the location of the long hand on the
minute number line.

   To write the time of day, we write the hour followed
by a colon. Then we write two digits to show the number
of minutes after the hour. We use the abbreviation a.m. for

the 12 hours before noon and p.m. for the 12 hours after noon. This form is referred to as *digital form*. Noon is written as 12:00 p.m. and midnight is 12:00 a.m.[†]

Example 1 If it is evening, what time is shown by the clock?

Solution Since the short hand is between the 9 and the 10, we know it is after 9 p.m. We count 5, 10, 15, 20 minutes after 9:00 p.m. It is **9:20 p.m.**

Since sixty minutes is one hour, thirty minutes is half an hour. So if the time is 7:30, we might say that the time is half past seven. Fifteen minutes is a quarter of an hour. At 6:15 we might say that the time is a quarter after six.

| 7:30 | 6:15 | 3:45 |
| "Half past seven" | "A quarter after six" | "A quarter to four" |

Sometimes when it is getting close to the next hour, we say how many minutes it is until the next hour. When the time is 5:50, we might say, "It is ten minutes to six." When it is 3:45, we might say, "It is a quarter to four."

Example 2 Use the digital form to show what time it is at a quarter to eight in the evening.

Solution A quarter to eight is 15 minutes before eight, which is **7:45 p.m.**

[†]The use of p.m. and a.m. to designate 12:00 is unclear. To avoid confusion, we refer to these times as *noon* and *midnight*.

Practice   If it is morning, what time is shown by each clock?

a.
b.
c.

d. Use the digital form to show what time it is at ten minutes to nine in the evening.

Problem set
23

1. On the first day Sarah sharpened fifty-one pencils.
(17) Then she sharpened some more pencils on the second day. She sharpened seventy-six pencils in all. How many pencils did she sharpen on the second day? Draw a SSM pattern.

2. Two hundred seventy ambassadors came on Monday.
(12) Three hundred two ambassadors came on Tuesday. One hundred eleven ambassadors came on Wednesday. How many ambassadors came in all? Draw a SSM pattern.

3. The hundreds' digit is 5. The ones' digit is 7. The
(5) number is greater than 540 and less than 550. What is the number?

4. Write 905 in expanded form.
(20)

5. Use digits and a comparison symbol to write "One
(15) hundred twenty is greater than one hundred twelve."

6. This clock shows that it is half
(23) past four. It is afternoon. Write the time shown in digital form.

7. What temperature is shown on the
(22) thermometer?

8. $468
(16) + $293

9. 468
(16) + 185

10. $187
(16) + $698

11.   14
(14) − A
    7

12.   8
(1) + B
    16

13.   C
(14) − 8
    7

14.   14
(14) − D
    9

15.   74
(19) − 58

16. $44
(19) − $28

17.   23
(19) − 18

18. $62
(19) − $43

19.   25
(21)   28
    46
  + 88

20.   45
(20) − P
    21

21.   13
(18) + B
    37

22.   F
(20) − 45
    32

23. How many quarters are equal to four dollars? Count by
(3) fours.

24. Write a number sentence for this
(1) picture.

25. Write the next three numbers in this sequence:
(3)
       8, 16, 24, _____, _____, _____, …

LESSON 24

Reading a Centimeter Scale

Facts Practice: 100 Addition Facts (Test A in Test Masters)

Mental Math: Review.

a. 63 + 21   b. 45 + 23
c. 65 + 30   d. 48 + 19 + 200
e. 36 + 29 + 30   f. 130 + 200 + 300
g. What number should be added to each of these numbers
   for the total to be 10: 8, 4, 3, 9, 5?

Problem Solving: The hour hand moves around the face of a
clock once in twelve hours. How many
times does the hour hand move around the
face of the clock in a week?

The scale on a ruler is used to measure length. One kind of scale used on a ruler is a **centimeter** scale. A centimeter is this long.

———

We use the letters "cm" to abbreviate the word *centimeter*. To measure lengths in centimeters, we match the length of the object we are measuring with the marks on the scale.

Example How long is this nail?

Solution The head of the nail is lined up on the "zero" of the centimeter scale. The point of the nail is closest to the 5-centimeter mark of the scale, so the nail is 5 centimeters long. We abbreviate this by writing **5 cm.**

Practice   Find the length of each object to the nearest centimeter:

a.

b.

c. Use the centimeter scale on your ruler to draw a line segment 10 cm long.

d. Use the centimeter scale on your ruler to measure how long this book is.

Problem set 24

1. Martine gathered a "whole bunch" of eggs one day. *(17)* She gathered twenty-one eggs on the second day. If she gathered seventy-two eggs in all, how many were in the whole bunch? Draw a SSM pattern.

2. Four hundred seventy-six children stood quietly in *(12)* one line. Three hundred ninety-seven children stood quietly in another line. Altogether, how many children stood quietly in line? Draw a SSM pattern.

3. The ones' digit is 5. The tens' digit is 6. The number is *(5)* between 600 and 700. What is the number?

4. Write 509 in expanded form. *(20)*

5. Use digits and a comparison symbol to compare 493 *(15)* and 439.

6. What temperature is shown on
(22) this thermometer?

7. It is a quarter after four in the
(23) afternoon. Write the time shown
in digital form.

8. How long is the pin?
(24)

9. $476
(16)   + $285

10. $185
(16)   + $499

11.   568
(16)   + 397

12.   478
(16)   + 196

13.   17
(14)   − A
        9

14.   14
(14)   − B
        14

15.   13
(14)   − C
        6

16. $35
(19)   − $28

17.   23
(19)   − 15

18.   63
(19)   − 36

19.   74
(19)   − 59

20.   M
(18)   + 22
        45

21.   K
(20)   − 15
        32

22.   47
(20)   − K
        34

23.   28
(21)   36
        44
    + 58

24.   49
(21)   28
        32
    + 55

25. Without a ruler, try to draw a line segment that is 3 cm
(24) long. Then use the centimeter scale on your ruler to
check your drawing.

LESSON 25

Triangles, Rectangles, Squares, and Circles

Facts Practice: 100 Subtraction Facts (Test B in Test Masters)

Mental Math: Add hundreds, then tens, and then ones.

a. 320	**b.** 645	**c.** 145	**d.** 632	**e.** 86	**f.** 360
+ 256	+ 32	+ 250	+ 55	+ 210	25
					+ 214

g. What number should be added to each of these numbers for the total to be 10: 2, 6, 7, 1, 5?

Patterns: On a hundred number chart, shade the squares that contain a multiple of 9. Then write these shaded numbers from 9 to 90 in a column. What patterns can you find in the column of numbers?

In this lesson we will practice drawing triangles, rectangles, squares, and circles.

Example 1 Draw a triangle that has all sides the same length.

Solution You may need to practice on scratch paper until you find out how to draw this triangle. A triangle has three sides. If you start out with a "square" corner, the third side will be too long.

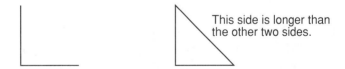

A triangle that has all sides the same length looks like this.

Example 2 Draw a rectangle that has all sides the same length.

Solution   A rectangle does not have to be longer than it is wide. A rectangle does have "square corners" and four sides. A rectangle with all sides the same length looks like this.

This may look like a square to you. It **is** a square. It is also a rectangle. **A square is a special kind of rectangle.**

Example 3   Draw a circle that is about 1 centimeter across the center.

Solution   First we will draw a line segment one centimeter long. Then we will draw a circle around the segment.

Circle drawing improves with practice.

Practice   **a.** Draw a triangle that has two sides that are the same length.

b. Draw a rectangle that is about twice as long as it is wide.

c. Draw a square. Inside the square draw a circle that just touches all four sides of the square.

Problem set 25

1. Roger had four hundred seventeen marbles. Harry had
(12) two hundred twenty-two marbles. How many marbles did Roger and Harry have in all? Draw a SSM pattern.

2. Susie put forty jacks into a pile. Jane put all of her
(17) jacks in the pile. Then there were seventy-two jacks in the pile. How many jacks did Jane put in? Draw a SSM pattern.

3. The ones' digit is 5. The number is greater than 640
(5) and less than 650. What is the number?

4. Write seven hundred fifty-three in expanded form.
(20)

5. Use digits and a comparison symbol to compare four
(15) hundred seventy-seven and five hundred forty-two.

6. The needle is pointing to what
(22) number on this scale?

7. How long is the pencil?
(24)

8.   493
(16)   + 278

9. $486
(16) + $378

10. $524
(16) + $109

11. Draw a triangle in which each side is 2 cm long.
(25)

12. Draw a square. Then draw a circle around the square
(25) so that the circle just touches each corner of the
square.

13.   17
(14)   − A
       ───
        9

14.   45
(19)   − 29
       ───

15.   15
(14)   − B
       ───
        6

16.   62
(19)   − 45
       ───

17.   24
(18)   + D
       ───
       45

18.   14
(14)   − B
       ───
        2

19.   Y
(20)   − 36
       ───
       56

20.   75
(20)   − P
       ───
       48

21.   46
(21)   35
          27
       + 39
       ───

22.   14
(21)   28
          77
       + 23
       ───

23.   14
(21)   23
          38
       + 64
       ───

24.   15
(21)   24
          36
       + 99
       ───

25. Write the next three numbers in this sequence:
(3)

28, 35, 42, _____, _____, _____, ...

LESSON 26

Rounding Whole Numbers to the Nearest Ten

Facts Practice: 100 Subtraction Facts (Test B in Test Masters)

Mental Math: Add hundreds, then tens, and then ones.
  a. 365 + 321   **b.** 650 + 45
  c. 40 + 300 + 25   **d.** 500 + 40 + 16
  e. 300 + 50 + 12   **f.** 400 + 80 + 11
  g. Seven can be split into 3 + 4. Seven can also be split into
       2 + ☐.

Problem Solving: The pair of numbers 1 and 8 have the sum
                    of 9. List three more pairs of counting
                    numbers that have a sum of 9.

One of the sentences below uses an **exact number.** The other sentence uses a **rounded number.** Can you tell which sentence uses the rounded number?

 • The radio cost about $70.

 • The radio cost $68.47.

The first sentence uses a rounded number. Rounded numbers usually end with a zero. Rounded numbers are often used in place of exact numbers because they are easy to understand and easy to work with.

   To round an exact number to the nearest ten, we choose the closest number that ends in zero. The number line can help us understand rounding.

We see that 67 is between 60 and 70. Since 67 is closer to 70 than it is to 60, we say that 67 is "about 70." When we say this, we have rounded 67 to the nearest ten.

Example   Round 82 to the nearest ten.

Solution   Rounding to the nearest ten means to round to a number
we would say when counting by tens (10, 20, 30, 40, and
so on). We will use a number line marked off in tens to
picture this problem.

We see that 82 is between 80 and 90. Since 82 is closer to
80 than it is to 90, we round 82 to **80.**

Practice   Round each number to the nearest ten. For each problem,
draw a number line to show your work.

    a. 78   **b.** 43   **c.** 61   **d.** 49

**Problem set
26**

1. Forty-four dogs were in front. Seventy-six dogs were
(12) in the middle. Twenty-three dogs brought up the rear.
How many dogs were there in all? Draw a SSM
pattern.

2. The smallest three-digit whole number is subtracted
(18) from two hundred twenty-four. What is the answer?

3. Amelda had twenty-six books. Then Grant gave her
(17) some more books. Now she has ninety-nine books.
How many books did Grant give to Amelda? Draw a
SSM pattern.

4. List the odd numbers between 740 and 750.
(11)

5. Write four hundred eleven in expanded form.
(20)

6. Use digits and a comparison symbol to write "Five
(15) hundred eighty is greater than five hundred eighteen."

7. Round 71 to the nearest ten.
(26)

8. How long is the AA battery?
(24)

9. Draw a triangle that has all sides the same length.
(25) Then draw a circle around the triangle that just
touches the "corners" of the triangle.

10.   387
(16) + 196

11. $496
(16) + $503

12.   762
(16) + 109

13. $458
(16) + $385

14.   129
(16) + 548

15. $43
(19) − $27

16.   42
(19) − 15

17.   52
(20) − Y
          27

18.   X
(20) − 29
          18

19.   73
(20) − C
          46

20.   14
(21)   28
            47
          + 33

21.   21
(21)   38
            46
          + 93

22. Write four addition/subtraction facts using the three
(7) numbers 5, 8, and 13.

Write the next three numbers in each sequence:

23. 14, 21, 28, _____, _____, _____, ...
(3)

24. 20, 24, 28, _____, _____, _____, ...
(3)

25. Without a ruler, try to draw a line segment that is 2 cm
(24) long. Then use your ruler to check your drawing.

LESSON
27

Metric Units of Length

Facts Practice: 100 Subtraction Facts (Test B in Test Masters)

Mental Math: Add hundreds, then tens, and then ones.
  a. 340 + 50 + 200   **b.** 200 + 50 + 432
  c. 560 + 200 + 25
Review:
  d. 56 + 19 + 200   **e.** 48 + 39 + 100   **f.** 36 + 9
  g. Complete each split: 6 = 2 + ☐   6 = 3 + ☐

Problem Solving: If the sun rose at 5:00 a.m. and then set at
                    7:00 p.m., how many hours of sunlight
                    were there?

The centimeter is a unit we use to measure short distances. To measure longer distances, we use the **meter** or the **kilometer.**

A meter is exactly 100 centimeters. An easy way to remember this fact is that there are 100 centimeters in 1 meter just as there are 100 cents in one dollar. Perhaps you have a meterstick in your classroom. A meterstick is a ruler that is 1 meter long. Notice it is also 100 centimeters long. If you took a **big step,** your step would be about **1 meter.**

From the word *meter* comes the word *metric*. The **metric system** of measurement uses meters, fractions of meters, and multiples of meters to measure distances.

A much larger unit of length in the metric system is the kilometer. *Kilo-* means "1000." **A kilometer is 1000 meters.** If you took **1000 big steps,** you would walk about **1 kilometer.**

We often use the abbreviations "cm," "m," and "km" to stand for "centimeters," "meters," and "kilometers."

Metric Units of Length

100 cm = 1 m
1000 m = 1 km

Activities (a) Use a meterstick to measure the height and width of a classroom door.

(b) Estimate the length and width of the classroom by "pacing off" the distance between opposite walls. Then measure the distance using a meterstick.

Practice **a.** If Simon said, "Take 5 giants steps," about how many meters would you walk?

b. One meter is how many centimeters?

c. One kilometer is how many meters?

Problem set **1.** When the bell rang, three hundred forty-two students
27   *(12)* came. When the bell rang again, two hundred fourteen students came. How many students came in all? Draw a SSM pattern.

2. The small horn sounded 46 times. The big horn
(17) sounded many times. If the horns sounded a total of 98 times, how many times did the big horn sound? Draw a SSM pattern.

3. Write seven hundred forty-two in expanded form.
(20)

4. Simon was twelfth in line. Mandy was seventh in line.
(6) How many people were between Simon and Mandy?

5. Round sixty-eight to the nearest ten.
(26)

6. A door is about how many meters wide?
(27)

7. What temperature is shown on the
(22) thermometer?

8. Draw a rectangle that is 2 centimeters long and 1
(25) centimeter wide.

9. Use digits and a comparison symbol to write "Three
(15) hundred twenty-seven is less than three hundred
thirty."

10. $43   **11.** $278   **12.**   61   **13.**   72
(19) $\underline{-\ \$27}$ (16) $\underline{+\ \$569}$ (19) $\underline{-\ 37}$ (19) $\underline{-\ 29}$

14.   389   **15.**   47   **16.**   43   **17.**   389
(16) $\underline{+\ 256}$ (20) $\underline{-\ Q}$ (18) $\underline{+\ S}$ (18) $\underline{-\ 256}$
                        14   74

18. 486 + 276   **19.** 91 − 76
(16)   (19)

20. 42 + 23 + 86 + 98   **21.** 95 + 87 + 24 + 38
(21)   (21)

Write the next three numbers in each sequence:

22. 24, 30, 36, _____, _____, _____, ⋯
(3)

23. 28, 32, 36, _____, _____, _____, ⋯
(3)

24. 24 + 26 + 35 + 27 + 15
(21)

25. 36 + 15 + 43 + 55 + 23
(21)

LESSON
28

Naming Fractions • Adding Dollars and Cents

Facts Practice: 100 Subtraction Facts (Test B in Test Masters)

Mental Math: Add from the left with regrouping. For example, 35 + 26 is 50 plus 11, which is 61.

a.	55	**b.**	36	**c.**	48	**d.**	37	**e.**	235	**f.**	156
	+ 25		+ 26		+ 22		+ 45		+ 145		+ 326

g. Complete each split: 8 = 1 + □   8 = 3 + □

Problem Solving: Jennifer has three coins in her left pocket that total 65¢. What coins does Jennifer have in her left pocket?

Naming fractions

Part of a whole can be named with a fraction. A fraction is written with two numbers. The bottom number of a fraction is called the **denominator.** The denominator tells how many equal parts are in the whole. The top number of a fraction is called the **numerator.** The numerator tells how many of the parts are being counted. When naming fractions, we name the numerator first; then we name the denominator using the ordinal number. Some fractions and their names are given here.

$\frac{1}{2}$ one half $\frac{3}{5}$ three fifths

$\frac{1}{3}$ one third $\frac{5}{6}$ five sixths

$\frac{2}{3}$ two thirds $\frac{7}{8}$ seven eighths

$\frac{1}{4}$ one fourth $\frac{1}{10}$ one tenth

Example 1   What fraction of the circle is shaded?

Solution   There are four equal parts, and three are shaded. Therefore, the fraction of the circle that is shaded is three fourths, which we write

$$\frac{3}{4}$$

Adding dollars and cents We add dollars and cents just like we add whole numbers. The dot, called a **decimal point,** separates dollars from cents. To add dollars to dollars and cents to cents, we align the decimal points. We remember the dollar sign and the decimal point when we write the sum.

Example 2 Add:　$3.56
+ $2.75

Solution We add the pennies, add the dimes, and add the dollars. Since ten pennies equal a dime and ten dimes equal a dollar, we regroup when the total in any column is ten or more.

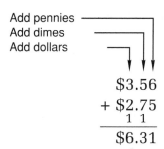

```
Add pennies ─────────┐
Add dimes ────────┐  │
Add dollars ───┐  │  │
               ▼  ▼  ▼
              $3.56
            + $2.75
               1  1
             ─────────
              $6.31
```

Practice What fraction of each shape is shaded?

a. 1/3

b. 5/9

c. 3/8

d. 1/4

Add:

e.　$2.75
+ $2.75

f.　$3.65
+ $4.28

Problem set 28

1. The first four odd numbers are 1, 3, 5, and 7. What is
(1)　their sum?

2. James was 49 inches tall at the beginning of summer.
(12)　He grew 2 inches over the summer. How tall was James at the end of summer? Draw a SSM pattern.

3. Use the digits 1, 2, and 3 once each to make an odd
(11) number less than 200.

Write the next three numbers in each sequence:

4. 80, 72, 64, _____, _____, _____, ...
(3)

5. 60, 54, 48, _____, _____, _____, ...
(3)

Find the missing number in each sequence:

6. 18, _____, 36, 45, ...   **7.** 18, _____, 22, 24, ...
(3)   (3)

8. What is the place value of the 9 in 891?
(5)

9. Write 106 in expanded form.
(20)

10. Write 160 using words.
(8)

11. Use digits and symbols to write that eighteen minus
(15) nine equals five plus four.

12. Round 28 to the nearest ten.
(26)

13. A bicycle is about how many meters long?
(27)

14. The needle is pointing to what
(22) number on this scale?

15. Draw a circle that is 2 centimeters
(25) across the center.

16. What fraction of the rectangle is
(28) shaded?

17. The door was two meters high. Two meters is how
(27) many centimeters?

18. 51 − 43   **19.** 70 − 44   **20.** 37 − 9
(19)   (19)   (19)

21. $8.79 + $0.64   **22.** $5.75 + $2.75
(28)   (28)

23.
(18)
$$\begin{array}{r} N \\ + \ 13 \\ \hline 17 \end{array}$$

24.
(20)
$$\begin{array}{r} X \\ - \ 42 \\ \hline 27 \end{array}$$

25.
(20)
$$\begin{array}{r} 31 \\ - \ O \\ \hline 14 \end{array}$$

LESSON 29

Parallel and Perpendicular Lines · Right Angles

Facts Practice: 100 Subtraction Facts (Test B in Test Masters)

Mental Math: Add hundreds, then tens, and then ones, regrouping ones.

a. 25 + 36

b. 147 + 225

c. 30 + 25 + 26

d. 356 + 26

e. 46 + 10 + 28

f. 350 + 35 + 7

g. Complete each split: 9 = 3 + ☐   9 = 4 + ☐

Problem Solving: The two-digit numbers 18 and 81 are written with digits whose sum is nine. On your paper, list in order the eight two-digit numbers which have the sum of nine, from 18 to 81.

18, ___ , ___ , ___ , ___ , ___ , ___ , 81

Parallel and perpendicular lines

Lines that go in the same direction and stay the same distance apart are **parallel lines.**

Pairs of parallel lines

When lines cross, we say they **intersect.**

Pairs of intersecting lines

Intersecting lines that form "square corners" are **perpendicular.**

Pairs of perpendicular lines

Right angles   The corners are called **angles.** Square corners are called **right angles.**

Example 1   Which of these angles is a right angle?

A.   /   B. |_   C.   \

Solution   Angle B makes a square corner, so **angle B is a right angle.**

Example 2   Which shape below has four right angles?

A.   ⌂   B.   ▭   C.   ◺

Solution   The shape labeled "B" has four square corners. Thus **shape B has four right angles.**

Example 3   Draw a triangle that has one right angle.

Solution   We begin by drawing two line segments to make a right angle. Then we draw the third side.

Practice   **a.** Draw two lines that intersect but are not perpendicular.

b. Draw two lines that are perpendicular.

c. Are train tracks parallel or perpendicular?

d. A triangle has how many angles?

e. Which of these angles is not a right angle?

1. ⌐   (2.) ╱   3. ¬

**Problem set
29**

1. Twenty-eight children were in the first line. Forty-two
(12) children were in the second line. How many children
were in both lines? Draw a SSM pattern.

2. Tina knew that there were 28 books in two stacks. In
(17) the first stack Tina counted 12 books. Then she
figured out how many books were in the second stack.
How many books were in the second stack? Draw a
SSM pattern.

3. Use the digits 1, 2, and 3 once each to make an odd
(11) number greater than 300.

Write the next three numbers in each sequence:

4. 40, 36, 32, _____, _____, _____, ···
(3)

5. 30, 27, 24, _____, _____, _____, ···
(3)

6. Use digits and a comparison symbol to write that six
(15) hundred thirty-eight is less than six hundred eighty-
three.

7. Round 92 to the nearest ten.
(26)

8. A nickel is 2 centimeters across the center. If 10
(3) nickels are laid in a line, how long will the line be? Count by twos.

9. How long is this rectangle?
(24)

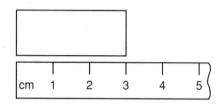

10. Draw a pair of perpendicular lines.
(29)

11. What fraction of this triangle is
(28) shaded?

1/3

12. If it is afternoon, what time is it?
(23)

2:15 pm

13. (19)	$83 − $27	**14.** (19)	42 − 27	**15.** (19)	72 − 36	**16.** (28)	$4.28 + $1.96

13. $83
(19) − $27

14. 42
(19) − 27

15. 72
(19) − 36

16. $4.28
(28) + $1.96

17. $4.36
(28) + $2.95

18. 57
(18) + K
        88

19. 67
(20) − B
        48

20. K
(20) − 22
        22

21. 42 − 27
(19)

22. 55 − 48
(19)

23. 31 − 14
(19)

24. 4 + 3 + 2 + 5 + 7 + 6 + 3 + 8 + 5 + 4
(1)

25. 25 + 25 + 25 + 25
(21)

More About Missing Addends

LESSON 30

Facts Practice: 100 Addition Facts (Test A in Test Masters)

Mental Math: Review.

  a. 54 + 36   **b.** 54 + 19   **c.** 54 + 120
  d. 350 + 30 + 200   **e.** 210 + 25 + 35   **f.** 48 + 29
  g. Complete each split: 5 = 1 + □   5 = 3 + □

Problem Solving: At 12:00 the hands of the clock point in the same direction. At 6:00 the hands point in opposite directions. At what hours do the hands of a clock form right angles?

We have found missing addends by asking an addition question. We can also find missing addends by asking a subtraction question.

What number plus
five equals
fourteen?

$$\begin{array}{r} N \\ + 5 \\ \hline 14 \end{array}$$

Fourteen minus
five equals what
number?

Sometimes the subtraction question is easier to answer.

Example 1 Find the missing addend:

$$\begin{array}{r} W \\ + 26 \\ \hline 63 \end{array}$$

Solution We will ask the subtraction question "Sixty-three minus twenty-six equals what number?"

$$\begin{array}{r} \overset{5}{\cancel{6}}\overset{1}{3} \\ - 2\,6 \\ \hline 3\,7 \end{array}$$

We find that the missing addend is **37.** Now we try 37 in the original problem to check our answer.

$$\begin{array}{r} 1 \\ 37 \\ + 26 \\ \hline 63 \end{array}$$

The answer checks.

Example 2   Find the missing addend:

$$\begin{array}{r} 37 \\ +\ M \\ \hline 84 \end{array}$$

Solution   Remember that with subtraction problems we may "subtract down" or "add up." With addition problems we may "add down" or "subtract up." Some people just remember that we can turn addition or subtraction problems and do the opposite operation.

ADD, OR TURN AND SUBTRACT   SUBTRACT, OR TURN AND ADD

$$\begin{array}{r} 5 \\ +\ 3 \\ \hline 8 \end{array} \qquad \begin{array}{r} 8 \\ -\ 3 \\ \hline 5 \end{array} \qquad\qquad \begin{array}{r} 15 \\ -\ 7 \\ \hline 8 \end{array} \qquad \begin{array}{r} 8 \\ +\ 7 \\ \hline 15 \end{array}$$

For this problem we may add, or turn and subtract.

$$\begin{array}{r} 37 \\ +\ M \\ \hline 84 \end{array} \qquad \begin{array}{r} 84 \\ -\ M \\ \hline 37 \end{array}$$

We will answer the subtraction problem as we have practiced.

$$\begin{array}{r} 84 \\ -\ M \\ \hline 37 \end{array} \quad > \quad \begin{array}{r} {}^{7}\!\!\!\not{8}{}^{1}4 \\ -\ 3\ 7 \\ \hline 4\ 7 \end{array}$$

Now we try 47 in the original problem.

$$\begin{array}{r} {}^{1} \\ 37 \\ +\ 47 \\ \hline 84 \end{array}$$

The answer checks. The missing addend is **47**.

Practice   Find the missing addends:

a. $\begin{array}{r} 23 \\ +\ M \\ \hline 42 \end{array}$ **b.** $\begin{array}{r} Q \\ +\ 17 \\ \hline 45 \end{array}$ **c.** $\begin{array}{r} 28 \\ +\ W \\ \hline 53 \end{array}$ **d.** $\begin{array}{r} Y \\ +\ 36 \\ \hline 54 \end{array}$

Problem set 30

1. Two hundred seventy-five fans sat in the first row.
   $^{(12)}$ Three hundred sixty-two fans sat in the second row. How many fans sat in the first two rows? Draw a SSM pattern.

2. There were 47 apples in the big tree. There was a total
   $^{(17)}$ of 82 apples in the big tree and in the little tree. How many apples were in the little tree? Draw a SSM pattern.

3. All the students lined up in two equal rows. Which
   $^{(11)}$ could not be the total number of students?

   A. 36   B. 45   C. 60

Find the missing numbers in each sequence:

4. 9, 18, _____, _____, 45, _____, ...
   $^{(3)}$

5. 7, 14, _____, _____, 35, _____, ...
   $^{(3)}$

6. Compare: 15 − 9 ⊘ 13 − 8
   $^{(15,7)}$
   $\qquad\qquad\quad 6 \qquad\qquad 5$

7. Round 77 to the nearest ten. 80
   $^{(26)}$

8. A professional basketball player is about how many
   $^{(27)}$ meters tall?

9. If it is morning, what time is
   $^{(23)}$ shown on this clock?

   7:10 AM

10. Which street is parallel to Elm?
    $^{(29)}$

11. What fraction of this shape is shaded?
₍₂₈₎

12. Draw a rectangle that is 3 centimeters long and 2 centimeters wide.
₍₂₅₎

13. Which of these angles is a right angle?
₍₂₉₎

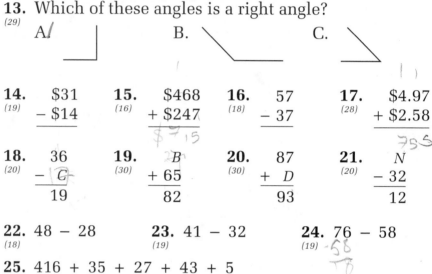

A.   B.   C.

14. ₍₁₉₎	**15.** ₍₁₆₎	**16.** ₍₁₈₎	**17.** ₍₂₈₎
$31 − $14	$468 + $247	57 − 37	$4.97 + $2.58

18. ₍₂₀₎	**19.** ₍₃₀₎	**20.** ₍₃₀₎	**21.** ₍₂₀₎
36 − C 19	B + 65 82	87 + D 93	N − 32 12

22. 48 − 28   **23.** 41 − 32   **24.** 76 − 58
₍₁₈₎   ₍₁₉₎   ₍₁₉₎

25. 416 + 35 + 27 + 43 + 5
₍₂₁₎

LESSON 31

"Some Went Away" Word Problems

Facts Practice: 100 Subtraction Facts (Test B in Test Masters)

Mental Math: We can split numbers to help us add. Adding 35 and 8, we may notice that 35 needs 5 more to make 40, and that 8 splits into 5 + 3. So to add 35 and 8, we could add 35 + 5 + 3.

a. 35 + 7   **b.** 26 + 8   **c.** 38 + 5
d. 47 + 6   **e.** 68 + 7   **f.** 45 + 8

Problem Solving: Tom has seven coins in his right pocket. He does not have a half dollar in his right pocket. What is the lowest possible value of all seven coins? What is the highest possible value of all seven coins?

We have practiced "some and some more" story problems. The "some and some more" pattern is an addition pattern.

In this lesson we will begin practicing **"some went away"** story problems. The "some went away" pattern is a subtraction pattern. In this book we will sometimes use the initials SWA to stand for "some went away." Read this "some went away" story:

John had 7 marbles. Then he lost 3 marbles. He has 4 marbles left.

We will write the information from this story in a "some went away" story pattern. We use a subtraction sign in this pattern.

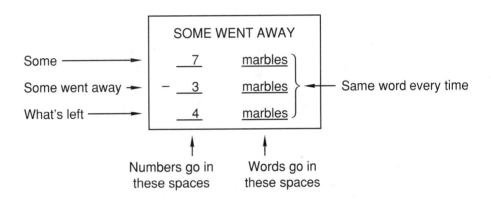

In a subtraction pattern, the top number is the largest number. The top number is the sum of the other two numbers. If we know two numbers in the pattern, we can find the missing number.

Example 1   Jimmy had some marbles. Then he lost 15 marbles. He has 22 marbles left. How many marbles did he have in the beginning?

Solution   He had some marbles. Then **some marbles went away.** The pattern for a "some went away" problem is a subtraction pattern. To make a subtraction pattern, we use six lines and a minus sign.

$$- \ \underline{\hspace{3em}} \quad \underline{\hspace{3em}}$$
$$ \ \underline{\hspace{3em}} \quad \underline{\hspace{3em}}$$
$$ \ \underline{\hspace{3em}} \quad \underline{\hspace{3em}}$$

The same word goes in the three spaces on the right. This problem is about marbles, so the word is "marbles."

		marbles
−	_____	marbles
	_____	marbles

He began with some marbles. Then 15 marbles went away. **In a "some went away" problem, the number that went away has the minus sign.** Then he had 22 marbles left.

Some	N	marbles
Some went away	− 15	marbles
What's left	22	marbles

We can find the missing number in this subtraction pattern by asking an **addition question.**

22 marbles + 15 marbles = how many marbles?

The answer is **37 marbles.**

Now we check the answer.

$$\begin{array}{r} 37 \text{ marbles} \\ - 15 \text{ marbles} \\ \hline 22 \text{ marbles} \quad \text{check} \end{array}$$

Example 2   Celia had 42 marbles. She lost some marbles. She has 29 marbles left. How many marbles did she lose?

Solution   **Some marbles went away.** "Some went away" problems have a subtraction pattern. Since some marbles were lost, the minus sign goes with those "some went away" marbles.

Some	42	marbles
Some went away	− N	marbles
What's left	29	marbles

Now we must find the missing number in the pattern. To find the middle number, we subtract. Let's subtract 29 from 42.

$$\begin{array}{r} 42 \\ - 29 \\ \hline 13 \end{array}$$

Now let's see if **13 marbles** makes the pattern correct.

$$\begin{array}{r} 42 \text{ marbles} \\ - 13 \text{ marbles} \\ \hline 29 \text{ marbles} \end{array}$$

Now we check. We can check two ways.

$$42 - 13 = 29 \quad \text{check}$$

$$29 + 13 = 42 \quad \text{check}$$

Example 3   Rebecca had 65 marbles. Then she lost 13 marbles. How many marbles does she have left?

Solution   This problem has the thought that **some went away**. This problem has a subtraction pattern. The number that went away has the minus sign.

Some	65	marbles
Some went away −	13	marbles
What's left	W	marbles

Now we have the pattern. To find the missing number, we subtract 13 from 65 and get 52.

$$\begin{array}{r} 65 \text{ marbles} \\ - 13 \text{ marbles} \\ \hline \mathbf{52 \text{ marbles}} \end{array}$$

To check, we note that 52 plus 13 equals 65. This means that our answer is correct.

Practice   Draw a "some went away" pattern for each problem. Then answer each question.

   a. Marko had 42 marbles. Then he lost some marbles. Now he has 26 marbles. How many marbles did he lose?

   b. Karen lost 42 marbles. Now she has 26 marbles. How many marbles did she have in the beginning?

c. Barbara had 75 cents. Then she spent 27 cents. Now how many cents does Barbara have?

**Problem set
31**

1. Micky had 75 rocks. Then she lost some rocks. Now
(31) she has 27 rocks. How many rocks did she lose? Draw a "some went away" pattern.

2. Sixty-three birds sat in the tree. Then fourteen birds
(31) flew away. How many birds remained in the tree? Draw a SWA pattern.

3. There were many cats in the alley at noon. Seventy-
(31) five cats ran away. Forty-seven cats remained. How many cats were in the alley at noon? Draw a SWA pattern.

4. There are 12 months in a whole year. How many
(6) months are in half of a year?

5. Find the missing numbers in this sequence:
(3)
5, 10, _____, _____, 25, _____, ...

6. Use digits and a comparison symbol to write that
(15) seven hundred sixty-two is less than eight hundred twenty-six.

7. Round 78 to the nearest ten.
(26)

8. Use a centimeter scale to measure the width of the
(24) cover of this book.

9. If it is afternoon, what time is it?
(23)
1:20 pm

10. Which street is perpendicular to Elm?
(29)

11. What fraction of this shape is shaded?
(28)

12. Draw a square whose sides are 2 cm long.
(25)

13. To what number is the arrow pointing?
(13)

14. $52
(19) − $14

15. 476
(16) + 177

16. 62
(19) − 38

17. $4.97
(28) + $2.58

18. 36
(20) − G
      ——
      18

19. 55
(18) + B
      ——
      87

20. D
(20) − 23
      ——
      58

21. Y
(30) + 14
      ——
      32

22. 42 − 37
(19)

23. 52 − 22
(18)

24. 73 − 59
(19)

25. 900 + 90 + 9
(21)

LESSON
32

Drawing Pictures of Fractions

Facts Practice: 100 Subtraction Facts (Test B in Test Masters)

Mental Math: Practice splitting the second number to add.

  a. 36 + 8   **b.** 48 + 6   **c.** 47 + 9

Review:

  d. 67 + 19 + 100   **e.** 350 + 40 + 200   **f.** 38 + 45 + 200

Patterns: In some sequences the count from one number to the next increases. In this sequence, from 1 to 4 is 3, from 4 to 9 is 5, and from 9 to 16 is 7. (Notice that the increase itself forms a sequence.) Continue this sequence to the tenth term, which is 100.

1, 4, 9, 16, ...

We can understand fractions better if we learn to draw pictures that represent fractions.

Example 1   Draw a rectangle and shade two thirds of it.

Solution   On the left, we draw a rectangle. In the center, we divide the rectangle into **3 equal parts.**

    Rectangle   3 equal parts   2 parts shaded

On the right, we shade any two of the equal parts. We have shaded two thirds of the rectangle.

    There are many ways to divide the rectangle into three parts. Here is another way.

    Rectangle   3 equal parts   2 parts shaded

Again we have shaded two thirds of the rectangle.

Example 2   Draw a circle and shade one fourth of it.

Solution   First we draw a circle. Then we divide the circle into **four equal parts.** Then we shade any one of the parts. We have shaded one fourth of the circle.

    Circle   4 equal parts   1 part shaded

Practice   Follow your teacher's example as you do these exercises:

    a. Draw a square and shade one half of it.

    b. Draw a rectangle and shade one third of it.

    c. Draw a circle and shade three fourths of it.

    d. Draw a circle and shade two thirds of it.

Problem set 32   **1.** Mary had 42 pebbles. She threw some in the lake.
(31) Then she had 27 pebbles left. How many pebbles did she throw in the lake? Draw a SWA pattern.

2. Demosthenes had a bag of pebbles when the sun came
(31) up. He put 17 pebbles in his mouth. Then there were 46 pebbles left in the bag. How many pebbles were in the bag when the sun came up? Draw a SWA pattern.

3. Franklin saw one hundred twelve stars. Eleanor
(17) looked the other way and saw some more. If they saw three hundred seventeen stars in all, how many did Eleanor see? Draw a SSM pattern.

4. Use the digits 4, 5, and 6 once each to write an even
(11) number less than 500.

Find the missing numbers in each sequence:

5. 14, 21, _____, 35, _____, _____, ...
(3)

6. 16, 24, _____, 40, _____, _____, ...
(3)

7. Use digits and symbols to show that twenty-seven
(15) plus eleven equals eleven plus twenty-seven.

8. Round 19 to the nearest ten. 20
(26)

9. One meter equals how many centimeters? 100
(27)

10. If it is before noon, what time is
(23) shown by this clock?

11:35 AM.

11. Which street makes a right angle
(29) with Oak?

12. What fraction of this figure is
(28) shaded?

13. This scale shows weight in
(22) pounds. How many pounds does
the needle show?

14. Y **15.** $\$486$ **16.** $\$68$ **17.** $\$5.97$
(30) $+ 63$ (16) $+ \$277$ (19) $- \$39$ (28) $+ \$2.38$
       $\overline{81}$

18. 71 **19.** 87 **20.** 27 **21.** E
(19) $- 42$ (20) $- N$ (18) $+ C$ (20) $- 14$
                        $\overline{65}$ $\overline{48}$ $\overline{25}$

22. $42 - 29$ **23.** $77 - 37$ **24.** $41 - 19$
(19)   (18)   (19)

25. $4 + 7 + 15 + 21 + 5 + 4 + 3$
(21)

LESSON
33

Multiplication as Repeated Addition • Elapsed Time

Facts Practice: 100 Subtraction Facts (Test B in Test Masters)

Mental Math: Practice splitting the second number to add.
   a. 58 + 7   **b.** 65 + 9   **c.** 37 + 6
Review:
   d. 46 + 29 + 100   **e.** 650 + 35 + 200   **f.** 340 + 43 + 207

Problem Solving: Johnna has seven coins in her right pocket. She does not have a half dollar, but she does have at least one penny, one nickel, one dime, and one quarter. What is the lowest possible value of all seven coins? What is the highest possible value of all seven coins?

Multiplication as repeated addition

Suppose we want to find the total number of dots shown on these four number cubes.

There are several ways we can find the total number of dots. One way is to count the number of dots one by one. Another way is to recognize that there are five dots in each group and that there are four groups. We can find the answer by adding four fives.

$$5 + 5 + 5 + 5 = 20$$

We can also use multiplication to show that we want to add five four times.

$$4 \times 5 = 20 \qquad \text{or} \qquad \begin{array}{r} 5 \\ \times\ 4 \\ \hline 20 \end{array}$$

If we find the answer this way, we are using multiplication. We call the × a **multiplication sign.** We read 4 × 5 as "Four times five."

Example 1   Change this addition problem to a multiplication problem:

$$6 + 6 + 6 + 6 + 6$$

Solution   We see five sixes. We can change this addition problem to a multiplication problem by writing either

$$\textbf{5} \times \textbf{6} \qquad \text{or} \qquad \begin{array}{r} \textbf{6} \\ \underline{\times\,\textbf{5}} \end{array}$$

Elapsed time   Elapsed time is time that has gone by. To find elapsed time, we must find the difference between two times.

Example 2   If it is afternoon, what time will it be in 3 hours and 20 minutes?

Solution   First we count forward on the clock face 20 minutes. From that point we count forward 3 hours.

     Step 1.   From 1:45 p.m. we count forward 20 minutes. This makes it 2:05 p.m.

     Step 2.   From 2:05 p.m. we count forward 3 hours. This makes it **5:05 p.m.**

Example 3   If it is afternoon, what time was it 4 hours and 25 minutes ago?

Solution   First count back the number of minutes. Then count back hours.

     Step 1.   We count back 25 minutes from 1:15 p.m. This makes it 12:50 p.m.

     Step 2.   From 12:50 p.m. we count back 4 hours. This makes it **8:50 a.m.**

Practice   Change each addition problem to a multiplication problem:

   a. 3 + 3 + 3 + 3   **b.** 9 + 9 + 9

   c. 7 + 7 + 7 + 7 + 7 + 7

   d. 5 + 5 + 5 + 5 + 5 + 5 + 5 + 5

Use this clock to answer these questions.

   e. If it is morning, what time will it
   be in 2 hours and 25 minutes?
   1:00 pm

   f. If it is morning, what time was it 6
   hours and 30 minutes ago?
   4:05AM

Problem set   **1.** Just before high noon, Nancy saw seventy-eight elves
33   (31) playing in the valley. At high noon, there were only
forty-two elves playing in the valley. How many elves
had left the valley by high noon? Draw a SWA pattern.

   2. According to the ancient Greeks, dryads were wood
   (17) nymphs. Penelope went one way and saw forty-six
   dryads. Perseus went the other way and saw some
   more dryads. Altogether, they saw seventy-three
   dryads. How many dryads did Perseus see? Draw a
   SSM pattern.

   3. List the even numbers between 31 and 39.
   (11)

Find the missing numbers in each sequence:

   4. 8, _____, _____, 20, 24, _____, ...
   (3)

   5. 24, _____, _____, 15, 12, _____, ...
   (3)

   6. Write 265 in expanded form.
   (20)

   7. Use words to write 613.
   (8)

   8. Round 63 to the nearest ten.
   (26)

9. Compare: 392 ◯ 329
(15)

10. The arrow is pointing to what number?
(13)

11. Draw a square and shade one fourth of it.
(32)

12. What fraction of this figure is shaded?
(28)

13. It is afternoon. What will be the time 3 hours from now?
(33)

14. (19) $67 − $29	**15.** (16) 483 + 378	**16.** (19) 71 − 39	**17.** (28) $5.88 + $2.39

18. (30) D + 19 = 36	**19.** (18) 66 + F = 87	**20.** (20) 87 − R = 67	**21.** (20) B − 14 = 27

22. 400 − 300
(18)

23. 663 − 363
(18)

24. Change this addition problem to a multiplication problem:
(33)

$$9 + 9 + 9 + 9$$

25. 5 + 7 + 3 + 6 + 4 + 8 + 7 + 2 + 5 + 6 + 4 + 8
(1)

LESSON
34

The Multiplication Table

Facts Practice: 100 Subtraction Facts (Test B in Test Masters)

Mental Math: Practice splitting the second number to add.
   a. 57 + 8   **b.** 78 + 6   **c.** 49 + 4

Review:
   d. 300 + 520 + 70   **e.** 63 + 19 + 200 **f.** 354 + 220 + 18

Patterns: Here we show 4 squares. The smallest is 1 small square. The next have 4, 9, and 16 small squares, respectively. Draw the next 2 squares in the pattern.

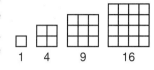

If we count by zeros, ones, twos, and threes, we get the sequences shown below.

Zeros	0	0	0	0	0	0	0	0	0	0	0	0
Ones	1	2	3	4	5	6	7	8	9	10	11	12
Twos	2	4	6	8	10	12	14	16	18	20	22	24
Threes	3	6	9	12	15	18	21	24	27	30	33	36

If we count by fours, fives, sixes, sevens, eights, and nines,[†] and put all these sequences in a box, we have a **multiplication table.**

Multiplication Table

	0	1	2	3	4	5	6	7	8	9
0	0	0	0	0	0	0	0	0	0	0
1	0	1	2	3	4	5	6	7	8	9
2	0	2	4	6	8	10	12	14	16	18
3	0	3	6	9	12	15	18	21	24	27
4	0	4	8	12	16	20	24	28	32	36
5	0	5	10	15	20	25	30	35	40	45
6	0	6	12	18	24	30	36	42	48	54
7	0	7	14	21	28	35	42	49	56	63
8	0	8	16	24	32	40	48	56	64	72
9	0	9	18	27	36	45	54	63	72	81

[†]Multiplication by tens, elevens, and twelves is considered in Appendix A.

From a multiplication table we can find the answer to multiplications such as 3 × 4 by using rows and columns. Rows run left to right and columns run top to bottom. We start by finding the row which begins with the 3 and the column which begins with the 4. Then we look for the number where that row and column meet.

Column

	0	1	2	3	4	5	6	7	8	9
0	0	0	0	0	0	0	0	0	0	0
1	0	1	2	3	4	5	6	7	8	9
2	0	2	4	6	8	10	12	14	16	18
3	0	3	6	9	12	15	18	21	24	27
4	0	4	8	12	16	20	24	28	32	36
5	0	5	10	15	20	25	30	35	40	45
6	0	6	12	18	24	30	36	42	48	54
7	0	7	14	21	28	35	42	49	56	63
8	0	8	16	24	32	40	48	56	64	72
9	0	9	18	27	36	45	54	63	72	81

Row →

Each of the two numbers multiplied is called a **factor.** The answer to a multiplication problem is called a **product.** In this problem, 3 and 4 are factors and 12 is the product. In multiplication problems, the order of the factors does not matter. Thus, the product of 4 × 3 also equals 12.

Practice Use the multiplication table to find the following products:

$$
\textbf{a.} \quad
\begin{array}{r}
9 \\
\times\, 3 \\
\hline
\end{array}
\qquad
\textbf{b.} \quad
\begin{array}{r}
3 \\
\times\, 9 \\
\hline
\end{array}
\qquad
\textbf{c.} \quad
\begin{array}{r}
6 \\
\times\, 4 \\
\hline
\end{array}
\qquad
\textbf{d.} \quad
\begin{array}{r}
4 \\
\times\, 6 \\
\hline
\end{array}
$$

$$
\textbf{e.} \quad
\begin{array}{r}
7 \\
\times\, 8 \\
\hline
\end{array}
\qquad
\textbf{f.} \quad
\begin{array}{r}
8 \\
\times\, 7 \\
\hline
\end{array}
\qquad
\textbf{g.} \quad
\begin{array}{r}
5 \\
\times\, 8 \\
\hline
\end{array}
\qquad
\textbf{h.} \quad
\begin{array}{r}
8 \\
\times\, 5 \\
\hline
\end{array}
$$

Problem set   **1.** Hansel ate seventy-two pieces of gingerbread. Then
34   *(12)* Gretel ate three hundred forty-two pieces of gingerbread. How many pieces of gingerbread did they eat in all? Draw a SSM pattern.

2. Sherry needs $35 to buy a baseball glove. She has
(17) saved $18. How much more money does she need? Draw a SSM pattern.

3. All of the men walked to the meeting. Then forty-two
(31) men got mad and went home. Only twenty-three men were left at the meeting. How many men walked to the meeting? Draw a SWA pattern.

Find the missing numbers in each sequence:

4. 12, _____, _____, 30, 36, _____, ...
(3)

5. 36, _____, _____, 24, 20, _____, ...
(3)

6. Use words to write 265.
(8)

7. Round 28 to the nearest ten.
(26)

8. A right triangle has one right angle. Draw a right
(29,24) triangle. Draw the two perpendicular sides 3 cm long and 4 cm long.

9. It is morning. What time will it be
(33) 10 minutes from now?

10. What fraction of the group is
(28) shaded?

11. Write 417 in expanded form.
(20)

12. How long is this arrow?
(24)

13. 76
(19) − 29

14. $286
(16) + $388

15. $73
(19) − $39

16. $5.87
(28) + $2.43

17. 46
(20) − C
19

18. N
(30) + 48
87

19. 29
(30) + Y
57

20. D
(20) − 14
37

21. 78 − 43
(18)

22. 77 − 17
(18)

23. 53 − 19
(19)

24. Change this addition problem to a multiplication
(33) problem:

$$6 + 6 + 6 + 6 + 6 + 6 + 6$$

25. 4 + 3 + 6 + 5 + 2 + 3 + 7 + 4 + 5 + 2 + 8 + 9
(1)

LESSON 35

Multiplication Facts (0, 1, 2, 5)

Facts Practice: 100 Subtraction Facts (Test B in Test Masters)

Mental Math: Practice splitting the second number to add.
  a. 49 + 6   **b.** 65 + 8   **c.** 38 + 8

Review:
  d. 920 + 38 + 7   **e.** 57 + 29 + 100   **f.** 350 + 40 + 500

Problem Solving: Tom has seven coins in his right pocket. He does not have a half dollar, but he has at least one penny, one nickel, one dime, and one quarter. However, Tom has no more than two of any one kind of coin. What are the possible values of all seven coins? (There are four possibilities.)

We must memorize all the multiplication facts. Sixty-four of the 100 multiplication facts in the multiplication table shown in Lesson 34 have 0, 1, 2, or 5 as one of the factors. These facts are the easiest to learn.

Zero times any number equals zero.

$$0 \times 5 = 0 \qquad 5 \times 0 = 0 \qquad 7 \times 0 = 0 \qquad 0 \times 7 = 0$$

One times any number equals the number.

$$1 \times 5 = 5 \qquad 5 \times 1 = 5 \qquad 7 \times 1 = 7 \qquad 1 \times 7 = 7$$

Two times any number doubles the number.

$$2 \times 5 = 10 \quad 2 \times 7 = 14 \quad 2 \times 6 = 12 \quad 2 \times 8 = 16$$

Until we have memorized the facts, we can find multiples of 2 by counting by twos. So 6×2 is the sixth number we say when counting by twos: 2, 4, 6, 8, 10, 12. **Counting by twos is not a substitute for memorizing the facts.**

**Five times any number equals a
number that ends in zero or in five.**

$$5 \times 1 = 5 \quad 5 \times 3 = 15 \quad 5 \times 8 = 40 \quad 5 \times 7 = 35$$

Until we have memorized the facts, we can find multiples of 5 by counting by fives. The sixth number we say when counting by fives is 30, so $6 \times 5 = 30$.

Practice Do the Facts Practice "Multiplication Facts: 0, 1, 2, 5" (Test C in Test Masters).

**Problem set
35**

1. Two hundred sixty-two soldiers were in the vanguard.
(12) Three hundred seventy-five were in the main body. One hundred seven were in the rear guard. How many soldiers were there in all? Draw a SSM pattern.

2. Ninety-two blackbirds squawked noisily in the tree.
(31) Then some flew away. Twenty-four blackbirds remained. How many blackbirds flew away? Draw a SWA pattern.

3. Robill threw 42 rocks. Then Buray threw some rocks.
(17) They threw 83 rocks in all. How many rocks did Buray throw? Draw a SSM pattern.

Find the missing numbers in each sequence:

4. 8, _____, _____, 32, 40, _____, ...
(3)

5. 14, _____, _____, 35, 42, ...
(3)

6. Use the digits 4, 5, and 6 once each to write a three-
(11) digit odd number that is less than 640.

7. Use digits and a comparison symbol to write that two
(15) hundred nine is greater than one hundred ninety.

8. It is afternoon. What time will it
(33) be in 6 hours?

9. Draw a rectangle and shade two
(32) thirds of it.

10. 2 × 8   **11.** 5 × 7   **12.** 2 × 7   **13.** 5 × 8
(35,34)   *(35,34)*   *(35,34)*   *(35,34)*

14. $83   **15.** $286   **16.**   72   **17.** $5.87
(19) − $19   *(16)* + $387   *(19)* − 38   *(28)* + $2.79

18.   19   **19.**   88   **20.**   88   **21.** G
(30) + Q *(20)* − N *(20)* − M *(18)* + 14
      ——— 46   ——— 37   ——— 47   ——— 47

22. 870 − 470   **23.** 525 − 521
(18)   *(18)*

24. Change this addition problem to a multiplication
(33) problem:

$$8 + 8 + 8$$

25. 2 + 5 + 3 + 7 + 8 + 5 + 6 + 4 + 3 + 2 + 1 + 5 + 4
(1)

**LESSON
36**

Multiplication Patterns

Facts Practice: Multiplication Facts: 0, 1, 2, 5 (Test C in Test Masters)

Mental Math: Subtract numbers ending in one or two zeros.

   a. 60 − 40   **b.** 80 − 30   **c.** 800 − 300

Review:

   d. 67 + 7   **e.** 67 + 19 + 100   **f.** 340 + 35 + 115

Patterns: These dots are arranged in square patterns of 2 rows of 2, 3 rows of 3, and so on. Copy these patterns and continue the sequence to 8 rows of 8.

4   9   16   25

We can draw patterns that help us understand multiplication. The patterns have the shapes of rectangles. The patterns have rows and columns. One of the numbers in the multiplication pattern is the number of rows. The other number is the number of columns.

To make our first pattern, we will use X's to show the multiplication of 3 times 4. We will use 3 rows and 4 columns. The total number of X's is the answer.

$$\begin{array}{c} \xleftarrow{\quad} 4 \xrightarrow{\quad} \\ \uparrow \ \ X \ X \ X \ X \\ 3 \ \ X \ X \ X \ X \\ \downarrow \ \ X \ X \ X \ X \end{array} \qquad 3 \times 4 = 12$$

We do not have to use X's. Another method is to draw a rectangle with small squares. We will use 3 rows of small squares. There are 4 columns of small squares.

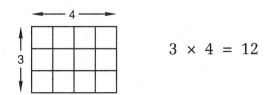

$$3 \times 4 = 12$$

Example 1 Draw a pattern of X's to show the multiplication of 4 × 5.

Solution One of the numbers is the number of rows, and the other number is the number of columns. It does not matter which is which. We show both patterns.

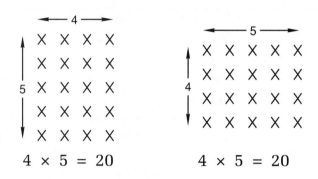

Example 2 Draw a rectangle to show the multiplication fact 2 × 4 = 8.

Solution We will draw a rectangle that is 2 small squares wide and 4 small squares long.

Practice   **a.** Draw a pattern of X's to show the multiplication fact 6 × 3 = 18.

b. Draw a rectangle to show the multiplication fact 2 × 5 = 10.

Write a multiplication fact for each pattern below:

c.   **d.**

e. X X X X X X
       X X X X X X
       X X X X X X
       X X X X X X
       X X X X X X

f.

Problem set **1.** Twenty-eight boys sat in the first row. Thirty-five boys
36 (12) sat in the second row. Fifty boys sat in the third row.
How many boys sat in the first three rows? Draw a
SSM pattern.

2. Forty crayons were in the box. Fran took some crayons
(31) out of the box. Nineteen crayons were left in the box.
How many crayons did Fran take out of the box? Draw
a SWA pattern.

3. William had some crayons when he came to school.
(17) Then Fran gave him 36 crayons. William now has 72
crayons. How many crayons did William have when
he came to school? Draw a SSM pattern.

4. The first eight counting numbers are 1, 2, 3, 4, 5, 6, 7,
(1) and 8. What is the sum of the first eight counting
numbers?

5. Find the missing numbers in this sequence:
(3)
45, _____, _____, 72, 81, _____, ...

6. It is evening. What time was it 10
(33) hours ago?

7. Write 703 in expanded form. Then use words to write
(20,8) this number.

8. Use digits and symbols to write that eight times zero
(15) equals nine times zero.

9. This metal object was found in a park. About how long
(24) is it?

10. A 2 is in the ones' place. The number is between 742
_(5)_ and 762. What is the number?

11. Draw a pattern of X's to show the multiplication of
_(36)_ 2 × 7.

12. 4 × 5   **13.** 2 × 5   **14.** 5 × 8
_(35,34)_   _(35,34)_   _(35,34)_

15.   93   **16.** $386   **17.** $61   **18.** $5.86
_(19)_ − 29   _(16)_ + $275   _(19)_ − $38   _(28)_ + $3.76

19.   C   **20.**   84   **21.**   C   **22.**   N
_(18)_ + 14   _(20)_ − A   _(20)_ − 76   _(30)_ + 28
        37   37   14   63

23. 486 + 294 + 8
_(21)_

24. Change this addition problem to a multiplication
_(33)_ problem:

7 + 7 + 7 + 7 + 7 + 7

25. 2 + 3 + 5 + 7 + 4 + 8 + 5 + 3 + 7 + 6 + 5 + 4
_(1)_

LESSON 37

Subtracting Three-Digit Numbers with Regrouping

Facts Practice: 100 Addition Facts (Test A in Test Masters)

Mental Math: Subtract numbers ending in one or two zeros.
   a. 600 − 300   **b.** 65 − 30   **c.** 650 − 300
Review:
   d. 58 + 4 + 100   **e.** 36 + 29 + 200   **f.** 520 + 36 + 126

Problem Solving: Refer to Lesson 35 for information about the coins in Tom's pocket. Although he has an odd number of coins in his right pocket, their total value is an even number of cents. What is the value of the coins?

Up to this point, we have subtracted three-digit numbers without regrouping. In this lesson we will discuss subtracting three-digit numbers with regrouping.

Example 1 Find the difference: $365 − $187

Solution We write the first number on top. We line up the last digits. We cannot subtract 7 ones from 5 ones.

$$\begin{array}{r} \$365 \\ -\ \$187 \\ \hline (?) \end{array}$$

We exchange 1 ten for 10 ones. Now there are 15 ones, and we can subtract the ones.

$$\begin{array}{r} {}^{5}{}_{1} \\ \$3\,\cancel{6}\,5 \\ -\ \$1\,8\,7 \\ \hline 8 \end{array}$$

We cannot subtract 8 tens from 5 tens. This time we exchange 1 hundred for 10 tens. Now we have 15 tens and we can subtract.

$$\begin{array}{r} 2\ {}^{1}5{}_{1} \\ \$\cancel{3}\,\cancel{6}\,5 \\ -\ \$1\,8\,7 \\ \hline 7\,8 \end{array}$$

We subtract 1 hundred from 2 hundreds to finish. The difference is **$178.**

$$\begin{array}{r} 2\ {}^{1}5{}_{1} \\ \$\cancel{3}\,\cancel{6}\,5 \\ -\ \$1\,8\,7 \\ \hline \$1\,7\,8 \end{array}$$

Example 2
$$\begin{array}{r} \$4.10 \\ -\ \$1.12 \\ \hline \end{array}$$

Solution We subtract pennies, then dimes, and then dollars.

$$\begin{array}{r} 0{}_{1} \\ \$\,4.\cancel{1}\,0 \\ -\ \$\,1.1\,2 \\ \hline 8 \end{array} \qquad \begin{array}{r} 3\ {}^{1}0{}_{1} \\ \$\,\cancel{4}.\cancel{1}\,0 \\ -\ \$\,1.1\,2 \\ \hline .9\,8 \end{array} \qquad \begin{array}{r} 3\ {}^{1}0{}_{1} \\ \$\,\cancel{4}.\cancel{1}\,0 \\ -\ \$\,1.1\,2 \\ \hline \$\,2.9\,8 \end{array}$$

Practice
a.
$$\begin{array}{r} \$365 \\ -\ \$287 \\ \hline \end{array}$$
b.
$$\begin{array}{r} \$4.30 \\ -\ \$1.18 \\ \hline \end{array}$$
c.
$$\begin{array}{r} 563 \\ -\ 356 \\ \hline \end{array}$$

d. 240 − 65 e. 459 − 176 f. 157 − 98

Problem set 37 **1.** The room was full of students when the bell rang.
(31) Then forty-seven students ran away. Twenty-two students remained. How many students were there when the bell rang? Draw a SWA pattern.

2. Fifty-six children peered through the window of the
(17) pet shop. Then the store owners brought the puppies
out. Now there were seventy-three children peering
through the window. How many children came to the
window when the store owners brought the puppies
out? Draw a SSM pattern.

3. A nickel is worth 5¢. Gilbert has an even number of
(11) nickels in his pocket. Which of the following **could
not be** the value of his nickels?

   A. 45¢   B. 70¢   C. 20¢

4. It is morning. What time will it be
(33) in 15 minutes?

5. Draw a rectangle and shade one fifth of it.
(32)

6. To what number is the arrow pointing?
(13)

7. Write a multiplication fact for this
(36) pattern.

8. Write 843 in expanded form. Then use words to write
(20,8) 843.

9. 6 × 8   **10.** 4 × 2   **11.** 4 × 5   **12.** 6 × 5
(34)   (35,34)   (35,34)   (35,34)

13.   746   **14.** $3.86   **15.**   61   **16.** $4.86
(37) − 295   (28) + $2.78   (19) − 48   (37) − $2.75

17.   51   **18.**   86   **19.**   25   **20.**   Q
(30) + M   (20) − A   (18) + Y   (20) − 24
     ────   ────   ────   ────
      70   43   36   37

21. Write four addition/subtraction facts using the three
(7)   numbers 8, 3, and 11.

22. 25¢ + 25¢ + 25¢ + 25¢
(21)

23. There are 100 cents in a dollar. How many cents are in
(28)   half of a dollar?

24. Change this addition problem to a multiplication
(33)   problem:

$$7 + 7 + 7 + 7 + 7 + 7 + 7$$

25. 4 + 3 + 8 + 4 + 2 + 5 + 7 + 6 + 3 + 7 + 2 + 5
(1)

LESSON 38

"Larger-Smaller-Difference" Word Problems

Facts Practice: Multiplication Facts: 0, 1, 2, 5 (Test C in Test
Masters)

Mental Math: Subtract numbers ending in one or two zeros.
  a. 750 − 200   **b.** 86 − 50   **c.** 245 − 200
Review:
  d. 78 + 7 + 10   **e.** 43 + 9 + 110   **f.** 630 + 45 + 210

Patterns: This multiplication pattern sequence is 1 × 1, 2 × 2,
3 × 3,.... Use a multiplication table to help you
continue this pattern sequence to 100.

  1, 4, 9, 16, ___, ___, ___, ___, ___, 100

There are 43 apples in the large basket.

There are 19 apples in the small basket.

When we compare the number of apples in the two baskets, we see that 43 is **greater than** 19. To find **how much greater** 43 is than 19, we can subtract.

$$\begin{array}{r} 43 \\ -\ 19 \\ \hline 24 \end{array}$$

As we think about this problem, we realize that it is not a "some went away" problem because nothing went away. This is a different kind of problem. In this problem we are **comparing** two numbers. The thinking pattern we use to help us compare numbers is called the **"larger-smaller-difference"** pattern. We will sometimes use the abbreviation L-S-D to stand for "larger-smaller-difference."

The "larger-smaller-difference" pattern is a subtraction pattern. We write the two numbers we are comparing on the first two lines with the larger number on top. The smaller number is written on the second line. **The smaller number has a minus sign.** The bottom number tells us **how much larger** the top number is than the middle number. The bottom number also tells us **how much smaller** the middle number is than the top number.

Below we have drawn a "larger-smaller-difference" pattern box. Inside we have written the number of apples in the two baskets.

The difference tells us how many more. It also tells us how many fewer. There are **24 more** apples in the large basket than there are in the small basket. We can say this comparison another way. There are **24 fewer** apples in the small basket than there are in the large basket.

Example 1   Forty-two apples is how many more than 13 apples?

Solution   To find out **how many more,** we use the "larger-smaller-difference" thinking pattern. The two numbers we are comparing are 42 and 13. We write these on the first two lines with the larger number on top. The minus sign goes with the smaller number.

Larger number	42	apples
Smaller number	− 13	apples
Difference	N	apples

To find the bottom number in this pattern, we subtract.

$$\begin{array}{r} 42 \text{ apples} \\ - 13 \text{ apples} \\ \hline 29 \text{ apples} \end{array} \qquad \begin{array}{r} 29 \\ + 13 \\ \hline 42 \end{array} \text{ check}$$

Forty-two apples is **29 apples** more than 13 apples.

Example 2   Seventeen apples is how many fewer than 63 apples?

Solution   Whether we are finding how many more or how many fewer, we still use the "larger-smaller-difference" thinking pattern. We are comparing 17 and 63. We write "63" on top.

Larger number	63	apples
Smaller number	− 17	apples
Difference	N	apples

To find the bottom number, we subtract.

$$\begin{array}{r} 63 \text{ apples} \\ - 17 \text{ apples} \\ \hline 46 \text{ apples} \end{array} \qquad \begin{array}{r} 46 \\ + 17 \\ \hline 63 \end{array} \text{ check}$$

Seventeen apples is **46 apples** fewer than 63 apples.

Example 3   Seventeen is how much less than 42?

Solution   Problems about numbers that ask **how much less** or **how much greater** also have a "larger-smaller-difference" pattern. Since we are just comparing numbers, there are no words to write in the pattern.

Larger number	42	_____
Smaller number	− 17	_____
Difference	N	_____

We find the bottom number by subtracting.

$$
\begin{array}{r} 42 \\ -\ 17 \\ \hline 25 \end{array}
\qquad
\begin{array}{r} 25 \\ +\ 17 \\ \hline 42 \end{array}
\quad \text{check}
$$

Seventeen is **25** less than 42.

Practice   Draw a "larger-smaller-difference" pattern for each problem. Then answer each question.

a. Forty-three is how much greater than twenty-seven?

b. Mary has 42 peanuts. Frank has 22 peanuts. How many fewer peanuts does Frank have?

c. Roger had 53 shells. Juanita had 95 shells. How many more shells did Juanita have?

Problem set 38

1. There were 43 parrots in the tree. Some flew away.
$^{(31)}$ Then there were 27 parrots in the tree. How many flew away? Draw a SWA pattern.

2. One hundred fifty is how much greater than twenty-
$^{(38)}$ three? Draw a "larger-smaller-difference" pattern.

3. Twenty-three apples is how many fewer than seventy-
$^{(38)}$ five apples? Draw a L-S-D pattern.

4. It is evening. What time will it be 3
$^{(33)}$ hours from now?

5. Write 412 in expanded form. Then use words to write
(20,8) the number 412.

6. What fraction of this figure is
(28) shaded?

7. Matt drew a triangle that had two sides each 3 cm
(29,24) long. These sides made a right angle. Draw this
triangle.

8. 2 × 5   **9.** 5 × 7   **10.** 2 × 7
(35,34)   (35,34)   (35,34)

11. To what number is the arrow pointing?
(13)

12. 5 × 8   **13.** 2 × 8   **14.** 5 × 9
(35,34)   (35,34)   (35,34)

15. $4.22   **16.**   909   **17.** $422   **18.**   703
(37)   − $2.95   (37)   − 27   (37)   − $144   (37)   − 471

19. $4.86   **20.**   370   **21.**   22   **22.**   76
(28)   + $2.95   (37)   − 209   (18)   + N   (20)   − C
                                          ___   ___
                                           37   28

23. 24 + 48 + 65 + 93
(21)

24. Change this addition problem to a multiplication
(33) problem:

$$2 + 2 + 2 + 2 + 2$$

25. Draw a pattern of X's to show 3 × 5.
(36)

LESSON
39

Multiplication Facts (Squares)

Facts Practice: Multiplication Facts: 0, 1, 2, 5 (Test C in Test Masters)

Mental Math: Subtract numbers ending in one or two zeros.
  a. 840 − 200   **b.** 840 − 20   **c.** 845 − 220
Review:
  d. 75 + 7 + 200   **e.** 36 + 39 + 10   **f.** 300 + 620 + 50

Problem Solving: A checkerboard has 64 small squares. There are 8 squares along each side. If a square checkerboard had only 36 small squares, how many squares would there be along each side?

Squares are the multiplication facts that have the same factor twice: 1 × 1, 2 × 2, 3 × 3, and so on. They are called **squares** because squares can be used to illustrate these facts.

1 × 1 = 1   2 × 2 = 4   3 × 3 = 9   4 × 4 = 16   5 × 5 = 25

These are squares that we will memorize:

0 × 0 = 0	7 × 7 = 49
1 × 1 = 1	8 × 8 = 64
2 × 2 = 4	9 × 9 = 81
3 × 3 = 9	10 × 10 = 100
4 × 4 = 16	11 × 11 = 121
5 × 5 = 25	12 × 12 = 144
6 × 6 = 36	

To memorize facts, it is helpful to practice saying the facts out loud. Say these facts out loud two or three times a day. Get used to the sounds. The sounds help us remember the facts.

Example   What multiplication fact is illustrated by this square?

Solution   The length is 6 and the width is 6. Counting, we find there are 36 squares. This is a picture of **6 × 6 = 36**.

Practice   **a.** 3 × 3   **b.** 6 × 6   **c.** 9 × 9

d. 4 × 4   **e.** 8 × 8   **f.** 7 × 7

g. Draw a square to show 3 × 3.

Problem set 39

1. Forty-two is how much greater than twenty-seven? Draw a L-S-D pattern.
(38)

2. Forty-six is how much less than seventy? Draw a "larger-smaller-difference" pattern.
(38)

3. Seven hundred fifteen cheerful hikers began the long march. Three hundred seventeen cheerful hikers finished the long march. How many cheerful hikers did not finish the long march? Draw a SWA pattern.
(31)

4. Write 483 in expanded form. Then use words to write this number.
(20,8)

5. Draw a rectangle whose length is 5 cm and whose width is 3 cm.
(25,24)

6. It is evening. What time will it be 13 hours from now?
(33)

7. What fraction of this shape is
(28) shaded?

2/5

8. The addition problem 5 + 5 + 5 can be written as a
(33) multiplication problem by writing 3 × 5. Write a
multiplication problem for 7 + 7 + 7 + 7.

9. Round 38 to the nearest ten. Round 44 to the nearest
(26) ten. Then add the rounded numbers.

10. The digit in the tens' place is 4. The digit in the ones'
(5) place is 2. The number is greater than 500 and less
than 600. What is the number?

11. To what number is the needle
(22) pointing?

12. 4 × 4   **13.** 6 × 6   **14.** 7 × 7   **15.** 9 × 9
(39)   (39)   (39)   (39)

16.   433   **17.**   807   **18.**   406   **19.** $7.22
(37) − 268   (37) − 45   (37) − 241   (37) − $4.44

20.   C   **21.** $3.27   **22.**   747   **23.**   85
(30) + 248   (28) + $4.68   (20) −   B   (20) −   B
        486   414   27

24. Draw a square to show 4 × 4.
(36)

25.   21   **26.**   7   **27.**   13
(21)   5   (1)   7   (21)   25
           7   7   14
          43   7   7
          56   7   8
           4   7   12
        + 17   7   + 6
                          + 7

LESSON
40

Squares and Square Roots

Facts Practice: Multiplication Facts: 2, 5, Squares (Test D in Test Masters)

Mental Math: Subtract numbers ending in one or two zeros.

  a. 780 − 200   **b.** 870 − 230   **c.** 458 − 30

Review:

  d. 58 + 6   **e.** 157 + 19   **f.** 435 + 35 + 200

Problem Solving: The rectangle is divided into four areas, *A*, *B*, *C*, and *D*. Area *C* is the same size as Area *D*. Areas *C* and *D* together are the same size as Area *B*. Areas *B*, *C*, and *D* together are the same size as Area *A*. What fraction of the whole rectangle is each area?

To **square** a number, we multiply the number by itself. If we square five, we get 25 because 5 × 5 is 25. Likewise, six squared is 36 since 6 × 6 is 36. A picture of a square can help us understand this idea.

Five squared is 25.   Six squared is 36.

A side is 5.   A side is 6.

25 squares in all   36 squares in all

To find a **square root** of a number, we find a number which, when multiplied by itself, equals the original number. A square root of 25 is five. A square root of 36 is six. Again, a picture of a square can help us understand the idea. When searching for a square root, we know the number of squares in all, and we are looking for the length of a side.

A square root of 25 is 5.

25 squares in all

A side is 5.

A square root of 36 is 6.

36 squares in all

A side is 6.

We can show that we mean the square root of a number by using a square root symbol.

We can read this symbol as "the square root of."

$$\sqrt{25} = 5$$

"The square root of twenty-five equals five."

Example   (a) What is the square of 9?

(b) What is a square root of 9?

Solution   Carefully read both questions and understand the difference between them.

(a) We square a number by multiplying the number by itself. It is like knowing the length of a side of a square and finding the number of squares in all. Since 9 × 9 = 81, the square of 9 is **81.**

(b) A square root of 9 is a number which, when multiplied by itself, equals 9. Since 3 × 3 = 9, a square root of 9 is **3.**

Practice   Square each number:

a. 4   **b.** 7   **c.** 10

Find each square root:

d. $\sqrt{4}$ **e.** $\sqrt{16}$ **f.** $\sqrt{64}$

Problem set 40

1. Two hundred thirty-three is how much greater than
(38)   seventy-six? Draw a L-S-D pattern.

2. One hundred twenty-three is how much less than five
(38)   hundred seventy-two? Draw a L-S-D pattern.

3. The first shipment contained 223 beds. The second
(12) shipment contained 243 beds. The third shipment
contained only 175 beds. What was the total number
of beds in all three shipments? Draw a SSM pattern.

4. Write the number 780 in expanded form.
(20)

5. Draw two perpendicular lines.
(29)

6. It is early in the morning. What
(33) time will it be in 30 minutes?

7. What fraction of this shape is
(28) shaded?

8. Change this addition problem to a multiplication
(33) problem:

$$8 + 8 + 8 + 8 + 8 + 8 + 8$$

9. Compare: three squared $\bigcirc$ the square root of 36
(40,15)

10. The digit in the hundreds' place is 4. The digit in the
(5) ones' place is 2. The number is between 450 and 460.
What is the number?

11. To what number is the arrow pointing?
(13)

12. 7 × 7	**13.** 9 × 9	**14.** 6 × 6	**15.** $\sqrt{64}$
(39)	(39)	(39)	(40)

16. $444	**17.** 927	**18.** 345	**19.** $7.25
(37) − $268	(37) − 48	(30) + C	(37) − $5.66
		421	

20. 478	**21.** $4.28	**22.** B	**23.** Z
(37) − 259	(37) − $3.29	(20) − 48	(20) − 328
		37	404

24. 88 + 24 + 35 + 66 + 58 + 229
(21)

25. Draw a rectangle to show 3 × 4.
(36)

LESSON
41

Multiplication Facts (9's)

Facts Practice: Multiplication Facts: 2, 5, Squares (Test D in Test Masters)

Mental Math: Add dollars to another amount of money.
  a. $3.45 + $1.00   **b.** $5.75 + $2.00   **c.** $0.85 + $2.00
Review:
  d. 365 − 120   **e.** 45 + 8 + 120   **f.** 56 + 19 + 200

Problem Solving: We can make a dollar with two coins—two half dollars. We can make a dollar with three coins—a half dollar and two quarters. We can make a dollar with four coins—four quarters. What coins do we need to make a dollar with five coins?

The 9's multiplication facts have patterns that can help us learn these facts.

Below we have listed some 9's multiplication facts. **Notice that the first digit of each answer is one less than the number that is multiplied by nine.**

$$9 \times 2 = 18 \qquad (1 + 8 = 9)$$
$$9 \times 3 = 27 \qquad (2 + 7 = 9)$$
$$9 \times 4 = 36 \qquad (3 + 6 = 9)$$
$$9 \times 5 = 45 \qquad (4 + 5 = 9)$$
$$9 \times 6 = 54 \qquad (5 + 4 = 9)$$
$$9 \times 7 = 63 \qquad (6 + 3 = 9)$$
$$9 \times 8 = 72 \qquad (7 + 2 = 9)$$
$$9 \times 9 = 81 \qquad (8 + 1 = 9)$$

Notice also that the two digits of the answer add up to nine.

These two patterns can help us quickly find the answer to a 9's multiplication. The first digit of the answer is one less than the number multiplied. The two digits add up to nine.

Example 1 What is the **first digit** of each answer?

(a) $\begin{array}{r} 9 \\ \times 6 \\ \hline ?\_\_ \end{array}$
(b) $\begin{array}{r} 3 \\ \times 9 \\ \hline ?\_\_ \end{array}$
(c) $\begin{array}{r} 9 \\ \times 7 \\ \hline ?\_\_ \end{array}$
(d) $\begin{array}{r} 4 \\ \times 9 \\ \hline ?\_\_ \end{array}$
(e) $\begin{array}{r} 9 \\ \times 8 \\ \hline ?\_\_ \end{array}$

Solution The first digit is one less than the number multiplied by nine.

(a) $\begin{array}{r} 9 \\ \times 6 \\ \hline 5\_\_ \end{array}$
(b) $\begin{array}{r} 3 \\ \times 9 \\ \hline 2\_\_ \end{array}$
(c) $\begin{array}{r} 9 \\ \times 7 \\ \hline 6\_\_ \end{array}$
(d) $\begin{array}{r} 4 \\ \times 9 \\ \hline 3\_\_ \end{array}$
(e) $\begin{array}{r} 9 \\ \times 8 \\ \hline 7\_\_ \end{array}$

Example 2 Complete these two-digit numbers so that the sum of the digits is nine:

(a) 3 __   (b) 6 __   (c) 4 __   (d) 5 __

(e) 8 __   (f) 1 __   (g) 2 __   (h) 7 __

Solution We find the second digit so that the two digits add up to nine.

(a) 36   (b) 63   (c) 45   (d) 54

(e) 81   (f) 18   (g) 27   (h) 72

Practice Find the answer to each multiplication fact. Remember, the first digit is one less than the number multiplied, and the two digits add up to nine.

a. $\begin{array}{r} 9 \\ \times 6 \\ \hline \end{array}$
b. $\begin{array}{r} 5 \\ \times 9 \\ \hline \end{array}$
c. $\begin{array}{r} 9 \\ \times 8 \\ \hline \end{array}$
d. $\begin{array}{r} 3 \\ \times 9 \\ \hline \end{array}$

e. $\begin{array}{r} 9 \\ \times 4 \\ \hline \end{array}$
f. $\begin{array}{r} 7 \\ \times 9 \\ \hline \end{array}$
g. $\begin{array}{r} 9 \\ \times 2 \\ \hline \end{array}$
h. $\begin{array}{r} 9 \\ \times 9 \\ \hline \end{array}$

Problem set 41

1. There are two hundred fifteen pages in the book. Ted
(31) has read eighty-six pages. How many more pages are left to read? Draw a SWA pattern.

2. Use the digits 7, 8, and 9 once each to make an even
(11) number greater than 800.

3. Use digits and a comparison symbol to show that four
(15) hundred eighty-five is less than six hundred ninety.

4. This is a sequence of square numbers. What are the
(39,3) next three numbers in the sequence?

$$1, 4, 9, 16, \underline{\quad}, \underline{\quad}, \underline{\quad}, \ldots$$

5. If it is morning, what time is
(23) shown on this clock?

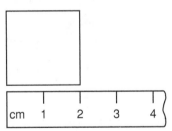

6. Use words to write 697.
(8)

7. Write 729 in expanded form.
(20)

8. Round 66 to the nearest ten.
(26)

9. Each side of this square is how long?
(24)

10. Find a letter of the alphabet formed with just two
(29) perpendicular line segments.

11. $12 - W = 7$
(14)

12. What fraction of this rectangle is
(28) shaded?

13. Draw a pattern of X's to show the multiplication
(36) 5×5.

14. Is the value of three nickels and two dimes an even
(11)   number of cents or an odd number of cents?

15. The arrow is pointing to what number on this number
(13)   line?

16. 9×6 **17.** 9×8 **18.** 9×4
(41)   (41)   (41)

19. $\sqrt{81}$ **20.** $3.60 - $1.37
(40)   (37)

21. $413 - 380$ **22.** $875 - 218$
(37)   (37)

23. Compare: $47 + 36 \bigcirc 57 + 26$
(15)

24. Five squared is how much more than the square root
(40,38) of 25?

25. Change this addition problem to a multiplication
(33)   problem:

$$6 + 6 + 6 + 6 + 6 + 6 + 6$$

LESSON 42

Writing Numbers Through 999,999: Part 1

Facts Practice: Multiplication Facts: 2, 5, 9, Squares (Test E in Test Masters)

Mental Math: To add 99¢ or 98¢ or 95¢ to another amount of money, add a dollar; then subtract 1¢ or 2¢ or 5¢.

  a. $3.45 + $0.99   **b.** $5.75 + $0.98   **c.** $0.85 + $0.95

Review:

  d. 438 − 20   **e.** 58 + 6 + 200   **f.** 78 + 9 + 300

Problem Solving: Jill's mom cut an orange in half. Then she cut each half in half. Jill ate three of the orange slices. What fraction of the orange did Jill eat?

We remember that the places in a three-digit number are the hundreds' place, the tens' place, and the ones' place. The places to the left of the hundreds' place are the thousands' place (1,000s), the ten-thousands' place (10,000s), and the hundred-thousands' place (100,000s). We notice that as we move to the left, each new place has one more zero.

hundred-thousands' place 100,000	ten-thousands' place 10,000	thousands' place 1,000	,	hundreds' place 100	tens' place 10	ones' place 1

Example 1 Write 75,634 in expanded form.

Solution The 7 is in the ten-thousands' place and has a value of 70,000. So we write

$$70,000 + 5000 + 600 + 30 + 4$$

We usually use a comma to write a number equal to or greater than one thousand. A comma helps us read numbers that have four, five, or six digits. It is not necessary, but we often use a comma to write four-digit numbers. However, a comma should be inserted when writing numbers with five or more digits. To read

4507 34507 234507

we place a comma three digits from the right-hand end of the numbers.

4,507 34,507 234,507

The comma is the thousands' comma. **The digits to the left of this comma tell the number of thousands.** First we read the part of the number to the left of the comma. Then we read the thousands' comma by saying "thousand." Then we read the part of the number to the right of the comma.

4,507	is read	four **thousand,** five hundred seven
34,507	is read	thirty-four **thousand,** five hundred seven
234,507	is read	two hundred thirty-four **thousand,** five hundred seven

When we write the number in words, we must remember to place a comma after the word *thousand*, **as we did in these examples.**

Example 2 Use words to write 123456.

Solution First we place a comma three places from the right-hand end of the number.

123,456

Now we write the part of the number to the left of the comma.

One hundred twenty-three

Next we write **"thousand"** and **put a comma after this word.**

One hundred twenty-three thousand,

Finally, we write the part of the number to the right of the comma.

> **One hundred twenty-three thousand, four hundred fifty-six**

Practice Use words to write:

a. 907,411

b. 223,512

c. 14,518

d. Write 5,280 in expanded form.

Problem set 42

1. Wilbur saw that there were one hundred forty-two goldfish in the first tank. There were three hundred fifteen goldfish in the second tank. How many more goldfish were in the second tank? Draw a L-S-D pattern.
   (38)

2. The square root of 49 is how much less than four squared?
   (40,38)

3. When Linda looked the first time, she saw 211 elves frolicking in the glen. When she looked the second time, there were 272 elves frolicking in the glen. How many more elves did she see the second time? Draw a L-S-D pattern.
   (38)

4. Write the number 3,425 in expanded form. Then write this number using words.
   (42)

5. Draw two parallel lines. Then draw a line that makes right angles when it crosses the parallel lines.
   (29)

6. It is evening. What time will it be 2 hours and 25 minutes from now?
   (33)

7. What fraction of this figure is
(28) shaded?

8. Change this addition problem to a multiplication
(33) problem:

$$9 + 9 + 9 + 9 + 9$$

9. Compare: $9 \times 4 \bigcirc \sqrt{36}$
(15)

10. The digit in the thousands' place is 4. The digit in the
(42) ones' place is 6. The digit in the tens' place is 7. The
number is between 4200 and 4300. What is the
number?

11. To what number is the arrow pointing?
(13)

12. 5×8 **13.** 8×8 **14.** 9×3 **15.** 9×4
(35)   (39)   (41)   (41)

16. $\$7.37$ **17.**   921   **18.**   464
(37) $- \$2.68$ (37) $- 58$ (16) $+ 247$

19.   329   **20.** $\$4.88$ **21.**   555
(30) $+ Z$ (28) $+ \$2.69$ (20) $- C$
     547   222

22. Janet's birth date is 5/23/54. In what month was she
(6) born?

23. Use words to write 416,803.
(42)

24.   4   **25.**   5
(21)   8   (21)   8
   12   7
   16   14
   14   6
   28   21
$+ 37$ $+ 15$

LESSON
43

Writing Numbers Through
999,999: Part 2

Facts Practice: Multiplication Facts: 2, 5, Squares (Test D in Test Masters)

Mental Math: Practice adding 99¢, 98¢, or 95¢.
  a. $5.85 + $0.99   **b.** $8.63 + $0.98   **c.** $4.98 + $0.95
Review:
  d. 574 − 200   **e.** 77 + 6 + 110   **f.** 460 + 300 + 24

Problem Solving: The two hands of a clock are together at noon. The next time the hands of a clock are together is about how many minutes later?

In Lesson 42, we practiced using words to write numbers through 999,999. In this lesson we will use digits to write numbers through 999,999.

We use a comma to help us write thousands. We write the number of thousands in front of the comma and the rest of the number behind the comma. The form looks like this.

_____ , _____

Example 1 Use digits to write eight hundred ninety-five thousand, two hundred seventy.

Solution It is a good idea to read the entire number before we begin writing it. We see the word *thousand*, so we know it will have a **thousands' comma** after the digits that tell how many thousands.

_____ , _____

Then we go back and read the part of the number in front of the word *thousand* and write this number in front of the comma. For "eight hundred ninety-five thousand" we write:

895, _____

Now, to the right of the comma, we write the last part of the number.

895,270

When writing thousands, we must be sure there are **three digits after** the thousands' comma. Sometimes it may be necessary to use one or more zeros to be sure there are three digits after the comma.

Example 2 Use digits to write thirty-five thousand.

Solution We see the word *thousand*, so it will have this form.

$$\underline{\hspace{2cm}} , \underline{\hspace{1.5cm}}$$

In front of the word *thousand*, we read "thirty-five," so for thirty-five thousand we write

$$35, \underline{\hspace{1.5cm}}$$

There is nothing written after the word *thousand*—no hundreds, no tens, no ones. However, we need to have three digits, so we write three zeros.

35,000

Example 3 Use digits to write seven thousand, twenty-five.

Solution For "seven thousand," we write

$$7, \underline{\hspace{1.5cm}}$$

After the word *thousand*, we read "twenty-five." It would not be correct to write

7,25   NOT CORRECT

We need to write three digits after the thousands' comma because there are three whole number places after the comma: hundreds, tens, and ones. Since there are no hundreds, we put a zero in the hundreds' place.

7,025   CORRECT

Practice   Use digits to write each number:

      a. One hundred twenty-one thousand, three hundred forty

      b. Twelve thousand, five hundred seven

      c. Five thousand, seventy-five

      d. Eighty-two thousand, five hundred

      e. Seven hundred fifty thousand

      f. Two thousand, one

Problem set 43

1. Four hundred sixty-five is how much greater than twenty-four? Draw a L-S-D pattern.
(38)

2. Marcie had four hundred twenty marbles. Robert had one hundred twenty-three marbles. How many fewer marbles did Robert have? Draw a L-S-D pattern.
(38)

3. Terry has forty-two marbles. Mary has one hundred thirty marbles. How many marbles do Mary and Terry have together? Draw a SSM pattern.
(12)

4. Write the number 25,463 in expanded form.
(42)

5. Draw a circle that is about 3 centimeters across the center.
(25)

6. It is afternoon. What time will it be in four and a half hours?
(33)

7. What fraction of the circles is shaded?
(28)

8. Change this addition problem to a multiplication
(33) problem:

$$8 + 8 + 8 + 8 + 8$$

9. Round 76 to the nearest ten. Round 59 to the nearest
(26,15) ten. Use digits and a symbol to compare the rounded
numbers.

10. The digit in the ones' place is 5. The digit in the tens'
(5) place is 6. The number is between 166 and 364. What
is the number?

11. To what number is the arrow pointing?
(13)

<table>
<tr><td>2000</td><td>2100</td><td>2200</td><td>2300</td></tr>
</table>

12. 9×9 **13.** 5×7 **14.** 6×6 **15.** $\sqrt{16}$
(39)   (35)   (39)   (40)

16.   535   **17.**   908   **18.**   471
(37) $- 268$ (37) $- \ 43$ (37) $- 346$

19. C **20.** C **21.**   \$3.49
(30) $+ 329$ (20) $- 127$ (28) $+ \$4.28$
    715   398

22. Five squared is how much more than 5 + 5?
(40)

23. How many sides are on eight triangles? Count by
(3) threes.

24. Use words to write 365,123.
(42)

25. Use digits to write nine hundred forty thousand, ten.
(43)

LESSON
44

Naming Mixed Numbers

Facts Practice: Multiplication Facts: 2, 5, Squares (Test D in Test Masters)

Mental Math: To add $1.99 to an amount of money, we may add two dollars, and then subtract one cent. Practice adding $1.99, $1.98, and $1.95.

   a. $5.85 + $1.98   **b.** $6.73 + $1.99   **c.** $4.85 + $1.95

Review:

   d. 687 − 350   **e.** 36 + 8 + 140   **f.** 56 + 34 + 200

Patterns: This is the sequence of numbers we say when we count by halves. Copy this sequence on your paper and continue the sequence to the whole number 8.

$$\tfrac{1}{2}, 1, 1\tfrac{1}{2}, 2, 2\tfrac{1}{2}, 3, \ldots$$

A **mixed number** is a **whole number** followed by a **fraction.** The mixed number $3\tfrac{1}{2}$ is read "three and one half."

Example 1 How many circles are shaded?

Solution Two whole circles are shaded and one fourth of another circle is shaded. The total number of shaded circles is two and one fourth, which we write as

$$2\frac{1}{4}$$

Example 2 Use words to write $21\tfrac{1}{2}$.

Solution We *do* use the word *and* when naming mixed numbers.

Twenty-one and one half

Practice What mixed numbers are pictured here?

e. Use words to name $34\frac{3}{4}$.

Problem set 44

1. There were seventy-one birds in the first tree. There
(38) were forty-two birds in the second tree. How many more birds were in the first tree? Draw a L-S-D pattern.

2. At first there were four hundred ten screaming
(31) students. Then some quieted down, and only two hundred eighty-seven students were screaming. How many students quieted down? Draw a SWA pattern.

3. Ninety-seven oranges were in the first bunch, fifty-
(12) seven oranges were in the second bunch, and forty-eight oranges were in the third bunch. How many oranges were in all three bunches? Draw a SSM pattern.

4. What mixed number is pictured
(44) in this figure?

5. Write the number 506,148 in expanded form.
(42)

6. Use words to write $56\frac{5}{6}$.
(44)

7. Which letter below has no right angles?
(29)

    T   H   E   N

8. It is morning. What time will it be
(33) 5 hours and 20 minutes from now?

9. Change this addition problem to a multiplication
(33) problem:

$$4 + 4 + 4 + 4 + 4 + 4 + 4 + 4$$

10. Round 176 to the nearest ten.
(26)

11. To what number is the arrow pointing?
(13)

12. 9 × 7   **13.** 9 × 6   **14.** 6 × 7   **15.** $\sqrt{36}$
(41)   (41)   (34)   (40)

16. $7.32   **17.** $4.89   **18.**   464
(37)   − $3.45   (28)   + $2.57   (37)   − 238

19.   548   **20.**   487   **21.**   250
(16)   + 999   (30)   +   Z   (20)   −   C
                         721   122

22.   C   **23.**   87
(20)   − 338   (20)   −   B
        238   54

24. 22 + 46 + 84 + 97 + 96 + 47
(21)

25. Use digits to write nine hundred seven thousand,
(43) seventy.

LESSON
45

Two Forms of Money

Facts Practice: Multiplication Facts: 2, 5, 9, Squares (Test E in Test Masters)

Mental Math: Practice adding amounts ending in 99¢, 98¢, or 95¢.

   a. $4.65 + $2.99   **b.** $3.86 + $1.95   **c.** $6.24 + $2.98

Review:

   d. 520 − 120   **e.** 350 + 400 + 35 **f.** 37 + 29 + 220

Problem Solving: We can quickly add or subtract some numbers on a calendar. Select a number from the middle part of a monthly calendar. If we move straight up from that number, we subtract 7. If we move straight down, we add 7. We can add or subtract two other numbers if we move diagonally. Which numbers do we add or subtract when we move in these directions?

We can tell how much money there is by using a number and a cent sign (¢). If we put the cent sign behind the number, we are telling how many cents.

(a) 324¢   (b) 20¢   (c) 4¢

We can also use a dollar sign ($) to tell how much money there is. We always put the dollar sign in front of the number. Then we put a **decimal point** two places from the end of the number. The number to the left of the decimal point tells how many dollars. The number to the right of the decimal point tells how many cents.

(a) $3.24   (b) $0.20   (c) $0.04

The first amount is three dollars and twenty-four cents. The second amount is twenty cents. Since there were no dollars, we wrote a zero for dollars. We do not read the zero. The third amount is four cents.

The decimal point must be two digits from the end. If there is just one digit, we insert another zero in front of that digit.

$0.04 means the same as 4¢

We do not read the zeros in $0.04. We just say "Four cents."

Example 1 Write three hundred fifteen dollars and twenty-five cents using a dollar sign and a decimal point.

Solution When we use a dollar sign, we put a decimal point two places from the end.

$315.25

Example 2 Use words to write $30.76.

Solution We write the number of dollars, write "and," and then write the number of cents.

Thirty dollars and seventy-six cents

Example 3 Use a dollar sign and a decimal point to write seven cents.

Solution To show cents with a dollar sign, we use a decimal point. The decimal point goes two places from the end. If we write the seven,

7

we have only one digit, so we put a zero between the seven and the decimal point.

$.07

We may put another zero in front of the decimal point because there are no dollars.

$0.07

Example 4 Tommy has one quarter, one dime, and one nickel. Write how much money he has using a cent sign. Then write the amount again using a dollar sign and a decimal point.

Solution First we find how many cents. A quarter is twenty-five cents, a dime is ten cents, and a nickel is five cents.

$$25¢ + 10¢ + 5¢ = \textbf{40¢}$$

Now we write forty cents using a dollar sign and a decimal point.

$0.40

Practice Write these amounts with a cent sign instead of a dollar sign:

   a. $0.17   **b.** $0.05   **c.** $4.60

Write these amounts with a dollar sign instead of a cent sign:

   d. 195¢   **e.** 8¢   **f.** 30¢

   g. Write the value of two quarters, two dimes, and one nickel with a dollar sign. Then use a cent sign to write this amount again.

Use words to write each amount:

   h. $0.77

   i. $12.25

   j. $20.05

Problem set 45 **1.** The king saw two hundred seventy peasants. The *(38)* queen saw one hundred fifty-five peasants. How many more peasants did the king see? Draw a L-S-D pattern.

2. The king saw five hundred sixty-seven peasants the *(38)* first time he looked. Then he saw eight hundred forty-two peasants the second time he looked. How many fewer peasants did he see the first time he looked? Draw a L-S-D pattern.

3. Jimbo had four dollars and sixty-five cents. Use a
(45) dollar sign and a decimal point to write this amount.
Then write this amount again using a cent sign.

4. What temperature is shown on
(22) this thermometer?

5. Which one of these angles does not look like a right
(29) angle?

A.   B.   C.   D.

6. What mixed number is pictured?
(44)

7. The square root of 81 is how much less than seven
(40,38) squared?

8. Write 250,516 in expanded form. Then use words to
(42) write this number.

9. It is evening. What time will it be
(33) 2 hours and 20 minutes from
now?

10. The digit in the ones' place is 5. The digit in the tens'
(5) place is 6. The number is between 390 and 490. What
is the number?

11. To what number is the arrow pointing?
(13)

12. Use words to write $1.43. Then use a cent sign to write
(45) the same amount.

13. 6 × 9   **14.** 4 × 9   **15.** 8 × 9   **16.** 3 × 9
(41)   (41)   (41)   (41)

17. $6.05   **18.**   489   **19.** $5.32
(37)   − $2.53   (30) +   Z   (28) + $3.44
                        ‾‾‾‾‾
                         766

20.   C   **21.**   423   **22.**   670
(30) + 294   (37) − 245   (20) −   Z
      ‾‾‾‾‾   ‾‾‾‾‾   ‾‾‾‾‾
       870   352

23. 46 + 24 + 87 + 96
(21)

24. Draw a rectangle that shows 2 × 5. Shade three tenths
(36,32) of the rectangle.

25. Use digits to write four hundred twenty-seven
(43) thousand, five hundred two.

LESSON 46

Reading Fractions and Mixed Numbers from a Number Line

Facts Practice: Multiplication Facts: 2, 5, 9, Squares (Test E in Test Masters)

Mental Math: Subtract without regrouping.

    a. 563 − 242   **b.** $5.75 − $2.50   **c.** $8.98 − $0.72

Review:

    d. $4.85 + $1.99   **e.** 48 + 7 + 20   **f.** 54 + 19 + 320

Problem Solving: The hands of a clock are together at 12:00. The hands of a clock are not together at 6:30, because the hour hand is halfway between the 6 and the 7 at 6:30. The hands come together at about 6:33. Name nine more times that the hands of a clock come together.

To find mixed numbers on a number line, we must find the number of **spaces** between consecutive whole numbers. If there are four spaces between the whole numbers, each space equals $\frac{1}{4}$. If there are six spaces between the whole numbers, each space equals $\frac{1}{6}$.

Example 1   The arrow points to what number?

Solution   There are three **spaces** between 5 and 6. Each space equals $\frac{1}{3}$. The arrow points to **$5\frac{2}{3}$**.

Example 2   The arrow points to what number on each number line?

Solution   (a) There are five spaces between the whole numbers. Each space equals $\frac{1}{5}$. The arrow points to **$17\frac{3}{5}$**.

(b) There are six spaces between the whole numbers. Each space equals $\frac{1}{6}$. The arrow points to $36\frac{5}{6}$.

Practice Name the fraction or mixed number marked by the arrows on these number lines:

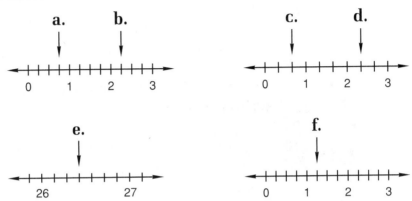

Problem set 46

1. On the way to school, Ted saw four hundred twenty-seven petunia blossoms. Karen saw seven hundred fifteen petunia blossoms. How many more petunia blossoms did Karen see? Draw a L-S-D pattern.
   (38)

2. Circe had two hundred seventy-five pigs. After Odysseus came, Circe had four hundred sixty-two pigs. How many pigs did she get from Odysseus? Draw a SSM pattern.
   (17)

3. Four hundred seventy-five thousand, three hundred forty-two is a big number. Use digits to write this number.
   (43)

4. The money in the piggy bank was worth seven dollars and sixty-five cents. Use a dollar sign to write this amount. Then use a cent sign to write this amount.
   (45)

5. The arrow is pointing to what number?
   (46)

6. Draw a rectangle whose length is 5 cm and whose
(25) width is 3 cm.

7. What mixed number is shown by
(44) the shaded rectangles?

8. Use words to write $32\frac{2}{3}$.
(44)

9. Write 257,026 in expanded form. Then use words to
(42) write this number.

10. It is early morning. What time
(33) will it be 2 hours and 35 minutes
from now?

11. Write each amount using a dollar sign. Then write
(45) each amount again using a cent sign.
(a) One dollar and forty-seven cents
(b) Seven cents

12. Draw a rectangle pattern to show 4 × 6.
(36)

13. 7 × 9   **14.** 6 × 9   **15.** 4 × 9
(41)   (41)   (41)

16. $\sqrt{81}$ **17.** $6.63 − $3.55
(40)   (37)

18. $4.99 + $2.88   **19.** $A − 247 = 321$
(28)   (20)

20. $Z + 296 = 531$ **21.** $523 − Z = 145$
(30)   (20)

22. 28 + 46 + 48 + 64 + 32 + 344
(21)

23. Y **24.**   74   **25.**   67
(20) $- 14$ (20) $- B$ (30) $+ Y$
         $\overline{37}$ $\overline{48}$ $\overline{83}$

LESSON
47

Multiplication Facts (Memory Group)

Facts Practice: Multiplication Facts: 2, 5, 9, Squares (Test E in Test Masters)

Mental Math: Subtract a number ending in five from a number ending in zero.

   a. $80 - 5$ **b.** $80 - 25$ (Subtract 20. Then subtract 5 more.)

Review:

   c. $6.23 + 2.98$ **d.** $340 + 26 + 216$ **e.** $65 + 8 + 200$

Patterns: Counting by halves we say, "One half, one, one and one half, two." Count by halves from one half to ten. Then write this sequence on a piece of paper. What number is halfway between two and five?

There are only 10 multiplication facts we have not practiced. We call these facts the **memory group.**

$$3 \times 4 = 12 \qquad 4 \times 7 = 28$$
$$3 \times 6 = 18 \qquad 4 \times 8 = 32$$
$$3 \times 7 = 21 \qquad 6 \times 7 = 42$$
$$3 \times 8 = 24 \qquad 6 \times 8 = 48$$
$$4 \times 6 = 24 \qquad 7 \times 8 = 56$$

These facts must be memorized. Sounds are often helpful when we memorize things. If we say these facts out loud in a sing-song manner, the sounds become familiar. When you practice facts, you should say the facts softly to yourself.

The multiplication facts should be practiced by doing **timed written tests** on a daily basis. A suggested goal is to complete a 100-facts written test in 4 minutes with no more than three errors. Then you should continue to practice often so you remember the facts.

Practice Multiplication Facts: Memory Group (Test F in Test Masters)

Problem set 47

1. There were two hundred twenty toys in the first pile.
   ⁽³⁸⁾ There were four hundred five toys in the second pile.
   How many more toys were in the second pile? Draw a
   L-S-D pattern.

2. Five hundred seventy-five thousand, five hundred
   ⁽⁴³⁾ forty-two people lived in the city. Use digits to write
   this number.

3. Write 472,503 in expanded form. Then use words to
   ⁽⁴²⁾ write this number.

4. There were four hundred thirty-two boys. There were
   ⁽¹⁷⁾ nine hundred eighteen boys and girls. How many girls
   were there? Draw a SSM pattern. (*Hint:* The number
   of boys is one part. The number of girls is another part.
   The number of boys and girls is the total.)

5. The arrow is pointing to what number?
   ⁽⁴⁶⁾

6. Which street is parallel to Broad
   ⁽²⁹⁾ Street?

7. What mixed number is shown by
   ⁽⁴⁴⁾ the shaded circles?

8. Round 624 to the nearest ten.
   ⁽²⁶⁾

9. It is morning. What time will it be
   ⁽³³⁾ 5 hours and 15 minutes from
   now?

10. Use a dollar sign and a decimal point to write each of
(45) these amounts:

(a) 1256¢   (b) 4¢

11. Draw shaded circles to show $2\frac{3}{4}$.
(44)

12. Draw a pattern of X's to show 4 × 7.
(36)

13. 4 × 7   **14.** 4 × 8   **15.** 4 × 6   **16.** 7 × 8
(47)   (47)   (47)   (47)

17. $7.23   **18.** $5.42   **19.**   943
(37) − $2.54   (28) + $2.69   (37) − 276

20.   478   **21.**   Z   **22.**   117
(16) + 249   (20) − 581   (30) + 843
                    222   960

23. 28 + 36 + 78 + $\sqrt{49}$
(40,21)

24.   14   **25.**   29
(21)   18   (21)   5
       6   13
       4   27
    18   63
+ 15   + 76

LESSON
48

Reading an Inch Scale to the Nearest Fourth

Facts Practice: Multiplication Facts: Memory Group (Test F in Test Masters)

Mental Math: Subtract a number ending in five from a number ending in zero.

   a. 70 − 5   **b.** 70 − 45   **c.** 370 − 125

Review:

   d. $5.96 + $3.95   **e.** 76 + 9 + 200   **f.** 560 + 24 + 306

Vocabulary: Copy these two patterns on a piece of paper. In each of the six boxes write either "factor" or "product."

An **inch** is a unit used for measuring length. An inch is this long.

We use the letters "in." to abbreviate the word *inch*. To avoid confusing the abbreviation for *inch* with the word *in*, we write the abbreviation with a period. To measure lengths in inches, we use an inch scale. Inch scales are found on rulers and on tape measures. An inch scale has marks between the inch marks. These marks let us read the inch scale to the nearest half inch, nearest quarter inch, or nearest eighth inch. One quarter inch is the same as one fourth inch. In this lesson we will practice reading to the nearest quarter inch.

When reading an inch scale, we should remember that $\frac{2}{4}$ is equal to $\frac{1}{2}$. The two circles below show that equal parts of the circles are shaded.

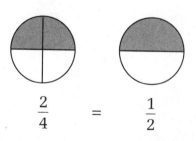

$$\frac{2}{4} \quad = \quad \frac{1}{2}$$

The fraction $\frac{1}{2}$ is the reduced form of $\frac{2}{4}$. Instead of naming a fraction $\frac{2}{4}$, we will use the fraction $\frac{1}{2}$. Half inch marks are usually drawn slightly longer than quarter inch marks.

Example   How long is the toothpick to the nearest quarter inch?

Solution   The toothpick is 2 inches plus a fraction. It is closest to $2\frac{2}{4}$ inches. Instead of writing $\frac{2}{4}$, we use $\frac{1}{2}$. The toothpick is $2\frac{1}{2}$ inches long. We abbreviate this by writing **$2\frac{1}{2}$ in.**

Practice   **a.** Draw a picture that shows that $\frac{2}{4}$ equals $\frac{1}{2}$.

Name each point marked by an arrow on this inch scale:

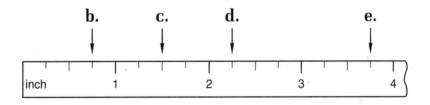

Problem set 48

1. Ann is twelve years old. Ann's mother is thirty-five
(38)   years old. Ann's mother is how many years older than Ann? Draw a L-S-D pattern.

2. Four hundred sixty-eight thousand, five hundred two
(43)   boxes were in the warehouse. Use digits to write this number.

3. Write the number 3,905 in expanded form. Then use
(42)   words to write this number.

4. Dan smashed two hundred forty-three pop cans with
(12,11)   his right foot and smashed three hundred sixty-four pop cans with his left foot. Was the total number of smashed cans an even number or an odd number?

5. Use words to write the mixed number $102\frac{1}{2}$.
(44)

6. Use digits and a comparison symbol to show that
(15) seven hundred eighty-six is greater than seven hundred sixty-eight.

7. Use a dollar sign to write the value of two dollars, one
(45) quarter, two dimes, and three nickels. Write the value again using a cent sign.

8. It is morning. What time will it be
(33) 10 minutes from now?

9. One kilometer is how many meters?
(27)

10. How many of these circles are
(44) shaded?

11. Find the length of this screw to the nearest quarter
(48) inch.

12. (41) $\begin{array}{r} 9 \\ \times\ 8 \\ \hline \end{array}$	**13.** (47) $\begin{array}{r} 6 \\ \times\ 7 \\ \hline \end{array}$	**14.** (47) $\begin{array}{r} 8 \\ \times\ 6 \\ \hline \end{array}$	**15.** (47) $\begin{array}{r} 6 \\ \times\ 4 \\ \hline \end{array}$

16. (47) $\begin{array}{r} 7 \\ \times\ 3 \\ \hline \end{array}$	**17.** (28) $\begin{array}{r} \$4.86 \\ +\ \$2.47 \\ \hline \end{array}$	**18.** (37) $\begin{array}{r} \$4.86 \\ -\ \$2.47 \\ \hline \end{array}$	**19.** (16) $\begin{array}{r} 293 \\ +\ 678 \\ \hline \end{array}$

20. (37) $\begin{array}{r} 893 \\ -\ 678 \\ \hline \end{array}$	**21.** (20) $\begin{array}{r} 463 \\ -\ \ Y \\ \hline 411 \end{array}$	**22.** (30) $\begin{array}{r} 463 \\ +\ \ Q \\ \hline 527 \end{array}$

23. 418
(20) − _T_
——————
216

24. 24
(21) 36
84
125
+ 127
——————

25. Draw a rectangle that shows 3 × 5. Then shade four
(36,32) fifteenths of it.

LESSON
49

U.S. Units of Length

Facts Practice: Multiplication Facts: Memory Group (Test F in
Test Masters)

Mental Math: Subtract a number ending in five from a number
ending in zero.
a. $0.80 − $0.35   **b.** $1.60 − $0.25   **c.** $4.50 − $1.15
Review:
d. $6.28 + $0.99   **e.** 68 + 6 + 20   **f.** 43 + 29 + 310

Patterns: This is the sequence of numbers we say when we
count by fourths. Copy this sequence on your paper
and continue the sequence to the whole number 5.
$\frac{1}{4}$, $\frac{1}{2}$, $\frac{3}{4}$, 1, $1\frac{1}{4}$, $1\frac{1}{2}$, $1\frac{3}{4}$, 2, ...

In Lesson 27 we described some units of length in the
metric system. In the United States we also use other units
of length. Some of these are inches, feet, yards, and miles.
In Lesson 48, we said that an inch is this long.

——————

Twelve inches equal 1 **foot.** You may have a 1-foot ruler
for use at your desk. A **yard** is 3 feet. One *big* step is about
1 yard. So a yard is about the same length as a meter.
Actually, a yard is about $3\frac{1}{2}$ inches less than a meter. A
mile is 1760 yards, which is 5280 feet.

We often use the abbreviations "in.," "ft," "yd," and "mi" to stand for *inches*, *feet, yards*, and *miles*.

U. S. Units of Length

12 in. = 1 ft
36 in. = 1 yd
3 ft = 1 yd
5280 ft = 1 mi
1760 yd = 1 mi

Activity   Use a yardstick and a 1-foot ruler to measure objects in the classroom. How tall and how wide is the door? How long and how wide is the room? Tables, desks, cabinets, and countertops can be measured. Compare a yardstick and a meterstick. Which is longer and by how much? A 1-foot ruler is about how many centimeters long?

Example 1   How many 1-foot rulers laid end to end would it take to equal 2 yards?

Solution   A yard is 3 feet long. So it would take 3 one-foot rulers to reach 1 yard. To reach another yard would take 3 more one-foot rulers. Therefore, to reach 2 yards would take **6 one-foot rulers.**

Example 2   How many *big* steps would it take to walk a mile?

Solution   A mile is 1760 yards, which is about **1760 *big* steps.**

Practice   **a.** How many 1-foot rulers laid end to end would it take to reach 3 yards?

b. A mile is how many feet?

c. One yard is how many inches?

**Problem set
49**

1. Use the digits 4, 5, and 6 once each to make an even
   number greater than 600.
   (11)

2. Myrtle the Turtle laid one hundred fifty eggs in the
   sand. Her friend Gertle laid one hundred seventy-five
   eggs. Together, how many eggs did they lay? Draw a
   SSM pattern.
   (12)

3. Jill is 6 years younger than her brother. If her brother
   is 15 years old, how old is Jill? Draw a L-S-D pattern.
   (38)

4. What numbers are missing in this sequence?
   (3)
   _____, 40, _____, _____, 64, 72, ...

5. Use words to write the mixed number $23\frac{2}{3}$.
   (44)

6. $219 = N + 10 + 9$
   (2)

7. Write 809,742 in expanded form. Then use words to
   write this number.
   (42)

8. Compare: three squared $\bigcirc$ $\sqrt{81}$
   (40,15)

9. Round 128 to the nearest ten.
   (26)

10. Write the value of three quarters and three dimes with
    a dollar sign. Then use words to write this amount of
    money.
    (45)

11. Find the length of this rectangle to the nearest quarter
    inch.
    (48)

12. Draw a square and shade one ninth of it. (*Hint:* Draw a
    square. Then draw an evenly spaced tic-tac-toe pattern
    inside the square.)
    (32)

13. Three one-foot rulers laid end to end reach how many
(49) inches?

14. Compare: one mile ◯ 1000 yards
(49,15)

15. 3   **16.** 4   **17.** 6   **18.** 7   **19.** 8
(47) × 7   (47) × 6   (47) × 7   (47) × 8   (41) × 9

20. $7.20   **21.** $4.26   **22.** 463   **23.** 436
(37) − $4.25   (28) + $1.57   (37) − 286   (37) − 147

24. $36 + 42 + 8 + \sqrt{81} + N = 100$
(40,2)

25. Draw a pattern of X's to show 6 × 7.
(36)

LESSON 50

Lines and Segments • Missing Factors

Facts Practice: Multiplication Facts: Memory Group (Test F in Test Masters)

Mental Math: Subtract a number ending in 50 from a number ending in two zeros.

  a. 300 − 50   **b.** $4.00 − $0.50   **c.** $5.00 − $1.50

Review:

  d. $7.90 + $1.95   **e.** 536 + 45   **f.** 59 + 6 + 210

Problem Solving: The digits 1, 2, 3, and 4, in order, can be written with an equal sign and a times sign to make a multiplication fact.

$$12 = 3 \times 4$$

Write another multiplication fact using four different digits written in order.

Lines and segments   A pencil line has two ends. We say that a mathematical line has no ends. A mathematical line just goes on and on in both directions. Sometimes we draw arrowheads on a pencil line to show this idea.

A line never ends.

Part of a mathematical line is a **line segment** or just a **segment.** A segment has two endpoints.

A line segment is part of a line. It has two ends.

Sometimes the endpoints of a segment are labeled with letters, and the segment is named using the letters. When we write the name of a segment, either letter can come first.

This is segment *AB*. This is also segment *BA*.

We can also write segment *AB* as $\overline{AB}$ and segment *BA* as $\overline{BA}$. Notice that the bar replaces the word *segment.* When there is more than one segment in a picture, we use the letters to make it clear which segment we are talking about.

Example 1   The length of $\overline{AB}$ is 3 cm. The length of $\overline{BC}$ is 4 cm. What is the length of $\overline{AC}$?

Solution   Two short segments can form a longer segment. From *A* to *B* is one segment. From *B* to *C* is a second segment. Together they form the third segment, segment *AC*. We are told the lengths of $\overline{AB}$ and $\overline{BC}$. If we add these lengths together, the sum will equal the length of $\overline{AC}$.

$$3 \text{ cm} + 4 \text{ cm} = 7 \text{ cm}$$

The length of $\overline{AC}$ is **7 cm.**

Since this problem is drawn to scale, we can check our answer with a ruler. However, we should not assume that all problems are drawn to scale. Therefore, we should always find the length mathematically instead of measuring with a ruler.

Missing factors   Recall that numbers that are multiplied are called *factors* and the answer is called the *product*.

$$\text{Factor} \times \text{factor} = \text{product}$$

If we know one factor and the product, we can figure out the other factor.

Example 2   Find the missing factors:

(a) $5 \times N = 40$ (b) $A \times 4 = 36$

Solution   (a) Five times what number is 40? Since $5 \times 8 = 40$, the missing factor is **8**.

(b) Since $9 \times 4 = 36$, the missing factor is **9**.

Practice   **a.** The length of segment AB is 5 cm. The length of segment BC is 4 cm. What is the length of segment AC?

A   B   C

b. The length of $\overline{RS}$ is 4 cm. The length of $\overline{RT}$ is 10 cm. What is the length of $\overline{ST}$? (*Hint*: This time you will need to subtract.)

R   S   T

Find each missing factor:

c. $8 \times W = 32$ **d.** $P \times 3 = 12$

Problem set 50

1. A group of quail is called a *covey*. A group of cows is
(38) called a *herd*. A group of fish is called a *school*. There are twenty-five fish in the small school. There are one hundred twelve fish in the big school. How many fewer fish are in the small school? Draw a L-S-D pattern.

2. A 36-inch yardstick was divided into two pieces. One
(31) piece was 12 inches long. How many inches long was the other piece? Draw a SWA pattern.

3. Mrs. Green mailed forty-seven postcards from Paris.
(12) Her husband mailed sixty-two postcards from Paris. Her son mailed seventy-five postcards from Paris. In all, how many postcards did the Greens mail from Paris? Draw a SSM pattern.

4. Write the number 416,528 in expanded form. Then
(42) use words to write this number.

5. Use digits and a comparison symbol to write that one
(15) thousand, four hundred sixty is less than one thousand, six hundred forty.

6. Use a dollar sign and a decimal point to write the
(45) value of three dollars, two quarters, one dime, and two nickels. Then write this amount of money using words.

7. Find each missing factor:
(50)
(a) $5 \times N = 20$ (b) $W \times 3 = 21$

8. How many squares are shaded?
(44)

9. Find the length of the segment to the nearest quarter
(48) inch.

10. The length of segment AB is 3 cm. The length of seg-
(50) ment BC is 4 cm. What is the length of segment AC?

11. It is evening. What time will it be
(33) 1 hour and 50 minutes from now?

12. Use a comparison symbol to compare 294 and 302.
(15)

13. Draw a circle that is about 2 centimeters across the
(25) center.

14. (41)	**15.** (47)	**16.** (47)	**17.** (39)	**18.** (47)
9 $\times$ 7	7 $\times$ 3	6 $\times$ 8	6 $\times$ 6	4 $\times$ 8

19.   416
(20) $-$ Z
          179

20. $4.98
(28)   + $7.65

21.   536
(30) $+$ Z
          721

22. $\sqrt{1} + \sqrt{4} + \sqrt{9} + N = 10$
(40,2)

23. Draw a pattern of X's to show 3 $\times$ 7.
(36)

24. Use digits to write four hundred fifteen thousand,
(43) seven.

25. (1)
4
5
8
9
6
5
+ 4

26. (21)
9
3
14
7
8
5
+ 24

27. (1)
7
2
8
9
4
7
+ 6

LESSON
51

Subtracting Across Zero

Facts Practice: Multiplication Facts: Memory Group (Test F in Test Masters)

Mental Math: Add hundreds, then tens, and then ones, regrouping tens.

  a. 365 + 240   **b.** 456 + 252   **c.** 584 + 41

Review:

  d. $6.00 − $1.50   **e.** $4.56 + $1.99   **f.** 47 + 29 + 100

Problem Solving: Counting by fourths we say, "One fourth, one half, three fourths, one." Count by fourths from one fourth to four. Write this sequence on a sheet of paper. What number is between $2\frac{1}{2}$ and 3? What number is halfway between 3 and 4?

In the problem below we must regroup twice before we can subtract the first time.

$$
\begin{array}{r}
\$405 \\
- \$126 \\
\hline
\end{array}
$$

We cannot exchange a ten for ones because there are no tens. The first step is to exchange 1 hundred for 10 tens.

$$
\begin{array}{r}
\$\overset{3}{\cancel{4}}\overset{1}{0}5 \\
- \$126 \\
\hline
\end{array}
$$

Now we have 10 tens. The next step is to exchange 1 of the tens for 10 ones.

$$
\begin{array}{r}
\$\overset{3}{\cancel{4}}\overset{9}{\cancel{0}}\overset{1}{5} \\
- \$126 \\
\hline
\end{array}
$$

Now we subtract.

$$
\begin{array}{r}
\$\overset{3}{\cancel{4}}\overset{9}{\cancel{0}}\overset{1}{5} \\
- \$126 \\
\hline
\$279 \\
\end{array}
$$

We check by adding.

$$\begin{array}{r} \$126 \\ + \$279 \\ \hline \$405 \quad \text{check} \end{array}$$

Example Tom had $3.00 and spent $1.23. How much money did he have left?

Solution First we change 3 dollars to 2 dollars and 10 dimes. Next we change 10 dimes to 9 dimes and 10 pennies. Then we subtract.

$$\begin{array}{r} \$\,3.0\,0 \\ -\$\,1.2\,3 \\ \hline \end{array} \qquad \begin{array}{r} \$\,\overset{2}{\cancel{3}}{\overset{1}{.}}0\,0 \\ -\$\,1.2\,3 \\ \hline \end{array} \qquad \begin{array}{r} \$\,\overset{2}{\cancel{3}}{.}\overset{9}{\cancel{0}}\overset{1}{0} \\ -\$\,1.2\,3 \\ \hline \$\,1.7\,7 \end{array}$$

Now we check by adding.

$$\begin{array}{r} \$1.23 \\ + \$1.77 \\ \hline \$3.00 \quad \text{check} \end{array}$$

Practice

a. $\begin{array}{r} \$3.00 \\ - \$1.32 \\ \hline \end{array}$

b. $\begin{array}{r} \$405 \\ - \$156 \\ \hline \end{array}$

c. $\begin{array}{r} 201 \\ - 102 \\ \hline \end{array}$

d. $4.00 − $0.86   e. $304 − $128   f. 703 − 198

Problem set 51

1. There were one hundred forty-seven birds in the first
(38) flock. There were six hundred forty-three birds in the second flock. How many more birds were in the second flock? Draw a L-S-D pattern.

2. Kevin had a dime, a quarter, and a penny. Write this
(45) amount with a dollar sign and a decimal point.

3. San Francisco is 400 miles north   • San Francisco
(50) of Los Angeles, as shown. Santa
Barbara is 110 miles north of Los
Angeles. How far is it from Santa
Barbara to San Francisco?   • Santa Barbara
                                        • Los Angeles

4. Use the digits 5, 6, and 7 once each to make an odd
_(11)_ number greater than 700.

5. Use digits and a comparison symbol to show that five
_(15)_ hundred ninety-four is greater than five hundred
forty-nine.

6. It is dark now. What time will it
_(33)_ be 7 hours from now?

7. Find the missing factor:
_(50)_ $W \times 5 = 40$

8. Draw a rectangle and shade one fourth of it.
_(32)_

9. There is a 6 in the ones' place and a 7 in the tens'
_(42)_ place. The number is between 4000 and 4100. What is
the number?

10. Which letter below has no right angles?
_(29)_
F   E   Z   L

11. Find the length of segment _BC_.
_(50)_

12. The arrow points to what number on this inch scale?
_(48)_

13.   7
_(47)_ $\times 8$

14.   9
_(41)_ $\times 6$

15.   _M_
_(50)_ $\times 8$
____
64

16.   6
_(47)_ $\times 7$

17.   9
_(41)_ $\times 8$

18.   _Z_
_(30)_ + 179
____
496

19. (30)
$$\begin{array}{r} 251 \\ + \quad C \\ \hline 426 \end{array}$$

20. (20)
$$\begin{array}{r} 405 \\ - \quad P \\ \hline 123 \end{array}$$

21. (20)
$$\begin{array}{r} W \\ - 297 \\ \hline 486 \end{array}$$

22. (40,2) Six squared + $\sqrt{64}$ + N = 50

23. (43) Use digits to write seven hundred thousand, seventeen.

24. (21)
$$\begin{array}{r} 27 \\ 4 \\ 16 \\ 28 \\ 7 \\ + 15 \\ \hline \end{array}$$

25. (21)
$$\begin{array}{r} 19 \\ 81 \\ 5 \\ 7 \\ 14 \\ + 21 \\ \hline \end{array}$$

26. (21)
$$\begin{array}{r} 31 \\ 14 \\ 28 \\ 15 \\ 6 \\ + 7 \\ \hline \end{array}$$

LESSON 52

Rounding Numbers to the Nearest Hundred • Multiplying by Multiples of 10 and 100

Facts Practice: Multiplication Facts: Memory Group (Test F in Test Masters)

Mental Math: Add hundreds, then tens, and then ones, regrouping tens.

  a. 466 + 72   **b.** $3.59 + $2.50   **c.** 572 + 186

Review:

  d. 400 + 160 + 30   **e.** $4.60 + $2.45   **f.** $6.24 + $2.98

Problem Solving: The hands of a clock point in opposite directions at 6:00. They also point in opposite directions at about 12:33. Name nine more times the hands of a clock point in opposite directions.

Rounding numbers to the nearest hundred

We have practiced rounding numbers to the nearest ten. Now we will learn to round numbers to the nearest hundred. To round numbers to the nearest hundred, we find the hundred number to which the number is nearest.

The hundred numbers are the numbers in this sequence.

100, 200, 300, 400, ...

A number line can help us understand rounding to the nearest hundred.

Example 1   Round 472 to the nearest hundred.

Solution   The number 472 is between the hundred numbers 400 and 500. Halfway between 400 and 500 is 450. Since 472 is greater than 450, it is nearest 500. We see this on the number line below.

Rounding 472 to the nearest hundred gives us **500.**

Example 2   Round 362 and 385 to the nearest hundred. Then use a comparison symbol to compare the rounded numbers.

Solution   The number 362 is closer to 400 than it is to 300. The number 385 is closer to 400 than it is to 300. Both 362 and 385 round to **400.** If we compare the rounded numbers, we get

400 = 400

Multiplying by multiples of 10 and 100   The multiples of 10 are the numbers we say when we count by 10.

Multiples of 10: 10, 20, 30, 40, 50, ...

Likewise, the multiples of 100 are the numbers we say when we count by 100.

Multiples of 100: 100, 200, 300, 400, 500, ...

When multiplying by multiples of 10 and 100, we focus our attention on the first digit of the multiple of 10 or 100.

Example 3   Find the product: 3×200

Solution   We will show three ways.

$$\begin{array}{r} 200 \\ 200 \\ + 200 \\ \hline 600 \end{array}$$

$$\begin{array}{r} 2 \text{ hundred} \\ \times \qquad 3 \\ \hline 6 \text{ hundred} \end{array}$$

$$\begin{array}{r} 200 \\ \times \quad 3 \\ \hline 600 \end{array}$$

We will look closely at the method on the right.

$$\begin{array}{r} 2\,0\,0 \quad \longleftarrow \text{ Two zeros here} \\ \times \quad 3 \\ \hline 2 \times 3 = 6 \longrightarrow 6\,0\,0 \quad \longleftarrow \text{ Two zeros here} \end{array}$$

By focusing on the first digit and by counting ending zeros, we can multiply by multiples of 10 and 100 mentally.

Example 4   Multiply: 6×40

Solution   We will practice two mental math methods.

$$6 \times 4 \,0 = 240$$

$$\begin{array}{r} 4\,0 \\ \times \quad 6 \\ \hline 2\,4\,0 \end{array}$$

Practice   Round each number to the nearest hundred:

a. 813   **b.** 685   **c.** 427   **d.** 573

Find each product:

e. $\begin{array}{r} 50 \\ \times\ 7 \\ \hline \end{array}$ **f.** $\begin{array}{r} 600 \\ \times\ \ 3 \\ \hline \end{array}$ **g.** 7×40 **h.** 4×800

Problem set 52

1. Two hundred fifty-two cowboys came when the bell
(17) rang once. Then some more cowboys came when the bell rang twice. Four hundred two cowboys came in all. How many cowboys came when the bell rang twice? Draw a SSM pattern.

2. Wilbur had sixty-seven grapes. He ate some grapes.
(31) Then he had thirty-eight grapes. How many grapes did
he eat? Draw a SWA pattern.

3. The distance from Whery to Radi-
(50) cal is 42 km. The distance from
Whery to Appletown through
Radical is 267 km. How far is it
from Radical to Appletown?

4. It is afternoon. What time will it
(33) be in half an hour?

5. Write the next three numbers in this sequence of
(39,3) square numbers:

1, 4, 9, 16, 25, 36, 49, _____, _____, _____, ...

6. Round 673 to the nearest hundred.
(52)

7. How many squares are shaded?
(44)

8. Find the length of the screw to the nearest quarter
(48) inch.

9. The length of $\overline{AB}$ is 7 cm. The length of $\overline{AC}$ is 12 cm.
(50) How long is $\overline{BC}$?

A   B   C

10. One way to remember the difference between the
(29) words *parallel* and *perpendicular* is to look at the
three l's in *parallel*. The l's are parallel. Now here's
the question. Are the line segments in a plus sign
parallel or perpendicular?

11. To what number is the arrow pointing?
(13)

12. Use the digits 4, 7, and 8 once each to write an odd
(11) number greater than 500.

13. 6 × 80   **14.** 7 × 700   **15.** 9 × 80   **16.** 7 × 600
(52)   (52)   (52)   (52)

17. Z **18.** $4.06   **19.**   705
(30)   + 338   (51)   − $2.28   (20)   − N
         ‾‾‾‾‾   ‾‾‾‾‾‾‾   ‾‾‾‾‾
          507   416

20. N **21.** 55 + 555 + 378
(20)   − 422   (21)
         ‾‾‾‾‾
          305

22. 293 + 58 + 681
(21)

23. 8 + 56 + 78 + 24 + 55 + 387
(21)

24. Draw a pattern of X's to show 6 × 8.
(36)

25. Write each amount of money with a dollar sign and a
(45) decimal point.

(a) 77¢   (b) 8¢   (c) 430¢

26. Use words to write 703,742.
(42)

27. Use digits to write nine hundred two thousand, five
(43) hundred seven.

LESSON
53

More Adding and Subtracting Money

Facts Practice: 64 Multiplication Facts (Test G in Test Masters)

Mental Math: Add hundreds, then tens, and then ones, regrouping tens and ones.

    a. 258 + 154   **b.** $367 + $265   **c.** 587 + 354

Review:

    d. 54 + 19 + 110   **e.** 620 + 40 + 115   **f.** 480 − 115

Problem Solving: From Point *A* to Point *B* is $1\frac{1}{4}$ inches. How far is it from Point *B* to Point *C*?

To add or subtract money written with a dollar sign, we first line up the decimal points.

Example 1 (a) $3.45 + $0.75   (b) $5.35 − $2

Solution (a) First we line up the decimal points.

$$\begin{array}{r} \$3.45 \\ + \$0.75 \\ \hline \end{array}$$

Now we add, remembering to write the dollar sign and decimal point.

$$\begin{array}{r} \$3.45 \\ + \$0.75 \\ \hline \mathbf{\$4.20} \end{array}$$

(b) First we use a decimal point to write $2. To do this, we put a decimal point and two zeros behind the $2.

$2 means $2.00

Now we line up the decimal points and subtract.

$$\begin{array}{r} \$5.35 \\ - \$2.00 \\ \hline \mathbf{\$3.35} \end{array}$$

Example 2 (a) 67¢ − 59¢   (b) 45¢ + 80¢

Solution To add or subtract money in cent form, we line up the last digits and add or subtract as the sign shows. If the answer equals $1 or more, we usually change from cent form to dollar form.

$$
\text{(a)} \quad \overset{5}{\cancel{6}}{}^{1}7¢ \qquad \text{(b)} \quad 45¢
$$
$$
\underline{-\ 5\ 9¢} \qquad\qquad \underline{+\ 80¢}
$$
$$
8¢ \qquad\qquad 125¢ = \mathbf{\$1.25}
$$

Example 3 $3.75 + $4 + 15¢

Solution If both forms of money are in the problem, we change to one form first. Most people change the cent form to the dollar form. We make these changes.

$4	means	$4.00
15¢	means	$0.15

Then we line up the decimal points and add.

$$
\begin{array}{r}
\$3.75 \\
\$4.00 \\
+\ \$0.15 \\
\hline
\mathbf{\$7.90}
\end{array}
$$

Practice
a. $6.32 + $5   b. $3.25 − $1.75

c. 46¢ + 64¢   d. 98¢ − 89¢

e. $1.46 + 87¢   f. 76¢ − $0.05

Problem set 53

1. One hundred pennies are separated into two piles. In one pile there are thirty-five pennies. How many pennies are in the other pile? Draw a SWA pattern.
   (31)

2. Maria skied three hundred forty-two kilometers the first month. She skied seven hundred fifteen kilometers the second month. How many more kilometers did she ski the second month? Draw a L-S-D pattern.
   (38)

3. The apple cost 35¢. Harry gave the vendor a dollar
(53) bill. How much change did he get back?

4. Purcell is a town between Chickasha and Konawa. It is
(50) 61 miles from Chickasha to Konawa through Purcell. It
is 24 miles from Chickasha to Purcell. How far is it
from Purcell to Konawa? Draw a sketch of this
problem.

5. Round 572 to the nearest hundred.
(52)

6. Write the number 7,284 in expanded form. Then use
(42) words to write the number.

7. Are railroad tracks parallel or perpendicular?
(29)

8. Draw a square to show 3 × 3. Then shade two ninths
(36,32) of the square.

9. It is morning. What time was it 2
(33) hours ago?

10. To what number is the arrow pointing?
(13)

11. $2.45 + $3   **12.** $3.25 − $2.47
(53)   (53)

13. $2.15 + $3 + 7¢   **14.** 4¢ + 23¢ + 7¢
(53)   (53)

15.   507   **16.**   N   **17.** $4.86
(20)   −   N   (20)   − 207   (28)   + $9.57
        ─────   ─────   ─────────
          456   423

18. 6 × 80   **19.** 4 × 300   **20.** 7 × 90
(52)   (52)   (52)

21. $4 \times N = 32$ **22.** $\sqrt{100}$
(50)   (40)

23. Use digits to write four hundred two thousand, five
(43) hundred two.

24.
(21)
```
    5
    7
    5
   14
   17
   17
   21
    8
 +  6
```

25.
(21)
```
   19
   42
   17
    5
    2
    8
    9
    5
 +  6
```

LESSON 54

Multiplying Two-Digit Numbers, Part 1

Facts Practice: 64 Multiplication Facts (Test G in Test Masters)

Mental Math: Add hundreds, then tens, and then ones, regrouping tens and ones.

  a. 589 + 46   **b.** 375 + 425   **c.** $5.64 + $1.46

Review:

  d. $389 + $195   **e.** 76 + 9 + 10   **f.** 500 + 43 + 264

Problem Solving: One way to make a dollar with six coins is with a half dollar and five dimes. Find two more ways to make a dollar with six coins.

If there are 23 children in each classroom, then how many children are in 3 classrooms?

One way to find the answer to this question is to multiply 3 × 23. Here are two ways to multiply using pencil and paper.

23 is 20 + 3

MULTIPLY 3 × 20.   MULTIPLY ONES.

MULTIPLY 3 × 3.   MULTIPLY TENS.

$$\begin{array}{r} 20 + 3 \\ \times 3 \\ \hline 60 + 9 = 69 \end{array} \qquad \begin{array}{r} 23 \\ \times 3 \\ \hline 69 \end{array}$$

→

THEN ADD.

The method on the left is helpful when multiplying mentally. The method on the right is a quick way to multiply using pencil and paper.

Example   Multiply: 42 × 3

Solution   We put 42 above and 3 below, under the 2. First we multiply 2 by 3 and get 6. Then we multiply 4 (for 40) by 3 and get 12. The product is 126.

$$\begin{array}{r} 42 \\ \times 3 \\ \hline \mathbf{126} \end{array}$$

Practice
a. $\begin{array}{r} 31 \\ \times 2 \\ \hline \end{array}$
b. $\begin{array}{r} 31 \\ \times 4 \\ \hline \end{array}$
c. $\begin{array}{r} 42 \\ \times 4 \\ \hline \end{array}$

d. $\begin{array}{r} 30 \\ \times 2 \\ \hline \end{array}$
e. $\begin{array}{r} 30 \\ \times 4 \\ \hline \end{array}$
f. $\begin{array}{r} 24 \\ \times 0 \\ \hline \end{array}$

Problem set 54

1. Juan compared two numbers. The first number was forty-two thousand, three hundred seventy-six. The second number was forty-two thousand, eleven. Use digits and a comparison symbol to show the comparison. *(43,15)*

2. Sally found two hundred forty-three pinecones. Jane
(38) found four hundred ninety-six pinecones. How many
more pinecones did Jane find? Draw a L-S-D pattern.

3. The ticket cost $3.25. The man paid for the ticket with
(53,51) a $5 bill. How much change did he get?

4. Nine squared is how much more than the square root
(40,38) of nine?

5. Find the missing factor: $8 \times M = 48$
(50)

6. The length of segment RT is 9 cm. The length of
(50) segment ST is 5 cm. What is the length of segment RS?

7. How many circles are shaded?
(44)

8. Find the length of this bottle to the nearest quarter
(48) inch.

9. Compare: $4 \times 60 \bigcirc 3 \times 80$
(52,15)

10.(51) $4.03 − $1.68	**11.**(28) $4.33 + $5.28	**12.**(37) $5.22 − $2.46	**13.**(51) $7.08 − $0.59

14.(54) 21 × 6	**15.**(52) 40 × 7	**16.**(54) 73 × 2	**17.**(54) 51 × 6

18. $2 + 47¢ + 21¢
(53)

19. $3.42 + 75¢ + 68¢
(53)

20.
(20)
$$\begin{array}{r} 462 \\ -\ \ N \\ \hline 143 \end{array}$$

21.
(20)
$$\begin{array}{r} N \\ -\ 472 \\ \hline 246 \end{array}$$

22. Write this addition problem as a multiplication
(33) problem:

$$21 + 21 + 21 + 21 + 21 + 21$$

23. Use words to write 815,002.
(42)

24.
(30)
$$\begin{array}{r} 426 \\ +\ \ N \\ \hline 521 \end{array}$$

25.
(30)
$$\begin{array}{r} N \\ +\ 628 \\ \hline 793 \end{array}$$

LESSON
55

Parentheses

Facts Practice: 100 Multiplication Facts (Test H in Test Masters)

Mental Math: Add hundreds, then tens, and then ones, regrouping tens and ones.

  a. 396 + 145   **b.** $2.75 + $2.75   **c.** $6.38 + $2.86

Review:

  d. $4.80 − $1.55   **e.** $3.90 + $2.95   **f.** 48 + 39 + 200

Problem Solving: Chad bought a pizza and gave half of it to Charles. Charles gave half of his portion to Diane. Diane gave half of hers to Trinh. Draw a diagram of the divided pizza. Each person ended up with what fraction of the pizza?

When parentheses are in an arithmetic problem, we do the work inside the parentheses first.

$$2 \times (3 + 4)$$

In this problem, we first add 3 and 4 and get 7. Then we multiply 2 times 7. The answer is 14.

Example 1 $(3 \times 4) + 5$

Solution First we multiply 3×4 and get 12. Then we add 5 to 12.

$$12 + 5 = \mathbf{17}$$

Example 2 $3 \times (4 + 5)$

Solution We add $4 + 5$ and get 9. Then we multiply 9 by 3.

$$3 \times 9 = \mathbf{27}$$

Practice   **a.** $8 - (4 + 2)$ **b.** $(8 - 4) + 2$

c. $9 - (6 - 3)$ **d.** $(9 - 6) - 3$

e. $10 + (2 \times 3)$ **f.** $3 \times (10 + 20)$

Problem set 55

1. There were four hundred twenty-four carrots in the
(17) first bunch. There were seven hundred forty-two
carrots in the first two bunches combined. How many
carrots were in the second bunch? Draw a SSM
pattern.

2. A whole hour is 60 minutes. How many minutes is
(23) half of an hour?

3. The space shuttle orbited 155 miles above the earth.
(38) The weather balloon floated 25 miles above the earth.
The space shuttle was how much higher than the
weather balloon? Draw a L-S-D pattern.

4. How much change should you get back if you give the
(53,51) clerk $5.00 for a box of cereal that costs $2.85?

5. Use the digits 4, 5, 6, and 7 once each to write an odd
(11) number between 4700 and 4790.

6. Use digits and a comparison symbol to show that five
(15) hundred sixteen is less than five hundred sixty.

7. It is morning. What time was it 20
(33) minutes ago?

8. Write 72,856 in expanded form. Then use words to
(42) write this number.

9. How many circles are shaded?
(44)

10. Use shaded circles to show the mixed number $4\frac{3}{4}$.
(44)

11. Use a ruler to measure this line segment to the nearest
(48) quarter inch.

————————————

12. Use a centimeter scale to measure the segment in
(24) Problem 11 to the nearest centimeter.

13. 8 × (40 + 30)   **14.** (8 × 4) + 3
(55)   (55)

15. $4.07   **16.** $5.02   **17.** $5.83   **18.** $3.92
(37)   − $2.26   (51)   − $2.47   (37)   − $2.97   (28)   + $5.14
      ————   ————   ————   ————

19.   42   **20.**   83   **21.**   40   **22.**   41
(54)   × 3   (54)   × 2   (52)   × 4   (54)   × 6
      ———   ———   ———   ———

23. $2 + 42¢ + 7¢   **24.** $5.24 + 23¢ + 2¢
(53)   (53)

25. $\sqrt{36}$ + 18 + 26 + 200 + N = 300
(40,2)

26. Write this addition problem as a multiplication
(33) problem:

$$40 + 40 + 40 + 40$$

27. Eight times four is how much less than six squared?
(39,38)

28. Find the missing factor: 6 × W = 42
(50)

LESSON 56

Division

Facts Practice: 100 Multiplication Facts (Test H in Test Masters)

Mental Math: Subtract a multiple of 10 from 100.

   a. $100 - 40$ **b.** $100 - 70$ **c.** $100 - 20$

Review:

   d. $465 + 175$ **e.** $\$3.50 - \$1.35$ **f.** $346 + 29$

   g. What number should be added to each of these numbers for the total to be 9: 6, 4, 7, 1?

Problem Solving: On Christmas Day, 1995, Stacy's brother turned eighteen months old. What was the date of her brother's birth?

Remember that multiplication problems have three numbers. The multiplied numbers are **factors.** The answer is the **product.**

$$\text{Factor} \times \text{factor} = \text{product}$$

If we know the two factors, we multiply to find the product. If the factors are 4 and 3, the product is 12.

$$4 \times 3 = 12$$

If we know one factor and the product, we can find the other factor.

$$4 \times W = 12 \qquad N \times 3 = 12$$

The process of finding the missing factor is called *division.*

We know how to use a multiplication table to find the product of 3 and 4. We locate the proper row and column. Where they meet, we find the product.

	0	1	2	3	(4)
0	0	0	0	0	0
1	0	1	2	3	4
2	0	2	4	6	8
(3)	0	3	6	9	(12)
4	0	4	8	12	16

We may also use a multiplication table to find a missing factor. If we know that one factor is 3 and the product is 12, we move across the row that starts with 3 until we get to 12. Then we look up to the top of the column with 12 and find 4, which is the missing factor.

We write the numbers 3, 4, and 12 with a division box this way.

$$3\overline{)12}^{\;4}$$

We say "Twelve divided by three is four."

Example 1 Divide: $4\overline{)32}$

Solution The problem is to find the missing factor. We think, "Four times what number is thirty-two?" We show how to find the missing factor in the multiplication table below. First we find the row beginning with 4. Then we follow this row across until we see 32. Then we go up this column and find that the answer is **8.**

Multiplication Table

	0	1	2	3	4	5	6	7	8	9
0	0	0	0	0	0	0	0	0	0	0
1	0	1	2	3	4	5	6	7	8	9
2	0	2	4	6	8	10	12	14	16	18
3	0	3	6	9	12	15	18	21	24	27
4	0	4	8	12	16	20	24	28	32	36
5	0	5	10	15	20	25	30	35	40	45
6	0	6	12	18	24	30	36	42	48	54
7	0	7	14	21	28	35	42	49	56	63
8	0	8	16	24	32	40	48	56	64	72
9	0	9	18	27	36	45	54	63	72	81

Example 2 $2\overline{)18}$

Solution   We search for the number that goes above the box. We think, "Two times what number is eighteen?" We remember that $2 \times 9 = 18$, so the answer is **9**. We write "9" above the 18.

$$\begin{array}{r} 9 \\ 2\overline{)18} \end{array}$$

Practice   Find the answer to each division:

    a. $2\overline{)12}$ **b.** $3\overline{)21}$ **c.** $4\overline{)20}$ **d.** $5\overline{)30}$

    e. $6\overline{)42}$ **f.** $7\overline{)28}$ **g.** $8\overline{)48}$ **h.** $9\overline{)36}$

Problem set 56

1. Four hundred ninety-five oil drums were on the first
(17) train. Seven hundred sixty-two oil drums were on the first two trains combined. How many oil drums were on the second train? Draw a SSM pattern.

2. There were one hundred twenty-five fish in the first
(38) tank. There were three hundred forty-two fish in the second tank. How many fewer fish were in the first tank? Draw a L-S-D pattern.

3. Cyrus baled 82 bales of hay on the first day. He baled
(12) 92 bales of hay on the second day. He baled 78 bales of hay on the third day. How many bales of hay did he bale in all three days? Draw a SSM pattern.

4. Use the digits 6, 7, and 8 once each to write an odd
(11) number greater than 856.

5. Draw shaded rectangles to picture the mixed
(44) number $4\frac{1}{3}$.

6. The first five odd numbers are 1, 3, 5, 7, and 9. What is
(1) their sum?

7. It is morning. What time was it 12
(33) hours ago?

8. To the nearest quarter inch, how long is this rectangle?
(48)

9. Martin took two dozen *big* steps. About how many
(27) meters did he walk?

10. To what number is the arrow pointing?
(46)

11. 64 + (9 × 40)
(55)

12. $6.25 + 39¢ + $3
(53)

13. $4.02
(51)   − $2.47
‾‾‾‾‾‾‾

14. $5.07
(51)   − $2.48
‾‾‾‾‾‾‾

15.   N
(30)   + 223
‾‾‾‾‾‾‾
        715

16.   938
(20)   −   C
‾‾‾‾‾‾
        223

17.   42
(54)   ×   3
‾‾‾‾‾‾

18.   81
(54)   ×   5
‾‾‾‾‾‾

19.   30
(52)   ×   4
‾‾‾‾‾‾

20. 6)‾30‾
(56)

21. 7)‾21‾
(56)

22. 8)‾56‾
(56)

23. 9)‾81‾
(56)

24. 7)‾28‾
(56)

25. 3)‾15‾
(56)

26. 4)‾24‾
(56)

27. 8)‾24‾
(56)

28. 5)‾40‾
(56)

LESSON 57

Other Ways to Show Division

Facts Practice: 100 Multiplication Facts (Test H in Test Masters)

Mental Math: Subtract a multiple of 10 from a multiple of 100.

a. 200 − 30   b. 300 − 60   c. 400 − 90

Review:

d. $2.48 + $2.99   e. 384 + 167   f. 46 + 7 + 30

g. What number should be added to each of these numbers for the total to be 9: 8, 2, 5, 3?

Problem Solving: A loop is worth five points and a tip is worth three points. Sal made four loops and two tips. Cheryl made three loops and five tips. How many points did each person score?

We have different ways to show division. Here we show "fifteen divided by three" three different ways.

$$3\overline{)15} \qquad 15 \div 3 \qquad \frac{15}{3}$$

The first way uses a division box. The second way uses a division sign. The third way uses a division bar. We should be able to solve problems in any form and be able to change from one form to another form.

Example 1 Use digits and division symbols to show "twenty-four divided by six" in three ways.

Solution
$$6\overline{)24} \qquad 24 \div 6 \qquad \frac{24}{6}$$

Example 2 Solve: (a) $28 \div 4$ (b) $\dfrac{27}{3}$

Solution (a) We read this as "Twenty-eight divided by four." It means the same as $4\overline{)28}$.

$$28 \div 4 = 7$$

(b) We read this as "Twenty-seven divided by three." It means the same as $3\overline{)27}$.

$$\frac{27}{3} = 9$$

A multiplication fact has three numbers. The same three numbers form a division fact. Multiplication facts and division facts should be practiced together. Frequent timed written tests on multiplication and division facts will help you memorize these facts.

Practice

a. $49 \div 7$

b. $45 \div 9$

c. $40 \div 8$

d. $\dfrac{36}{6}$

e. $\dfrac{32}{8}$

f. $\dfrac{27}{3}$

Use digits and three different division symbols to show:

g. Twenty-seven divided by nine

h. Twenty-eight divided by seven

Problem set 57

1. Frank hit the target two hundred forty-three times.
   $^{(38)}$ Vanessa hit the target five hundred seven times. How many more times did Vanessa hit the target than Frank hit the target? Draw a L-S-D pattern.

2. The numbers 3, 4, and 12 are a multiplication and
   $^{(57)}$ division fact family.

$$\begin{array}{cc} 3 & 4 \\ \times\ 4 & \times\ 3 \\ \hline 12 & 12 \end{array} \qquad \begin{array}{l} 12 \div 4 = 3 \\ 12 \div 3 = 4 \end{array}$$

Write the four multiplication/division facts using the numbers 4, 5, and 20.

3. Altogether, how many days are there in the last three
   $^{(6)}$ months of the year?

4. Use the digits 1, 5, 6, and 8 once each to write an even
   $^{(11)}$ number greater than 8420.

5. Draw shaded circles to picture the mixed number $4\frac{2}{3}$.
(44)

6. To the nearest quarter inch, how long is the stick of
(48) gum?

7. It is evening. What time was it 2
(33) hours and 25 minutes ago?

8. One sixth of this rectangle is
(32) shaded. Draw another rectangle
and shade five sixths of it.

9. The length of segment PQ is 2 cm. The length of
(50) segment PR is 11 cm. How long is segment QR?

P   Q   R

10. $95 - \left(7 \times \sqrt{64}\right)$
(55,40)

11. $2.53 + 45¢ + $3
(53)

12. $3.04
(37) $- 1.22

13. $8.46
(37) $- 3.58

14.   842
(20) $- \quad Z$
       $\overline{215}$

15. N
(20) $- 516$
       $\overline{293}$

16.   40
(52) $\times \quad 3$

17.   51
(54) $\times \quad 5$

18. $28 \div 7$
(57)

19. $81 \div 9$
(57)

20. $35 \div 7$
(57)

21. $16 \div 4$
(57)

22. $\dfrac{28}{4}$
(57)

23. $\dfrac{42}{7}$
(57)

24. $\dfrac{48}{8}$
(57)

25. $\dfrac{45}{5}$
(57)

26. Five squared is how much less than 28?
(40,38)

LESSON
58

Multiplying Two-Digit Numbers, Part 2

Facts Practice: 90 Division Facts (Test I in Test Masters)

Mental Math: Nine dimes plus ten pennies total one dollar. We can use this fact to find change back from a dollar. For example, if you pay a dollar for an item that costs 47¢, you should get back 53¢. Notice that the 4 of 47¢ and the 5 of 53¢ equal 9 dimes. The 7 and the 3 equal 10 pennies. Find the change back from a dollar for items with these prices.

   a. 46¢   **b.** 64¢   **c.** 28¢   **d.** 52¢   **e.** 17¢   **f.** 85¢

Problem Solving: From Point *A* to Point *B* is $1\frac{1}{4}$ inches. From Point *B* to Point *C* is how many inches?

We have practiced multiplying two-digit numbers by multiplying the digit in the ones' place and then multiplying the digit in the tens' place.

MULTIPLY ONES	MULTIPLY TENS
12	12
× 4	× 4
8	48

Often when we multiply the ones, the result is a two-digit number. We do not write both digits below the line. Instead we write the last digit below the line in the ones' column and **carry** the first digit above the tens' column.

$$\begin{array}{r} 1 \\ 12 \\ \times\ \ 8 \\ \hline 6 \end{array}$$

Then we multiply the tens' digit and **add** the digit we wrote above this column.

We think, "Eight times one is eight, plus one is nine."

$$\begin{array}{r} 1 \\ 12 \\ \times\ \ 8 \\ \hline 96 \end{array}$$

Example   Find the product: 8 × $64

Solution   We write the two-digit number over the one-digit number. We think of $64 as 6 tens and 4 ones. We multiply 8 × 4 ones and get 32 ones ($32). We write the 2 of $32 below the line. The 3 of $32 is 3 tens. We write the 3 above the tens' column.

$$\begin{array}{r} \overset{3}{} \\ \$64 \\ \times \quad 8 \\ \hline 2 \end{array}$$

Then we multiply 8 × 6 tens, which is 48 tens. We add the 3 tens to this, making 51 tens. We write "51" below the line. The product is **$512.**

$$\begin{array}{r} \overset{3}{} \\ \$64 \\ \times \quad 8 \\ \hline \$512 \end{array}$$

Practice
a. $\begin{array}{r} 16 \\ \times \ 4 \\ \hline \end{array}$ **b.** $\begin{array}{r} 24 \\ \times \ 3 \\ \hline \end{array}$ **c.** $\begin{array}{r} 45 \\ \times \ 6 \\ \hline \end{array}$

d. 53 × 7   **e.** 35 × 8   **f.** 64 × 9

Problem set 58

1. Write four multiplication/division facts using the
(57)   numbers 3, 5, and 15.

2. There were four hundred seventy-two birds in the first
(38)   flock. There were one hundred forty-seven birds in the second flock. How many fewer birds were in the second flock? Draw a L-S-D pattern.

3. Rae hiked forty-two miles. Then she hiked seventy-
(12)   five more miles. How many miles did she hike in all? Draw a SSM pattern.

4. Use the digits 1, 3, 6, and 8 once each to write an odd
(11)   number between 8000 and 8350.

5. Write 306,020 in expanded form. Then use words to
(42)   write this number.

6. Draw shaded circles to picture the number $2\frac{1}{8}$.
(44)

7. How many feet are in 1 mile?
(49)

8. To what number is the arrow pointing on this inch
(48) scale?

9. How many centimeters are in a meter?
(27)

10. To what mixed number is the arrow pointing?
(46)

11. 100 + (4 × 50)
(55,52)

12. $3.25 + 37¢ + $3   **13.** $\sqrt{4} \times \sqrt{9}$
(53)   *(40)*

14.   33   **15.**   24   **16.**   90   **17.**   42
(58) × 6   *(58)* × 5   *(52)* × 6   *(58)* × 7

18. $5.06   **19.** $3.28   **20.** $5.27   **21.**   14
(51) − $2.28   *(28)* + $4.33   *(37)* − $3.68   *(21)*   28
                                                                45
                                                                36
22. 28 ÷ 7   **23.** 5$\overline{)35}$ 92
(57)   *(56)*   + 47

24. 6$\overline{)54}$ **25.** $\dfrac{63}{7}$
(56)   *(57)*

LESSON
59

"Equal Groups" Problems, Part 1

Facts Practice: 90 Division Facts (Test I in Test Masters)

Mental Math: Find the change back from a dollar for items with
these prices.

   a. 41¢   **b.** 89¢   **c.** 19¢   **d.** 34¢   **e.** 62¢

Review:

   f. 537 + 100 + 19   **g.** $5.62 + $3.98   **h.** 396 + 437

Problem Solving: One way to make a dollar with seven coins is
with two quarters and five dimes. Can you
find three more ways to make a dollar with
seven coins?

We have found that some story problems have an addition
pattern. The addition pattern has three numbers. If we
know two of the numbers, we can find the third number.

$$
\begin{array}{r}
5 \text{ marbles} \\
+\ 7 \text{ marbles} \\
\hline
12 \text{ marbles}
\end{array}
$$

Some story problems have a subtraction pattern. The
subtraction pattern has three numbers. If we know two of
the numbers, we can find the third number.

$$
\begin{array}{r}
12 \text{ marbles} \\
-\ 7 \text{ marbles} \\
\hline
5 \text{ marbles}
\end{array}
$$

Some story problems have a multiplication pattern. The
multiplication pattern has three numbers. If we know two
of the numbers, we can find the third number.

$$
\begin{array}{r}
5 \text{ marbles in each bag} \\
\times\ 7 \text{ bags} \\
\hline
35 \text{ marbles}
\end{array}
$$

    Stories that have a multiplication pattern are often
"equal groups" stories. We will often use the abbreviation
EG to stand for "equal groups." Look at this pattern
carefully. It looks different from the other patterns we

have practiced. The top number of the pattern is the number in each equal group. The second number of the pattern is the number of groups. The bottom number is the total number in all the groups.

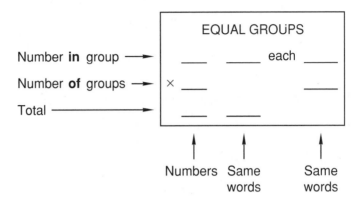

To find the bottom number in the "equal groups" pattern, we multiply. To find the first or second number, we divide.

Example   Ted has 5 cans of tennis balls. There are 3 balls in each can. How many tennis balls does he have?

Solution   The words *in each* are a clue to this problem. The words *in each* usually mean that the problem is an "equal groups" problem. We write the number and the words that go with *in each* on the first line. This is the number in each group.

Number **in** group   3   balls   each   can

× ——   ——

—— ——

The other number and word in the problem is *5 cans*. This is the number of groups. The word *cans* lines up with the word *can* in the first line of the pattern.

Number **in** group   3   balls   each   can
Number **of** groups   ×   5   cans
                              N   balls

To find the bottom number, we multiply the first two numbers. The word on the bottom line is the same as the word above it on the first line. We complete the "equal groups" pattern and answer the question. Ted has **15 tennis balls.**

Number **in** group		3	balls	each	can
Number **of** groups	×	5			cans
Total		15	balls		

Practice

a. There were 8 birds in each flock. There were 6 flocks in all. How many birds were there in all?

b. There are 6 people in each car. There are 9 cars. How many people are there in all?

Problem set 59

1. There were 8 boys in each row. There were 4 rows. How many boys were there? Draw an "equal groups" pattern.
(59)

2. There were 7 girls in each row. There were 9 rows. How many girls were in all 9 rows? Draw an EG pattern.
(59)

3. Write four multiplication/division facts using the numbers 5, 6, and 30.
(57)

4. The big animal weighed four hundred seventy-five pounds. The small animal weighed one hundred eleven pounds. How much more did the big animal weigh? Draw a L-S-D pattern.
(38)

5. Shade circles to picture the number $6\frac{3}{4}$.
(44)

6. To what number is the arrow pointing?
(46)

452   453

7. It is evening. What time will it be 7
(33) hours and 22 minutes from now?

8. Draw a rectangle and shade $\frac{7}{8}$ of it.
(32)

9. Use digits to write three hundred forty-nine thousand,
(43) eight hundred eleven.

10. Seven times eight is how much less than eight
(39,38) squared?

11. $4.63 + 23¢ + $6 + 6¢
(53)

12. $3.07
(51) − $2.28
————

13. $4.78
(28) + $3.96
————

14.   707
(20) −   N
————
    485

15.   C
(20) − 23
————
    48

16. 403 − (5 × 80)
(55,54)

17. (4 + 3) × $\sqrt{64}$
(55,40)

18. $N × 6 = 30$
(50)

19. (587 − 238) + 415
(55)

20.   45
(58) × 6

21.   23
(58) × 7
————

22.   34
(58) × 8

23.   83
(58) × 5

24. 56 ÷ 7
(57)

25. 64 ÷ 8
(57)

26. 6$\overline{)30}$
(57)

27. $\frac{45}{9}$
(57)

LESSON
60

Perimeter

The distance around a shape is its **perimeter.** To find the
perimeter of a shape, we add the lengths of all of its sides.

Example 1 Claudia ran around the perimeter of the block. How far did
Claudia run?

Solution We are told Claudia ran around the perimeter, so we know
that she ran all the way around. We find that distance by
adding all four sides.

      80 yards
      40 yards
      80 yards
   + 40 yards
    240 yards

Claudia ran **240 yards.**

Example 2   What is the perimeter of this square?

Solution   We are told the shape is a square. That means all four sides are the same length. We see that each side is 2 centimeters long. The perimeter is the distance all the way around. We add all four sides.

$$2 \text{ cm} + 2 \text{ cm} + 2 \text{ cm} + 2 \text{ cm} = 8 \text{ cm}$$

The perimeter of the square is **8 cm.**

Practice   Find the perimeter of each shape:

a.

3 cm
5 cm
4 cm

b.   8 m

5 m

c.

6 in.
3 in.
5 in.
3 in.
5 in.

d. What is the perimeter of this square?

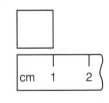

e. What does the word *perimeter* mean?

Problem set
60

1. Each of the 3 lifeboats carried 12 people. How many
(59) people were in the 3 lifeboats? Draw an EG pattern.

2. The tape cost $6.98. The tax was 42¢. What was the
(12) total price? Draw a SSM pattern.

3. Sarah did six hundred twenty sit-ups. Syd did four
(38) hundred seventeen sit-ups. Sarah did how many more
sit-ups than Syd? Draw a L-S-D pattern.

4. The coach separated 28 players into 4 equal teams.
(56) How many players were on each team? (*Hint*: Four times what number is 28?)

5. Justin ran the perimeter of the block. How far did
(60) Justin run?

6. Shade circles to draw a picture of $3\frac{3}{8}$.
(44)

7. Use the digits 1, 2, 3, and 4 once each to write an odd
(11) number between 4205 and 4223.

8. Six times seven is how much less than nine times
(38) five?

9. It is evening. What time will it be
(33) 9 hours and 30 minutes from
now?

10. To what number is the arrow pointing?
(46)

11. (4 × 50) + 203
(55)

12. $4.63 + $2 + 47¢ + 65¢
(53)

13.   43   **14.**   54   **15.**   37   **16.**   40
(58)   × 6   (58)   × 8   (58)   × 3   (54)   × 4

17. 47 + 55 + 84 + 63 + 24 + 27
(21)

18. $6.08 − $4.29   **19.** $7.03 − $4.26
(53)   (53)

20. $3.25   **21.**   472   **22.** N
(28)   + $1.98   (16)   + 348   (20)   − 279
          ————   ————   ————
                                                             484

23.   462   **24.** 3)‾24‾   **25.** 4)‾24‾
(30)   + C (57)   (57)
          ————
           529

26. 36 ÷ 6   **27.** $\dfrac{36}{9}$
(57)   (57)

LESSON
61

Adding Numbers with More Than Three Digits • Checking One-Digit Division

Facts Practice: 90 Division Facts (Test I in Test Masters)

Mental Math: Subtract cents from dollars.
   a. $1.00 − $0.42   **b.** $1.00 − $0.67   **c.** $2.00 − $0.25
Review:
   d. $3.45 + $4.65   **e.** 370 − 135   **f.** 76 + 19 + 100

Problem Solving: Sarah paid a dollar for an item that cost 63 cents. What four coins did she get back in change?

Adding numbers with more than three digits

To add numbers that have more than three digits, we add in the ones' column first. Then we add in the tens' column, the hundreds' column, the thousands' column, the ten-thousands' column, and so forth. When the sum of the digits in one column is a two-digit number, we record the second digit below the line. We write the first digit above or below the column to the left.

Example 1   Add: 43,287
                    + 68,595

Solution   We add the digits in the ones' column   1   11
first. When the sum is a two-digit   43,287
number, we write the last digit below   + 68,595
the line and the first digit above or   ─────────
below the next column. The sum is   111,882
111,882.

Example 2   Add: 456 + 1327 + 52 + 3624

Solution   When we write the numbers in a   111
column, we are careful to line up the   456
last digit in each number. We add the   1327
digits one column at a time, starting   52
from the right. The sum is **5459.**   + 3624
                                             ──────
                                               5459

Checking   We can check division by multiplying. We multiply the
one-digit   numbers outside the division box.
division

$$\text{DIVISION:}\quad 3\overline{)12}\overset{4}{}\qquad \begin{array}{r}4\\ \times\ 3\\ \hline 12\end{array}\quad \text{check}$$

We see that the multiplication answer matches the
number inside the division box. We usually show this by
writing the multiplication answer under the number in the
division box.

$$\begin{array}{r}4\\ 3\overline{)12}\\ 12\end{array}$$ ←   **Step 1.** Divide 12 by 3 and write "4."
                         ←   **Step 2.** Multiply 4 by 3 and write "12."

Example 3   Divide. Check the answer by multiplying.

(a) $3\overline{)18}$ (b) $4\overline{)32}$

Solution   First we divide and write the answer above the box. Then
we multiply and write the product below the box.

(a) $\begin{array}{r}6\\ 3\overline{)18}\\ 18\end{array}$ (b) $\begin{array}{r}8\\ 4\overline{)32}\\ 32\end{array}$

Practice

a.   4356
    + 5644

b.   46,027
    + 39,682

c.   360,147
    + 96,894

d. 436 + 5714 + 88

e. 43,284 + 572 + 7635

Divide. Check the answer by multiplying.

f. 3)‾21

g. 7)‾42

h. 6)‾48

Problem set 61

1. The coach had forty-two players. The coach wanted to
(56) make six equal teams. How many players should be on
each team? (*Hint*: Six times what number is 42?)

2. There were 7 pancakes in each stack. There were 6
(59) stacks of pancakes. How many pancakes were there in
all? Draw an EG pattern.

3. Five hundred forty-two clowns laughed out loud.
(12) Nine hundred thirty-three clowns merely smiled.
What was the total of the smilers and the laughers?
Draw a SSM pattern.

4. Write four multiplication/division facts using the
(57) numbers 6, 7, and 42.

5. Compare: 1 + 3 + 5 + 7 + 9 ◯ five squared
(40,15)

6. What is the smallest four-digit odd number that has
(11) the digits 1, 2, 3, and 4 once each?

7. How many circles are shaded?
(44)

8. Which of these angles does not appear to be a right
(29) angle?

A. └   B. ┘   C. \/   D. ∠

9. This is a rectangle.
(60,25)

(a) What is the length?

(b) What is the width?

(c) What is the perimeter?

4 ft

2 ft

10. Thirty is how much more than four times seven?
(38)

11. 3864 + 598 + 4237 + 12
(61)

12.   63,285
(61)   + 97,642

13. $5.00
(51)   − $4.81

14. N
(30)   + 398
        614

15.   85
(58)   × 5

16.   37
(58)   × 7

17.   40
(54)   × 8

18. F
(50)   × 8
      72

19.   478
(20)   − C
        203

20.   462,586
(61)   +   39,728

21. Z
(20)   − 478
        263

22. Compare: $7 \times 6 \bigcirc 44$
(15)

Divide. Check each answer by multiplying.

23. $2\overline{)18}$
(61)

24. $7\overline{)21}$
(61)

25. $\dfrac{56}{8}$
(61)

LESSON 62

Subtracting Numbers with More Than Three Digits • "Equal Groups" Problems, Part 2

Facts Practice: 90 Division Facts (Test J in Test Masters)

Mental Math: Subtract dollars and cents from dollars.
  a. $1.00 − $0.85   **b.** $2.00 − $0.63   **c.** $5.00 − $1.25

Review:
  d. 340 + 500 + 32   **e.** $5.47 + $1.95   **f.** 400 − 30

Problem Solving: In this addition problem some digits are missing. Copy this problem on your paper and fill in the missing digits.

$$\begin{array}{r} 5\_3 \\ + \ 28\_ \\ \hline \_50 \end{array}$$

Subtracting numbers with more than three digits

To subtract numbers with more than three digits, we begin by subtracting in the ones' column. We regroup if it is necessary. Then we move one column to the left and subtract in the tens' column, regrouping if necessary. Then we move one column at a time to the hundreds' column, the thousands' column, the ten-thousands' column, and so on. Sometimes we must subtract across several zeros.

Example 1   Subtract: 36,152 − 9,415

Solution   We write the first number on top. We write the second number below. We line up digits with the same place value. We begin by subtracting in the ones' column. Then we subtract in the other columns.

$$\begin{array}{r} {}^{2}\ {}^{1}5\ \ \ {}^{4} \\ \cancel{3}\ \cancel{6},{}^{1}1\ \cancel{5}{}^{1}2 \\ -\quad 9,4\,1\,5 \\ \hline 2\,6,7\,3\,7 \end{array}$$

Example 2   Subtract: 5000
                              − 2386

Solution   We need to find some ones for the ones' place before we can subtract. We can only get ones from the tens' place, but there are no tens. We can only get tens from the hundreds' place, but

$$\begin{array}{r} {}^{4}\ {}^{9}\ {}^{9}\ {}^{1} \\ \cancel{5}\ \cancel{0}\ \cancel{0}\ 0 \\ -\ 2\ 3\ 8\ 6 \\ \hline 2\ 6\ 1\ 4 \end{array}$$

there are no hundreds. To get hundreds, we go to the thousands' place. We exchange 1 thousand for 10 hundreds, 1 hundred for 10 tens, and 1 ten for 10 ones. Then we can subtract.

"Equal groups" problems, part 2

"Equal groups" stories have a multiplication pattern. If we know the number of groups and the number in each group, then we multiply to find the total. However, if we know the total, then we need to divide to find the number of groups or the number in each group. Carefully follow the following examples.

Example 3

Ted has 21 tennis balls in cans. There are 3 balls in each can. How many cans does he have?

Solution

There are two numbers in this problem. The words *in each* are a clue. They show us the number and words to write on the first line.

Number **in** group		3 balls	each can
Number **of** groups	×		
Total			

The other number is 21 and the other word is *balls*. We need to decide if this is the number of groups or the total. The pattern shows us how the words should line up. Altogether, Ted had 21 tennis balls. This is the total.

Number **in** group		3 balls	each can
Number **of** groups	×	N	cans
Total		21 balls	

Now we need to find the missing number. **To find the first or second number of an "equal groups" pattern, we divide.**

$$\frac{7}{3\overline{)21}}$$

We complete the pattern, matching the words, and then answer the question.

Number **in** group		3	balls each	can
Number **of** groups	×	7		cans
Total		21	balls	

Seven times 3 balls is 21 balls, so our answer is correct. Ted has **7 cans.**

Example 4   Ted has 5 cans of rubber balls. He has 40 rubber balls in all. How many balls are in each can if the same number of balls is in each can?

Solution   The words *in each* shows us that this is an "equal groups" problem. We are not given an *in each* number, but we are given the other words that go with *in each*, which we can write on the first line.

Number **in** group		N	balls each	can
Number **of** groups	×	5		cans
Total		40	balls	

Now we need to find the missing number on the first line. **To find the first or second number in an "equal groups" pattern, we divide.**

$$\frac{8}{5)\overline{40}}$$

We complete the pattern and answer the question.

Number **in** group		8	balls each	can
Number **of** groups	×	5		cans
Total		40	balls	

We see that 5 times 8 balls equals 40 balls, so our answer is correct. There are **8 rubber balls in each can.**

     "Equal groups" problems are easy after we find out where to put the numbers in the pattern.

Practice

a.
$$\begin{array}{r} 4783 \\ -\ 2497 \\ \hline \end{array}$$

b.
$$\begin{array}{r} 4000 \\ -\ 527 \\ \hline \end{array}$$

c. There were 35 people. There were 7 cars. The number of people in each car was the same. How many people were in each car?

Problem set 62

1. There were 8 buses. Each bus could seat 60 students. How many students could ride in all the buses? Draw an EG pattern.
(59)

2. Each van could carry 9 students. There were 63 students. How many vans were needed? Draw an EG pattern.
(62)

3. Fifty-six Easter eggs were to be divided into 7 equal piles. How many eggs would be in each pile? Draw an EG pattern.
(62)

4. There are 10 swimmers in the race. Only 3 can win medals. How many swimmers will not win a medal? Draw a SWA pattern.
(31)

5. There were two hundred sixty-seven apples in the first bin. There were four hundred sixty-five apples in the second bin. How many fewer apples were in the first bin? Draw a L-S-D pattern.
(38)

6. Write four multiplication/division facts using the numbers 7, 8, and 56.
(57)

7. Compare: $1 + 2 + 3 + 4 \bigcirc \sqrt{100}$
(40,15)

8. Use shaded circles to draw a picture of $3\frac{3}{4}$.
(44)

9. This shape has four sides, but it is not a rectangle. What is the perimeter of this shape in meters?
(60)

10. 849 + 73 + 615
(61)

11.   47,586
(61)   + 23,491

12. $5.00
(51)   − $3.26

13. N
(30)   + 258
        604

14.   49
(58)   × 6

15.   84
(58)   × 5

16.   70
(54)   × 8

17.   35
(58)   × 9

18. $\sqrt{64}$
(40)

19.   400
(20)   − N
        256

20.   4000
(62)   − 2468

21. Use a dollar sign and a decimal point to show each
(45) amount of money.

   (a) 54¢   (b) 6¢   (c) 340¢

22. Thirteen is how much more than four times three?
(38)

23. Compare: 4 × 8 $\bigcirc$ 31
(15)

Divide, and then check each answer by multiplying:

24. 3)$\overline{27}$
(61)

25. 7)$\overline{28}$
(61)

26. 8)$\overline{72}$
(61)

27. $\dfrac{54}{6}$
(61)

LESSON
63

One-Digit Division with a Remainder

Facts Practice: 90 Division Facts (Test J in Test Masters)

Mental Math: Subtract dollars and cents from dollars.

  a. $5.00 − $2.25   **b.** $5.00 − $1.63   **c.** $5.00 − $3.35

Review:

  d. 560 − 200   **e.** 35 + 49 + 110   **f.** $6.58 + $0.72

Problem Solving: From Point A to Point B is $1\frac{1}{4}$ inches. From Point B to Point C is how many inches?

We can divide 12 objects into equal groups of four. Here we show 12 dots divided into equal groups of four.

12 dots   3 equal groups

However, we cannot divide 13 dots into equal groups of four because there is one dot too many. We call the extra dot the **remainder.**

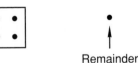

13 dots   3 equal groups   Remainder

We can show that 13 is to be divided into groups of four by writing

$$4\overline{)13}$$

As we look at this problem, we may wonder what to write for the answer. The answer is not exactly three because 3 × 4 is 12, which is less than 13. However, the answer is not four because 4 × 4 is 16, which is more than 13. Since we *can* make three groups of four, we write "3" for our answer. Then we multiply 3 × 4 and write "12" below the 13.

$$\begin{array}{r} 3 \\ 4\overline{)13} \\ 12 \end{array}$$ ← three groups

We see that 13 is more than 12. Now we find out how much is left over after making three groups of four. To do this, we subtract 12 from 13.

$$\begin{array}{r} 3 \\ 4\overline{)13} \\ -12 \\ \hline 1 \end{array}$$ ← three groups

subtract

← 1 left over (remainder)

There is one left over. The amount left over is the **remainder.** We use the letter *r* to stand for **remainder.** We can write the answer as

$$\begin{array}{r} \mathbf{3\,r\,1} \\ 4\overline{)13} \\ -12 \\ \hline 1 \end{array}$$

Example 1   Divide: $3\overline{)16}$

Solution   This problem tells us to divide 16 into three groups. Three groups of six is 18. This is too much. Three groups of five is 15. This is less than 16. We write "5."

$$\begin{array}{r} 5 \\ 3\overline{)16} \end{array}$$

Since three groups of five is 15, we write "15" below the 16. Then we subtract and find that the remainder is 1.

$$\begin{array}{r} 5 \\ 3\overline{)16} \\ -15 \\ \hline 1 \end{array}$$ ← remainder

The answer is **5 r 1.**

Example 2   Divide: $20 \div 6$

Solution   First we write the problem using a division box.

$$6\overline{)20}$$

Now we think, "Six times four equals twenty-four." This is too much. We think "Six times three equals eighteen." This is less than 20. We will use three.

$$6\overline{)20}^{\,3}$$

Next we multiply, and then we subtract.

$$\begin{array}{r} 3 \\ 6\overline{)20} \\ -18 \\ \hline 2 \end{array} \leftarrow \text{remainder}$$

We write the answer as **3 r 2.**

Practice   Divide and write the answer with a remainder:

a. $3\overline{)17}$ **b.** $5\overline{)12}$ **c.** $4\overline{)23}$

d. $15 \div 2$ **e.** $20 \div 6$ **f.** $25 \div 3$

Problem set 63

1. Harry had 56 washers. He wanted to put them into equal piles of 8 washers. How many piles would he have? Draw an EG pattern.
(62)

2. There were 42 children waiting for a ride. There were 7 cars available. If the same number rode in each car, how many children would be in each car? Draw an EG pattern.
(62)

3. Write four multiplication/division facts using the numbers 4, 7, and 28.
(57)

4. Which months have exactly 30 days?
(6)

5. Six squared is how much more than $\sqrt{64}$?
(40,38)

6. Round 4725 to the nearest hundred.
(52)

7. Write the time for a quarter after four in the afternoon in digital form.
(23)

8. One side of a square is 4 feet long. What is the perimeter of the square?
(60)

9. How many circles are shaded?
(44)

10. $\sqrt{64} + (42 \div 6)$ **11.** $6.35 + $12.49 + 42¢
(55)   (53)

12. $100.00 - $59.88   **13.** 51,438 − 47,495
(53)   (62)

14.   60   **15.**   57
(54)   × 9   (58)   × 4

Divide and write the answer with a remainder:

16. 25 ÷ 4   **17.** 22 ÷ 5   **18.** 6)‾39   **19.** 7)‾30
(63)   (63)   (63)   (63)

20.   46   **21.**   38   **22.** Z
(58)   × 8   (58)   × 7   (20)   − 165
                                                    ‾‾‾‾‾
                                                     402

23.   400   **24.** Use words to write 87,906.
(20)   − C (42)
        ‾‾‾‾‾
         283

25.   3   **26.**   3
(21)   48   (21)   43
          76   58
          25   9
         336   6
          98   454
       + 75   + 28
       ‾‾‾‾‾   ‾‾‾‾‾
       6·58   598

LESSON 64

Years, Decades, Centuries

Facts Practice: 90 Division Facts (Test J in Test Masters)

Mental Math: Subtract dollars and cents from dollars.
  a. $5.00 − $3.95   **b.** $5.00 − $1.39   **c.** $10.00 − $8.75

Review:
  d. $4.36 + $2.98   **e.** 475 − 125   **f.** 46 + 320 + 200

Problem Solving: Can you find three ways to make a dollar with
          eight coins?

A year is the number of days it takes for the earth to go around the sun. It takes the earth almost exactly $365\frac{1}{4}$ days to go around the sun. To make the days come out even, we have 3 years in a row that have 365 days each. These years are called **common years.** Then we have a year that has 366 days. The year with 366 days is called a **leap year.** We put the extra day in February.

February has 28 or 29 days. Four months have 30 days. All the rest have 31 days. If we say the four months that have 30 days, we can remember the number of days in the other months. The following jingle helps us remember which months have 30 days.

> Thirty days hath September,
> April, June, and November.
> All the rest have 31, except February.
> February has 28 or 29.

A **decade** is ten years. A **century** is one hundred years.

Example 1   How many days does December have?

Solution   "Thirty days hath September, April, June, and November." This tells us that December does not have 30 days. December must have **31 days.**

Example 2   According to this calendar, May 10, 2014, is what day of the week?

MAY 2014						
S	M	T	W	T	F	S
				1	2	3
4	5	6	7	8	9	10
11	12	13	14	15	16	17
18	19	20	21	22	23	24
25	26	27	28	29	30	31

Solution   The letters across the top of the calendar stand for "Sunday," "Monday," "Tuesday," "Wednesday," "Thursday," "Friday," and "Saturday." We see that May 10 is a **Saturday,** the second Saturday of the month.

Example 3   How many years were there from 1620 to 1776?

Solution   To find the number of years from one date to another, we may subtract.[†] This is like a "larger-smaller-difference" problem except we use the words "later-earlier-difference" (L-E-D). We subtract the earlier date from the later date. In this problem we subtract 1620 from 1776.

$$\begin{array}{r} 1776 \\ -\ 1620 \\ \hline 156 \end{array}$$

We find that there were **156 years** from 1620 to 1776.

Practice   **a.** How many days long is a leap year?

b. According to the calendar in Example 2, what is the date of the fourth Friday of the month?

c. How many years were there from 1918 to 1943?

d. A century is how many decades?

[†]Years have been numbered forward (A.D.) and backward (B.C.) from the birth of Jesus of Nazareth. In this book, all year dates should be considered years A.D.

Problem set 64

1. There were 7 students in each row. If there were 56 students in all, how many rows were there? (Use the EG pattern.)
(62)

2. There were 7 nails in each board. If there were 42 boards, how many nails were there? (Use the EG pattern.)
(59)

3. How many years is 5 decades?
(64)

4. How many years were there from 1921 to 1938? (Use the "later-earlier-difference pattern.")
(64)

5. According to this calendar, what day of the week was December 25, 1957?
(64)

DECEMBER 1957						
S	M	T	W	T	F	S
1	2	3	4	5	6	7
8	9	10	11	12	13	14
15	16	17	18	19	20	21
22	23	24	25	26	27	28
29	30	31				

6. Round 523 to the nearest hundred. Round 692 to the nearest hundred. Then add the rounded numbers.
(52)

7. One side of a rectangle is 10 kilometers long. Another side is 20 kilometers long. Draw a picture of the rectangle and show the lengths of the sides. What is the perimeter of the rectangle?
(60,25)

8. How many circles are shaded?
(44)

9. To what number is the arrow pointing?
(46)

10. When Elmer emptied his bank, he found 17 pennies, 4 nickels, 5 dimes, and 2 quarters. What was the value of the coins in his bank?
(45)

11. 794,150
(61)   + 9,863

12. $51,786
(61)   + $36,357

13.   876
(21)   40
        317
         55
         11
      +   5

14. $20.00
(51)   − $18.47

15. 41,315
(62)   − 29,418

16. 46   **17.** 54   **18.** 39   **19.** 58   **20.** 30
(58)   × 7   (58)   × 8   (58)   × 9   (58)   × 6   (54)   × 4

21. $\dfrac{36}{4}$
(57)

22. 43 ÷ 7
(63)

23. 9)$\overline{64}$
(63)

24. $\sqrt{64}$
(40)

25. $Y \times 4 = 32$
(50)

26. $6 \times N = 42$
(50)

27. Use digits to write four hundred forty-two thousand,
(43) nine hundred seventy-six.

**LESSON
65**

Multiples • Percent

Facts Practice: 90 Division Facts (Test J in Test Masters)

Mental Math: Subtract dollars and cents from dollars.
   a. $5.00 − $3.89   **b.** $10.00 − $7.25   **c.** $10.00 − $8.67
Review:
   d. 126 + 49   **e.** $5.95 + $3.76   **f.** 480 − 225

Problem Solving: This question is written in code: 1 is A, 2 is B, 3 is C, and so on. Write the answer to this question in the same code.
23-8-1-20   4-1-25   9-19   20-8-9-19?

Multiples If we multiply 4 by the numbers 1, 2, 3, 4, 5, 6, …, we get

4, 8, 12, 16, 20, 24, …

These numbers are **multiples of 4.** The multiples of 4 are the numbers we get if we count by fours.

The following numbers are the multiples of 6.

6, 12, 18, 24, 30, 36, ...

The multiples of any number are the answers we get when we multiply the number by 1, 2, 3, 4, 5, 6, ...

Example 1 List the first four multiples of 7.

Solution To find the first four multiples of 7, we multiply 7 by 1, then by 2, then by 3, and then by 4.

$$\begin{array}{r} 7 \\ \times\,1 \\ \hline 7 \end{array} \qquad \begin{array}{r} 7 \\ \times\,2 \\ \hline 14 \end{array} \qquad \begin{array}{r} 7 \\ \times\,3 \\ \hline 21 \end{array} \qquad \begin{array}{r} 7 \\ \times\,4 \\ \hline 28 \end{array}$$

The first four multiples of 7 are **7, 14, 21,** and **28.** The multiples of 7 are the numbers we say when we count by 7.

Example 2 (a) What is the fourth multiple of 6?

(b) What is the third multiple of 8?

Solution (a) To find the fourth multiple of 6, we multiply 6 by 4. The fourth multiple of 6 is **24.**

(b) To find the third multiple of 8, we multiply 8 by 3. The third multiple of 8 is **24.**

Percent We use fractions and percents to describe parts of a whole. We often use the symbol % to stand for *percent.* If your score on a test is 100%, that means you have every answer right since 100% means the whole thing. If 50% of the children in the class are girls, then half of the children are girls since 50% is half of 100%. So 50% is half of the whole group.

We can use shaded squares to illustrate percentages.

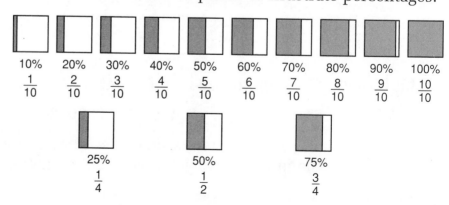

Thinking about money can help us understand percents. Twenty-five cents is $\frac{1}{4}$ of a whole dollar and it is 25% of a whole dollar. Likewise, seventy-five cents is $\frac{3}{4}$ of a whole dollar and it is 75% of a whole dollar.

Example 3   Draw a square and shade 50% of it.

Solution   Since 50% is half of 100%, we shade half of the square. Here are three ways.

Fifty percent of each square is shaded.

Example 4   Forty percent of the children in the class are girls. Are there more boys or more girls in the class?

Solution   Since 50% is half, 40% must be less than half. Since girls are less than half of the class, there must be **more boys than girls in the class.**

Practice   **a.** List the first five multiples of 6.

b. List the third, fourth, and fifth multiples of 9.

c. What is the seventh multiple of 8?

d. Draw a square and shade 25% of it.

e. The chance of rain is 20%. What is the chance that it will not rain?

Problem set 65   **1.** Kent bought a toy for $1.85 and sold it for 75¢ more. For what price did he sell the toy? (Use the SSM pattern.)
(12)

2. Two thousand people entered the contest. Only seven will win prizes. How many will not win prizes? Draw a SWA pattern.
(31)

3. Sixty percent of the students in the class were boys.
(65) Were there more girls or more boys in the class?

4. Twenty-seven thousand people lived in the big town.
(38) Only eight thousand, four hundred seventy-two people lived in the small town. How many more people lived in the big town? (Use the L-S-D pattern.)

5. Draw a rectangle that is 4 cm long and 3 cm wide.
(60,25) What is the perimeter of the rectangle?

6. Fiona found the third multiple of 4. Then she
(65) subtracted two from this number. What was her answer?

7. Compare: $\frac{1}{2}$ ◯ 50%
(65,15)

8. If it is afternoon, what time was it
(33) 30 minutes ago?

9. How many years were there from
(64) 1776 to 1789? (Use the L-E-D pattern.)

10. What is the length of $\overline{ST}$?
(50)

R   S   T

cm   1   2   3   4   5   6   7   8   9   10

11. (51)	**12.** (37)	**13.** (61)
400 − 222	705 − 423	4587 + 2364

14. (37)	**15.** (58)	**16.** (54)
$25.42 − $7.25	64 × 5	70 × 6

17. 89
(58) × 4

18. 63
(58) × 7

19. 46
(21) 295
329
746
761
+ 356

20. 8)15
(63)

21. 5)32
(63)

22. $\frac{63}{7}$
(57)

23. 33 ÷ 6
(63)

24. 44 ÷ 7
(63)

25. $\sqrt{64}$ ÷ 8
(56,40)

26. Use digits to write seventy thousand, seven hundred
(43) two.

27. 7 + 5 + 4 + 3 + 2 + 6 + 9 + 5 + N = 44
(2)

LESSON 66

Using Pictures to Compare Fractions

Facts Practice: 64 Multiplication Facts (Test G in Test Masters)

Mental Math: Multiply by ten.
  a. 6 × 10   **b.** 16 × 10   **c.** 160 × 10
Review:
  d. $5.00 − $1.58   **e.** $4.64 + $1.99   **f.** 56 + 29 + 300

Problem Solving: Marco paid a dollar for an item that cost 54¢. What four coins did he get back in change?

We have practiced comparing whole numbers using comparison symbols. In this lesson we will compare fractions. To begin, we will compare one half and one third.

$$\frac{1}{2} \bigcirc \frac{1}{3}$$

One way to compare fractions is to draw pictures of the fractions and compare the pictures. We will draw two circles of the same size. We shade $\frac{1}{2}$ of one circle and $\frac{1}{3}$ of the other circle.

$$\frac{1}{2} \qquad\qquad \frac{1}{3}$$

As we study the pictures, we see that more of the circle is shaded when $\frac{1}{2}$ is shaded than when $\frac{1}{3}$ is shaded. So $\frac{1}{2}$ is greater than $\frac{1}{3}$.

$$\frac{1}{2} > \frac{1}{3}$$

When drawing pictures to compare fractions, the figures that we draw should be **congruent.** Congruent figures are the same shape and size.

Example Compare: $\frac{1}{4} \bigcirc \frac{1}{3}$. Draw two rectangles to show the comparison.

Solution We draw two congruent rectangles. We shade $\frac{1}{4}$ of one rectangle and $\frac{1}{3}$ of the other rectangle. We see that $\frac{1}{4}$ is slightly less than $\frac{1}{3}$.

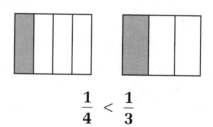

$$\frac{1}{4} < \frac{1}{3}$$

Practice Compare these fractions. Draw a pair of congruent figures to illustrate each comparison.

a. $\frac{1}{2} \bigcirc \frac{2}{3}$ **b.** $\frac{1}{2} \bigcirc \frac{1}{4}$ **c.** $\frac{2}{5} \bigcirc \frac{1}{3}$

Problem set 66

1. James had fifty-six pies. Seven pies would fit on one
   (62) tray. How many trays did he need? Use the EG pattern.

2. Five hundred forty-seven birds were on the lake. At
(31) sunrise some flew away. Then only two hundred fourteen birds were left. How many flew away? Use the SWA pattern.

3. Three hundred forty-two rabbits munched grass in the
(17) meadow. That afternoon some more rabbits came. Then seven hundred fifty-two rabbits munched grass in the meadow. How many rabbits came in the afternoon? Use the SSM pattern.

4. Write four multiplication/division facts using the
(57) numbers 3, 8, and 24.

5. List the seven months of the year that have 31 days.
(64)

6. Find the eighth multiple of six. Then add one. What is
(65,40) the square root of the answer?

7. Compare these fractions. Shade two congruent
(66) rectangles to show the fractions.

$$\frac{1}{4} \bigcirc \frac{1}{6}$$

8. Round 497 to the nearest hundred.
(52)

9. What is the perimeter of this
(60) rectangle?

7 miles

4 miles

10. $10.00
(51) − $5.46

11. 36,024
(62) − 15,539

12. 43,675
(61) + 52,059

13. 73
(58) × 9

14. 46
(58) × 7

15. 84
(58) × 6

16. 40
(54) × 5

17. 56 ÷ 5
(63)

18. 7)48
(63)

19. $\frac{63}{7}$
(57)

20. $7\overline{)25}$　　　　**21.** $9\overline{)60}$　　　　**22.** $N \times 6 = 54$
(63)　　　　　　　　(63)　　　　　　　　　(50)

23.　　　N　　　**24.**　　　4　　　**25.**　　　5
(20)　$- 942$　　　(2)　　　7　　　(2)　　　8
　　　$\overline{517}$　　　　　　　8　　　　　　　13
　　　　　　　　　　　　　21　　　　　　　14
　　　　　　　　　　$+\ N$　　　　　　$+\ N$
　　　　　　　　　　$\overline{49}$　　　　　　　$\overline{47}$

26. Draw a rectangle and shade 50% of it.
(65)

LESSON
67

Rate Word Problems

Facts Practice: 90 Division Facts (Test I in Test Masters)

Mental Math: Multiply by ten.
　a. 12×10　　　**b.** 120×10　　　**c.** 10×10

Review:
　d. $48 + 250$　　　**e.** $\$1.00 - \$0.36$　　　**f.** $\$3.75 + \$3.75$

Problem Solving: The whole circle has been divided into quarters. What percent of the circle is shaded? What percent is not shaded?

A **rate** tells **how far** or **how many are in one time group.**

The car went 30 miles per hour.

This statement tells us that the car's rate is 30 miles each hour. **Rate problems have the same pattern that "equal groups" problems have.**

Example 1　Brad drove the car 30 miles per hour for 4 hours. How far did Brad drive in 4 hours?

Solution   This is a rate problem. A rate problem is an "equal groups" problem. Let's draw the pattern.

		each	
Number **in** time group	___ ___	each	___
Number **of** time groups	× ___		___
Total	___ ___		

We do not see the words *in each* in a rate problem, but there are words that mean *in each*. The words *miles per hour* mean *miles **each** hour.*

			each	
Number **in** time group		30	miles each	hour
Number **of** time groups	×	4		hours
Total		N	miles	

Now we find the missing number. To find the bottom number of an "equal groups" pattern, we multiply.

$$\begin{array}{r} 30 \\ \times\ 4 \\ \hline 120 \end{array}$$

We complete the pattern and answer the question.

			each	
Number **in** time group		30	miles each	hour
Number **of** time groups	×	4		hours
Total		120	miles	

Brad drove **120 miles** in 4 hours.

Example 2   Nalcomb earns 3 dollars a week for doing chores. How much money does he earn in 7 weeks?

Solution   This is a rate problem. A rate problem is an "equal groups" problem. The words *3 dollars a week* mean *3 dollars **each** week.*

			each	
Number **in** time group		3	dollars each	week
Number **of** time groups	×	7		weeks
Total		N	dollars	

We need to find the missing number. We find the bottom number of an "equal groups" pattern by multiplying.

$$\begin{array}{r} 3 \\ \times\ 7 \\ \hline 21 \end{array}$$

We complete the pattern and answer the question.

Number **in** time group		3	dollars each	week
Number **of** time groups	×	7		weeks
Total		21	dollars	

Nalcomb earns **21 dollars** in 7 weeks.

Practice

a. Tammy drove 55 miles in one hour. At that rate, how far can she drive in 6 hours?

b. Jeff swims 20 laps every day. How many laps will he swim in 1 week?

Problem set 67

1. Marybeth could jump 42 times each minute. How
(67) many times could she jump in 8 minutes? Use the EG pattern.

2. Robo could run 7 miles in 1 hour. At that rate, how far
(67) could Robo run in 3 hours? Use the EG pattern.

3. Write four multiplication/division facts using the
(57) numbers 8, 9, and 72.

4. What is the sum of $\sqrt{36}$ and $\sqrt{64}$?
(40)

5. Compare: $\frac{1}{3} \bigcirc 50\%$
(66,65)

6. Round 582 to the nearest hundred. Then subtract 18.
(52) What is the answer?

7. It is afternoon. What time was it 6
(33) hours and 5 minutes ago?

8. Find the fourth multiple of 6.
(65) Then find the third multiple of 8.
What is the sum of these two
numbers?

9. How many years were there from 1492 until 1800? Use
(64) the "later-earlier-difference" pattern.

10. A square has one side that is 7 inches long. What is the
(60) perimeter of the square?

11. $\quad$ 70,003
(62) $\quad$ − 36,418

12. $\quad\quad N$
(20) $\quad$ − 432
$\quad\quad$ 257

13. $\quad$ \$861.34
(28) $\quad$ + \$764.87

14. $\quad$ 93
(58) $\quad \times\ 5$

15. $\quad$ 84
(58) $\quad \times\ 6$

16. $\quad$ 77
(58) $\quad \times\ 7$

17. $\quad$ 80
(54) $\quad \times\ 8$

18. $\dfrac{56}{8}$
(57)

19. $7\overline{)65}$
(63)

20. $45 \div 6$
(63)

21. $7\overline{)51}$
(63)

22. $7 \times N = 42$
(50)

23. $R \times 8 = 48$
(50)

24. Compare these fractions. Draw a picture to show each
(66) fraction.

$$\frac{2}{3} \bigcirc \frac{3}{4}$$

25. $\quad$ 423
(2)
$\quad\quad$ 7
$\quad\quad$ 8
$\quad\quad$ 15
$\quad$ + $\quad N$
$\quad\quad$ 458

26. $\quad\quad$ 2
(2)
$\quad\quad$ 24
$\quad\quad$ 36
$\quad\quad\quad N$
$\quad$ + 14
$\quad\quad$ 82

27. $\quad\quad$ 7
(2)
$\quad\quad$ 5
$\quad\quad$ 4
$\quad\quad$ 3
$\quad$ + N
$\quad\quad$ 30

LESSON
68

Multiplying Three-Digit Numbers

Facts Practice: 90 Division Facts (Test I in Test Masters)

Mental Math: Multiply three numbers, including ten.

  a. $6 \times 7 \times 10$ **b.** $5 \times 8 \times 10$ **c.** $12 \times 10 \times 10$

Review:

  d. $\$6.47 + \$1.85$ **e.** $400 + 37 + 210$ **f.** $\$10.00 - \$6.87$

Patterns: In this sequence the count from one number to the next increases. Copy this sequence and find the next three terms.

  1, 3, 6, 10, 15, ___, ___, ___

When we multiply three-digit numbers, we multiply the ones' digit first. Then we multiply the tens' digit. Then we multiply the hundreds' digit.

In the next problem, we get 18 when we multiply the ones' digit. We write the eight in the ones' column and write the one above the tens' column. Then we multiply the tens' digit.

Three times five is 15, plus one is 16. We write the six below the line and write the one above the hundreds' column. Then we multiply the hundreds. Three times four is 12, plus one equals 13. The product is 1368.

Example 1   Multiply: 654 × 7

Solution
$$
\begin{array}{r}
^{3\,2} \\
654 \\
\times \quad 7 \\
\hline
4578
\end{array}
$$

Example 2
$$
\begin{array}{r}
\$3.75 \\
\times \quad 3 \\
\hline
\end{array}
$$

Solution   Imagine multiplying pennies, dimes, and dollars. We multiply three times five pennies and get 15 pennies, which equals one dime and five pennies. We write "5" below the line and "1" above the dimes.

$$
\begin{array}{r}
^{1} \\
\$3.75 \\
\times \quad 3 \\
\hline
5
\end{array}
$$

Next we multiply three times seven dimes and get 21 dimes. We add the one dime from multiplying pennies for a total of 22 dimes. Since 22 dimes equals two dollars and two dimes, we write a two below the line and a two above the dollars.

$$
\begin{array}{r}
^{2\,1} \\
\$3.75 \\
\times \quad 3 \\
\hline
25
\end{array}
$$

Finally, we multiply three times three dollars and get nine dollars. We add the two dollars, making 11 dollars. The total is **$11.25.**

$$
\begin{array}{r}
^{2\,1} \\
\$3.75 \\
\times \quad 3 \\
\hline
\$11.25
\end{array}
$$

Practice
a.
$$
\begin{array}{r}
234 \\
\times \quad 3 \\
\hline
\end{array}
$$

b.
$$
\begin{array}{r}
\$340 \\
\times \quad 4 \\
\hline
\end{array}
$$

c.
$$
\begin{array}{r}
\$4.25 \\
\times \quad 5 \\
\hline
\end{array}
$$

d. Explain the steps of multiplying 5 × $4.25 by imagining multiplying dollars, dimes, and pennies.

Problem set 68

1. Elizabeth pays 9 dollars every week for karate lessons.
(67) How much does she pay for 4 weeks of karate lessons? Use the EG pattern.

2. It takes 4 apples to make 1 pie. How many apples does
(59) it take to make 5 pies? Use the EG pattern.

3. Elmer has to get up at 6 a.m. What time should he go
(33) to bed in order to get 8 hours of sleep?

4. Nine hundred seventy-three raccoons were hiding in
(31) the forest. Hoover found three hundred eighty-eight of
them. How many raccoons were still hiding in the
forest? Use the SWA pattern.

5. Write the number 8,402 in expanded form. Then use
(42) words to write the number.

6. Find the fourth multiple of 7. Then find the sixth
(65,40) multiple of 6. Add these multiples. What is the square
root of the answer?

7. According to this calendar, what
(64) is the date of the second Tuesday
in September 2042?

SEPTEMBER 2042						
S	M	T	W	T	F	S
	1	2	3	4	5	6
7	8	9	10	11	12	13
14	15	16	17	18	19	20
21	22	23	24	25	26	27
28	29	30				

8. If $5 + N = 23$, what number is N?
(30)

9. What is the perimeter of this fig-
(60) ure? Dimensions are in feet.

10. Compare these fractions. Shade two circles to show
(66) the fractions.

$$\frac{1}{2} \bigcirc \frac{2}{4}$$

11. The arrow points to what number on this number
(46) line?

12. Draw a rectangle and shade about 30% of it.
(65)

13. $3 + $4.39 + $12.62   **14.** 47 + 362 + 85 + 454
(53)   (21)

15. $20.00 − $7.29   **16.** 41,059 − 36,275
(51)   (62)

17.   768   **18.** $2.80   **19.**   436
(68) × 3   (68)   × 4   (20) − Z
                                                       252

20. 5)$\overline{36}$ **21.** 7)$\overline{45}$ **22.** 4)$\overline{35}$
(63)   (63)   (63)

23. 17 ÷ 3   **24.** 49 ÷ 6   **25.** 57 ÷ 8
(63)   (63)   (63)

26.   6   **27.**   N   **28.**   4
(2)   5   (2)   5   (2)   7
      N   7   8
      4   3   N
      7   2   3
    + 3   + 12   + 16
      31   38   44

LESSON 69

Two-Step Equations

Facts Practice: 90 Division Facts (Test J in Test Masters)

Mental Math: Multiply four numbers, including two tens.
a. 6 × 4 × 10 × 10   **b.** 3 × 4 × 10 × 10
c. 4 × 5 × 10 × 10

Review:
d. $5.00 − $3.25   **e.** $7.59 + $0.95   **f.** 470 − 30

Problem Solving: Fifty percent of the students in Gabriel's class are girls. Do we know how many students are in this class? Do we know whether there are more boys or more girls in the class? Do we know if the number of students in the class is an odd or even number?

We have used letters to stand for numbers in arithmetic problems. Problems like we have practiced are sometimes called *equations*. Some equations can be solved in one step while others require several steps to solve.

Example $3 \times 5 = 2 + N$

Solution   The equal sign shows that the answer to 3×5 equals the answer to $2 + N$. For the first step, we multiply 3×5 and find that the left-hand side of the equation is 15.

STEP 1
$$3 \times 5 = 2 + N$$
$$15 = 2 + N$$

Since the left-hand side of the equation is 15, the right-hand side must also total 15. So the second step is to find this missing addend.

STEP 2
$$15 = 2 + N$$
$$15 = 2 + 13$$

So N is **13**.

Practice   **a.** $2 + 17 = N + 5$ **b.** $W + 3 = 5 \times 3$

Problem set 69

1. *(59)* There were forty-two apples in each big basket. There were seven big baskets. How many apples were in the seven big baskets? Use the EG pattern.

2. *(62)* There were forty-eight pears in all. Six pears were in each box. How many boxes were there? Use the EG pattern.

3. *(12)* One thousand, nine hundred forty-two ducks were in the first flight. Two thousand, seven hundred five ducks were in the second flight. How many ducks were in both flights? Use the SSM pattern.

4. *(57)* Write four multiplication/division facts using the numbers 3, 9, and 27.

5. *(65,40)* Compare: 50% of $16 \bigcirc \sqrt{16}$

6. *(65)* Find the sum of the fourth multiple of 10, the third multiple of 7, and the second multiple of 100.

7. How many years were there from 1492 to 1701? Use
(64) the L-E-D pattern.

8. It is dark outside. What time was
(33) it 3 hours and 10 minutes ago?

9. Compare these fractions. Shade rectangles to show the
(66) fractions.

$$\frac{2}{5} \bigcirc \frac{1}{4}$$

10. Janine could pack 40 packages in 1 hour. How many
(67) packages could she pack in 5 hours? Use the EG
pattern.

11. If $25 + N = 5 \times 7$, what number is N?
(69)

12. One side of a rectangle is 2 miles long. Another side is
(60,25) 3 miles long. Draw a picture of the rectangle and show
the length of each side. What is the perimeter of the
rectangle?

13. *(28)*	$37.75 + $45.95	**14.** *(61)*	43,793 + 76,860	**15.** *(61)*	480 97 126 53 + 2362
16. *(51)*	$50.00 − $42.87	**17.** *(62)*	43,793 − 26,860		

18. 483×4
(68)

19. 360×4
(68)

20. 207×8
(68)

21. $8\overline{)43}$
(63)

22. $5\overline{)43}$
(63)

23. $7\overline{)43}$
(63)

24. $29 \div 4$
(63)

25. $\dfrac{32}{8}$
(57)

26. $55 \div 9$
(63)

27. $5 + 7 + N + 4 + 7 + 8 + 7 + 6 + 3 = 52$
(2)

LESSON
70

Estimating Arithmetic Answers •
More About Rate

Facts Practice: 90 Division Facts (Test J in Test Masters)

Mental Math: Multiply two numbers ending in zero.
Example: 30 × 40 equals 3 × 10 times 4 × 10.
This equals 3 × 4 × 10 × 10, which is 1200.
 a. 40 × 40   **b.** 30 × 50   **c.** 60 × 70   **d.** 40 × 50

Problem Solving: This question is written in code. When you
figure out the question, write the answer in
the same code.
23-8-9-3-8   3-15-9-14   5-17-21-1-12-19
8-1-12-6   15-6   1   4-9-13-5?

**Estimating
arithmetic
answers**
We can **estimate** arithmetic answers by using round
numbers instead of exact answers to do the arithmetic.
Estimating does not give us the exact answer, but it gives
us an answer that is close to the exact answer. Estimating
is a way to find if our exact answer is **reasonable.**

Example 1 Estimate the sum of 396 and 512.

Solution To estimate, we first change the exact numbers to round
numbers. We round 396 to 400. We round 512 to 500.
Then we do the arithmetic with the round numbers. We
find the sum by adding, so we add 400 and 500.

$$\begin{array}{r} 400 \\ + 500 \\ \hline 900 \end{array}$$

The estimated sum of 396 and 512 is **900.** The exact sum
of 396 and 512 is 908. The estimated answer is not exact,
but it is close to the exact number.

Example 2 Estimate the product of 72 and 5.

Solution We round the two-digit number but
not the one-digit number. The
estimated product of 72 and 5 is **350.**

$$\begin{array}{r} 70 \\ \times\ \ 5 \\ \hline 350 \end{array}$$

More about rate In Lesson 67, we learned that rate problems have the same pattern as "equal groups" problems. The rate tells how many are in each time group. If we know two numbers in the problem, we can find the third number. We have practiced problems in which we were given the rate and time. We multiplied to find the total. In this lesson we will practice problems in which we are given the total. We will divide to find the number we are not given.

Example 3 Stanley can read 2 pages in 1 minute. How long will it take him to read 18 pages?

Solution This is a rate problem. A rate problem is an "equal groups" problem. Let's draw the pattern.

Number **in** time group _____ _____ each _____

Number **of** time groups × _____ _____

Total _____ _____

We are told that the rate is 2 pages in 1 minute. This means 2 pages each minute. We are told that the total number of pages is 18.

Number **in** time group 2 pages each minute

Number **of** time groups × N minutes

Total 18 pages

Now we find the missing number. **To find the first or second number in an "equal groups" pattern, we divide.**

$$\frac{9}{2\overline{)18}}$$

We complete the pattern and answer the question.

Number **in** time group 2 pages each minute

Number **of** time groups × 9 minutes

Total 18 pages

It would take Stanley **9 minutes** to read 18 pages.

Practice Estimate the answer to each arithmetic problem. Then find the exact answer.

      a. $59 + 68 + 81$ **b.** $607 + 891$

      c. $585 - 294$ **d.** $82 - 39$

      e. 59×6 **f.** 397×4

      g. Miguel can sharpen 5 pencils in a minute. How long will it take Miguel to sharpen 40 pencils?

Problem set 70

1. Fifty percent of an hour is how many minutes?
$^{(65)}$

2. There were two hundred fourteen parrots, seven hundred fifty-two crows, and two thousand, forty-two blue jays. How many birds were there in all? Use the SSM pattern.
$^{(12)}$

3. Letha could make four burritos with one pound of beans. How many pounds of beans would she need to make a dozen burritos? Use the EG pattern.
$^{(62)}$

4. Harry could paint 36 signs in 3 hours. How many signs could he paint in 1 hour? Use the EG pattern.
$^{(70)}$

5. Round each number to the nearest hundred; then add to estimate the sum of 286 and 415.
$^{(70)}$

6. What is the sum of the fourth multiple of 100 and the seventh multiple of 10?
$^{(65)}$

7. Write the digital form for a quarter to seven in the morning.
$^{(23)}$

8. $140 + N = 28 \times 5$
$^{(69)}$

9. The product of 6 and 7 is how much greater than the sum of 6 and 7?
$^{(38)}$

10. What is the length of segment *BC*?
(50)

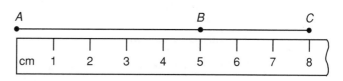

11. Compare: $(32 \div 8) \div 2 \bigcirc 32 \div (8 \div 2)$
(57,55)

12. $6.49 + $12 + $7.59 + 8¢
(53)

13. 3742 + 5329 + 8415   **14.** $30.00 − $29.17
(61)   (51)

15.   350   **16.**   204   **17.**   463
(68) × 5   (68) × 7   (68) × 6

18. 4)‾3‾7‾   **19.** 6)‾3‾9‾   **20.** 3)‾2‾8‾
(63)   (63)   (63)

21. $\sqrt{49} \div 7$ **22.** 48 ÷ 5   **23.** $\dfrac{48}{8}$
(56,40)   (63)   (57)

24.   5   **25.**   4   **26.**   5
(1)   1   (2)   2   (2)   2
         2   *N*   42
         3   15   3
         8   12   *N*
         4   3   16
       + 7   + 5   + 4
      ‾‾‾‾‾   ‾‾‾‾‾‾   ‾‾‾‾‾‾
                               44   75

LESSON

71

Remaining Fraction

If a whole has been divided into parts and we know the size of one part, then we can figure out the size of the other parts.

Example 1 (a) What fraction of the circle is shaded?

(b) What fraction of the circle is **not** shaded?

Solution We see that the whole circle has been divided into eight parts. Three of the parts are shaded, so five of the parts are not shaded.

(a) The fraction that is shaded is $\frac{3}{8}$.

(b) The fraction that is **not** shaded is $\frac{5}{8}$.

Example 2 The pizza was cut into eight equal slices. After Bill, Tony, and Jenny each took a slice, what fraction of the pizza was left?

Solution The whole pizza was cut into eight equal parts. Since three of the eight parts were taken, five of the eight parts remained. The fraction that was left was $\frac{5}{8}$.

Example 3 Two fifths of the crowd cheered. What fraction of the crowd did not cheer?

Solution We think of the crowd as though it were divided into five parts. We are told that two of the five parts cheered. So there were three parts that did not cheer. The fraction that did not cheer was $\frac{3}{5}$.

Practice **a.** What fraction of this rectangle is not shaded?

b. Three fifths of the race was over. What fraction of the race was left?

Problem set **1.** The first number was one thousand, three hundred
71 $^{(38)}$ forty-two. The second number was five hundred fourteen. The second number was how much less than the first number? Use the L-S-D pattern.

2. Five little people could crowd into each one of the
$^{(59)}$ spaces. If there were thirty-five spaces, how many little people could crowd in? Use the EG pattern.

3. Only two big people could crowd into one of the
$^{(62)}$ spaces. If there were sixty-four big people standing in line, how many spaces would it take to hold them? Use the EG pattern.

4. The Gilbreth family drank 39 quarts of milk in 3 days.
$^{(70)}$ That amounts to how many quarts of milk each day? Use the EG pattern.

5. Carl weighed 88 pounds. He put on his clothes, which
$^{(12)}$ weighed 2 pounds, and his shoes, which weighed 1 pound each. Finally, he put on a jacket that weighed 3 pounds and stepped on the scale again. Then how much did the scale show that he weighed? Use the SSM pattern.

6. What fraction of this rectangle is
$^{(71)}$ not shaded?

7. The pumpkin pie was sliced into 6 equal parts. After 1
(71) slice was taken, what fraction of the pie was left?

8. Compare these fractions. Shade parts of circles to
(66) show each fraction.

$$\frac{2}{3} \bigcirc \frac{3}{4}$$

9. Use rounded numbers to estimate the sum of 507 and
(70) 384.

10. If 60% of the answers were true, then were there more
(65) true answers or more false answers?

11. What is the perimeter of this
(60) rectangle?

4 cm

8 cm

12. $62.59
(28) + $17.47

13. z
(20) − 417
      268

14. 976
(61)   434
        129
      ] 85
    + 1140
        769

15. 1000 − (110 × 9)
(55)

16. 413,216
(62) − 127,159
      286,057

17.   670
(68) ×   4

18.   703
(68) ×   6

19.   346
(68) ×   9

20. 5)39
(63)

21. 7)39
(63)

22. 4)39
(63)

23. 16 ÷ 3
(63)

24. 26 ÷ 6
(63)

25. 36 ÷ $\sqrt{36}$
(57,40)

LESSON
72

Multiplying Three Factors • Exponents

Facts Practice: 90 Division Facts (Test J in Test Masters)

Mental Math: Multiply numbers ending in two zeros by numbers ending in one zero.

    a. 200 × 10   **b.** 300 × 20   **c.** 400 × 50

Review:

    d. 250 × 10   **e.** $1.00 + $0.29   **f.** $4.47 + $2.95

Patterns: Counting by fives from five, we say this sequence:

$$5, 10, 15, 20, 25, 30, \ldots$$

If we count by fives from **one,** we say this sequence:

$$1, 6, 11, 16, 21, 26, \ldots$$

What sequence do we say when we count by fives from **two?**

Multiplying three factors
To multiply three numbers, we first multiply two of the numbers. Then we multiply the answer we get by the third number.

Example 1 3 × 4 × 5

Solution First we multiply two numbers and get an answer. Then we multiply that answer by the third number. If we multiply 3 × 4 first, we get 12. Then we multiply 12 × 5 and get 60.

$$
\begin{array}{cc}
\textbf{First} & \textbf{Then} \\
3 & 12 \\
\underline{\times\,4} & \underline{\times\,5} \\
12 & \textbf{60}
\end{array}
$$

It does not matter which numbers we multiply first. If we multiply 5 × 4 first, we get 20. Then we multiply 20 × 3 and get 60 again.

$$
\begin{array}{cc}
\textbf{First} & \textbf{Then} \\
5 & 20 \\
\underline{\times\,4} & \underline{\times\,3} \\
20 & \textbf{60}
\end{array}
$$
 ← same answer

Exponents   An exponent is a number that shows how many times another number is to be used as a factor. An exponent is written above and to the right of the other number.

$$5^2 \leftarrow \text{exponent}$$

$$5^2 \text{ means } 5 \times 5.$$

$$5^2 \text{ equals } 25.$$

We read 5^2 as "five squared."

Example 2 $5^2 + 2^3$

Solution   We read 2^3 as "two cubed." We will find the value of 5^2 and 2^3 and then add.

$$5^2 \text{ means } 5 \times 5, \text{ which is } 25.$$

$$2^3 \text{ means } 2 \times 2 \times 2, \text{ which is } 8.$$

Now we add 25 and 8.

$$5^2 + 2^3$$

$$25 + 8 = \textbf{33}$$

Practice   **a.** $2 \times 3 \times 4$ **b.** $2 \times 4 \times 6$

c. 8^2 **d.** 3^3

Problem set 72

1. There were twice as many peacocks as peahens. If there were 12 peacocks, how many peahens were there?
   (56)

2. Beth's dance class begins at 6 p.m. It takes 20 minutes to drive to dance class. What time should she leave home to get to dance class on time?
   (33)

3. Samantha bought a package of paper for $1.98 and 2 pens for $0.49 each. The tax was 18¢. What was the total price? Use the SSM pattern.
   (12)

4. Nalcomb earns $3 a week for washing the car. How
(67) much money does he earn in a year? (There are 52
weeks in a year.) Use the EG pattern.

5. Two thirds of the race was over. What fraction of the
(71) race was left?

6. Estimate the difference: 887 − 291
(70)

7. In the equation 9 × 11 = 100 − *y*, the letter *y* stands
(69) for what number?

8. Compare: $\frac{2}{4} \bigcirc \frac{4}{8}$. Draw and shade two circles to show
(66) the comparison.

9. What is the sum of the eighth multiple of 5 and the
(65) fourth multiple of 10?

10. According to this calendar, the
(64) Fourth of July, 2014, is what day
of the week?

JULY 2014						
S	M	T	W	T	F	S
		1	2	3	4	5
6	7	8	9	10	11	12
13	14	15	16	17	18	19
20	21	22	23	24	25	26
27	28	29	30	31		

11. Write four multiplication/divi-
(57) sion facts using the numbers 6, 3,
and 18.

12. 5 × 6 × 7   **13.** 4^3
(72)   (72)

14.   476,385   **15.** $20.00   **16.**
(61)   + 259,518   (51)   − $17.84   (20)   − 19,434
                           $2.16   ‾‾‾‾‾‾‾‾
                                             45,579

17.   417   **18.**   470   **19.**   608
(68)   ×   8   (68)   ×   7   (68)   ×   4
   ‾‾‾‾‾‾‾‾   ‾‾‾‾‾‾‾‾   ‾‾‾‾‾‾‾‾

20. 4)29   **21.** 8)65   **22.** 5)29
(63)   (63)   (63)

23. 65 ÷ 7   **24.** 29 ÷ 5   **25.** 65 ÷ 9
(63)   (63)   (63)

26. If 40% of the students are boys, then what percent of
(65) the students are girls?

LESSON   **Polygons**
73

Facts Practice: 90 Division Facts (Test I in Test Masters)

Mental Math: Multiply three numbers ending in zero.
   a. 10 × 10 × 10   **b.** 10 × 20 × 30   **c.** 20 × 30 × 40
Review:
   d. $6.48 + $2.84   **e.** 320 + 200 + 60   **f.** $5.00 − $3.79

Problem Solving: Mathea exercised for 50% of an hour. For
                   50% of her exercise time she was running.
                   For how many minutes was Mathea
                   exercising? For how many minutes was she
                   running?

Polygons are closed, flat shapes formed by straight lines.

Example 1 Which of these shapes is a polygon?

A.   B.   C.   D.

Solution Figure A is not a polygon because it is not closed. Figure B
is not a polygon because it is not flat. Figure C is not a
polygon because not all of its sides are straight. **Figure D is
a polygon.**

The name of a polygon tells how many sides the
polygon has. The sides do not have to have the same
lengths. If the sides do have the same lengths and all

angles are the same size, they are called **regular** polygons. The right-most figure in each row illustrates a regular polygon.

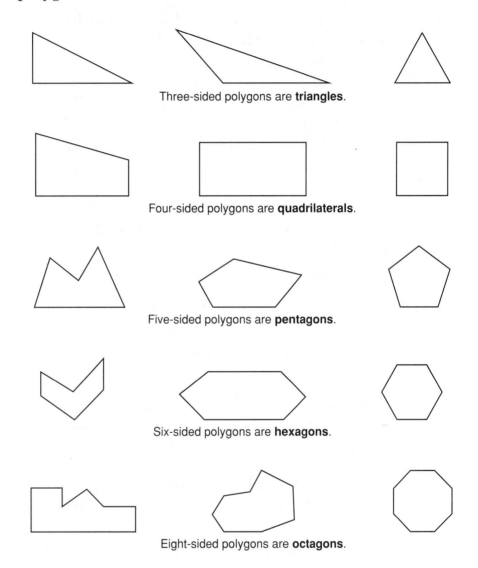

Three-sided polygons are **triangles**.

Four-sided polygons are **quadrilaterals**.

Five-sided polygons are **pentagons**.

Six-sided polygons are **hexagons**.

Eight-sided polygons are **octagons**.

Example 2   What kind of a polygon is a square?

Solution   A square has four sides, so a square is a **quadrilateral.**

Practice   Draw an example of each kind of polygon:

    a. triangle   **b.** quadrilateral

    c. pentagon   **d.** hexagon   **e.** octagon

Problem set   **1.** Three feet equals one yard. A car that is 15 feet long is
      73   (62) how many yards long? Use the EG pattern.

2. Write four multiplication/division facts using the
(57) numbers 3, 10, and 30.

3. Roberta had six quarters, three dimes, and fourteen
(45) pennies. How much money did she have in all?

4. What is the sum of the even numbers that are greater
(11) than 10 but less than 20?

5. Estimate the sum of 715 and 594 by rounding these
(70) numbers to the nearest hundred before adding.

6. Seven bugs could fit into one small space. There were
(62) 56 bugs in all. How many small spaces were needed to
hold them all? Use the EG pattern.

7. The arrow points to what number?
(46)

8. The cake was cut into 12 pieces. Seven of the pieces
(71) were eaten. What fraction of the cake was left?

9. The product of 4 and 3 is how much greater than the
(38) sum of 4 and 3?

10. What is the sum of 9^2 and $\sqrt{9}$?
(40,1)

11. (a) What is the name of this
(73,60)   polygon?

   (b) Each side is the same length.
       What is the perimeter of this
       polygon?

12. Roger could pick 56 flowers in 8 minutes. How many
(70) flowers could he pick in 1 minute? Use the EG pattern.

13. Sarah could pick 11 flowers in 1 minute. How many
(67) flowers could she pick in 5 minutes? Use the EG pattern.

14. $3 \times 5 \times 7$ **15.** 5^3 **16.**   2415
(72)   *(72)*   *(61)*   3621
                                                 157
                                                 642

17. $40.00   **18.**   64,150 $+$ 93
(20) $-$ D *(62)* $- 48{,}398$
          $2.43

19. 349×8 **20.** 760×7 **21.** $6\overline{)34}$
(68)   *(68)*   *(63)*

22. $8\overline{)62}$ **23.** $5\overline{)24}$ **24.** $\dfrac{63}{7}$
(63)   *(63)*   *(57)*

25. $5 \times N = 15 + \sqrt{25}$ **26.**   7
(69)   *(2)*   8
                                                  4
                                                  3
                                                  6
                                                  5

27. If 60% of the flowers Sarah   1
(65) picked were red, then what per-   3
cent of the flowers Sarah picked $+\ N$
were not red?   44

LESSON
74

Division with Two-Digit Answers, Part 1

Facts Practice: 90 Division Facts (Test I in Test Masters)

Mental Math: Multiply three numbers.
  a. $12 \times 10 \times 10$ **b.** $12 \times 2 \times 10$ **c.** $12 \times 3 \times 10$

Review:
  d. $20 \times 20 \times 20$ **e.** $\$5.36 + \$1.98$ **f.** $56 + 9 + 120$

Problem Solving: In this addition problem some digits are missing. Copy this problem on your paper and fill in the missing digits.

$$\begin{array}{r} 7\_6 \\ +\ \_4\_ \\ \hline \_45 \end{array}$$

In this lesson we will learn a pencil-and-paper method for dividing a two-digit number by a one-digit number. To show the method, we will divide 78 by 3.

$$3\overline{)78}$$

For the first step we ignore the 8 and divide 7 by 3. We write the 2 above the 7. Then we multiply 2×3 and write "6" below the 7. We subtract and write "1."

$$\begin{array}{r} 2 \\ 3\overline{)78} \\ 6 \\ \hline 1 \end{array}$$

Then we "bring down" the 8, as we show here. Together, the 1 and 8 form 18.

$$\begin{array}{r} 2 \\ 3\overline{)78} \\ 6\downarrow \\ \hline 18 \end{array}$$

Now we divide 18 by 3 and get 6. We write the 6 above the 8 in 78. Then we multiply 6 by 3 and write "18" below the 18.

$$\begin{array}{r} 26 \\ 3\overline{)78} \\ 6 \\ \hline 18 \\ 18 \\ \hline 0 \end{array}$$

When we subtract, we find the remainder is zero. This shows that if we divide 78 into 3 parts, there will be 26 in each part.

Example   Divide: $3\overline{)87}$

Solution   For the first step we ignore the 7. We divide 8 by 3, multiply, and then subtract. Now we bring down the 7. This forms 27. Now we divide 27 by 3, multiply, and subtract again.

$$
\begin{array}{r}
29 \\
3\overline{)87} \\
6\downarrow \\
\hline
27 \\
27 \\
\hline
0
\end{array}
$$

When we divide 87 into 3 parts, there are **29** in each part.

Practice   **a.** $3\overline{)51}$ **b.** $4\overline{)52}$ **c.** $5\overline{)75}$

d. $3\overline{)72}$ **e.** $4\overline{)96}$ **f.** $2\overline{)74}$

Problem set 74

1. Franco liked to run. He ran the course two thousand, (12) three hundred times the first year. He ran the course one thousand, nine hundred forty-two times the second year. How many times did he run the course in all? Use the SSM pattern.

2. William Tell's target was one hundred thirteen paces (59) away. If each pace was 3 feet, how many feet away was the target? Use the EG pattern.

3. Tracy's baseball card album will hold five hundred (31) cards. Tracy has three hundred eighty-four cards. How many more cards will fit in the album? Use the SWA pattern.

4. The trip lasted 21 days. How many weeks is that? (62)

5. A stop sign has the shape of an octagon. How many (73) sides are on seven stop signs?

6. Find the length of this hairpin to the nearest quarter
⁽⁴⁸⁾ inch.

7. Write 406,912 in expanded form. Then use words to
⁽⁴²⁾ write this number.

8. One foot equals 12 inches. If each side of a square is
⁽⁶⁰⁾ one foot long, what is the perimeter of the square in
inches?

9. Estimate the sum of 586 and 797 by rounding the
⁽⁷⁰⁾ numbers to the nearest hundred and then adding the
rounded numbers.

10. Compare: $\frac{3}{6} \bigcirc \frac{1}{2}$. Draw and shade two circles to show
⁽⁶⁶⁾ the comparison.

11. Compare: 50% of 100 $\bigcirc \sqrt{100}$
^(65,40)

12. Some birds sat on the wire at sunup. Later, 47 more
⁽¹⁷⁾ birds came. Then there were 112 birds sitting on the
wire. How many birds sat on the wire at sunup? Use
the SSM pattern.

13. $32.47
⁽²⁸⁾ + $67.54

14. 51,036
⁽⁶²⁾ − 7,648

15. 536
⁽⁶¹⁾ 29
  974
  88
+ 4361

16. 5)75
⁽⁷⁴⁾

17. 3)84
⁽⁷⁴⁾

18. 257
⁽⁶⁸⁾ × 5

19. 709
⁽⁶⁸⁾ × 3

20. 334
⁽⁶⁸⁾ × 9

21. 4)92
⁽⁷⁴⁾

22. 6)58
⁽⁶³⁾

23. 2)36
⁽⁷⁴⁾

24. $N \times 4 = 36$
⁽⁵⁰⁾

25. $4^2 + 2^3$
⁽⁷²⁾

LESSON 75

Division with Two-Digit Answers, Part 2

Facts Practice: 90 Division Facts (Test I in Test Masters)

Mental Math: Multiply three numbers.

    a. $21 \times 2 \times 10$ **b.** $25 \times 2 \times 10$ **c.** $12 \times 4 \times 10$

Review:

    d. $30 \times 30 \times 30$ **e.** $\$10.00 - \$2.99$ **f.** $\$7.16 + \$1.99$

Problem Solving: The parking lot charged $1.50 for the first hour and 75¢ for each additional hour. Harold parked the car in the lot from 11 a.m. to 3 p.m. How much did he have to pay?

To perform the following division, we begin by dividing $3\overline{)23}$.

$$3\overline{)234}$$

We write "7" above the 3 of 23. Then we multiply. Then we subtract.

$$
\begin{array}{r}
7 \\
3\overline{)234} \\
\underline{21} \\
2
\end{array}
$$

Next, we bring down the 4.

$$
\begin{array}{r}
7 \\
3\overline{)234} \\
\underline{21}\downarrow \\
24
\end{array}
$$

Now we divide 24 by 3. We write the 8 above the 4. Then we multiply and finish by subtracting.

$$
\begin{array}{r}
78 \\
3\overline{)234} \\
\underline{21} \\
24 \\
\underline{24} \\
0
\end{array}
$$

We see that 234 divides into 3 equal groups of 78.

Example Divide: 174 ÷ 3

Solution We begin by dividing 3)‾1‾7‾. We write the 5 above the 7 in 17. Then we multiply. Then we subtract.

$$\begin{array}{r} 5 \\ 3\overline{)174} \\ 15 \\ \hline 2 \end{array}$$

Then we bring down the 4. Now we divide 24 by 3.

$$\begin{array}{r} 58 \\ 3\overline{)174} \\ 15\downarrow \\ \hline 24 \\ 24 \\ \hline 0 \end{array}$$

We see that 174 divides into 3 equal groups of **58.**

Practice   **a.** 3)‾1‾4‾4‾   **b.** 4)‾1‾4‾4‾   **c.** 6)‾1‾4‾4‾

d. 225 ÷ 5   **e.** 455 ÷ 7   **f.** 200 ÷ 8

Problem set 75

1. *(62)* The chef used 3 eggs for each omelet. How many omelets would be made from 24 eggs? Use the EG pattern.

2. *(31)* Seventy-two young knights met peril in the forest. Twenty-seven fought bravely, but the others fled. How many young knights fled? Use the SWA pattern.

3. *(59)* Brian wore braces for 3 years. How many months is that?

4. *(67)* Fango could walk 3 miles in 1 hour. At that rate, how many miles could he walk in 10 hours? Use the EG pattern.

5. Fanga ran 28 miles in 4 hours. She ran at a rate of how
(70) many miles per hour?

6. Andrea bought dance shoes for $37.95 and tap shoes
(12) for $6.85. How much did she pay for both pairs of
shoes? Use the SSM pattern.

7. What fraction of this hexagon has
(71) not been shaded?

8. Each side of the hexagon in prob-
(60) lem 7 is 1 cm long. What is its
perimeter?

9. Jim began walking in the morning. He stopped
(33) walking later that morning. How long did he walk?

10. Use rounded numbers to estimate the difference
(70) between 903 and 395.

11. How long is segment *BC*?
(50)

12. How much greater than two hundred ninety-seven
(38) thousand, one hundred fifteen is three hundred
eighty-four thousand, two hundred? Use the L-S-D
pattern.

13. Compare: $27 \div 3^2 \bigcirc 27 \div \sqrt{9}$
(72,40)

14. $97.56
(28) + $8.49

15. $60.00
(51) − $54.78

16.   3764
(61)   2945
             301
        + 7538

17. 168 ÷ 3
(75)

18. 378 ÷ 7
(75)

19. 840 × 3
(68)

20. 4 × 564
(68)

21. 304 × 6
(68)

22. 4)‾136‾
(75)

23. 2)‾132‾
(75)

24. 6)‾192‾
(75)

25. N × 7 = 56
(50)

26. 4 × N = 56
(74,50)

LESSON 76

Area, Part 1

Facts Practice: 90 Division Facts (Test I in Test Masters)

Mental Math: Review.
   a. 300 × 30   **b.** 240 × 10   **c.** 11 × 4 × 10
   d. $10.00 − $9.28   **e.** $3.75 + $2.95   **f.** 467 − 63

Problem Solving: Henry has ten coins that total one dollar, but only one of the coins is a dime. What are the other nine coins?

We can find the **area** of a shape by counting the number of squares of a certain size that are needed to cover the shape. The surface within this rectangle is covered with squares that are 1 cm on each side. By counting the squares, we see that the area of the rectangle is 12 square centimeters.

4 cm

3 cm

1 cm

1 cm

This is one square centimeter

Notice that area is not the same as perimeter. Perimeter is the measure of the distance around a shape. Area is the measure of the surface within the shape.

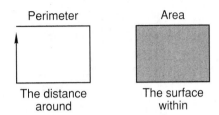

In this lesson we will practice finding areas of rectangles by counting squares.

Example Find the perimeter and the area of this rectangle.

Solution The length of the rectangle is 5 units. The width of the rectangle is 3 units. The perimeter is the distance around, so **the perimeter is 16 units.** The area is the number of square units that cover the surface within the rectangle. We count three rows of squares with five squares in each row. **The area is 15 square units.**

Practice Find the perimeter and area of each rectangle:

a.

b.

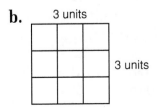

Problem set
76

1. With his bow and arrow, William Tell split 10 apples
(32) in half. How many apple halves were there?

2. Every third bead on the necklace was red. There were
(62) one hundred forty-one beads in all. How many beads
were red? (Make equal groups of three.)

3. Twenty-five percent of this square
(71,65) is shaded. What percent of the
square is not shaded?

4. Big Fox chased Little Rabbit 20 kilometers north, then
(50) 15 kilometers south. How far was Big Fox from where
he started? (Draw a diagram.)

5. At 11:45 a.m. Jason glanced at the clock. His doctor's
(33) appointment was in $2\frac{1}{2}$ hours. At what time was his
appointment?

6. Find the perimeter and area of this rectangle.
(76)

6 units

3 units

7. The car could go 30 miles on 1 gallon of gas. How far
(67) could the car go on 8 gallons of gas? Use the EG
pattern.

8. Two sevenths of the crowd cheered wildly. The rest of
(71) the crowd stood silently. What fraction of the crowd
stood silently?

9. $N + 2 = 3 \times 12$
(69)

10. Forty-two glops were required to make a good glue.
(59) Jean needed nine good glues. How many glops did she
need? Use the EG pattern.

11. Compare: $\frac{1}{2} \bigcirc \frac{2}{5}$. Draw and shade two rectangles to
(66) show the comparison.

12. 46,278 + 148,095
(61)

13. 48 + 163 + $\sqrt{81}$ + 83 + 3425
(61,40)

14. $10 − 10¢   **15.** 43,016 − 5987
(53)   (62)

16. 5 × 6 × 8
(72)

17.   486   **18.**   307   **19.**   460
(68)   × 7   (68)   × 8   (68)   × 9

20. 2)152   **21.** 6)264   **22.** 4)56
(75)   (75)   (74)

23. 230 ÷ 5   **24.** 91 ÷ 7   **25.** 135 ÷ 3
(75)   (74)   (75)

26. Write each amount of money by using a dollar sign
(45) and decimal point:

(a) 17¢   (b) 8¢   (c) 345¢

LESSON 77

Multiplying by Multiples of 10

Facts Practice: 90 Division Facts (Test I in Test Masters)

Mental Math: Review.

a. 5 × 6 × 10   b. 500 × 20   c. 21 × 3 × 10
d. 300 − 50   e. $5.00 − $1.95   f. 456 + 87

Patterns: Counting by fives from one we say this sequence:

1, 6, 11, 16, 21, 26, ...

What sequence do we say when we count by fives from three? Which two digits appear as final digits?

We remember that the multiples of 10 are the numbers we use when we count by tens. The last digit in every multiple of 10 is a zero. The first five multiples of 10 are

10, 20, 30, 40, 50

To multiply a whole number by a multiple of 10, we may write the multiple of 10 so that the zero "hangs out" to the right, as we show here.

$$
\begin{array}{r}
34 \\
\times \quad 20 \\
\end{array}
$$
← zero "hangs out" to the right

Next, we write a zero in the answer directly below the zero that we let hang out.

$$
\begin{array}{r}
34 \\
\times \quad 20 \\
\hline
0 \\
\end{array}
$$

Then we multiply by the first digit.

$$
\begin{array}{r}
34 \\
\times \quad 20 \\
\hline
680 \\
\end{array}
$$

Example 1 Multiply: 30 × 34

Solution We set up the problem so that the multiple of 10 is the bottom number. We let the zero "hang out."

$$
\begin{array}{r}
34 \\
\times \quad 30 \\
\end{array}
$$

Next, we write a zero in the answer directly below the zero in 30. Then we multiply by the first digit. Our answer is **1020.**

$$
\begin{array}{r}
1 \\
34 \\
\times \quad 30 \\
\hline
1020 \\
\end{array}
$$

Example 2 Multiply: $1.43 × 20

Solution We set up the problem so that the zero "hangs out." We write a zero below the line, and then multiply by the 2. We place the decimal point so that there are two digits after it. Finally, we write a dollar sign in front to get **$28.60.**

$$
\begin{array}{r}
\$1.43 \\
\times \qquad 20 \\
\hline
\$28.60 \\
\end{array}
$$

Practice   **a.** 75 × 10   **b.** 10 × 32   **c.** 10 × 53¢

d.   26   **e.** $1.64   **f.**   45
     × 20   ×   30   ×   50

Problem set
77

1. Find the perimeter and area of this rectangle.
(76)

8 units

3 units

2. Seventy-five beans were equally divided into five
(62) pots. How many beans were in each pot? Use the EG
pattern.

3. Five thousand, seven hundred people listened to the
(31) concert. Then some went home. Three thousand,
forty-two remained. How many people went home?
Use the SWA pattern.

4. James could go 7 miles on 1 sandwich. He wanted to
(70) go 84 miles. How many sandwiches did he need? Use
the EG pattern.

5. The starting time was before dawn. The stopping time
(33) was in the afternoon. What was the difference in the
two times?

Starting   Stopping

6. One hundred forty thousand is how much less than
(38) two hundred thousand? Use the L-S-D pattern.

7. What fraction of this pentagon is
(71) not shaded?

8. Is the shaded part of this pentagon
(65) more than 50% or less than 50%
of the pentagon?

9. According to this calendar, what
(64) is the date of the last Saturday in
July, 2019?

JULY 2019						
S	M	T	W	T	F	S
	1	2	3	4	5	6
7	8	9	10	11	12	13
14	15	16	17	18	19	20
21	22	23	24	25	26	27
28	29	30	31			

10. To what number is the arrow pointing?
(46)

7   8

11. Estimate the product of 78 and 4 by rounding 78 to the
(70) nearest ten before multiplying by 4.

12. Compare: $2^3 \bigcirc 2 \times 3$
(72,15)

13. $6.25 + $4 + $12.78
(53)

14. 142 + 386 + 570 + 864
(21)

15. $30.25   **16.**   149,384   **17.**   409
(20) $-\quad\quad B$ (62) $-\quad 98,765$ (77) $\times\quad 70$
       30.25
       ‾‾‾‾‾‾‾
       $13.06

18. 5 × $3.46   **19.** $0.79 × 6
(68)   (68)

20. 10 × 39¢   **21.** 6)‾90‾
(77)   (74)

22. 4)‾96‾   **23.** 8)‾456‾
(74)   (75)

24. 95 ÷ 5   **25.** 234 ÷ 3   **26.** 364 ÷ 7
(74)   (75)   (75)

LESSON
78

Division with Two-Digit Answers and a Remainder

Facts Practice: 100 Multiplication Facts (Test H in Test Masters)

Mental Math: Multiply two-digit numbers by numbers ending in zero.

   a. 12 × 20   **b.** 12 × 30   **c.** 12 × 40

Review:

   d. 36 + 29 + 230   **e.** $4.87 + $3.98   **f.** $1.00 − 36¢

Problem Solving: Segment *AC* is how much longer than segment *AB*?

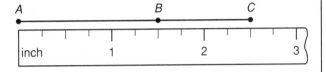

The method we use for dividing has four steps. These steps are divide, multiply, subtract, and bring down. Then we repeat the steps as necessary.

    Step 1. Divide.   ÷

    Step 2. Multiply.   ×

    Step 3. Subtract.   −

    Step 4. Bring down.   ↓

For each step we write a number. When we finish Step 4, we go back to Step 1 and repeat the steps until there are no digits left to bring down. Then whatever is left after the last subtraction is the remainder. We will continue to write the remainder after the division answer with a small "r" in front.

Example $5\overline{)137}$

Solution   **Step 1.** We divide $5\overline{)13}$ and write "2."

Step 2. We multiply 2 × 5 and write "10."

Step 3. We subtract 13 − 10 and write "3."

Step 4. We bring down 7 to make 37.

$$\begin{array}{r} 2 \\ 5\overline{)137} \\ -10 \\ \hline 37 \end{array}$$

Now we repeat the same four steps:

Step 1. We divide 37 by 5 and write "7."

Step 2. We multiply 7 × 5 and write "35."

Step 3. We subtract 37 − 35 and write "2."

Step 4. There are no more digits to bring down, so we are finished. We write the 2 as a remainder. Our answer is **27 r 2.**

$$\begin{array}{r} 27 \\ 5\overline{)137} \\ -10 \\ \hline 37 \\ -35 \\ \hline 2 \end{array}$$

If we divide 137 into 5 equal groups, there will be 27 in each group. There will also be 2 extra.

Practice   **a.** $3\overline{)134}$ **b.** $7\overline{)240}$ **c.** $5\overline{)88}$

d. 259 ÷ 8   **e.** 95 ÷ 4   **f.** 325 ÷ 6

Problem set 78

1. Find the perimeter and area of this rectangle.
(76)

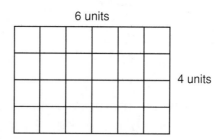

6 units

4 units

2. It took four spoonfuls to make one complete batch. How many spoonfuls were required to make 40 batches? Use the EG pattern.
(59)

3. The first number was forty-two thousand, five
(38) hundred. The second number was eighteen thousand,
forty-two. How much greater was the first number?
Use the L-S-D pattern.

4. Olive ran $\frac{3}{5}$ of the course but walked the rest of the
(71) way. What fraction of the course did she walk?

5. In problem 4, did Olive run more than 50% of the
(65) course or less than 50% of the course?

6. Jimmy had an octagon and a pentagon. What was the
(73) total of the number of sides in these two polygons?

7. The arrow points to what mixed number on this
(46) number line?

8. Mount Rainier stands four thousand, three hundred
(43) ninety-two meters above sea level. Use digits to write
this number.

9. Mickey could make 35 prizes in 7 minutes. How many
(70) prizes could he make in 1 minute? Use the EG pattern.

10. Estimate the sum of 681 and 903 by rounding each
(70) number to the nearest hundred before adding.

11. $12 + $8.95 + 75¢   **12.** 3627 + 5314 + 729
(53)   (61)

13. $30.00 − $21.49   **14.** 36,157 − 29,448
(51)   (62)

15.   43¢   **16.** $3.05   **17.** $2.63
(58) × 8   (68) ×   5   (68) ×   7

18. 47 × 30
(77)

19. 60 × 39
(77)

20. 85 × 40
(77)

21. 5)‾96‾
(78)

22. 7)‾156‾
(78)

23. 3)‾246‾
(75)

24. $\frac{216}{6}$
(75)

25. 156 ÷ 4
(75)

26. 195 ÷ 8
(78)

LESSON
79

Millimeters

Facts Practice: 100 Multiplication Facts (Test H in Test Masters)

Mental Math: Multiply two-digit numbers by numbers ending in zero.

   a. 21 × 20   **b.** 25 × 30   **c.** 25 × 20

Review:

   d. $10.00 − $2.98   **e.** 48 + 19 + 310   **f.** 490 − 125

Problem Solving: John figures that about 50% of the calories he consumes are from carbohydrates. John consumes about 2000 calories each day. About how many of those calories are from carbohydrates?

A centimeter is this long.

———

If we divide a centimeter into 10 equal lengths, each equal length is 1 millimeter long. A dime is about 1 millimeter thick.

 ◄─── 1 millimeter thick

The words *centimeter* and *millimeter* are based on Latin words. *Centum* is the Latin word for "hundred." This is why we say there are 100 cents in a dollar. The Latin word for "feet" is *pede*. A centipede looks like it has 100 feet. **There are 100 centimeters in 1 meter.**

Mille is the Latin word for "thousand." A millipede looks like it has 1000 feet. **There are 1000 millimeters in 1 meter. It takes 10 millimeters to equal 1 centimeter.**

Here we show a millimeter scale and a centimeter scale.

Millimeter | mm 10   20   30   40   50   60

Centimeter | cm 1   2   3   4   5   6

We use the letters "mm" to abbreviate the word *millimeter*.

Example 1   This segment is how many millimeters long?

mm 10   20   30   40   50   60

Solution   The length of the segment is **35 mm**.

Example 2   This paper clip is 3 cm long. How many millimeters long is it?

Solution   Each centimeter is 10 mm. We multiply 3 × 10 mm and find that the length of the paper clip is **30 mm**.

Practice   **a.** The thickness of a dime is about 1 mm. How many dimes would it take to form a stack that is 1 cm high?

b. How long is this segment?

mm 10   20   30   40

c. Each side of this square is 1 cm long. What is the perimeter of this square in millimeters?

Problem set 79

1. In the morning one hundred forty-two thousand,
   (12) seven hundred fifty-three athletes came. In the
   afternoon ninety-six thousand, five hundred twenty-
   two athletes came. How many athletes came in all?
   Use the SSM pattern.

2. Tracy has three hundred eighty-four baseball cards.
   (38) Nathan has two hundred sixty baseball cards. Tracy
   has how many more cards than Nathan? Use the L-S-D
   pattern.

3. Forty-two students could get on 1 bus. There were 30
   (59) buses. How many students could get on all the buses?
   Use the EG pattern.

4. To what number is the arrow pointing?
   (13)

```
     200                    400
```

5. Copy this hexagon and shade one
   (32) sixth of it.

6. (a) This match is how many centimeters long?
   (79)
   (b) This match is how many millimeters long?

7. Twenty-five percent of the students earned an A. What
   (65) percent of the students did not earn an A?

8. One yard equals 3 feet. If each side of a square is 1
(60) yard long, then what is the perimeter of the square in
feet?

9. Estimate the sum of 412, 695, and 379 by rounding
(70) each of the three numbers to the nearest hundred
before adding.

10. Segment *AB* is 35 mm long. Segment *AC* is 115 mm
(50) long. How long is segment *BC*?

A   B   C

11. Hugo could go 125 miles in 5 hours. How many miles
(70) could Hugo go in 1 hour? Use the EG pattern.

12. Urgo could go 21 miles in one hour. How many miles
(67) could Urgo go in 7 hours? Use the EG pattern.

13. $96.89
(28)   + $26.56

14.   *E*
(20)   − 28,165
     15,246

15.   362
(61)   47
    159
  1484
    305
  +   60

16. $10.00
(51)   − $1.73

17.   36,428
(62)   − 27,338

18.   78
(77)   ×   60

19. 9 × $4.63
(68)

20. 80 × 29¢
(77)

21. 4)328
(75)

22. 7)375
(78)

23. 5)320
(75)

24. $\frac{256}{8}$
(75)

25. 250 ÷ 6
(78)

26. 100 ÷ 9
(78)

27. *A* × 5 = 25 + 25
(69)

28. 4 × *W* = 60
(74,50)

LESSON 80

"Fraction-of-a-Group" Problems, Part 1

Facts Practice: 100 Multiplication Facts (Test H in Test Masters)

Mental Math: Multiply by 100.

    a. 25×100 **b.** 100×40 **c.** $12 \times 3 \times 100$

Review:

    d. $567 - 230$ **e.** $\$20.00 - \$12.50$ **f.** $\$6.49 + \$2.99$

Problem Solving: The charge for the taxi ride was $2.50 for the first mile and $1.50 for each additional mile. What was the charge for an 8-mile taxi ride?

We know that the fraction $\frac{1}{2}$ means that a whole has been divided into 2 parts. To find the number in $\frac{1}{2}$ of a group, we divide the total number in the group by 2. To find the number in $\frac{1}{3}$ of a group, we divide the total number in the group by 3. To find the number in $\frac{1}{4}$ of a group, we divide the total number in the group by 4.

Example 1 One half of the carrot seeds sprouted. If 84 seeds were planted, how many sprouted?

Solution We will begin by drawing a picture. The large rectangle stands for all the seeds. We are told that $\frac{1}{2}$ of the seeds sprouted, so we divide the large rectangle into 2 parts (into halves). Then we divide 84 by 2 and find that **42 seeds sprouted.**

Example 2 One third of the 27 students earned an A on the test. How many students earned an A on the test?

Solution   We start with a picture. The whole rectangle stands for all of the students. Since $\frac{1}{3}$ of the students earned an A, we divide the rectangle into 3 equal parts. To find how many students are in each part, we divide 27 by 3 and find that **9 students** earned an A on the test.

Example 3   One fourth of the team's 32 points were scored by Cliff. Cliff scored how many points?

Solution   We draw a rectangle. The whole rectangle stands for all 32 points. Cliff scored $\frac{1}{4}$ of the points, so we divide the rectangle into 4 parts. We divide 32 by 4 and find that each part is 8 points. **Cliff scored 8 points.**

$$\begin{array}{r} 8 \text{ points} \\ 4\overline{)32 \text{ points}} \end{array}$$

	32 points
$\frac{1}{4}$ scored by Cliff	8 points
$\frac{3}{4}$ not scored by Cliff	8 points
	8 points
	8 points

Example 4   What is $\frac{1}{5}$ of 40?

Solution   We sketch a rectangle to stand for 40. We divide the rectangle into five parts, and we divide 40 by 5. Each part is 8, so $\frac{1}{5}$ **of 40 is 8.**

$$\begin{array}{r} 8 \\ 5\overline{)40} \end{array}$$

Practice   **a.** What is $\frac{1}{3}$ of 60?   **b.** What is $\frac{1}{2}$ of 60?

           c. What is $\frac{1}{4}$ of 60?   **d.** What is $\frac{1}{5}$ of 60?

Problem set 80

1. Nine hundred forty-two thousand is how much greater than two hundred forty-two thousand? Use the L-S-D pattern.
   (38)

2. There were 150 seats at the Round Table. If 128 seats were taken, how many seats were empty? Use the SWA pattern.
   (31)

3. There were 3 surf riders for each child. How many surf riders were there for 17 children? Use the EG pattern.
   (59)

4. Stuart bought his lunch Monday through Friday. If each lunch cost $1.25, how much did he spend on lunch for the week? Use the EG pattern.
   (67)

5. Find the perimeter and area of this rectangle.
   (76)

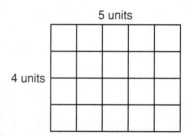

6. Rhonda read 30 pages a day on Monday, Tuesday, and Wednesday. She read 45 pages on Thursday and 26 pages on Friday. How many pages did she read in all?
   (12)

7. One half of the cabbage seeds sprouted. If 74 seeds were planted, how many sprouted? Draw a picture.
   (80)

8. In problem 7, what percent of the seeds sprouted?
   (65)

9. What is $\frac{1}{6}$ of 60? Draw a picture.
   (80)

10. The machine made 39 buttons in 1 minute. How many buttons would it make in 1 hour (60 minutes)? Use the EG pattern.
    (67)

11. An older machine made 160 buttons in 4 minutes.
(70) How many buttons could it make in 1 minute? Use the
EG pattern.

12. (a) This shirt button is how many
(79)   centimeters across?

(b) This shirt button is how many
       millimeters across?

13. Segment *AB* is 27 mm long. Segment *BC* is 48 mm
(50) long. How long is segment *AC*?

$$A \qquad\qquad B \qquad\qquad\qquad C$$

14. $8 + $9.48 + 79¢
(53)

15. 285 + 37 + 962 + 215
(21)

16. $100.00
(51) − $59.47

17.   37,102
(62)   − 18,590

18. $\sqrt{49} \times 2^3$
(72,40)

19. $1.63 × 40
(77)

20. 60 × 39
(77)

21. 7 × $2.56
(68)

22. 3$\overline{)89}$
(78)

23. 9$\overline{)234}$
(75)

24. $\dfrac{90}{6}$
(74)

25. 243 ÷ 7
(78)

26. 355 ÷ 5
(75)

27.   7
(2)   6
           3
           4
           2
           8
        + *N*
        ——
          54

LESSON
81

Division Answers Ending with Zero

Facts Practice: 100 Multiplication Facts (Test H in Test Masters)

Mental Math: The sum of 38 and 17 is 55. If we make 38 larger by 2 and 17 smaller by 2, then the addition is 40 + 15. The sum is still 55, but the mental addition is easier. Before adding these numbers, make one number larger and the other number smaller so that one of the numbers ends in zero.

    a. 38 + 27   **b.** 48 + 24   **c.** 59 + 32   **d.** 57 + 26

Problem Solving: In this subtraction problem some digits are missing. Copy this problem on your paper and fill in the missing digits.

$$\begin{array}{r} 123 \\ -\ 4\_ \\ \hline \_4 \end{array}$$

Sometimes two-digit division answers have a zero in them before the division is complete. It is important to continue the division until it is completed. Look at this problem.

Two hundred pennies are separated into 4 equal piles. How many pennies are in each pile?

This problem can be answered by dividing 200 by 4. We begin by dividing 4 into 20. We put a 5 on top. Then we multiply, and then we subtract.

$$\begin{array}{r} 5 \\ 4\overline{)200} \\ \underline{20} \\ 0 \end{array}$$

It may look like the division is complete, but it is not. The answer is not "five pennies in each pile." That would total only 20 pennies. There is another zero inside the division box that we have not used. **We have not finished dividing.** So we bring down the zero and divide again. Of course, 4 goes into zero 0 times, and zero times four equals zero.

$$
\begin{array}{r}
50 \\
4\overline{)200} \\
20\!\downarrow \\
\hline
00 \\
0 \\
\hline
0
\end{array}
$$

The answer is 50 pennies in each pile.

    Sometimes a two-digit division answer will end with a zero, yet there will be a remainder. We show this in the following example.

Example $3\overline{)121}$

Solution   We begin by dividing $3\overline{)12}$. After we subtract, we bring down the next digit, which is 1. Now we divide $3\overline{)1}$ (or $3\overline{)01}$, which means the same thing). Since 1 is less than 3, the answer is 0. We write this on top above the 1. Since 0 × 3 is 0, we write "0" below the 1 and subtract. The remainder is 1.

$$
\begin{array}{r}
4 \\
3\overline{)121} \\
12 \\
\hline
0
\end{array}
$$

$$
\begin{array}{r}
40 \ \text{r } 1 \\
3\overline{)121} \\
12 \\
\hline
01 \\
0 \\
\hline
1
\end{array}
$$

Practice   **a.** $3\overline{)120}$ **b.** $4\overline{)240}$ **c.** $5\overline{)152}$

            d. $4\overline{)121}$ **e.** $3\overline{)91}$ **f.** $2\overline{)41}$

Problem set 81

1. *(38)* The first number was one hundred forty-two thousand. The second number was one hundred eight thousand. How much larger was the first number?

2. *(31)* Four hundred eleven people waited to buy tickets. When the rain began, some went home. Then there were only two hundred forty-two in line. How many people went home when the rain began?

3. Each cookie contained 5 chocolate chips. How many
(59) chocolate chips would be in 115 cookies?

4. Harry could hop 420 spaces in 7 minutes. How many
(70) spaces could he hop in 1 minute?

5. What is the value of 5 pennies, 3 dimes, 2 quarters,
(45) and 3 nickels?

6. One fourth of the students earned an A. There were
(80) 280 students in all. How many students earned an A?
Draw a picture.

7. What percent of the students in problem 6 earned
(65) an A?

8. What is $\frac{1}{2}$ of 560? Draw a picture.
(80)

9. (a) The line segment shown is how many centimeters
(79)   long?

(b) The segment is how many millimeters long?

```
mm  10    20    30    40    50    60
   |||||||||||||||||||||||||||||||||||||

cm   1     2     3     4     5     6
```

10. It is evening. What time was it 6
(33) hours and 10 minutes ago?

11. Compare: $\frac{2}{3} \bigcirc \frac{2}{5}$. Draw and shade
(66) two rectangles to show the com-
parison.

12. Jenny could hop 72 spaces in 1 minute. How many
(67) spaces could she hop in 9 minutes?

13. $375.48
(28) + $536.70

14. 367,419
(61) + 90,852

15. 423
(21) 571
289
964
+ 380

16. $20.00
(51) − $19.39

17. 310,419
(62) − 250,527

18. 608
(68) × 7

19. 86
(77) × 40

20. 59¢
(58) × 8

21. 3)$\overline{180}$
(81)

22. 8)$\overline{241}$
(81)

23. 5)$\overline{323}$
(78)

24. $184 \div 6$
(81)

25. 7
(2) 6
4
5
9
4
3
7
+ N
56

26. 8
(2) 5
3
4
7
8
2
3
+ N
56

27. $279 \div 4$
(78)

28. $423 \div 7$
(81)

29. $9 \times M = 27 + 72$
(69)

30. $N \times 6 = 90$
(74,50)

LESSON 82

Finding Information to Solve Problems

Facts Practice: 100 Multiplication Facts (Test H in Test Masters)

Mental Math: Before adding, make one number larger and the other number smaller.

  a. 49 + 35   **b.** 57 + 35   **c.** 28 + 44

Review:

  d. 400 × 30   **e.** $10.00 − $4.98   **f.** 350 + 47 + 200

Problem Solving: Which day of the week is 7 days after Monday? Which day of the week is 71 days after Monday? Which day of the week is 699 days after Monday?

Part of the problem-solving process is finding the information needed to solve the problem. We may find information in graphs, tables, books, or other places. In this lesson we will practice solving problems in which we need to choose the information needed to solve the problem.

Example Read this information. Then answer the questions.

> *The school elections were held on Friday, February 2. Kim, Dan, and Miguel ran for president. Dan received 146 votes, and Kim received 117 votes. Miguel received 35 more votes than Kim.*

(a) How many votes did Miguel receive?

(b) Who won the election?

(c) Speeches were given on the Tuesday before the election. What was the date on which the speeches were given?

Solution (a) We read that Miguel received 35 more votes than Kim and that Kim received 117 votes. We add 35 and 117 and find that Miguel received **152 votes.**

(b) Miguel received the most votes, so the winner was **Miguel.**

(c) We read that the election was on Friday, February 2. The Tuesday before that is 3 days before that. We count back 3 days: February 1, January 31, January 30. The speeches were given on Tuesday, **January 30.**

Practice   Read this information. Then answer the questions.

> *Tom did yard work on Saturday. He worked for 3 hours in the morning and 4 hours in the afternoon. He was paid $4 for every hour he worked.*

a. How many hours did Tom work in all?

b. How much money did Tom earn in the morning?

c. How much money did Tom earn in all?

Problem set 82

1. Of the one thousand, six hundred forty-two fair
(17) maidens that Sir Lancelot rescued, only one hundred twenty-one remembered to thank him. How many did not thank Sir Lancelot?

2. Christie's car travels 18 miles on each gallon of gas.
(67) How far can it travel on 10 gallons of gas?

3. Humpty Dumpty weighed 160 pounds. If Humpty
(81) Dumpty broke into 8 equal pieces, how much did each piece weigh?

4. Soccer practice lasts for an hour and a half. If practice
(33) starts at 3:15 p.m., at what time does it end?

5. One third of the team's 36 points were scored by Lucy.
(80) How many points were scored by Lucy? Draw a picture.

6. Find the perimeter and area of this rectangle.
(76)

4 units

3 units

7. A dime is about 1 millimeter thick. A roll of 50 dimes
(79) is about how many centimeters long?

8. According to this calendar, the
(64) year 1902 began on what day of
the week?

DECEMBER 1901

S	M	T	W	T	F	S
1	2	3	4	5	6	7
8	9	10	11	12	13	14
15	16	17	18	19	20	21
22	23	24	25	26	27	28
29	30	31				

9. The chance of rain is 30%. What
(65) is the chance that it will not rain?

10. A meter equals 100 centimeters. If each side of a
(60) square is 1 meter, then what is the perimeter of the
square in centimeters?

11. $1.68 + 32¢ + $6.37 + $5
(53)

12. 43 + 24 + 8 + 67 + 4327
(61)

13. $10 − $8.63   **14.** 361,420 − 23,169
(51)   (62)

15. 5 × 4 × 5   **16.** 359 × 70   **17.** 50 × 74
(72)   (77)   (77)

18. 2)161   **19.** 5)400   **20.** 9)462
(81)   (81)   (78)

21. $\frac{216}{3}$ **22.** 159 ÷ 4   **23.** $\frac{490}{7}$
(75)   (78)   (81)

24. $\dfrac{126}{3}$
(75)

25. $360 \div \sqrt{36}$
(81,40)

26. $5 \times N = 120$
(75,50)

27. $\begin{array}{r} 473 \\ - N \\ \hline 274 \end{array}$
(20)

28.
(2)
$\begin{array}{r} 9 \\ 5 \\ 6 \\ 4 \\ 7 \\ 8 \\ 5 \\ 7 \\ + N \\ \hline 64 \end{array}$

29.
(2)
$\begin{array}{r} 4 \\ 3 \\ 7 \\ 6 \\ 8 \\ 2 \\ 9 \\ 1 \\ + N \\ \hline 64 \end{array}$

30. $\begin{array}{r} N \\ - 437 \\ \hline 943 \end{array}$
(20)

LESSON 83

Measuring Liquids

Facts Practice: 64 Multiplication Facts (Test G in Test Masters)

Mental Math: Before adding, make one number larger and the other number smaller.

  a. $55 + 47$ **b.** $24 + 48$ **c.** $458 + 33$

Review:

  d. $\$6.25 + \$1.95$ **e.** 15×30 **f.** $\$1.00 - \$0.38$

Patterns: Counting by fives from one we say this sequence:

$$1, 6, 11, 16, 21, 26, \dots$$

What sequence do we say when we count by fives from four? Which two digits appear as final digits?

Liquids like paint, milk, juice, and soda pop are measured in **liquid units. Ounces, pints, quarts,** and **gallons** are liquid units in the U.S. system. **Liters** and **milliliters** are liquid units in the metric system.

1 gallon

$\frac{1}{2}$ gallon

1 quart

2 liters

A liter is about the same amount as a quart.

The abbreviations for units of liquid measure are as follows:

oz	ounce	L	liter
pt	pint	mL	milliliter
qt	quart		
gal	gallon		

The chart below shows the number of units needed to equal the next larger unit.

Units of Liquid Measure

U.S. Units	Metric Units
16 oz = 1 pt 2 pt = 1 qt 4 qt = 1 gal	1000 mL = 1 L

Example 1   Two liters of water is how many milliliters?

Solution   From the chart we see that 1 liter is 1000 milliliters. Two liters would be twice as much. Thus, 2 liters of water equals **2000 milliliters of water.**

Example 2   A half gallon of milk is how many quarts?

Solution   One gallon of milk is 4 quarts. So a half gallon is half of 4 quarts. Since half of 4 is 2, a half gallon of milk is **2 quarts of milk.**

Practice   **a.** A quart is a "quarter" of a gallon. How many "quarters" make a whole?

b. Two pints equals a quart. How many ounces are in 2 pints?

c. Three liters is how many milliliters?

Choose the most reasonable measure:

d. Would a glass of chocolate milk be about 8 oz or 8 qt?

e. Would a can of pop be about 350 mL or 350 L?

Problem set 83

Use this information to answer questions 1–3:

Thirty students are going on a field trip. Each car can hold five students. The field trip will cost each student $5.

1. How many cars are needed for the field trip?
(82)

2. Altogether, how much money will be collected?
(82)

3. Don has saved $3.25. How much more does he need to go on the field trip?
(82)

4. During the summer the swim team practiced $3\frac{1}{2}$ hours a day. If practice started at 6:30 a.m., at what time did it end?
(33)

5. Half of the 48 pencils were sharpened. How many were not sharpened? What percent of the pencils were not sharpened?
(80,65)

6. What number is $\frac{1}{4}$ of 60? Draw a picture.
(80)

7. One gallon of water will be poured into 1-quart bottles. How many 1-quart bottles can be filled?
(83)

1 gal   1 qt

8. Each side of a regular polygon has the same length.
(79) This is a regular hexagon. How many **millimeters** is
the perimeter of this hexagon?

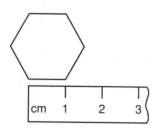

9. A mile is five thousand, two hundred eighty feet. The
(38) Golden Gate Bridge is four thousand, two hundred feet
long. The Golden Gate Bridge is how many feet less
than 1 mile long?

10. Estimate the product of 394 and 5 by rounding 394 to
(70) the nearest hundred before multiplying.

11. What number is halfway between 300 and 400?
(13) (*Hint:* Use a number line.)

12.
(20)
$$\begin{array}{r} z \\ -\ 476 \\ \hline 325 \end{array}$$

13.
(61)
$$\begin{array}{r} 37{,}156 \\ +\ 214{,}390 \\ \hline \end{array}$$

14.
(61)
$$\begin{array}{r} 1534 \\ 367 \\ 29 \\ 6 \\ +\ 142 \\ \hline \end{array}$$

15.
(51)
$$\begin{array}{r} \$100.00 \\ -\ \$31.53 \\ \hline \end{array}$$

16.
(62)
$$\begin{array}{r} 251{,}546 \\ -\ 37{,}156 \\ \hline \end{array}$$

17.
(68)
$$\begin{array}{r} 346 \\ \times\ \ 7 \\ \hline \end{array}$$

18.
(77)
$$\begin{array}{r} 96 \\ \times\ 30 \\ \hline \end{array}$$

19.
(68)
$$\begin{array}{r} \$0.59 \\ \times\ \ \ \ 8 \\ \hline \end{array}$$

20. $7\overline{)633}$
(81)

21. $5\overline{)98}$
(78)

22. $3\overline{)150}$
(81)

23. $329 \div 6$
(78)

24. $274 \div 4$
(78)

25. $247 \div 8$
(81)

26. $A \times 6 = 12 + 6$
(69)

27.
(2)

| 7 |
| 5 |
| 6 |
| 4 |
| 9 |
| 3 |
| 2 |
| + N |
| 54 |

28.
(2)

| 5 |
| 2 |
| 7 |
| 9 |
| 6 |
| 4 |
| 8 |
| + N |
| 61 |

29. $\sqrt{25} \times M = 135$
(75,50)

30.
(30)

$$\begin{array}{r} N \\ + 423 \\ \hline 618 \end{array}$$

LESSON
84

Fraction of a Set

Facts Practice: 64 Multiplication Facts (Test G in Test Masters)

Mental Math: Review.
  a. $77 + 14$ **b.** $87 - 40$ **c.** 35×100
  d. $\$5.00 - \$4.36$ **e.** $\$4.38 + \$2.99$ **f.** 120×10

Problem Solving: Segment AC is how much longer than segment AB?

There are seven circles in the set below. Three of the circles are shaded. The fraction of the set that is shaded is $\frac{3}{7}$.

$\dfrac{3}{7}$ Three circles are shaded.

          There are seven circles in all.

The number of members in the set is the bottom number (denominator) of the fraction. The number of members named is the top number (numerator) of the fraction.

Example 1   What fraction of the triangles is not shaded?

Solution   There are 9 triangles in all (denominator). There are 5 triangles that are not shaded (numerator). The fraction not shaded is $\frac{5}{9}$.

Example 2   In a class of 25 students, there are 12 girls and 13 boys. What fraction of the class is girls?

Solution   The total number of members in the class is 25 (denominator). The number of girls is 12 (numerator). The fraction of the class that is girls is $\frac{12}{25}$.

Practice   a. What fraction of the set is shaded?

b. What fraction of the set is not shaded?

c. In a class of 27 students, there are 14 girls and 13 boys. What fraction of the class is boys?

d. What fraction of the letters in the word ALABAMA is made up of A's?

Problem set 84

1. Michael caught sixty-two crawfish in the creek. James
   (12) caught seven crawfish, and Julie and John each caught twelve crawfish. Altogether, how many crawfish did these young people catch?

2. The Matterhorn is fourteen thousand, six hundred
   (38) ninety-two feet high. Mont Blanc is fifteen thousand, seven hundred eighty-one feet high. How much taller is Mont Blanc than the Matterhorn?

3. There are 25 squares on a bingo card. How many
(59) squares are there on 4 bingo cards?

4. Ninety-six books were placed on 4
(80) shelves so that there were the same number of books on each shelf. How many books were on each shelf?

96 books

5. One half of the 780 fans stood and cheered. How many
(65) fans stood and cheered? What percent of the fans stood and cheered?

6. How many years is ten centuries?
(64)

7. What fraction of this set is not
(84) shaded?

8. The 2-liter bottle contains how
(83) many milliliters of beverage?

9. Estimate the sum of 493 and 387.
(70)

10. What is the perimeter of this
(60) rectangle?

6 in.

4 in.

11. If this rectangle were to be cov-
(76) ered with squares with sides one inch long, how many squares would be needed?

12. $6.15 − ($0.57 + $1.20)
(55)

13. 3746 + 2357 + 489
(61)

14. $462 − Y = 205$
(20)

15. 43,160 − 8,459
(62)

16. 8 × 8 × 8
(72)

17. $3.54 × 6
(68)

18. 80×57
(77)

19. 704×9
(68)

20. $9\overline{)354}$
(78)

21. $7\overline{)285}$
(81)

22. $5\overline{)439}$
(78)

23. $515 \div 6$
(78)

24. $\dfrac{360}{4}$
(81)

25. $784 \div 8$
(75)

26. $50 = 5 \times R$
(50)

27.
(2)

$$\begin{array}{r} 4 \\ 7 \\ 8 \\ 5 \\ 7 \\ 6 \\ 4 \\ 3 \\ + N \\ \hline 56 \end{array}$$

28. $6^2 - \sqrt{36}$
(40)

29.
(30)
$$\begin{array}{r} 476 \\ + N \\ \hline 732 \end{array}$$

30.
(20)
$$\begin{array}{r} N \\ - 214 \\ \hline 638 \end{array}$$

LESSON 85

Pictographs and Bar Graphs • Tallying

Facts Practice: 64 Multiplication Facts (Test G in Test Masters)

Mental Math: Before adding, make one number larger and the other number smaller.

  a. $48 + 37$ **b.** $62 + 29$ **c.** $135 + 47$

Review:

  d. $30 \times 40 \times 20$ **e.** $\$20.00 - \$12.50$ **f.** $\$6.46 + \$1.98$

Problem Solving: Robby is mailing an envelope that weighs 6 ounces. Postage costs 32¢ for the first ounce and 23¢ for each additional ounce. Robby pays the postal clerk $2.00 for postage. How much money should he get back?

A **graph** is a picture that shows number information about the topic of the graph. There are many types of graphs. In this lesson we will look at **pictographs** and **bar graphs**.

Example 1   James made a pictograph to show the number of gummy bears of a certain color that he found in one package. According to this graph, what was the total number of yellow and green gummy bears in the package?

Gummy Bears in One Package

Solution   From the pictograph we can count the number of gummy bears of each color. There were 4 yellow gummy bears and 9 green gummy bears. To find the total of yellow and green gummy bears, we add 4 and 9 to get **13 yellow and green gummy bears.**

Example 2   This bar graph shows the same information as the pictograph, but in a different form. Use the bar graph to answer each question.

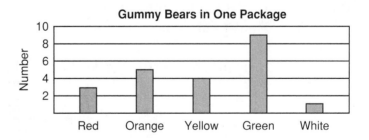

Gummy Bears in One Package

(a) How many red gummy bears were there?

(b) How many more gummy bears were green than were orange?

Solution   (a) The top of the bar showing the number of red gummy bears is halfway between 2 and 4 on the scale. So there were **3 red gummy bears.**

(b) There were 9 green gummy bears and 5 orange gummy bears. By subtracting, we find there were **4 more green gummy bears** than orange gummy bears.

Tallying   Tallying is a way of keeping track of a count. A tally mark is a short vertical mark that counts as one. Two marks count as two. Four marks with a diagonal line crossing them count as five.

I	II	III	IIII	JHT	JHT I
one	two	three	four	five	six

Practice   Use the information in the graphs from this lesson to answer questions a–c:

    a. How many gummy bears were in the package?

    b. The total of which two colors of gummy bears equals the number of green gummy bears?

    c. The total of which three colors of gummy bears equals the number of green gummy bears?

    d. What number is represented by this tally?   JHT JHT II

Problem set 85

    1. Pears cost 59¢ per pound. How much would 4 pounds of pears cost?
    (59)

    2. Find the perimeter and area of this rectangle.
    (76)

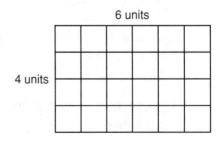

    3. There were three hundred twelve books on the floor. Frankie put one fourth of the books on a table. How many books did Frankie put on the table?
    (80)

4. What percent of the books in problem 3 were left on
(65) the floor?

5. To what number is the arrow pointing?
(46)

201   202

6. Estimate the sum of 272 and 483. Begin by rounding
(70) both numbers to the nearest hundred.

7. What fraction of this set is
(84) shaded?

8. One quart of milk is how many
(83) ounces?

9. One quart is a quarter of a gallon. So one quart is what
(65) percent of a gallon?

Use the information in this bar graph to answer questions
10 and 11:

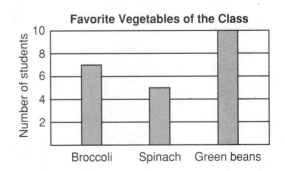

10. Spinach was the favorite vegetable of how many
(85) students?

11. Altogether, how many students said broccoli or
(85) spinach was their favorite vegetable?

12. $86.47
(28)   + $47.98

13.   362,458
(61)   + 179,682

14.   2358
(61)
     4715
      317
     2103
  +   62

15.   17,362
(62)   −   9,854

16. N
(20)   − $17.53
     $21.49

17. $6.95
(68)   ×   8

18.   46
(77)   ×   70

19.   460
(68)   ×   9

20. $8\overline{)716}$
(78)

21. $2\overline{)161}$
(81)

22. $7\overline{)434}$
(75)

23. $\dfrac{270}{9}$
(81)

24. $513 \div 6$
(78)

25. $\dfrac{267}{3}$
(75)

26. $3 \times A = 30 + 30$
(69)

27. $3^2 - 2^3$
(72)

28. $4 + 7 + 3 + 5 + 6 + 5 + 7 + 2 + N = 43$
(2)

LESSON
86

Division with Three-Digit Answers

Facts Practice: 64 Multiplication Facts (Test G in Test Masters)

Mental Math: Subtracting two-digit numbers is easier to do mentally if the second number ends in zero. By making both subtraction numbers larger, we can sometimes make subtraction easier while keeping the difference the same.

Instead of subtracting $\begin{array}{r} 45 \\ -\ 28 \\ \hline \end{array}$ we subtract $\begin{array}{r} 47 \\ -\ 30 \\ \hline \end{array}$

We added 2 to 28 so that the second number would end in zero. Then we added 2 to 45 to keep the difference the same.

a. $\begin{array}{r} 45 \\ -\ 39 \\ \hline \end{array}$ **b.** $\begin{array}{r} 56 \\ -\ 27 \\ \hline \end{array}$ **c.** $\begin{array}{r} 63 \\ -\ 48 \\ \hline \end{array}$ **d.** $\begin{array}{r} 82 \\ -\ 35 \\ \hline \end{array}$

We have practiced division problems that have two-digit answers. In this lesson we will practice division problems that have three-digit answers.

We remember that the method we use for dividing has four steps.

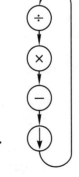

Step 1. Divide.

Step 2. Multiply.

Step 3. Subtract.

Step 4. Bring down.

For each step we write a number. When we finish Step 4, we go back to Step 1 and repeat the steps until there are no digits left to bring down.

Example 1 $3\overline{)794}$

Solution **Step 1.** Divide $3\overline{)7}$ and write "2."

Step 2. Multiply 2×3 and write "6."

Step 3. Subtract 6 from 7 and write "1."

Step 4. Bring down the 9, making 19.

REPEAT:

Step 1. Divide $3\overline{)19}$ and write "6."

Step 2. Multiply 6×3 and write "18."

Step 3. Subtract 18 from 19 and write "1."

Step 4. Bring down the 4, making 14.

REPEAT:

Step 1. Divide $3\overline{)14}$ and write "4."

Step 2. Multiply 4×3 and write "12."

Step 3. Subtract 12 from 14 and write "2."

Step 4. There are no digits to bring down. We are finished dividing. We write "2" as a remainder for a final answer of **264 r 2.**

```
  264 r 2
3)794
  6
  19
  18
  14
  12
   2
```

To divide dollars and cents by a whole number, we divide the digits just like we divide whole numbers. **The decimal point in the answer is placed directly above the decimal point inside the division box.** We write the dollar sign in front of the answer.

Example 2 $\$8.40 \div 3$

Solution We put a decimal point in the answer directly above the decimal point in the problem. Then we divide. We put a dollar sign in front of the answer.

```
   $2.80
3)$8.40
   6
   2 4
   2 4
    00
    00
     0
```

Practice

a. Copy this diagram and name the four steps of division.

b. 4)974

c. $7.95 ÷ 5

d. 6)1512

e. 8)$50.00

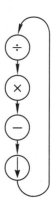

Problem set 86

1. Seven thousand, three hundred ninety-six is how much less than eleven thousand, eight hundred seventy-three?
(38)

2. Shannon has five days to read a 200-page book. If she wants to read the same number of pages each day, how many pages should she read each day?
(62)

3. Julie ordered a book for $2.99, a dictionary for $3.99, and a set of maps for $4.99. What was the price for all three items?
(12)

4. The prince searched 7 weeks for the princess. For how many days did he search?
(59)

5. One third of the books were placed on the first shelf. What fraction of the books were not placed on the first shelf?
(71)

6. What number is halfway between 2000 and 3000? (*Hint:* Use a number line.)
(13)

7. In the word HIPPOPOTAMI, what fraction of the letters is made up of P's?
(84)

8. Mary ran a 5-kilometer race. Five kilometers is how many meters?
(27)

9. $12 + 13 + 5 + N = 9 \times 8$
(69)

10. What is the perimeter of this
(60) triangle?

15 mm   20 mm

25 mm

11. The length of segment *AB* is 36 mm. The length of
(50) segment *AC* is 118 mm. What is the length of
segment *BC*?

A   B   C

12. $25 − ($19.71 + 98¢)   **13.** $365 + 10^2 + 3^3$
(55)   (72)

14. $5.00 − $2.92   **15.** 36,214 − 579
(51)   (62)

16. 5 × 6 × 9   **17.** 50 × 63   **18.** 478 × 6
(72)   (77)   (68)

19. 3)‾435‾   **20.** 7)‾867‾   **21.** 5)‾$13.65‾
(86)   (86)   (86)

22. 453 ÷ 6   **23.** 543 ÷ 4   **24.** $4.72 ÷ 8
(78)   (86)   (86)

25. $N × 6 = 120$ **26.** $4 × W = 132$
(50)   (50)

27. $4 + 8 + 7 + 6 + 4 + N + 3 + 6 + 5 = 55$
(2)

28. Find the perimeter and area of this rectangle.
(76)

5 units

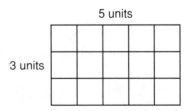

3 units

LESSON
87

Ounces, Pounds, and Tons

In Lesson 83 we used the word *ounce* to describe an amount of liquid. The word *ounce* can also describe an amount of weight. A liquid ounce of water weighs about one weight ounce. The units of weight of the U.S. system are **ounces, pounds,** and **tons.** A ton equals 2000 pounds. *Ounce* is abbreviated **oz.** *Pound* is abbreviated **lb.**

$$
\begin{array}{l}
16 \text{ oz} = 1 \text{ lb} \\
2000 \text{ lb} = 1 \text{ ton}
\end{array}
$$

Some boxes of cereal weigh 24 ounces. Some boys weigh 98 pounds. Some cars weigh 1 ton.

24 ounces   98 pounds   1 ton

Example 1   This book weighs about 2 pounds. Two pounds is how many ounces?

Solution   Each pound is 16 ounces, so 2 pounds is 2 × 16 ounces, which is **32 ounces.**

Example 2   The rhinoceros weighed 3 tons. Three tons is how many pounds?

Solution   Each ton is 2000 pounds, so 3 tons is 3 × 2000 pounds, which is **6000 pounds.**

Problem set 87   Use the information in this pictograph to answer questions 1–3:

Consumed by Matt in One Day

Water ▯▯▯▯▯▯
Soda ▯
Milk ▯▯▯▯
Juice ▯▯▯

▯ = 1 cup = 8 ounces

1. How many pints of liquid did Matt drink in 1 day?
(85)

2. Matt drank twice as much water as he did what other
(85) beverage?

3. Of which beverage did he drink exactly 1 quart?
(85)

4. There were 4 rooms. One fourth of the 56 guests
(80,65) gathered in each room. How many guests were in each room? What percent of the guests were in each room?

5. Which of these arrows could be pointing to 2500?
(13)

6. Estimate the sum of 682, 437, and 396.
(70)

7. What fraction of this set is
(84) shaded?

8. McGillicuddy weighed 9 pounds
(87) when he was born. How many
ounces is that?

9. (a) The segment is how many centimeters long?
(79) (b) The segment is how many millimeters long?

10. Four hundred forty-two thousand is how much greater
(38) than three hundred thousand?

11. If each side of a hexagon is 1 foot long, how many
(73) inches is its perimeter?

12. 93,417
(61) + 8,915

13. 42,718
(20) − K
     26,054

14. 1307
(61)   638
     5219
      138
   +   16

15. $100.00
(51) − $86.32

16. 405,158
(62) − 396,370

17. 567 × 8
(68)

18. 30 × 84¢
(77)

19. $2.08 × 4
(68)

20. 4$\overline{)\$15.00}$
(86)

21. $\frac{936}{6}$
(86)

22. 8$\overline{)4537}$
(86)

23. 452 ÷ 5
(81)

24. 378 ÷ 9
(75)

25. 960 ÷ 7
(86)

26. $\sqrt{16}$ × N = 100
(50)

27. 5 × B = 10^2
(50)

28.   4
(2)
       7
       3
       5
       4
       8
   + N
     45

29.   N
(20)   − 463
     214

30.   756
(20)   − N
     462

LESSON 88

Grams and Kilograms

Facts Practice: 90 Division Facts (Test I in Test Masters)

Mental Math: Find each difference by first enlarging both numbers so that the second number ends in zero.

  a. 72 − 58   **b.** 60 − 37   **c.** 83 − 35

Review:

  d. 76 + 19   **e.** 24 × 20   **f.** $6.98 + $1.49

Problem Solving: Which month is 12 months after May? Which month is 121 months after May? Which month is 1199 months after May?

Grams and kilograms are metric units of weight.[†] Recall that the prefix *kilo-* means "1000." Thus, a kilogram is 1000 grams.

$$1000 \text{ grams} = 1 \text{ kilogram}$$

This book weighs about 1 kilogram, so one of these pages weighs more than a gram. A dollar bill weighs about 1 gram. *Gram* is abbreviated **g.** *Kilogram* is abbreviated **kg.**

[†]There is a technical difference between the terms *weight* and *mass* that will be clarified in other coursework. In this book, we will use the word *weight* to include the meaning of both terms.

Example 1 Choose the more sensible measure:

(a) A pair of shoes   (b) A chicken   (c) A quarter
   1 g   1 kg   3 g   3 kg   5 g   5 kg

Solution (a) **1 kg**   (b) **3 kg**   (c) **5 g**

Example 2 Jason's rabbit weighs 4 kilograms. Four kilograms is how many grams?

Solution Each kilogram is 1000 grams. Four kilograms is 4 × 1000 grams, which is **4000 grams.**

Practice Choose the more sensible measure in these problems:

  a. Tennis ball   **b.** Cat   **c.** Bowling ball
    57 g   57 kg   6 g   6 kg   7 g   7 kg

  d. Seven kilograms is how many grams?

Problem set 88

1. Katie hit the ball seven hundred forty-two times on
(12) Monday, two hundred sixty-seven times on Tuesday, and eight hundred forty-seven times on Wednesday. How many times did she hit the ball in the 3 days?

2. Mickey bought apples at 5 cents per pound at the sale.
(62) She spent 95 cents. How many pounds of apples did she buy?

3. Bill placed 243 paint cans on the shelf. Ninety-five
(31) cans fell off during the earthquake. How many paint cans stayed on the shelf?

4. Pamela listened to half of a 90-minute tape. How
(80) many minutes of the tape did she hear?

5. One fourth of the guests gathered in the living room.
(71,65) What fraction of the guests did not gather in the living room? What percent of the guests did not gather in the living room?

6. Which of these arrows could be pointing to 2750?
(13)

7. Half of a gallon is a half gallon. Half of a half gallon is
(83) a quart. Half of a quart is a pint. Half of a pint is a cup.
A cup is what fraction of a quart?

8. Debbie weighed 3 kilograms when she was born. How
(88) many grams is that?

9. Estimate the product of 396 and 7.
(70)

10. It is afternoon. What time was it
(33) 12 hours ago?

11. Compare: $\frac{3}{4} \bigcirc \frac{4}{5}$. Draw and shade
(66) two rectangles to show the
comparison.

12. $4329 + 157 + (6385 - 9)$
(55)

13. $17.54 + 49¢ + $15
(53)

14. $36,147 - 16,280$
(62)

15. $50.00 - $42.60
(51)

16. $2\overline{)567}$ **17.** $6\overline{)\$34.56}$ **18.** $4\overline{)978}$
(86)   (86)   (86)

19. 398×6 **20.** 47×60 **21.** $8 \times \$6.25$
(68)   (77)   (68)

22. $970 \div \sqrt{25}$ **23.** $\dfrac{372}{3}$ **24.** $491 \div 7$
(86)   (86)   (81)

25. $8 \times N = 120$ **26.** $F \times 3^2 = 108$
(50)   (50)

27. $7 + 8 + 5 + 4 + N + 2 + 7 + 3 = 54$
(2)

28. Find the perimeter and area of this rectangle.
(76)

8 units

4 units

LESSON
89

Tables

Facts Practice: 90 Division Facts (Test I in Test Masters)

Mental Math: Before adding, make one number larger and the other number smaller.

  a. 38 + 46   **b.** 67 + 24   **c.** 44 + 28

Review:

  d. 30 × 50 × 10   **e.** $5.00 − $3.15

Problem Solving: How long is segment *AB*? How long is segment *BC*? Segment *AB* is how much longer than segment *BC*?

We have studied graphs that present number information in picture form. Another way of presenting number information is in a **table**.

Example   Use the information in the table to answer these questions.

Heights of Major Mountains

MOUNTAIN	FEET	METERS
Everest	29,028	8848
McKinley	20,320	6194
Kilimanjaro	19,340	5895
Matterhorn	14,691	4478
Pike's Peak	14,110	4301
Fuji	12,389	3776

(a) The Matterhorn is how many meters taller than Pike's Peak?

(b) Mount McKinley is how many feet taller than Mount Kilimanjaro?

Solution   We compare the heights by subtracting.

(a) We use the numbers from the meters column.

$$
\begin{array}{lr}
\text{Matterhorn} & 4478 \text{ m} \\
\text{Pike's Peak} & -\ 4301 \text{ m} \\
\hline
& \textbf{177 m}
\end{array}
$$

(b) We use the numbers from the feet column.

$$
\begin{array}{lr}
\text{McKinley} & 20{,}320 \text{ ft} \\
\text{Kilimanjaro} & -\ 19{,}340 \text{ ft} \\
\hline
& \textbf{980 ft}
\end{array}
$$

Practice   Use the information from the table given in the example to answer these questions:

a. Mount Kilimanjaro is how many meters taller than Mount Fuji?

b. Mount Everest is how many feet taller than the Matterhorn?

Problem set Use the information in this table to answer questions 1–4:
89

Average Yearly Rainfall

CITY	RAINFALL IN INCHES
Boston	43
Chicago	35
Denver	16
Houston	49
San Francisco	20

1. Which cities listed in the table average less than 2 feet
(89) of rain per year?

2. One year Houston received 62 inches of rain. This was
(89) how much more than its yearly average?

3. About how many inches of rain would Denver receive
(89) in 3 average years?

4. Copy and finish this bar graph to show the
(85) information in the rainfall table:

Average Yearly Rainfall

5. One fifth of the 60 eggs were
(80) placed in each box. How many
eggs were placed in each box?

6. Which of these arrows could be pointing to 2250?
(13)

7. Estimate the sum of 427, 533, and 764 by rounding
(70) each number to the nearest hundred before adding.

8. What fraction of this set is not
(84) shaded?

9. Forty-two oranges could be
(59) shipped in one box. Luther had 30
boxes. How many oranges could
he ship?

10. Only 5 apples would fit in one small box. If Roger had
(62) 145 apples, how many boxes did he need?

11. What is the perimeter of this
(60) square?

5 inches

12. If this square were to be covered
(76) with small squares one inch on
each side, how many squares
would be needed?

13. $20.10
(51)   − $16.45

14. $98.54
(28) + $9.85

15.   135
(61)   2416
    350
   4139
 +   67

16. 380 × 4
(68)

17. 97 × 80
(77)

18. 5)3840
(86)

19. $8.63 × 7
(68)

20. 8)$70.00
(86)

21. 6)3795
(86)

22. 4 × P = 160
(50)

23. $\dfrac{\sqrt{64}}{\sqrt{16}}$
(40)

24. $\dfrac{287}{7}$
(75)

25. $10 \times (6^2 + 2^3)$
(55)

Division with Zeros in Three-Digit Answers

Facts Practice: 90 Division Facts (Test I in Test Masters)

Mental Math: Before subtracting, make both numbers larger.

   a. 56 − 29   **b.** 43 − 18   **c.** 63 − 37

Review:

   d. 65 + 27   **e.** 365 × 10   **f.** $7.52 + $1.98

Patterns: Copy this pattern of dot triangles on your paper. Then continue the sequence by drawing the next three triangles in the pattern.

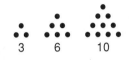

       3   6   10

Recall that the method we have used for dividing numbers has four steps.

Step 1. Divide.

Step 2. Multiply.

Step 3. Subtract.

Step 4. Bring down.

Every time we bring a number down, we return to Step 1 and divide again. Sometimes the answer to the next division is zero, and we end up with a zero in the answer.

Example 1 $3\overline{)618}$

Solution   **Step 1.** Divide $3\overline{)6}$ and write "2."

         Step 2. Multiply 2 × 3 and write "6."

         Step 3. Subtract 6 from 6 and write "0."

         Step 4. Bring down the 1, making 01 (which is 1).

$$\begin{array}{r} 2 \\ 3\overline{)618} \\ \underline{6} \\ 01 \end{array}$$

REPEAT:

Step 1. Divide $3\overline{)1}$ and write "0."

Step 2. Multiply 0×3 and write "0."

Step 3. Subtract 0 from 1 and write "1."

Step 4. Bring down the 8, making 18.

$$\begin{array}{r} \mathbf{206} \\ 3\overline{)618} \\ \underline{6} \\ 01 \\ \underline{0} \\ 18 \\ \underline{18} \\ 0 \end{array}$$

REPEAT:

Step 1. Divide $3\overline{)18}$ and write "6."

Step 2. Multiply 6×3 and write "18."

Step 3. Subtract 18 from 18 and write "0."

Step 4. There are no digits to bring down. The division is complete. The remainder is zero.

Example 2 $4\overline{)1483}$

Solution   **Step 1.** Divide $4\overline{)14}$ and write "3."

Step 2. Multiply 3×4 and write "12."

Step 3. Subtract 12 from 14 and write "2."

Step 4. Bring down the 8, making 28.

$$\begin{array}{r} \mathbf{370 \; r \; 3} \\ 4\overline{)1483} \\ \underline{12} \\ 28 \\ \underline{28} \\ 03 \\ \underline{0} \\ 3 \end{array}$$

REPEAT:

Step 1. Divide $4\overline{)28}$ and write "7."

Step 2. Multiply 7×4 and write "28."

Step 3. Subtract 28 from 28 and write "0."

Step 4. Bring down the 3, making 03 (which is 3).

REPEAT:

Step 1. Divide $4\overline{)03}$ and write "0."

Step 2. Multiply 0×4 and write "0."

Step 3. Subtract 0 from 3 and write "3."

Step 4. There are no digits to bring down. We are finished dividing. We write "3" as the remainder.

Practice **a.** List the four steps of division and draw the division diagram.

b. $4\overline{)815}$ **c.** $5\overline{)4152}$

d. $6\overline{)5432}$ **e.** $7\overline{)845}$

Problem set 90

1. If the chance of rain is 30%, then which is more likely—that it will rain or that it will not rain?
(65)

2. Monty's time for running the race was 12 seconds less than Ivan's time. Monty's time was 58 seconds. What was Ivan's time?
(82)

3. The whole rectangle is divided into 5 equal parts. Each part is what percent of the rectangle? (*Hint:* Divide 100 by 5.)
(80)

4. How many 6-inch-long sticks can be cut from a 72-inch-long stick of sugar cane?
(62)

5. One fifth of the leaves had fallen. What fraction of the leaves had not fallen?
(71)

6. Which of these arrows could be pointing to 5263?
(13)

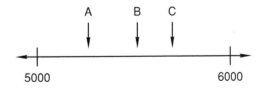

7. What fraction of the year is made up of months that have 31 days?
(84)

8. The prefix *kilo-* means what number?
(88)

9. Estimate the sum of 393, 589, and 241 by rounding each number to the nearest hundred before adding.
(70)

10. The sides of this triangle are equal
(79) in length. How many millimeters
is the perimeter of the triangle?

11. Three liters equals how many
(83) milliliters?

12. Wilma could run 5 miles in 1 hour. How long would it
(70) take her to run 40 miles?

13. 103,279
(61) + 97,814
	14. $36.14
	(28) + $27.95
		15. 3615
		(61) 294
		    18
		   378
		+ 4290

16. 39,420
(62) − 29,516

17. $60.50
(20) −   N
   $43.20

18. 604
(68) ×   9

19. 87
(77) × 60

20. $6.75
(68) ×   4

21. 3)618
(90)

22. 5)$21.50
(90)

23.   N
(30) + 1467
   2459

24. $\dfrac{600}{4}$
(90)

25. 543 ÷ 6
(81)

26. 472 ÷ 8
(75)

27. 9 × W = 9² + (9 × 2)
(69)

28.   4
(2)   2
   3
   N
   7
+ 2
  27

29.   5
(2)   2
   3
   1
   4
+ N
  27

30. N × 2 = 150
(50)

LESSON
91

Rounding to the Nearest Thousand

Facts Practice: 90 Division Facts (Test I in Test Masters)

Mental Math: Counting by 5's from 1, 2, 3, 4, or 5, we find five different final digit patterns: 1 and 6, 2 and 7, 3 and 8, 4 and 9, and 5 and 0. When a number ending in 5 is added to or subtracted from another number, the final digit of that number and of the answer will fit one of these five patterns.

a. 22	**b.** 22	**c.** 38	**d.** 38	**e.** 44	**f.** 44
+ 5	− 5	+ 5	− 5	+ 5	− 5

When we round a number to the nearest ten, we get a multiple of 10. The multiples of 10 are the numbers we get when we count by tens. **The multiples of 10 have a zero as the last digit.**

10, 20, 30, 40, 50, 60, …

When we round a number to the nearest hundred, we get a multiple of 100. The multiples of 100 are the numbers we get when we count by hundreds. **The multiples of 100 have zeros as the last two digits.**

100, 200, 300, 400, 500, 600, …

When we round a number to the nearest thousand, we get a multiple of 1000. The multiples of 1000 are the numbers we get when we count by thousands. **The multiples of 1000 have zeros as the last three digits.**

1000, 2000, 3000, 4000, 5000, 6000, …

We will use a number line to help us understand rounding to the nearest thousand.

Example Round 2781 to the nearest thousand.

Solution The number 2781 is between the thousand numbers 2000 and 3000. Halfway between 2000 and 3000 is 2500. As we see on the number line below, 2781 is nearer 3000 than 2000.

Rounding 2781 to the nearest thousand gives us **3000**.

Practice   Round each number to the nearest thousand:

    a. 5263   **b.** 4986   **c.** 7814   **d.** 8176

Problem set   **1.** Cecilia skated 27 times around the rink forward and
    91   (12) 33 times around the rink backward. In all, how many
    times did she skate around the rink?

    2. Nectarines cost 68¢ per pound. What is the price for 3
    (59) pounds of nectarines?

    3. In bowling, the sum of Amber's score and Beth's score
    (82) was equal to Sarah's score. If Sarah's score was 113
    and Beth's score was 55, what was Amber's score?

    4. One third of the 84 students were
    (80) assigned to each room. How many
    students were assigned to each
    room?

84 students

    5. Round 2250 to the nearest thousand.
    (91)

    6. What fraction of the letters in ARIZONA are not A's?
    (84)

    7. The African elephant weighed 7 tons. How many
    (87) pounds is that?

    8. The tip of this shoelace is how many millimeters long?
    (79)

9. Pick the more reasonable measure:
(88,83)   (a) Box of cereal: 400 g or 400 kg
     (b) Pail of water: 10 mL or 10 L

10. According to this calendar, what
(64) is the date of the last Tuesday in
February, 2019?

FEBRUARY 2019						
S	M	T	W	T	F	S
					1	2
3	4	5	6	7	8	9
10	11	12	13	14	15	16
17	18	19	20	21	22	23
24	25	26	27	28		

11. Forty-two thousand, seven hundred is how much
(38) greater than thirty-four thousand, nine hundred?

12. Find the perimeter and area of this rectangle.
(76)

10 units

5 units

13. Michelle could pack 75 packages in 3 hours. How
(70) many packages could she pack in 1 hour?

14. 6743 − (507 × 6)
(55)

15. $70.00 − $63.17
(51)

16. 3 × 7 × 0
(72)

17. $8.15 × 6
(68)

18. 67¢ × 10
(77)

19. 43,162 + 5,917
(61)

20. 2)$\overline{1216}$
(90)

21. 6)$\overline{4321}$
(90)

22. 8)$\overline{4537}$
(86)

23. 963 ÷ $\sqrt{9}$
(86)

24. 5^3 ÷ 5
(75)

25. $6.57 ÷ 9
(86)

26. 200 = 4 × B
(50)

27. D × 7 = 105
(50)

28.
(30)
```
   473
   286
+   N
------
   943
```

29.
(21)
```
    1
   12
    3
   14
    5
+ 26
```

30.
(21)
```
    2
   33
    4
   25
    6
+ 27
```

LESSON
92

Line Graphs

Facts Practice: 90 Division Facts (Test I in Test Masters)

Mental Math: Use the 5's patterns as you add.

   a. 36 + 15   **b.** 47 + 25   **c.** 28 + 35

Review:

   d. 40 × 40 × 10   **e.** \$10.00 − \$2.75   **f.** 72 − 39

Problem Solving: Estimate what percent of this circle is shaded.

Line graphs are often used to show how something has changed over a period of time.

Example   Sean kept a record of his test scores on a line graph. According to his line graph, how many correct answers did he have on Test 3?

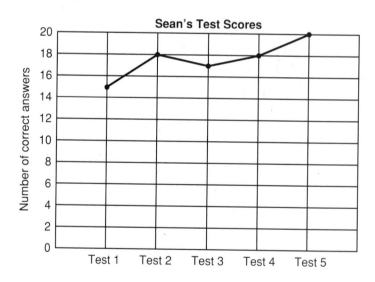

Solution   This line graph shows at a glance whether Sean's scores are going up or going down. To read this graph, we compare the level of a point with the scale on the left. The dot above Test 3 is halfway between 16 and 18 on the scale. This means that Sean's score on Test 3 was **17 correct answers.**

Practice   Use the graph of Sean's test scores from the example to answer questions a–d:

    a. From Test 1 to Test 2, Sean's score improved by how many answers?

    b. There were 20 questions on each test. How many questions did Sean miss on Test 4?

    c. On which test did Sean have a perfect score?

    d. Copy and finish this table using information from the line graph.

Sean's Test Scores

TEST	NUMBER OF CORRECT ANSWERS
1	15

    e. On Sherry's first five tests her scores were 18, 17, 20, 18, and 17. Draw a line graph that shows this information.

Problem set 92

    1. There were 35 students in the class but only 28 math
    (38) books. How many more math books did the class need?

    2. Each of the 7 children slid down the water slide 11
    (59) times. How many times did they slide in all?

    3. A bowling lane is 60 feet long. How many yards is
    (49) that?

    4. Justin carried the baton four hundred forty yards. Eric
    (12) carried it eight hundred eighty yards. Joe carried it one thousand, three hundred twenty yards, and Braulio carried it one thousand, seven hundred sixty yards. In all, how many yards was the baton carried?

5. One third of the members voted no. What fraction of
(71) the members did not vote no?

6. Round 6821 and 4963 to the nearest thousand. Then
(91,70) add the rounded numbers.

7. What fraction of the days of the week start with the
(84) letter S?

8. Together, Bob's shoes weigh about 1 kilogram. Each
(88) shoe weighs about how many grams?

Use the information in this line graph to answer
questions 9–11:

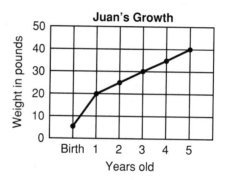

9. About how many pounds did Juan weigh on his
(92) second birthday?

10. About how many pounds did Juan gain between his
(92) third and fifth birthdays?

11. Copy and complete this table
(92,89) using information from the line
graph.

Juan's Growth	
AGE	WEIGHT
At birth	6 pounds
1 year	
2 years	

12. If 65% of the lights are on, then
(65) what percent of the lights are off?

13. $60.75
(28) + $95.75

14. $16.00
(51) − $15.43

15. $63.14
(28)   2.75
      39.81
       4.62
   +   0.87

16.   320
(77) ×   30

17.   465
(68) ×   7

18. $0.98
(68) ×   6

19. $425 \div 6$
(81)

20. $\$6.00 \div 8$
(75)

21. $625 \div 5$
(86)

22. $3 \times R = 150$
(50)

23. $10^2 + T = 150$
(72,30)

24. $1 + 7 + 2 + 6 + 9 + 4 + N = 37$
(2)

25. If the 3-inch square is covered
(76) with 1-inch squares, how many of
the 1-inch squares are needed?

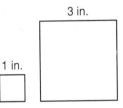

3 in.

1 in.

LESSON
93

Sales Tax • Change Back

Sales tax   Sales tax is an extra amount of money that must be paid when items are purchased. The amount of tax depends upon the amount purchased. The sales tax rate varies from state to state and sometimes from county to county.

Example 1   Sam bought six bolts for 89¢ each. The sales tax was 32¢. How much did Sam spend in all?

Solution   First we find the price of the six bolts. Then we add the sales tax.

$$
\begin{array}{r}
\overset{5}{89}¢ \\
\times\ \ 6 \\
\hline
534¢ = \$5.34
\end{array}
$$

The six bolts cost $5.34. To this we add the sales tax.

$$
\begin{array}{rl}
\$5.34 & \text{price of bolts} \\
+\ \$0.32 & \text{sales tax} \\
\hline
\$5.66 & \text{total price}
\end{array}
$$

The total price, including tax, was **$5.66.**

Change back   If we do not have the exact amount of money we need to buy something at a store, we pay more than the price and then we get money back. To find how much we should get in change, we subtract the total price from how much we paid.

Example 2   Midge bought a pair of pants for $23.99. The tax was $1.56. She paid the clerk $40.00. How much money should she get back?

Solution   First we figure out the total price.

$$
\begin{array}{rl}
\$23.99 & \text{price of pants} \\
+\ \$\ 1.56 & \text{sales tax} \\
\hline
\$25.55 & \text{total price}
\end{array}
$$

Now we subtract the total price from how much she paid.

$$
\begin{array}{rl}
\$40.00 & \text{how much she paid} \\
-\ \$25.55 & \text{total price} \\
\hline
\$14.45 & \text{change back}
\end{array}
$$

Midge should get **$14.45** back from the clerk.

Practice   **a.** Sarah bought three pairs of socks for $2.24 each pair. The sales tax was 34¢. What was the total price?

b. Mark paid $10.00 for a tape that cost $6.95. The sales tax was 49¢. How much money should Mark get back in change?

Problem set 93

1. Ali Baba brought home 30 bags. Each bag contained 320 gold coins. How many coins were there in all?
(59)

2. The movie was 3 hours long. If it started at 11:10 a.m., at what time did it end?
(33)

3. Tony is reading a 212-page book. If he has finished page 135, how many pages does he still have to read?
(31)

4. Brad, Jan, and Jordan each scored one third of the team's 42 points. They each scored how many points?
(80)

42 points

5. Round 4286 to the nearest thousand.
(91)

6. The shirt cost $16.98. The tax was $1.02. Sam paid $20. How much money should Sam get back?
(93)

7. What fraction of the letters in the following word is made up of I's?
(84)

SUPERCALIFRAGILISTICEXPIALIDOCIOUS

Use the information given to answer questions 8–10:

In the first 8 games of this season, the Rio Hondo football team won 6 games and lost 2 games. They won their next game by a score of 24 to 20. The team plays 12 games in all.

8. In the first 9 games of the season, how many games did Rio Hondo win?
(82)

9. Rio Hondo won its ninth game by how many points?
(82)

10. What is the greatest number of games Rio Hondo
(82) could win this season?

11. Compare: $3 \times 4 \times 5 \bigcirc 5 \times 4 \times 3$
(72,15)

12.
(20)
$$\begin{array}{r} M \\ -\ 13{,}728 \\ \hline 25{,}723 \end{array}$$

13.
(30)
$$\begin{array}{r} N \\ +\ 95{,}486 \\ \hline 568{,}372 \end{array}$$

14.
(28)
$$\begin{array}{r} \$\ 8.53 \\ 12.47 \\ 5.25 \\ 0.67 \\ +\ 14.37 \\ \hline \end{array}$$

15.
(77)
$$\begin{array}{r} 638 \\ \times\ \ \ \ 50 \\ \hline \end{array}$$

16.
(68)
$$\begin{array}{r} 472 \\ \times\ \ \ \ 9 \\ \hline \end{array}$$

17.
(68)
$$\begin{array}{r} \$6.09 \\ \times\ \ \ \ \ 6 \\ \hline \end{array}$$

18. $3\overline{)921}$
(90)

19. $5\overline{)678}$
(86)

20. $4\overline{)2400}$
(90)

21. $\$12.60 \div 5$
(86)

22. $\$14.34 \div 6$
(86)

23. $\$46.00 \div 8$
(86)

24. $9^2 = 9 \times N$
(69)

25. $5 \times W = 5 \times 10^2$
(69)

26.
(2)
$$\begin{array}{r} 5 \\ 4 \\ 3 \\ A \\ 4 \\ 7 \\ 6 \\ 5 \\ +\ 9 \\ \hline 62 \end{array}$$

27. One fourth of the months start with the letter J. What
(65) percent of the months start with the letter J?

LESSON
94

Area, Part 2

Facts Practice: 64 Multiplication Facts (Test G in Test Masters)

Mental Math: Use the 5's patterns as you subtract.

   a. 83 − 15   **b.** 29 + 35   **c.** 76 + 15

Review:

   d. 100 × 30   **e.** \$5.00 − \$4.38   **f.** 67 + 26

Problem Solving: How long is segment *AB*? How long is segment *BC*? Segment *BC* is how much longer than segment *AB*?

We can find the area of a figure by counting the number of squares of a certain size needed to cover the figure. We might use square centimeters, square meters, square inches, or square feet to measure an area. We even use square miles to measure large areas of land. We often use the letters "sq." as an abbreviation for the word *square*.

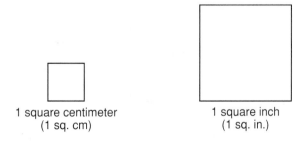

1 square centimeter
(1 sq. cm)

1 square inch
(1 sq. in.)

Large squares like square meters, square feet, and square miles are too large to fit on a page in this book, so we use scale drawings that are smaller than actual size. Here we show a scale drawing of a 4-feet-by-2-feet tabletop.

4 feet

2 feet

To find the area of this tabletop, we calculate the number of 1-foot-by-1-foot squares needed to cover it. The length of the sides of the tabletop show us that we could fit 2 rows of 4 squares on the table.

We find that the area is 8 square feet.

Example Morton Ranch is 4 miles long and 3 miles wide. What is the area of Morton Ranch?

Solution The area of the ranch is the number of square miles of land it occupies. Mile marks have been made on the illustration. By extending these marks across the drawing, we find that the area of the ranch is **12 square miles.**

Practice Find the area of each rectangle:

Problem set 94

1. If it is not a leap year, what is the total number of days in January, February, and March?
(64)

2. The shoemaker's wife made each of the 12 elves a pair of pants and 2 shirts. How many pieces of clothing did she make?
(59)

3. John did seven more chin-ups than Larry did. If John did eighteen chin-ups, how many chin-ups did Larry do?
(38)

4. Jan drove 200 miles on 8 gallons of gas. Her car
(70) averaged how many miles on each gallon of gas?

5. Melinda paid $20.00 for a book that cost $8.95. The
(93) tax was 54¢. How much money should she get back?

6. The tally for 8 is ⊥⊥⊥ |||. What is the tally for 9?
(85)

7. If each side of an octagon is 1 centimeter, what is its
(79) perimeter in millimeters?

8. $\sqrt{36} + N = 7 \times 8$
(69)

9. Illustrate this fraction-of-a-group problem: One third
(80) of the 18 marbles were cat's-eyes. How many of the
marbles were cat's-eyes?

10. Robert picked 46 peaches in 1 day. At that rate, how
(67) many peaches could he pick in 6 days?

11. Mary picked 3640 peaches in 7 days. She picked an
(70) average of how many peaches each day?

12.
(30)
$$\begin{array}{r} F \\ +\ 27{,}415 \\ \hline 271{,}052 \end{array}$$

13.
(28)
$$\begin{array}{r} \$96.47 \\ +\ \$5.85 \\ \hline \end{array}$$

14.
(21)
$$\begin{array}{r} 35 \\ 45 \\ 25 \\ 65 \\ 115 \\ 20 \\ +\ 25 \\ \hline \end{array}$$

15. $3 \times 6 \times 3^2$
(72)

16. $462 \times \sqrt{9}$
(68)

17.
(77)
$$\begin{array}{r} 36 \\ \times\ 50 \\ \hline \end{array}$$

18.
(68)
$$\begin{array}{r} 476 \\ \times\ 7 \\ \hline \end{array}$$

19. $\dfrac{524}{4}$
(86)

20. $6\overline{)4216}$
(90)

21. $5\overline{)\$26.30}$
(86)

22. $\$3.70 \div 2$
(86)

23. $786 \div 3$ **24.** $4902 \div 7$ **25.**
(86)   (90)
$$
\begin{array}{r}
4 \\
3 \\
2 \\
7 \\
6 \\
8 \\
+ \; N \\
\hline
47
\end{array}
$$

26. Find the perimeter and area of this square.
(94,60)

3 yards

3 yards

LESSON 95

Multiplying by Tens, Hundreds, and Thousands

Facts Practice: 64 Multiplication Facts (Test G in Test Masters)

Mental Math: Review.
  a. $10.00 − $7.50   **b.** 400×20 **c.** $58 + 35$
  d. 250×10 **e.** $7.68 + $1.95   **f.** $85 − 38$

Problem Solving: Sandra bought a CD for $12.95. Sales tax was $1.10. She paid for her purchase with a $10 bill and a $5 bill. Sandra got back five coins. What were the coins Sandra received in change?

When we multiply a whole number by 10, the answer has the same digits as the number that was multiplied, and the answer has an additional zero at the end.

$$
\begin{array}{r}
123 \\
\times \quad 10 \\
\hline
1230
\end{array}
$$

When we multiply a whole number by 100, there are two additional zeros at the end.

$$
\begin{array}{r}
123 \\
\times \quad 100 \\
\hline
12,300
\end{array}
$$

When we multiply a whole number by 1000, there are three additional zeros at the end.

$$
\begin{array}{r}
123 \\
\times \quad 1{,}000 \\
\hline
123{,}000
\end{array}
$$

When we multiply dollars and cents, we remember to place the decimal point two places from the right-hand side of the product.

Example   Multiply mentally:

(a) 37 × 10   (b) $6.12 × 100   (c) 45¢ × 1000

Solution   (a) We write "37" with one zero at the end: **370.**

(b) We write "612" with two zeros at the end, and then place the decimal point and dollar sign: **$612.00.**

(c) We write "45" with three zeros at the end. This makes 45000¢, which is **$450.00.**

Practice   Multiply mentally:

a. 365 × 10   **b.** 52 × 100   **c.** 7 × 1000

d. $3.60 × 10   **e.** 420 × 100   **f.** $2.50 × 1000

Problem set 95   Use the information in the graph to answer questions 1–3:

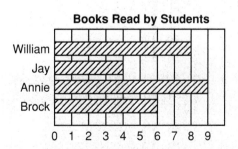

1. Which student has read exactly twice as many books as Jay?
(85)

2. Brock's goal is to read 10 books. How many more books does he need to read to reach his goal?
(85)

3. If the books Annie has read have an average of 160
(85) pages each, how many pages has she read?

4. Jim saw some pentagons. The pentagons had a total of
(73) 100 sides. How many pentagons did Jim see?

5. Tom bought a rectangular piece of land that was 3
(94) miles long and 2 miles wide. Fifty percent of the land
could be farmed. How many square miles could be
farmed?

6. Max bought 10 pencils for 24¢ each. The tax was 14¢.
(93) What was the total price?

7. A pitcher of orange juice is about:
(83)
    A. 2 ounces   B. 2 liters   C. 2 gallons

8. Draw a triangle so that two sides are perpendicular.
(29)

9. Illustrate this fraction-of-a-group problem: One fourth
(80) of the 48 gems were rubies. How many of the gems
were rubies?

10. What percent of the gems in problem 9 were not
(65) rubies?

11.   463,271   **12.**   728
(61)   + 175,349   (30) +   _C_
                                  1205

13.   68,418   **14.** $30.00
(62)   – 47,615   (51) – $14.75

15. 36 × 10   **16.** 100 × 42   **17.** $2.75 × 1000
(95)   (95)   (95)

18.   317   **19.**   206   **20.**   37
(68)   ×   4   (68)   ×   5   (77)   × 40

21. $3\overline{)492}$
(86)

22. $5\overline{)860}$
(86)

23. $6\overline{)\$9.30}$
(86)

24. $168 \div 2^3$
(75)

25. $\$20.00 \div 8$
(90)

26. $2315 \div \sqrt{16}$
(86)

27. Find the perimeter and area of
(94,60) this rectangle.

10 ft

6 ft

LESSON
96

Multiplying Round Numbers Mentally

Facts Practice: 64 Multiplication Facts (Test G in Test Masters)

Mental Math: Multiply by tens, hundreds, and thousands.

  a. 25×10 **b.** 25×100 **c.** 25×1000

Review:

  d. $\$10.00 - \$6.75$ **e.** $58 + 35$ **f.** $37 - 19$

Problem Solving: Estimate what percent of this circle is shaded.

If we have memorized the multiplication facts, we can multiply round numbers "in our heads." To do this, we multiply the first digits and count zeros. Study the multiplication below.

$$
\begin{array}{r}
40 \\
\times\ 30 \\
\hline
1200
\end{array}
$$

— two zeros

4×3 — two zeros

We can find the product of 40 and 30 by multiplying 4 and 3 and then attaching two zeros.

Example 1   Multiply mentally: 60 × 80

Solution   We multiply six times eight and get 48. There is one zero in 60 and one zero in 80. We attach two zeros to 48 and get 4800.

6 x 8 is 48

4800

Example 2   Multiply mentally: 30 × $7.00

Solution   We multiply three times seven and get 21. There are three zeros in the problem. We attach three zeros to 21 and get 21,000. Since we multiplied dollars and cents, we place the decimal point two places from the right and write a dollar sign.

3 x 7 is 21

$210.00

Example 3   Multiply mentally: 400 × 700

Solution   Four times seven is 28. We attach four zeros and get 280,000.

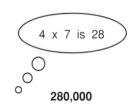

4 x 7 is 28

280,000

Practice   Multiply mentally:

    a. 70 × 80   **b.** 40 × 50

    c. 40 × $6.00   **d.** 30 × 800

Problem set 96

1. It takes Jennifer 20 minutes to walk to school. At what
(33) time should she start for school if she wants to arrive at 8:10 a.m.?

2. Before her haircut Rapunzel weighed 125 pounds.
(31) After her haircut she weighed 118 pounds. What was the weight of the hair that was cut?

3. Lucy bought a hamburger for $2.89, fries for $0.89,
(93) and a drink for 79¢. The tax was 28¢. She paid with a $5 bill. How much money should Lucy get back?

4. $5^2 + 5^2 + N = 10^2$
(69)

5. According to this calendar, Octo-
(64) ber 30, 1902, was what day of the week?

OCTOBER 1902						
S	M	T	W	T	F	S
						1
2	3	4	5	6	7	8
9	10	11	12	13	14	15
16	17	18	19	20	21	22
23	24	25	26	27	28	29
30	31					

6. The tally for 16 is ЖЖ ЖЖ ЖЖ |. What
(85) is the tally for 17?

7. Round three thousand, seven hundred eighty-two to
(91) the nearest thousand.

8. The limousine weighed 2 tons. How many pounds is 2
(87) tons?

9. Illustrate this fraction-of-a-group problem: One fifth
(80) of the 45 horses were pintos. How many of the horses were pintos?

10. What percent of the horses in
(80) problem 9 were pintos? (*Hint:* Find $\frac{1}{5}$ of 100%.)

11. Debby could run 90 laps in 3
(70) hours. How many laps could she run in 1 hour?

12. Mick could run 30 laps in 1 hour. How many laps
(67) could he run in 5 hours?

13.   17,414
(61) + 89,875

14. $36.47
(28) + $9.68

15.   6
(21)   8
            17
            23
           110
            25
        + 104

16.   31,425
(62) − 17,633

17. $30.00
(51) − $13.45

18.   476
(68) ×   7

19.   804
(68) ×   5

20. 100 × 23¢
(95)

21. 60 × 30
(96)

22. 70 × $2.00
(96)

23. 3)$6.27
(90)

24. 7)820
(86)

25. 6)333
(78)

26. 625 ÷ √25
(86)

27. 4000 ÷ 2³
(90)

28. 1370 ÷ 2
(86)

29. Find the perimeter and area of
(94,60)   this square.

10 m

LESSON 97

Multiplying Two Two-Digit Numbers, Part 1

Facts Practice: 64 Multiplication Facts (Test G in Test Masters)

Mental Math: Find half of each number.

  a. 10   **b.** 40   **c.** 48   **d.** 64   **e.** 86

Review:

  f. $3.54 + $2.99   **g.** 75 + 37   **h.** 86 − 38

Patterns: Fifteen dots can be arranged in a triangle pattern. Sixteen dots can be arranged in a square pattern. Thirty-six dots can be arranged in either a triangle pattern or a square pattern. Make a triangle and a square using 36 dots for each pattern.

15   16

When we multiply by a two-digit number, we take three steps. First we multiply by the ones' digit. Next we multiply by the tens' digit. Then we add the products together. To multiply 34 by 12, we multiply 34 by 2 and multiply 34 by 10. Then we add.

$$
\begin{array}{rl}
34 \times 2 = 68 & \text{product} \\
\underline{34 \times 10 = 340} & \text{product} \\
34 \times 12 = 408 & \text{total}
\end{array}
$$

It is easier to write the numbers one above the other when we multiply.

$$\begin{array}{r} 34 \\ \times\ 12 \end{array}$$

First we multiply 34 by 2 and write the answer with the last digit in the ones' column.

$$\begin{array}{r} 34 \\ \times\ 12 \\ \hline 68 \end{array}$$

Next we multiply 34 by 1. **Since this 1 is actually 10, we record the last digit of this multiplication in the tens' column, as we show on the left.** Then we add the results of the two multiplications and get 408.

$$\begin{array}{r} 34 \\ \times\ 12 \\ \hline 68 \\ 34 \\ \hline 408 \end{array} \quad \text{or} \quad \begin{array}{r} 34 \\ \times\ 12 \\ \hline 68 \\ 340 \\ \hline 408 \end{array}$$

On the right, we show another way. We put the zero after the 34 to show that 10 times 34 is 340. Then we add. We get the same answer both ways.

Example Multiply:
$$\begin{array}{r} 31 \\ \times\ 23 \end{array}$$

Solution We multiply 31 by 3 and write the last digit of the product in the ones' column.

$$\begin{array}{r} 31 \\ \times\ 23 \\ \hline 93 \end{array}$$

Now we multiply 31 by 2. Since this 2 is actually 20, we write the last digit of the product in the tens' column. Then we add to get **713**.

$$\begin{array}{r} 31 \\ \times\ 23 \\ \hline 93 \\ 62 \\ \hline 713 \end{array} \quad \text{or} \quad \begin{array}{r} 31 \\ \times\ 23 \\ \hline 93 \\ 620 \\ \hline 713 \end{array}$$

Practice

a. $\begin{array}{r} 32 \\ \times\ 23 \\ \hline \end{array}$	**b.** $\begin{array}{r} 24 \\ \times\ 32 \\ \hline \end{array}$	**c.** $\begin{array}{r} 43 \\ \times\ 12 \\ \hline \end{array}$	**d.** $\begin{array}{r} 34 \\ \times\ 21 \\ \hline \end{array}$
e. $\begin{array}{r} 32 \\ \times\ 32 \\ \hline \end{array}$	**f.** $\begin{array}{r} 23 \\ \times\ 14 \\ \hline \end{array}$	**g.** $\begin{array}{r} 13 \\ \times\ 32 \\ \hline \end{array}$	**h.** $\begin{array}{r} 33 \\ \times\ 33 \\ \hline \end{array}$

Problem set 97

Use this information to answer questions 1–3:

Freeman rode his bike 2 miles from his house to Daniel's house. Together, they rode 4 miles to the lake. Daniel caught 8 fish. At 3:30 p.m., they rode back to Daniel's house. Then Freeman rode home.

1. Altogether, how far did Freeman ride his bike?
(82)

2. It took Freeman an hour and a half to get home from the lake. At what time did he get home?
(82)

3. Daniel caught twice as many fish as Freeman. How many fish did Freeman catch?
(82)

4. Shep bought some feed for $12.97. Tax was 91¢. He paid $20.00. How much money should he get back?
(93)

5. Estimate the sum of 4876 and 3149. Round each number to the nearest thousand before adding.
(91)

6. This is the tally for what number?   ЖН ЖН |||
(85)

7. What is the perimeter of a pentagon if each side is 20 centimeters long?
(73,60)

8. Find the length of this segment to the nearest quarter inch.
(48)

9. Illustrate this fraction-of-a-group problem: One half of the 18 players were on the field. How many players were on the field?
(80)

10. A dime is $\frac{1}{10}$ of a dollar. What fraction of a dollar is a penny?
(28)

11. A dime is what percent of a dollar? (*Hint:* Find $\frac{1}{10}$ of
(80)   100%.)

12. 21,316 − 14,141   **13.** $20 − 20¢
(62)   (53)

14.   31   **15.**   32   **16.**   14
(97)   × 21   (97)   × 31   (97)   × 32

17.   11   **18.**   12   **19.** 30 × 800
(97)   × 11   (97)   × 14   (96)

20. 7)‾1000‾   **21.** 3)‾477‾   **22.** 5)‾2535‾
(86)   (86)   (90)

23. $64.80 ÷ 9   **24.** 716 ÷ 4   **25.** 352 ÷ 8
(90)   (86)   (75)

26. Find the perimeter and area of
(94,60)   this rectangle.

20 in.

10 in.

LESSON
98

Division Word Problems
with Remainders

Facts Practice: 90 Division Facts (Test I in Test Masters)

Mental Math: Find half of each number.
  a. 20   **b.** 24   **c.** 50   **d.** 46   **e.** 120

Review:
  f. $5.00 − $3.67   **g.** 52 + 39   **h.** 42 − 25

Problem Solving: A half-ton pickup truck can carry a load
                     weighing half of a ton. How many 100-pound
                     sacks of cement can a half-ton pickup truck
                     carry?

We have been practicing division word problems in which
there are no remainders. In this lesson we will begin
practicing division word problems in which there are
remainders. These problems should be read with special
care so that we know exactly what the question is.

Example   The packer placed 100 bottles into boxes that held 6 bottles each.

(a) How many boxes were **filled?**

(b) How many bottles were **left over?**

(c) How many boxes were needed to hold **all the bottles?**

Solution   These three questions have three different answers. To answer all three questions, we begin by dividing 100 by 6.

$$\begin{array}{r} 16 \text{ r } 4 \\ 6\overline{)100} \\ \underline{6} \\ 40 \\ \underline{36} \\ 4 \end{array}$$ This means that the 100 bottles can be separated into 16 groups of 6. Then there will be 4 extra bottles.

(a) The result 16 r 4 means that **16 boxes can be filled,** but there are still 4 more bottles.

(b) The result 16 r 4 means that after filling 16 boxes, there are still **4 bottles left over.**

(c) The result 16 r 4 means that after filling 16 boxes, there are still 4 more bottles. These 4 bottles will not fill another box, but another box is needed to hold them. Thus, in order to hold all the bottles, **17 boxes are needed.**

Practice   Tomorrow 32 students are going on a field trip. Each car can carry 5 students.

  a. How many cars can be filled?

  b. How many cars will be needed?

Rafik found 31 quarters in his bank. He made stacks of 4 quarters each.

  c. How many stacks of 4 quarters did he make?

  d. How many extra quarters did he have?

  e. If he made a "short stack" with the extra quarters, how many stacks were there in all?

Problem set 98

1. Peter packed 6 ping-pong balls in each package. There
(98) were 100 ping-pong balls to pack.

(a) How many packages could he fill?

(b) How many ping-pong balls were left over?

2. One hundred twenty-three is how much less than
(38) three hundred twenty-one?

3. Four giant pretzels are 59¢ each. Sales tax is 16¢. What
(93) is the total price?

4. Twenty-four inches is how many feet?
(49)

5. What is the length of segment *YZ* in millimeters? In
(79,50) centimeters?

6. $7 + 7 + N = 7^2$
(69)

7. It is morning. What time will it be
(33) 5 hours and 20 minutes from
now?

8. Write the number 7,528 in
(42) expanded form. Then use words
to write the number.

9. Illustrate this fraction-of-a-group problem: One fifth
(80) of the 25 band members missed the note. How many
band members missed the note?

10. What percent of the band members in problem 9
(80) missed the note?

11. $6.35 + $14.25 + $0.97 + $5
(53)

12. 16,456 − 7638
(62)

13. $10.00 − (46¢ + $1.30)
(55)

14. 28 × 1000
(95)

15.   13
(97)   × 13

16.   12
(97)   × 11

17. $8.67
(68)   ×   9

18.   31
(97)   × 31

19.   16
(97)   × 31

20. 7)3542
(90)

21. 6)$33.00
(90)

22. 8)4965
(90)

23. 482 ÷ 5
(78)

24. 2700 ÷ 9
(90)

25. 2700 ÷ $\sqrt{9}$
(90)

26. $3 × N = 6^2$
(69)

27.   4
(2)   2
           3
           5
           N
           8
           6
         + 3
        ————
          45

28. The classroom was 40 feet long
(94) and 30 feet wide. How many 1-
foot floor tiles were needed to
cover the floor?

40 ft

30 ft

LESSON
99

Mixed Numbers and Improper Fractions

Facts Practice: 90 Division Facts (Test I in Test Masters)

Mental Math: Find half of each number.

 a. 80   **b.** 140   **c.** 260   **d.** 420   **e.** 2800

Review:

 f. $2.95 + $6.38   **g.** 428 + 35   **h.** 75 − 39

Patterns: In this sequence, 25¢ is added to each term to make the next term. Copy this sequence and continue it to $3.00.

$0.25, $0.50, $0.75, $1.00, $1.25, ...

Here we show a picture of $1\frac{1}{2}$ shaded circles. Each whole circle has been divided into two half circles. We see that $1\frac{1}{2}$ is the same as **three halves,** which is written $\frac{3}{2}$.

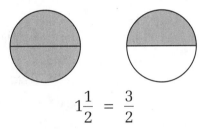

$$1\frac{1}{2} = \frac{3}{2}$$

The mixed number $1\frac{1}{2}$ equals the fraction $\frac{3}{2}$. The fraction $\frac{3}{2}$ is greater than 1. Fractions that are greater than or equal to 1 are called **improper fractions.** In this lesson we will draw pictures to show which mixed numbers and improper fractions are equal to each other.

Example   Draw circles to show that $2\frac{3}{4}$ equals $\frac{11}{4}$.

Solution   We begin by drawing 3 circles and shading $2\frac{3}{4}$.

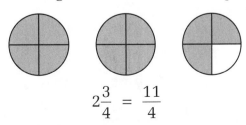

$$2\frac{3}{4} = \frac{11}{4}$$

We see that the fraction part of $2\frac{3}{4}$ is **fourths. So we divide all the circles into fourths.** We count 11 shaded fourths. This shows that $2\frac{3}{4}$ equals $\frac{11}{4}$.

Practice

a. Draw circles to show that $1\frac{3}{4} = \frac{7}{4}$.

b. Draw circles to show that $2\frac{1}{2} = \frac{5}{2}$.

c. Draw circles to show that $1\frac{1}{3} = \frac{4}{3}$.

Problem set 99

1. The coach divided 33 players as equally as possible into 4 teams.
(98)

(a) How many teams had exactly 8 players?

(b) How many teams had 9 players?

2. On the package there were two 25-cent stamps, two 20-cent stamps, and one 15-cent stamp. Altogether, how much did the stamps that were on the package cost?
(53)

3. Don read 20 pages each day. How many pages did he read in 2 weeks?
(59)

4. The Frog Prince leapt 27 feet to get out of the well. How many yards did he leap?
(49)

5. What is the perimeter of this triangle in centimeters?
(79,60)

20 mm   20 mm

30 mm

6. This is the tally for what number?
(85)

7. This dropperful of water is about:
(83)

A. 2 milliliters

B. 2 liters

C. 2 pints

8. $87 + 0 = 87 \times N$
(69)

9. Illustrate this fraction-of-a-group problem: One third
(80) of the 24 students finished early. How many students
finished early?

10. What percent of a dollar is a quarter?
(65)

11. $478.63   **12.**   137,140   **13.** $60.00
(28) + $32.47   (62) − 129,536   (51) − $24.38

14. 70 × 90   **15.**   11   **16.**   12
(96)   (97) × 13   (97) × 12

17. $4.76   **18.**   21   **19.**   17
(68) ×   8   (97) × 13   (97) × 21

20. 4)‾3‾0‾0‾0   **21.** 5)‾6‾3‾5   **22.** 7)‾4‾2‾6
(90)   (86)   (81)

23. 8)‾3‾6‾1‾4   **24.** $\frac{2736}{6}$
(86)   (86)

25. How much is one fourth of $10.00?
(80)

26. Draw and shade circles to show that $1\frac{1}{2}$ equals $\frac{3}{2}$.
(99)

27. Use a pencil and a ruler to sketch a rectangle that is
(25) 5 cm long and 4 cm wide.

28. What is the perimeter and area of the rectangle in
(94,60) problem 27?

LESSON
100

Multiplying Two Two-Digit Numbers, Part 2

Facts Practice: 90 Division Facts (Test I in Test Masters)

Mental Math: Find half of each product.
  a. Half of 10×12 **b.** Half of 10×24 **c.** Half of 10×480

Review:
  d. $20.00 - $17.50 **e.** $56 + 239$ **f.** $284 - 65$

Problem Solving: There were two gallons of punch for the class party. The punch was served in 8-ounce cups. Two gallons of punch was enough to fill how many cups? (Remember that 16 ounces is a pint, two pints is a quart, two quarts is a half gallon, and two half gallons is a gallon.)

We remember that three steps are required to multiply by a two-digit number:

1. Multiply by the ones' digit. Record the last digit of this product in the ones' column.

2. Multiply by the tens' digit. **Record the last digit of this product in the tens' column.**

3. Add to find the total.

In this lesson we will do multiplications that require carrying.

Example 1 Multiply: $\begin{array}{r} 46 \\ \times\ 27 \\ \hline \end{array}$

Solution First we multiply 46 by 7. This product is 322.

$$\begin{array}{r} \overset{4}{4}6 \\ \times\ 27 \\ \hline 322 \end{array}$$

Now we multiply 46 by the 2 of 27. First we multiply 6 by 2 and get 12. Since we are actually multiplying by 20, **we record the 2 in the tens' column** and write the 1 above the 4.

$$
\begin{array}{r}
1 \\
4 \\
46 \\
\times\ 27 \\
\hline
322 \\
2
\end{array}
$$

Then we multiply the 4 by 2 and add 1 to get 9. Then we add the products and get **1242.**

$$
\begin{array}{r}
1 \\
4 \\
46 \\
\times\ 27 \\
\hline
322 \\
92 \\
\hline
1242
\end{array}
\qquad \text{or} \qquad
\begin{array}{r}
1 \\
4 \\
46 \\
\times\ 27 \\
\hline
322 \\
920 \\
\hline
1242
\end{array}
$$

Example 2 Multiply:
$$
\begin{array}{r}
46 \\
\times\ 72 \\
\hline
\end{array}
$$

Solution First we multiply 46 by 2 and get 92.

$$
\begin{array}{r}
1 \\
46 \\
\times\ 72 \\
\hline
92
\end{array}
$$

Next we multiply 46 by 7 and add the products to get **3312.**

$$
\begin{array}{r}
4 \\
1 \\
46 \\
\times\ 72 \\
\hline
92 \\
322 \\
\hline
3312
\end{array}
\qquad \text{or} \qquad
\begin{array}{r}
4 \\
1 \\
46 \\
\times\ 72 \\
\hline
92 \\
3220 \\
\hline
3312
\end{array}
$$

Practice   **a.**   38   **b.**   49   **c.**   84   **d.**   65
              × 26   × 82   × 67   × 48

Problem set   Use the information in the graph to answer questions 1–3:
100

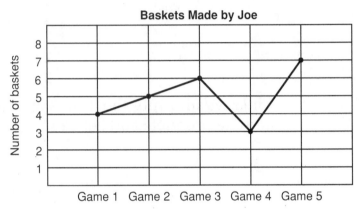

1. How many baskets did Joe make in the first game?
(92)

2. Each basket is worth 2 points. How many points did
(92)   Joe score in Game 5?

3. How many more points did Joe score in Game 5 than
(92)   in Game 3?

4. The 3-pound melon cost $1.44. What was the cost per
(62)   pound?

5. What is the product of the fourth multiple of 5 and the
(65)   tenth multiple of 7?

6. Sammy bought a pair of shoes for $47.99. The sales tax
(93)   was $2.88. Sammy gave the clerk $60.00. How much
      money should he get back?

7. If the perimeter of a square is 1 foot, how many inches
(60)   long is each side?

8. A dollar bill weighs about 1 gram. How many dollar
(88)   bills would it take to weigh 1 kilogram?

9. Illustrate this fraction-of-a-group problem: One fourth
(80) of the 64 clowns had red noses. How many clowns
had red noses?

10. What percent of the clowns in problem 9 did not have
(65) red noses?

11. Kerry knew that her trip would take about 7 hours. If
(33) she left at half past nine in the morning, at what time
would she plan to arrive?

12. Jill's boat would hold 42 containers. Each container
(59) would hold 8 big fish. How many big fish could Jill
put in her 42 containers?

13. Eighty-eight horseshoes are enough to shoe how many
(62) horses?

14. $37,134$
(61) $+ 52,891$

15. $\$85.00$
(51) $- \$68.65$

16.
(21)
$$
\begin{array}{r}
26 \\
32 \\
54 \\
213 \\
60 \\
143 \\
+ \quad 8 \\
\hline
536
\end{array}
$$

17. 47×100
(95)

18. 60×700
(96)

19. 328
(68) $\times \quad 4$

20. 43
(97) $\times 32$

21. 25
(100) $\times 35$

22. $5\overline{)4317}$
(86)

23. $8\overline{)\$44.00}$
(90)

24. $6\overline{)3963}$
(90)

25. $426 \div 3$
(86)

26. $2524 \div 4$
(86)

27. Draw and shade circles to show that $2\frac{1}{2}$ equals $\frac{5}{2}$.
(99)

28. $4 + 3 + 27 + 35 + 8 + N = 112$
(2)

LESSON 101

Decimal Place: Tenths

Facts Practice: 90 Division Facts (Test I in Test Masters)

Mental Math: Find half of each product.
   a. Half of 10 × 18   **b.** Half of 10 × 44   **c.** Half of 10 × 260

Review:
   d. $14.56 + $1.98   **e.** 37 − 18   **f.** 248 + 155

Patterns: Each number in this sequence is doubled to make the next number in the sequence. Find the next three numbers.

1, 2, 4, 8, __, __, __, ...

Part of this square is shaded. We show three ways to write how much of the square is shaded.

One tenth is shaded.

$\frac{1}{10}$ is shaded.

0.1 is shaded.

One tenth can be written with words.

One tenth can be written as a fraction: $\frac{1}{10}$

One tenth can be written as a decimal number: 0.1

We use **place value** to write "tenths" as a decimal number. We remember that the dot is called a **decimal point.** The digit just to the right of the decimal point is in the tenths' place. The digit in the tenths' place tells how many tenths. When we use a decimal point to help us write a number, we call the number a **decimal number** or just a **decimal.**

Decimal point

The digit in the tenths' place in 0.3 is 3. We read this number as "three tenths." We say the digit in the tenths' place and then say the word *tenths*. We usually write a zero in front of the decimal point.

.3 and 0.3 and $\frac{3}{10}$ are read as "three tenths"

.1 and 0.1 and $\frac{1}{10}$ are read as "one tenth"

.5 and 0.5 and $\frac{5}{10}$ are read as "five tenths"

Example 1 Write the shaded part of this square as a fraction and as a decimal number.

Solution The square is divided into 10 parts. Three of these parts are shaded. Three tenths of the square is shaded.

$\frac{3}{10}$ is the fraction   **0.3** is the decimal number

Example 2 Which of these fractions equals 0.7?

A. $\frac{1}{7}$ B. $\frac{7}{8}$ C. $\frac{7}{10}$

Solution The decimal number 0.7 is seven tenths. The correct choice is **C** because

$$0.7 = \frac{7}{10}$$

Practice **a.** What fraction names the shaded part of this square?

b. What decimal number names the shaded part of the square?

c. What fraction names the part that is not shaded?

d. What decimal number names the part that is not shaded?

e. Write a fraction equal to 0.6.

f. Write a decimal number equal to $\frac{4}{10}$.

g. Write seven tenths as a fraction and as a decimal number.

1. Three quarters, four dimes, two nickels, and seven
(45) pennies is how much money?

2. Trudy separated the 37 math books as equally as
(98) possible into 4 stacks.

  (a) How many stacks had exactly 9 books?

  (b) How many stacks had 10 books?

3. Martin paid $1 for a folder and received 52¢ back in
(93) change. If the tax was 3¢, how much did the folder
cost?

4. Frank wrote each of his 12 spelling words five times.
(59) In all, how many words did he write?

5. Round 5456 to the nearest thousand. Round 2872 to
(91) the nearest thousand. Find the sum of the two
rounded numbers.

6. What is the tally for 10?
(85)

7. Part of this square is shaded.
(101)
  (a) Use a fraction to write the
      shaded part.

  (b) Use a decimal number to write
      the shaded part.

8. Illustrate this fraction-of-a-group problem: One sixth
(80) of the 48 crayons are broken. How many crayons are
broken?

9. Segment *AB* is 32 mm long. Segment *BC* is 26 mm
(50) long. Segment *AD* is 91 mm long. How many
millimeters long is segment *CD*?

```
      A           B           C           D
      •───────────•───────────•───────────•
```

10. 39,279 − 9,816
(62)

11. $63.75 + $184.75
(28)

12. $60.00 − ($49.38 + 75¢)
(55)

13. $6.08
(68)   ×   8

14.   47
(100)   × 24

15.   36
(100)   × 62

16. 53 × 30
(100)

17. 63 × 37
(100)

18. 100 × 32
(95)

19. 4)3456
(86)

20. 8)6912
(86)

21. 7)$50.40
(90)

22. Draw and shade circles to show that $1\frac{1}{4}$ equals $\frac{5}{4}$.
(99)

23. $5^2 + \sqrt{25} + N = 30$
(72,2)

24. Draw a square with sides 4 cm long.
(25)

25. Shade 50% of the square in problem 24. How many
(94,65) square centimeters did you shade?

LESSON
102

Naming Hundredths with Decimal Numbers

Facts Practice: 90 Division Facts (Test I in Test Masters)

Mental Math: Five is half of 10. To multiply by 5 we may multiply by half of 10. For example, 5 × 12 equals half of 10 × 12. Find each product by multiplying by "half of 10."

   a. 5 × 16   **b.** 5 × 24   **c.** 5 × 28   **d.** 5 × 64

Problem Solving: About what percent of the circle is shaded? About what percent of the circle is not shaded?

The first place to the right of the decimal point is the tenths' place. If a 1 is written in the tenths' place, it has a value of one tenth.

$$0.1 \quad \text{means} \quad \frac{1}{10}$$

If a 3 is written in the tenths' place, it has a value of three tenths.

$$0.3 \quad \text{means} \quad \frac{3}{10}$$

The second place to the right of the decimal point is the **hundredths' place.** If a 1 is written in the hundredths' place, it has a value of one hundredth.

$$0.01 \quad \text{means} \quad \frac{1}{100}$$

If a 3 is written in the hundredths' place, it has a value of three hundredths.

$$0.03 \quad \text{means} \quad \frac{3}{100}$$

If we write "34" to the right of the decimal point, we mean thirty-four hundredths.

$$0.34 \quad \text{means} \quad \frac{34}{100}$$

When we write the fraction $\frac{34}{100}$, we **show** that the denominator is 100. When we write the decimal number 0.34, we **understand** that the denominator is 100. It is customary, but not necessary, to write a zero in front of the decimal point. The values of .34 and 0.34 are equal.

$$.34 = 0.34$$

Example 1   Part of this square is shaded.

(a) Use a fraction to write the shaded part.

(b) Use a decimal number to write the shaded part.

Solution   The square is divided into hundredths. Twenty-three hundredths are shaded.

(a) Twenty-three hundredths as a fraction is $\frac{23}{100}$.

(b) Twenty-three hundredths as a decimal number is **0.23.**

Example 2   (a) Write a fraction that equals 0.37.

(b) Write a decimal number that equals $\frac{29}{100}$.

Solution (a) The decimal number 0.37 is written with two places to the right of the decimal point. That means the denominator is 100. Thus, 0.37 equals $\frac{37}{100}$.

(b) A fraction with a denominator of 100 can be written as a decimal with two places to the right of the decimal point. So $\frac{29}{100}$ equals **0.29.**

Practice Write a fraction for each decimal number:

   a. 0.37   **b.** 0.07   **c.** 0.99   **d.** 0.03

Write a decimal number for each fraction:

   e. $\frac{61}{100}$ **f.** $\frac{9}{100}$ **g.** $\frac{25}{100}$ **h.** $\frac{4}{100}$

   i. What decimal number names the shaded part of this square?

   j. What decimal number names the part that is not shaded?

Problem set 102   Use the information given to answer questions 1–3:

   Mary invited 14 friends for lunch. She plans to make 12 tuna sandwiches, 10 bologna sandwiches, and 8 roast beef sandwiches.

   1. How many sandwiches will she make in all?
   (82)

   2. Including Mary, each person can have how many sandwiches?
   (82)

   3. If she cuts each tuna sandwich in half, how many halves will there be?
   (82)

   4. Five pounds of grapes cost $2.95. What was the cost per pound?
   (62)

   5. If each side of a hexagon is 4 inches long, what is the perimeter of the hexagon in feet?
   (73)

6. Nine hundred forty-seven thousand is how much
(38) greater than two hundred seventy-five thousand?

7. Part of this square is shaded.
(101)
    (a) Use a fraction to write the shaded part.
    (b) Use a decimal number to write the shaded part.

8. Use words to write $7572\frac{1}{8}$.
(44)

9. Illustrate this fraction-of-a-group problem: One fifth
(80) of the 80 chariots lost wheels in the chase. How many of the chariots lost wheels?

10. What percent of the chariots in problem 9 lost wheels?
(80,65)

11. Franca began the trip when it was still dark. She
(33) finished the trip a couple of hours later. How long did the trip take?

Start   Stop

12. James traveled 301 miles in 7 hours. He traveled an
(70) average of how many miles each hour?

13. Marvin bought 3 folders for $1.99 each. Sales tax was
(93) 33¢. He paid with a $20.00 bill. How much money should he get back?

14. $25 + $2.75 + $15.44 + 27¢
(53)

15. 21,631 − 5,716   **16.** $100.00 − $89.85
(62)   (51)

17. 60 × 900   **18.** 42 × 30   **19.** 21 × 17
(96)   (77)   (97)

20. $\begin{array}{r} 36 \\ \times\, 74 \\ \hline \end{array}$
(100)

21. $\begin{array}{r} 48 \\ \times\, 25 \\ \hline \end{array}$
(100)

22. $\begin{array}{r} \$4.79 \\ \times\qquad 6 \\ \hline \end{array}$
(68)

23. $9\overline{)2718}$
(90)

24. $5\overline{)4815}$
(86)

25. $6\overline{)4829}$
(90)

26. $\$50.00 \div 8$
(86)

27. $2121 \div 7$
(90)

28.
(2)
$\begin{array}{r} 7 \\ 8 \\ 5 \\ N \\ 6 \\ 2 \\ +\ 3 \\ \hline 47 \end{array}$

29. $\dfrac{2412}{3}$
(90)

30. Draw and shade rectangles to show that $1\frac{2}{3}$ equals $\frac{5}{3}$.
(99)

LESSON 103

Estimating Two-Digit Multiplication Answers

Facts Practice: 100 Multiplication Facts (Test H in Test Masters)

Mental Math: Find each product by multiplying by "half of 10."
a. 5×46 **b.** 5×62 **c.** 5×240

Review:
d. $\$24.87 + \$1.95$ **e.** $73 - 35$ **f.** $76 + 38$

Patterns: Each number in this sequence is one half of the preceding number. Find the next five numbers in this sequence.

..., 64, 32, 16, 8, __, __, __, __, __, ...

Estimation can help prevent mistakes. If we estimate the answer before we multiply, we can tell if our answer is reasonable.

Example 1   Jim multiplied 43 by 29 and got 203. Could this answer be correct?

Solution   Let's estimate the product by multiplying the rounded numbers 40 and 30.

$$40 \times 30 = 1200$$

Jim's answer of 203 and our estimate of 1200 are very different, **so Jim's answer of 203 is probably not correct.** He should check his multiplication.

Example 2   Estimate the product of 38 and 53. Then find an exact answer.

Solution   First we multiply the rounded numbers.

$$40 \times 50 = 2000$$

Now we will get an exact answer.

$$
\begin{array}{r}
38 \\
\times\, 53 \\
\hline
114 \\
190 \\
\hline
2014
\end{array}
$$

Our estimate of the product was **2000,** so our answer of **2014** is reasonable.

Practice   Estimate the product of each multiplication. Then find the exact answer.

a. 58 × 23   **b.** 49 × 51   **c.** 61 × 38

Problem set 103

1. Ninety-one students are divided as equally as possible
(98) among 3 classrooms.

   (a) How many classrooms have exactly 30 students?

   (b) How many classrooms have 31 students?

2. In 1970 it cost 6¢ to mail a letter. How much did it
(59) cost to mail 20 letters in 1970?

3. What number is seven hundred ninety more than two
(38) hundred ten?

4. George Washington was born in 1732 and died in
(64) 1799. How many years did he live?

5. A $1 bill weighs about 1 gram. How much would a $5
(88) bill weigh?

6. This is the tally for what number?   JHT JHT JHT IIII
(85)

7. Part of this square is shaded.
(101)

(a) Use a fraction to write the shaded part.

(b) Use a decimal number to write the shaded part.

8. Estimate the product of 49 and 62.
(103)

9. Illustrate this fraction-of-a-group problem: One half of
(80) the 32 chess pieces were still on the board. How many
chess pieces were still on the board?

10. Mary left home at 10:30 a.m. She traveled for 7 hours.
(33) What time was it when she arrived?

11. Mark traveled 42 miles in 1 hour. If he kept going at
(67) the same speed, how far would he travel in 20 hours?

12. Violet paid $40 for a toaster that cost $29.99 plus
(93) $1.80 in tax. How much money should she get back?

13. 3714 + 238 + 46 + 7   **14.** $15.27 + $85.75
(61)   *(28)*

15. $18.00 − $15.63   **16.** 10,141 − (363 + 99)
(51)   *(55)*

17. $2^3 \times \sqrt{25}$ **18.** 30 × 90   **19.** $7.50 × 8
(72,40)   *(96)*   *(68)*

20.   49   **21.**   54   **22.**   74
(100) × 62   *(100)* × 23   *(77)* × 40

23. 4)$6.36   **24.** 5)800   **25.** 6)1845
(86)   *(90)*   *(90)*

26. 4735 ÷ 8   **27.** 1800 ÷ 3   **28.**
(86)   (90)   (2)

$$
\begin{array}{r}
3 \\
5 \\
1 \\
4 \\
7 \\
N \\
8 \\
2 \\
3 \\
5 \\
+\ 2 \\
\hline
58
\end{array}
$$

29. Draw and shade circles to show
(99) that $2\frac{1}{4}$ equals $\frac{9}{4}$.

30. Find the perimeter and area of
(94,60) this rectangle.

50 ft

20 ft

LESSON 104

Two-Step Word Problems

Facts Practice: 100 Multiplication Facts (Test H in Test Masters)

Mental Math: Find half of each product.
  a. Half of 100×12 **b.** Half of 100×24 **c.** Half of 100×48
Review:
  d. $10.00 - $4.89   **e.** $151 - 27$ **f.** $340 + 60 + 200$

Problem Solving: On February 4, Edgar remembered that his two library books were due on January 28. The fine for late books is 15¢ per day. If he returns the books on February 4, what will be the total fine?

We have practiced two-step problems by finding total prices and change back. Starting with this lesson, we will practice other kinds of two-step problems. Many math problems require more than one step to solve. Writing down the information that is given or drawing a picture is often helpful in solving these problems.

Example 1 Jim is 5 years older than Tad. Tad is 2 years younger than Blanca. Blanca is 9 years old. How old is Jim?

Solution We will write down the information we have and see if that helps.

$$\text{Blanca} = 9 \text{ years old}$$

$$\text{Tad} = 2 \text{ years younger than Blanca}$$

$$\text{Jim} = 5 \text{ years older than Tad}$$

We see that Blanca is 9. Tad is 2 years younger than Blanca, so Tad is 7. Jim is 5 years older than Tad, so **Jim is 12 years old.**

Example 2 Jim paid for 5 pounds of apples with a $10 bill. He got back $6. What was the cost of 1 pound of apples?

Solution We begin by finding how much all 5 pounds of apples cost. If Jim paid for the apples with a $10 bill and got $6 back, then all 5 pounds must have cost $4.

$$
\begin{array}{rl}
\$10 & \text{amount paid} \\
- \ \$ 6 & \text{change back} \\
\hline
\$ 4 & \text{cost of 5 pounds of apples}
\end{array}
$$

To find the cost of 1 pound of apples, we divide $4 by 5.

$$
\begin{array}{r}
\$0.80 \\
5\overline{)\$4.00} \\
\underline{4\ 0} \\
00 \\
\underline{\ 0} \\
0
\end{array}
$$

Each pound of apples cost **$0.80.**

Practice Nancy paid for 4 pounds of peaches with a $5 bill. She got back $3. What was the cost of 1 pound of peaches? (First find the cost of 4 pounds of peaches.)

Problem set   **1.** Gabriel gave a $5 bill to pay for a half gallon of milk
104   *(93)*   that cost $1.06 and a box of cereal that cost $2.39. How
much money should he get back?

2. Eighty-one animals crossed the bridge. One third of
(104,80) them were billy goats. The rest were bears. How many
bears crossed the bridge? (First find how many billy
goats crossed the bridge.)

3. Johnny planted 8 rows of apple trees. There were 15
(59) trees in each row. How many trees did he plant?

4. Four pounds of bananas cost the Fairy Queen one
(104) hundred fifty-six trinkets. Each pound of bananas cost
how many trinkets?

5. The scale shows a weight of how
(22) many grams?

6. Write the tally for 16.
(85)

7. Part of this square is shaded.
(102)
    (a) Use a fraction to write the
shaded part.

    (b) Use a decimal number to write
the shaded part.

8. Estimate the product of 32 and 48.
(103) Then find the exact product.

9. Illustrate this fraction-of-a-group problem: One third
(80) of the 24 camels were Bactrian. How many camels
were Bactrian?

10. A quart is a quarter of a gallon. A quart is what percent
(65) of a gallon?

11. Five hundred seventy people sat in the bleachers.
(31) Then some went home. Only twenty-seven were left.
How many went home?

12. Matthew could travel 496 miles in 8 hours. How far
(70) could he travel in 1 hour?

13.
(30)
$$\begin{array}{r} N \\ +731 \\ \hline 398{,}548 \end{array}$$

14.
(28)
$$\begin{array}{r} \$46.39 \\ +\ \$54.60 \\ \hline \end{array}$$

15.
(21)
$$\begin{array}{r} 37 \\ 81 \\ 45 \\ 139 \\ 7 \\ 15 \\ +60 \\ \hline \end{array}$$

16.
(62)
$$\begin{array}{r} 96{,}410 \\ -9{,}641 \\ \hline \end{array}$$

17.
(19)
$$\begin{array}{r} \$37.81 \\ -\ \$16.79 \\ \hline \end{array}$$

18. 63×1000
(95)

19. $80 \times 50\cent$
(96)

20.
(100)
$$\begin{array}{r} 52 \\ \times\ 15 \\ \hline \end{array}$$

21.
(100)
$$\begin{array}{r} 36 \\ \times\ 27 \\ \hline \end{array}$$

22.
(100)
$$\begin{array}{r} 59 \\ \times\ 32 \\ \hline \end{array}$$

23. $2\overline{)714}$
(86)

24. $6\overline{)789}$
(86)

25. $4\overline{)2363}$
(90)

26. $2835 \div 7$
(90)

27. $\$29.00 \div 5$
(90)

28.
(2)
$$\begin{array}{r} 3 \\ 5 \\ 8 \\ 7 \\ 4 \\ N \\ +6 \\ \hline 53 \end{array}$$

29. Draw and shade rectangles to
(99) show that $1\frac{2}{5}$ equals $\frac{7}{5}$.

30. A room is 5 yards long and 4 yards
(94) wide. How many square yards of
carpet are needed to cover the
floor?

LESSON
105

"Fraction-of-a-Group" Problems, Part 2

Facts Practice: 100 Multiplication Facts (Test H in Test Masters)

Mental Math: Fifty is half of 100. Find each product by multiplying by half of 100.

  a. 50 × 16   **b.** 50 × 44   **c.** 50 × 26   **d.** 50 × 68

Review:

  e. $32.48 + $4.99   **f.** 96 − 29   **g.** 156 + 45

Patterns: Copy this sequence on your paper and continue it until you reach a number greater than 500.

$$1, 2, 4, 8, 16, \ldots$$

The fraction problems in this lesson are two-step problems. First we find the number in one part. Then we can find the number in more than one part.

Example 1 There were 30 leprechauns in the forest. Three fifths of them wore green jackets. How many leprechauns wore green jackets?

Solution The word *fifths* tells us there were 5 equal groups. We need to find the number in each group. Since there were 30 leprechauns in all, we divide 30 by 5.

$$5\overline{)30} \quad \begin{matrix} 6 \end{matrix}$$

There are 6 leprechauns in each group.

Three fifths wore green jackets. In three groups, there are 3 times 6 leprechauns. That is, **18 leprechauns wore green jackets.** We also see that two groups did not wear green jackets, so 12 leprechauns did not wear green jackets.

Example 2 Two thirds of the 24 elves worked in the toy factory. How many elves worked in the toy factory?

Solution First we divide 24 by 3 and find that the number of elves in **one** third is 8.

Then we multiply 8 by 2 and find that the number of elves in **two** thirds is 16. We have found that **16 elves** worked in the toy factory.

Practice Solve and illustrate each problem:

    a. Three fourths of the 24 checkers were still on the board. How many checkers were still on the board?

    b. Two fifths of the 30 leprechauns guarded the treasure. How many leprechauns guarded the treasure?

    c. Three eighths of the 40 students had perfect scores. How many students had perfect scores?

Problem set Use the information in this tally sheet to answer
105 questions 1–3:

Results of Class Election

Irma	卌 ‖
Brad	卌 ‖
Thanh	卌 ‖‖
Marisol	卌 卌 ‖

    1. Who was second in the election?
    (85)

    2. Who received twice as many votes as Brad?
    (85)

    3. Altogether, how many votes were cast?
    (85)

4. Two fifths of the 20 balloons were yellow. How many
(105) balloons were yellow? Illustrate the problem.

5. Tim is 5 years younger than Brad. Brad is 2 years older
(104) than Linda. Linda is 11 years old. How old is Tim?

6. Part of this group is shaded.
(101)

    (a) Write the shaded part as a fraction.

    (b) Write the shaded part as a decimal.

7. The fraction $\frac{1}{10}$ equals 10%. What percent of the group
(65) in problem 6 is shaded?

8. Estimate the product of 88 and 59. Then find the exact
(103) product.

9. Sue's birthday is May 2. Her birth-
(64) day will be on what day of the
week in the year 2047?

		MAY 2047				
S	M	T	W	T	F	S
		1	2	3	4	5	6
7	8	9	10	11	12	13
14	15	16	17	18	19	20
21	22	23	24	25	26	27
28	29	30	31			

10. Segment *AB* is 17 mm long. Segment *CD* is 36 mm
(50) long. Segment *AD* is 89 mm long. How long is
segment *BC*?

      A   *B*   *C*   *D*

11. $32.63 + $42 + $7.56   **12.** $86.45 − ($74.50 + $5)
(53)   (55)

13. 83 × 40   **14.** 1000 × 53   **15.** 9^3
(77)   (95)   (72)

16.   32   **17.**   67   **18.** $8.95
(100) × 16   (100) × 32   (68) ×   4

19. $3\overline{)625}$
(90)

20. $4\overline{)714}$
(86)

21. $6\overline{)1385}$
(90)

22. $\dfrac{900}{5}$
(90)

23. $3748 \div 9$
(86)

24. $\$28.56 \div 8$
(86)

25. This circle shows that $\frac{2}{2}$ equals 1.
(99) Draw a circle that shows that $\frac{3}{3}$
equals 1.

26.
(1)

```
  1 ⌐
  2 ⌐
  3 ⌐
  4 ⌐
  5 ⌐
  4 ⌐
  3 ⌐
  2 ⌐
  1 ⌐
  6 ⌐
+ 7
```

27.
(1)

```
  4 ⌐
  4 ⌐
  4 ⌐
  4 ⌐
  4 ⌐
  4 ⌐
  4 ⌐
  4 ⌐
  4 ⌐
  4 ⌐
+ 4
```

28. Find the perimeter and area of
(94,60) this rectangle.

LESSON 106

Average

Here we show three stacks of pancakes.

8   3   4

There are 15 pancakes in all. If we rearrange the pancakes to have an equal number in each stack, we get 5 in each stack.

5   5   5

We say that the **average** number of pancakes in each stack is 5. Finding an average is a two-step "equal groups" problem. First we find how many there are altogether. Then we find how many there would be in each group if the groups were equal.

Example   Four vans carried the team to the soccer field. There were 5 players in the first van, 4 players in the second van, 3 players in the third van, and 8 players in the fourth van. What was the average number of players in each van?

Solution   The average number of players in each van is the number there would be if there were the same number of players in each van. Imagine starting over and reloading the vans equally. First we need to find the total number of players. We find the total by adding the number in each van.

$$\begin{array}{r} 5 \text{ players} \\ 4 \text{ players} \\ 3 \text{ players} \\ + 8 \text{ players} \\ \hline 20 \text{ players} \end{array}$$

Since there are 4 vans, we divide the 20 players into 4 equal groups.

$$\frac{20 \text{ players}}{4 \text{ vans}} = 5 \text{ players in each van}$$

If the vans were loaded equally, there would be 5 players in each van. Even though the vans were not loaded equally, **the average number in each van was 5 players.**

Practice   In three classrooms there were 24, 26, and 28 children, respectively. What was the average number of children in each classroom?

Problem set   **1.** Freddie is 2 years older than Ivan. Ivan is twice as old
106   (104)   as Becky. Becky is 6 years old. How old is Freddie?

2. What is the total number of days in the first three
(64)   months of a leap year?

3. It cost $1.39 to mail the package. Marty put three 25-
(104)   cent stamps on the package. How much more postage does it need?

4. Thirty-two desks were arranged as equally as possible
(98) in 6 rows.

(a) How many rows had exactly 5 desks?

(b) How many rows had 6 desks?

5. Two thirds of the 21 riders rode bareback. How many
(105) riders rode bareback? Illustrate the problem.

6. (a) What decimal number names
(102) the shaded part of this square?

(b) What decimal number names
the part that is not shaded?

7. Each small square in problem 6 is
(65) 1% of the large square. What percent of the large square is shaded?

8. Round 3874 to the nearest thousand.
(91)

9. Beth opened a liter of milk and poured half of it into a
(83,65) pitcher. How many milliliters of milk did she pour
into the pitcher? What percent of the milk was still in
the container?

10. The sun was up when Mark started. It was dark when
(33) he stopped. How much time had gone by?

Start   Stop

11. For five days Jan recorded the high temperature. The
(106) temperatures were 79°F, 82°F, 84°F, 81°F, and 74°F,
respectively. What was the average high temperature
for those five days?

12. Mickey drove 368 miles in 8 hours. If she drove the
(70) same number of miles each hour, how far did she drive each hour?

13.   496,325
(61)   +   3,680

14. $36.00
(51)   − $30.78

15. $12.45
(28)   1.30
               2.00
               0.25
               0.04
               0.32
        +   1.29

16. $8.56 × 7
(68)

17. 60 × 300
(96)

18. $\dfrac{432}{6}$
(75)

19.   26
(100)   × 24

20.   25
(100)   × 25

21. 7)845
(90)

22. 9)1000
(86)

23. $16.40 ÷ 8
(90)

24. Draw and shade a circle that shows that $\frac{4}{4}$ equals 1.
(99)

25. The wall was 8 feet high and 12 feet wide. How many
(94) square feet of wallpaper were needed to cover the wall?

LESSON 107

Writing Mixed Numbers as Decimals

Facts Practice: 100 Multiplication Facts (Test H in Test Masters)

Mental Math: If we multiply the double of one factor by the half of the other factor, we can find the product.

$$4 \times 18$$
$$\text{double} \downarrow \qquad \downarrow \text{half}$$
$$8 \times 9 = 72$$

Find each product by the double and half method.

a. 3×14 **b.** 4×16 **c.** 5×22 **d.** 50×24

The figure below has three squares. Two and three tenths of the squares are shaded. We can describe the shaded parts by using either a mixed number or a decimal number. Both the mixed number and the decimal number are read "two and three tenths."

$2\frac{3}{10}$ is shaded   or   2.3 is shaded

In the decimal number, the whole number part is to the left of the decimal point and the fraction part is to the right of the decimal point.

In the next figure, one and thirty-three hundredths squares are shaded. We can name one and thirty-three hundredths as a mixed number or as a decimal (number).

$1\frac{33}{100}$ is shaded   or   1.33 is shaded

Both are read "one and thirty-three hundredths."

Example 1   Write each mixed number as a decimal number:

(a) $3\frac{7}{10}$ (b) $16\frac{17}{100}$ (c) $8\frac{9}{100}$

Solution   We write the whole number to the left of the decimal point and write the fraction to the right of the decimal point. Tenths are written one place to the right of the decimal point. Hundredths are written two places to the right of the decimal point.

(a) **3.7**   (b) **16.17**   (c) **8.09**

Example 2   Write each decimal number as a mixed number:

(a) 24.9   (b) 5.23   (c) 4.03

Solution   (a) $\mathbf{24\frac{9}{10}}$ (b) $\mathbf{5\frac{23}{100}}$ (c) $\mathbf{4\frac{3}{100}}$

Practice   **a.** Write the number of shaded squares as a mixed number.

b. Write the number of shaded squares as a decimal number.

Write each mixed number as a decimal number:

c. $9\frac{99}{100}$ **d.** $12\frac{3}{10}$ **e.** $10\frac{1}{100}$

Write each decimal number as a mixed number:

f. 60.3   **g.** 6.03   **h.** 5.67

Problem set 107

Use this chart to answer questions 1–4:

Mileage Chart

	Atlanta	Boston	Chicago	Kansas City	Los Angeles	New York City	Wash., D.C.
Chicago	730	975		499	2095	840	712
Dallas	805	1819	936	499	1403	1607	1372
Denver	1401	1989	1016	604	1134	1851	1696
Los Angeles	2197	3052	2095	1596		2915	2644
New York City	855	216	840	1319	2915		229
St. Louis	558	1178	288	253	1848	966	801

1. The distance from Los Angeles to Boston is how much greater than the distance from Los Angeles to New York City?
(89)

2. (a) Which two cities are the same distance from Kansas City?
(89)

   (b) How far apart are the two cities in the answer to (a)?

3. Rebecca is planning a trip from Chicago to Dallas to Los Angeles to Chicago. How many miles will her trip be?
(89)

4. There are 3 empty boxes in the chart. What number should go in these boxes?
(89)

5. Three fourths of the one thousand gold coins were doubloons. How many doubloons were there? Illustrate the problem.
(105)

6. What percent of the gold coins in problem 5 were doubloons?
(65)

7. Write each mixed number as a decimal:
(107)
   (a) $3\frac{5}{10}$ (b) $14\frac{21}{100}$ (c) $9\frac{4}{100}$

8. Estimate the product of 39 and 406. Then find the
(103) exact product.

9. What is the perimeter of this rect-
(60) angle in millimeters?

30 mm

10 mm

10. Use your answer to problem 9 to
(79) find the perimeter of the rectangle
in centimeters.

11. Find the area of the rectangle in problem 9.
(94)

12. James knew that his trip would take seven and a half
(33) hours. He left at 7 a.m. At what time will he arrive?

13. What is the average number of days per month in the
(106) first three months of a common year?

14. $2.74 + $0.27 + $6 + 49¢
(53)

15. $15.75 − ($2.47 + $10)
(55)

16. 25 × 40   **17.** 98¢ × 7   **18.** $\sqrt{36} \times \sqrt{4}$
(77)   (58)   (40)

19. $\dfrac{3^3}{3}$ **20.** 36   **21.** 35   **22.**
(72)   (100) × 34   (100) × 35   (2)

23. 8)$70.00   **24.** 6)1234
(86)   (90)

25. 800 ÷ 7   **26.** 487 ÷ 3
(86)   (86)

27. Draw and shade circles to show
(99) that $2\frac{1}{3}$ equals $\frac{7}{3}$.

$$
\begin{array}{r}
4 \\
2 \\
1 \\
3 \\
4 \\
7 \\
2 \\
2 \\
3 \\
4 \\
+ X \\
\hline
42
\end{array}
$$

LESSON
108

Naming Place Value • Naming Decimal Numbers

Facts Practice: 90 Division Facts (Test J in Test Masters)

Mental Math: Find each product by the double and half method.
  a. 3 × 18   **b.** 15 × 60   **c.** 50 × 48

Review:
  d. $5.00 − $1.75   **e.** 299 + 125   **f.** 76 − 48

Problem Solving: Robert can walk twice as fast as he can swim.
He can run twice as fast as he can walk. He
can ride a bike twice as fast as he can run. If
Robert can ride his bike a quarter mile in one
minute, how long would it take him to swim a
quarter mile?

In this lesson we will identify decimal place values and
write the names of the decimal numbers.

Naming place value
The chart below shows place values from hundreds to
hundredths. From the decimal point we find the value of
each place. To the left of the decimal point is the ones'
place, then the tens' place, and then the hundreds' place.
To the right of the decimal point is the tenths' ($\frac{1}{10}$) place,
and then the hundredths' ($\frac{1}{100}$) place.

Decimal point

Example 1   Name the place value of the 3 in each number:

(a) 23.4   (b) 2.34   (c) 32.4   (d) 4.23

Solution   (a) **Ones'**   (b) **Tenths'**

(c) **Tens'**   (d) **Hundredths'**

Example 2   Which digit in 23.47 is in the same place as the 5 in 8.5?

Solution   In 8.5, the 5 is in the tenths' place. The digit in 23.47 that is in the tenths' place is **4.**

Naming decimal numbers   To name a decimal number, we first name the whole number part. Then we name the decimal part.

To read the decimal number 562.35, we say the whole number part first.

Five hundred sixty-two

Next, we read the decimal point by saying "and."

Five hundred sixty-two **and**

Then we read the number to the right of the decimal point.

Five hundred sixty-two **and** thirty-five

Finally, we name the place value of the last digit.

Five hundred sixty-two **and** thirty-five **hundredths**

Example 3   Use words to name each number:

(a) 12.34   (b) 1.3   (c) 6.07

Solution   (a) **Twelve and thirty-four hundredths**

(b) **One and three tenths**

(c) **Six and seven hundredths**

Practice   Name the place value of the 7 in these numbers:

a. 17.26   **b.** 61.72

c. 26.17   **d.** 72.61

Which digit is in the tenths' place in these numbers?

e. 43.85   **f.** 438.5   **g.** 4.38   **h.** 1385.4

Use words to name each decimal number:

i. 4.38   **j.** 43.8

k. 10.6   **l.** 1.06

Problem set 108　Use the facts given to answer questions 1–3:

> *In the Jones family there are 3 children. John is 10 years old. James is 2 years younger than Jill. James is 4 years older than John.*

1. How old is James?
(104)

2. How old is Jill?
(104)

3. When James is 16, how old will Jill be?
(104)

4. Denise bought 6 pounds of carrots and an artichoke for $2.76. If the artichoke cost 84¢, how much was 1 pound of carrots? (First find the cost of all the carrots.)
(104)

5. Write each of these mixed numbers as a decimal number:
(107)

    (a) $5\frac{31}{100}$　　　　(b) $16\frac{7}{10}$　　　　(c) $5\frac{7}{100}$

6. Three fifths of the team's 40 points were scored in the first half. How many points did the team score in the first half? Illustrate the problem.
(105)

7. One fifth is 20%. What percent is three fifths?
(65)

8. Use words to write 7.68.
(108)

9. Use words to write 76.8.
(108)

10. Estimate the product of 78 and 91.
(103)

11. Name the number of shaded squares:
(107)

    (a) as a mixed number.

    (b) as a decimal.

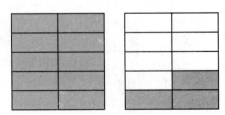

12. There were 24 people in one line and 16 people in the
(106) other line. What was the average number of people in
each line?

13. In the beginning it was dark. What
(33) time was it 5 hours and 20 minutes later?

Beginning

14. Mr. Toto could bake 27 pizzas in 3
(70) hours. How many could he bake
in 1 hour? How many could he
bake in 5 hours? (Multiply the
first answer by 5.)

$\frac{27}{3} = 9\ pizz - 1hr$
$45\ piz - 5hrs.$

15. $15 + $6.15 + $13.85   **16.** $13.70 − $6.85
(53)   (53)

17. 26 × 100   **18.** 9 × 87¢   **19.** 14 × 16
(95)   (58)   (100)

20.   15   **21.** $\frac{456}{6}$ **22.**   47
(100) × 15   (75)   (77) × 60

23. 6)4248   **24.** 1)163   **25.** 5)$49.00
(90)   (86)   (90)

26. 1 + 3 + 5 + P + 7 + 3 + 2 + 3 = 44
(2)

27. How many square foot floor tiles are needed to cover
(94) the floor of a room that is 15 feet long and 10 feet
wide?

28. A penny is what fraction of a dollar? $.01 dollar
(84)   1/100 of dollar

LESSON 109

Decimal Numbers and Money

Facts Practice: 90 Division Facts (Test J in Test Masters)

Mental Math: Find each product by the double and half method.

   a. 4 × 14   **b.** 25 × 80   **c.** 50 × 64

Review:

   d. $10.00 − $8.16   **e.** $4.68 + $2.95   **f.** 62 − 35

Problem Solving: Three of the 30 students in Marshall's class are left-handed. What percent of the students are left-handed? What percent are not left-handed?

We remember that there are two forms for writing money. In one form the unit is *cents*. For writing cents, we use a cent sign (¢) and no decimal point. When we write

25¢

we mean 25 **whole cents** (or 25 pennies). In the other form of money the unit is *dollars*. For writing dollars, we use a dollar sign ($). We also use a decimal point to show fractions of a dollar. When we write

$0.25

we mean twenty-five hundredths of a dollar (a fraction of a dollar).

A penny is 1 cent. A penny is also $\frac{1}{100}$ of a dollar.

1¢ = $0.01

Sometimes we see notations for money written incorrectly.

Example Something is wrong with this sign. What should be changed so that the sign is correct?

Solution The notation .50¢ is incorrect. We can use the ¢ sign and a whole number to tell how many cents. Or we can use a dollar sign and a decimal point to write the fractional part of a dollar.

50¢ is correct **$0.50 is also correct**

Practice At a vegetable stand Martin saw this incorrect sign. Draw two different signs to show ways to correct this error.

Corn
0.10¢
each
ear

Problem set 109

1. Robin divided his 53 merry men into groups of 6.
   (98)
   (a) How many groups of 6 could he make?

   (b) How many merry men were left over?

   (c) If the remaining merry men formed a group, how many groups were there in all?

2. Abraham Lincoln was born in 1809 and died in 1865.
   (64) How long did he live?

3. The parking lot charges $1.25 for the first hour. It
   (12) charges 50¢ for each additional hour. How much does it cost to park a car in the lot for 3 hours?

4. Two thirds of the team's 45 points were scored in the
   (105) second half. How many points did the team score in the second half? Draw a diagram to illustrate the problem.

5. Something is wrong with this sign. Draw two different signs to show ways to correct this error.
(109)

ICE CREAM BARS
0.25¢ each

6. What is the value of 3 ten-dollar bills, 4 one-dollar bills, 5 dimes, and 2 pennies?
(45)

$3 \times 10 = 30.00$
$4 \times 1 = 4.00$
$5 \times .1 = .50$
$2 \times 0.01 = .02$
$\$34.52$

7. Use words to write 6412.5.
(108)

8. Round 5139 to the nearest thousand. Round 6902 to the nearest thousand. Then add the rounded numbers.
(91)

9. James opened a gallon bottle of milk and poured out 1 quart. How many quarts of milk were left in the bottle?
(83)

10. What percent of the milk in problem 9 was left in the bottle?
(65)

11. Estimate the product of 39 and 41. Then find the exact product.
(103)

12. Thirteen little people came to the party every hour. After 11 hours, how many little people were at the party?
(67)

13. Five full buses held 240 students. What was the average number of students on each bus?
(106)

14. $68.57
(28) + $36.49

15. $100.00
(51) − $5.43

16.   15
(21)   24
         36
         75
         21
          8
         36
     + 420

17.   12
(97) × 12

18. $5.08
(68) ×   7

19. 1
(2)

   2

   3

   4

   P

   6

   7

   8

+ 9
―――
   56

20. 1
(1)

   2

   4

   6

   8

   6

   4

   3

+ 3
―――

21. 50^2
(72)

22. 49×51
(100)

23. 33×25
(100)

24. $\dfrac{848}{8}$
(90)

25. $9\overline{)6300}$
(90)

26. $\sqrt{144}$
(40)

27. $\$5.72 \div 4$
(86)

28. Draw and shade circles to show that $2\frac{2}{3}$ equals $\frac{8}{3}$.
(99)

29. Draw a rectangle that is three inches long and one inch wide.
(25)

30. What is the perimeter and area of the rectangle in problem 29?
(94,60)

LESSON 110

Circles: Radius and Diameter

Facts Practice: 90 Division Facts (Test I in Test Masters)

Mental Math: Review.

   a. 3×16 **b.** 600×40 **c.** $850 + 200 + 25$

   d. $\$20.00 - \$6.25$ **e.** $399 + 165$ **f.** $71 - 57$

Problem Solving: The library loans books for three weeks and will renew books once for three more weeks. If Salina borrows a book on April 22, when will the book be due? If she renews the book on the due date, what will be the final due date?

Many of the words we use in mathematics are based on Latin or Greek words. The Latin word for "ring" is *circus*. The Latin word for the spoke of a wheel is *radius*. The Greek word for "through-measure" is *diametron*.

     Circus   Radius   Diametron

From these Latin and Greek words we get the English words **circle, radius,** and **diameter.** The distance from the center to the circle is the *radius*. The distance across a circle through the center is the *diameter*.

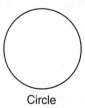

     Circle   Radius   Diameter

A diameter is twice as long as a radius. A radius is half as long as a diameter.

Example The diameter of this circle is 4 cm. What is its radius?

4 cm

Solution The radius is the distance from the center to the circle. The radius is half the diameter. Since half of 4 cm is 2 cm, the radius is **2 cm.**

Practice **a.** What is the name for the distance across the center of a circle?

b. What is the name for the distance from the center to the circle?

c. If the radius of a circle is 4 cm, what is its diameter?

Problem set 110

1. One hundred fifty feet equals how many yards?
(49)

2. Tammy gave the clerk $6 to pay for a record. She received 64¢ in change. Tax was 38¢. What was the price of the record?
(93)

3. Sergio is 2 years older than Rebecca. Rebecca is twice as old as Dina. Sergio is 12 years old. How old is Dina? (First find Rebecca's age.)
(104)

4. Write these decimal numbers as mixed numbers:
(107) (a) 3.29   (b) 32.9   (c) 3.09

5. Three fourths of the 84 contestants guessed wrong. How many contestants guessed wrong? Draw a diagram to illustrate the problem.
(105)

6. What percent of the contestants in problem 5 guessed wrong?
(65)

7. (a) What is the diameter of this circle?
(110) (b) What is the radius of this circle?

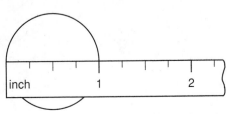

inch   1   2

8. Use words to write 8.75.
(108)

9. Estimate the product of 47 and 62. Then find the
(103) actual product.

10. The radius of a circle is 2 cm. How many centimeters
(110) is its diameter?

11. The first five odd numbers are 1, 3, 5, 7, and 9. What is
(106) the average of these five numbers?

12. $43.62 + $3.60 + 56¢   **13.** $16.25 − ($6 − 50¢)
(53)   (55)

14. 5 × 7 × 9   **15.** $7.83 × 6   **16.** 54 × 1000
(72)   (68)   (95)

17.   45   **18.**   32   **19.**   46
(100) × 45   (77)   × 40   (100) × 44

20. 6)3625   **21.** 5)3000   **22.** 7)987
(90)   (90)   (86)

23. $\dfrac{10^3}{\sqrt{25}}$ **24.** $13.76 ÷ 8   **25.** $\dfrac{234}{4}$
(90,72)   (86)   (78)

26. Draw and shade a circle to show that $\frac{8}{8}$ equals 1.
(99)

27. The perimeter of this square is 12
(60) inches. How long is each side of
the square?

28. What is the area of the square in
(94) problem 27?

Circle Graphs

Facts Practice: 90 Division Facts (Test J in Test Masters)

Mental Math: Thinking of quarters can make adding and subtracting numbers ending in 25, 50, and 75 easier to do mentally.

   a. 350 + 175   **b.** 325 − 150   **c.** $1.75 + $1.25

Review:

   d. 50 × 66   **e.** $10.00 − $1.95   **f.** 36 − 18

Problem Solving: Recall that 52 weeks is 364 days, that a common year is 365 days, and that a leap year is 366 days. If we know the day of the week on which a year begins, what rule will tell us the day of the week the year will end?

We have studied pictographs, bar graphs, and line graphs. Another kind of graph is the **circle graph.** This is often called a **pie graph** because the circle is divided into sections that look like slices of a pie.

Example Use the information in this circle graph to answer these questions:

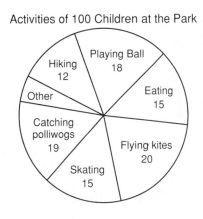

Activities of 100 Children at the Park

(a) How many children were there altogether?

(b) Which activity were most children doing?

(c) How many children were not catching polliwogs?

Solution (a) The title of the graph states that there were **100 children.**

(b) The numbers inside each "slice of pie" show how many children were doing each activity. The largest number of children were **flying kites.**

(c) Only 19 of the 100 children were catching polliwogs. The rest were not. We subtract 19 from 100 and find that **81 children** were not catching polliwogs.

Practice Use the information from the graph on the preceding page to answer these questions:

   a. How many children were either hiking or skating?

   b. How many more children were flying kites than were catching polliwogs?

   c. What number should be in the section named "other"?

Problem set 111 Use the information in the circle graph to answer questions 1–3:

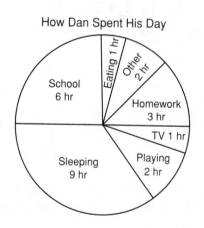

How Dan Spent His Day

1. What is the total number of hours shown in the graph?
(111)

2. What fraction of Dan's day was spent watching TV?
(111)

3. If Dan's school starts at 8:30 a.m., at what time does it end?
(111)

4. Five sixths of the 288 marchers were out of step. How
(105) many marchers were out of step? Illustrate the problem.

5. Something is wrong with this
(109) sign. Draw two different signs that show ways to correct this error.

6. (a) What is the radius of this
(110)   circle?

(b) What is the diameter of this circle?

7. The chance of rain is 60%. Is it more likely that it will
(65) rain or that it will not rain?

8. Estimate the product of 88 and 22. Then find the
(103) actual product.

9. Apples were priced at 53¢ per pound. What was the
(59) cost of 5 pounds of apples?

10. Write the number 3,708 in expanded form. Then use
(42) words to write this number.

11. Find the sum of two hundred ninety-three thousand
(61) and seven thousand.

12. Four pounds of pears cost $1.20. What did 1 pound of
(104) pears cost? What did 6 pounds of pears cost?

13. Mike drove his car 150 miles in 3 hours. What was his
(106) average speed in miles per hour?

14. $46.00
(51) − $45.56
_____

15.   10,165
(62) −   856
_____

16. $0.63
(28)   1.49
           12.24
            0.38
            0.06
            5.00
        +   1.20
_____

17. 70^2
(72)

18. 71 × 69
(100)

19.   37
(77) ×   60
_____

20.   56
(100) ×   42
_____

21. $5.97
(68) ×   8
_____

22. 4)$30.00
(90)

23. 3)263
(78)

24. 5)4080
(86)

25. $\dfrac{344}{8}$
(75)

26.   1
(2)   2
           4
           3
           5
           7
           8
           2
        + N
_____
          35

27.   9
(2)   8
           4
           A
           6
           2
           9
           4
        + 3
_____
          49

28. Draw and shade circles to show that 2 equals $\frac{4}{2}$.
(99)

29. Draw a square with sides 4 cm long.
(24)

30. Find the perimeter and the area of the square in
(94,60) problem 29.

LESSON
112

Decimal Number Line: Tenths

The arrow is pointing to three and one tenth on this number line. We may write three and one tenth as a mixed number or as a decimal.

$3\frac{1}{10}$ or 3.1

Centimeter scales are often divided into tenths. Since a millimeter is a tenth of a centimeter, each tenth of a centimeter mark on a centimeter scale also marks a millimeter.

Example 1 Find the length of this segment to the nearest tenth of a centimeter. Write the length as a decimal number.

Solution The length of the segment is 4 centimeters plus a fraction. The fraction is two tenths. The length of the segment is **4.2 cm.**

Example 2   (a) Find the length of the segment below in millimeters.

(b) Find the length of the segment below in centimeters.

Solution   (a) **23 mm**   (b) **2.3 cm**

Practice   Write the decimal number to which each arrow points:

Problem set 112

1. All 110 books must be packed in boxes. Each box will
   (98)   hold 8 books.

   (a) How many boxes can be filled?

   (b) How many boxes are needed to hold all the books?

2. What number is five more than the product of six and
   (104)   seven?

3. Gabriel gave the man $7 to pay for the tape. He got
   (93)   back a quarter and two dimes. Tax was 42¢. What was
   the price of the tape?

4. Four fifths of the 600 gymnasts did back handsprings.
   (105)   How many gymnasts did back handsprings? Illustrate
   the problem.

5. What percent of the gymnasts in problem 4 did not do
   (80)   back handsprings?

6. What is the value of 2 hundred-dollar bills, 5 ten-
   (45)   dollar bills, 4 one-dollar bills, 3 dimes, and 1 penny?

7. (a) Find the length of this line segment in millimeters.
(112)

    (b) Find the length of the segment in centimeters. Write the answer as a decimal number.

8. Use words to write 12.67.
(108)

9. Round 3834 to the nearest thousand.
(91)

10. The diameter of a circle is 1 meter. What is the radius of the circle in centimeters?
(110)

11. Find the sum of two hundred eighty-six thousand, five hundred fourteen and one hundred thirty-seven thousand, two.
(61)

12. Seven whirligigs cost $56. What did 1 whirligig cost? What would 12 whirligigs cost?
(104)

13. There were 36 children in one line and 24 children in the other line. What is the average number of children in each line?
(106)

14. $15 + $8.75 + $0.49
(53)

15. $10.00 − (37¢ + $6)
(55)

16. 40 × 50
(96)

17. 41 × 49
(100)

18. $2^3 \times 5 \times \sqrt{49}$
(72)

19.   32
(100) × 17

20.   38
(77) × 40

21. 7 + 4 + 6 + 8 + 5 + 2 + 7 + 3 + K = 47
(2)

22. 8)$\overline{3616}$
(86)

23. 4)$\overline{2482}$
(90)

24. 7)$\overline{3516}$
(90)

25. $4.38 ÷ 6   **26.** 7162 ÷ 9   **27.** $\dfrac{1414}{2}$
(75)   (86)   (90)

28. Draw and shade circles to show that 2 equals $\frac{8}{4}$.
(99)

29. What percent of a dollar is a dime?
(80,65)

30. How many square yards of carpet are needed to cover
(76) the floor of a classroom that is 15 yards long and 10
yards wide?

<table>
<tr><td>LESSON
113</td><td><h1>Fractions Equal to 1</h1></td></tr>
</table>

Facts Practice: 100 Addition Facts (Test A in Test Masters)

Mental Math: Think of quarters as you add or subtract.
  a. 750 + 250   **b.** 450 − 175   **c.** $6.75 + $2.50
Review:
  d. 50 × 42   **e.** $1.00 − 62¢   **f.** 463 − 45

Problem Solving: Which date occurs only once every four years?

Each of these circles equals 1 whole circle. The fraction
below each circle equals the number 1. If the top number
and the bottom number of a fraction are the same, the
fraction equals 1.

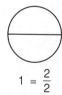

$1 = \dfrac{2}{2}$ $1 = \dfrac{3}{3}$ $1 = \dfrac{4}{4}$ $1 = \dfrac{5}{5}$

Example 1   Which of these fractions equals 1?

  A. $\frac{1}{6}$ B. $\frac{6}{6}$ C. $\frac{7}{6}$

Solution   A fraction equals 1 if its numerator and denominator are
equal. The fraction equal to 1 is **B.** $\frac{6}{6}$.

Example 2   Write a fraction equal to 1 that has a denominator of 7.

Solution   The denominator is the bottom number of the fraction. A fraction equals 1 if its top and bottom numbers are the same. So if the denominator is 7, the numerator must also be 7. We write $\frac{7}{7}$.

Practice   **a.** Write a fraction equal to 1 that has a denominator of 6.

b. Which of these fractions equals 1? $\frac{9}{10}, \frac{10}{10}, \frac{11}{10}$

What fraction name for 1 is shown by each picture?

c.   **d.**

Problem set 113

1. Find an even number between 79 and 89 that can be divided by 6 without a remainder.
(11)

2. How many minutes are in 3 hours?
(59,23)

3. Bill has $8. Jim has $2 less than Bill. How much money do they have altogether?
(104)

4. Write each fraction or mixed number as a decimal number:
(107)

(a) $\frac{3}{10}$ (b) $4\frac{99}{100}$ (c) $12\frac{1}{100}$

5. Five eighths of the 40 students earned an A on the test. How many students earned an A on the test? Illustrate the problem.
(105)

6. (a) What is the diameter of this circle?
(110)

(b) What is the radius of this circle?

7. The radius of a circle is what percent of the diameter?
(110,65)

8. Estimate the product of 49 and 68. Then find the actual product.
(103)

9. Jimbo found that 20 blocks would fill 4 containers.
(104) How many blocks could he put in 1 container? How many blocks could he put in 20 containers?

10. In Row 1 there were 6 students, in Row 2 there were 4
(106) students, in Row 3 there were 6 students, and in Row 4 there were 4 students. What was the average number of students in each row?

11. Gretchen paid $20 for five bottles of fruit juice. She
(104) received $6.00 in change. What was the price of one bottle of juice?

12. $37.50
(53)   − $26.35

13. $73.27
(28)   + $56.73

14.   16
(21)   15
            23
             8
           217
            20
             6
         + 317

15. $3.85
(68)   ×   7

16.   48
(100)   × 29

17. 60^2
(72)

18. 59 × 61
(100)

19.   5
(2)   4
             3
             7
             2
             5
             8
             1
             4
           + N
            45

20. $\dfrac{400}{5}$
(81)

21. 6)$\overline{5824}$
(90)

22. 9)$\overline{\$37.53}$
(86)

23. 7)$\overline{4205}$
(90)

24. Draw and shade circles to show that $3\frac{3}{4}$ equals $\frac{15}{4}$.
(99)

25. The perimeter of this square is 20
(94,60) inches. Find the length of each side. Then find the area.

LESSON
114

Changing Improper Fractions to Whole or Mixed Numbers

Facts Practice: 100 Addition Facts (Test A in Test Masters)

Mental Math: Think of one cent more or less than quarters.

   a. 425 + 374   **b.** 550 − 324   **c.** $4.49 + $2.26

Review:

   d. 15 × 40   **e.** $4.75 + $2.95   **f.** 83 − 35

Problem Solving: Todd wrapped a piece of tape around his front bicycle wheel. Then he rode his bicycle down his 50-foot driveway and counted eight full turns of the wheel. How many times will his wheel turn if he rides 100 yards?

If the top number of a fraction is as large as or larger than the bottom number, the fraction is an **improper fraction.** All of these fractions are improper fractions.

$$\frac{12}{4} \qquad \frac{10}{3} \qquad \frac{9}{4} \qquad \frac{3}{2} \qquad \frac{5}{5}$$

To write an improper fraction as a mixed number, we first need to find out how many wholes the number has. To do this, we divide. The division will tell us how many wholes we have. The remainder is the numerator of the fraction in the mixed number.

Example 1   Write $\frac{13}{5}$ as a mixed number. Draw a picture.

Solution   To find the number of wholes, we divide.

$$
\begin{array}{r}
2 \quad \leftarrow \text{ wholes} \\
5\overline{)13} \\
\underline{10} \\
3 \quad \leftarrow \text{ remainder of 3}
\end{array}
$$

This division tells us that $\frac{13}{5}$ equals two wholes and three fifths left over. We write this as $2\frac{3}{5}$. We can see this if we draw a picture.

$$\frac{13}{5} = 2\frac{3}{5}$$

Example 2   Write $\frac{10}{3}$ as a mixed number. Then draw a picture.

Solution   First we divide.

$$
\begin{array}{r}
3 \\
3\overline{)10} \\
\underline{9} \\
1
\end{array}
$$

We have three wholes and one third left over. We write $3\frac{1}{3}$. The picture shows us that $\frac{10}{3}$ equals $3\frac{1}{3}$.

       $\frac{10}{3} = 3\frac{1}{3}$

Example 3   Write $\frac{12}{4}$ as a whole number. Then draw a picture.

Solution   First we divide.

$$
\begin{array}{r}
3 \\
4\overline{)12} \\
\underline{12} \\
0
\end{array}
$$

We have three wholes and a remainder of zero.

    $\frac{12}{4} = 3$

Practice   Change each improper fraction to a whole number or to a mixed number. Then draw a picture.

a. $\frac{7}{2}$ b. $\frac{12}{3}$

c. $\frac{8}{3}$ d. $\frac{15}{5}$

Problem set 114   **1.** If the perimeter of a square is 280 feet, how long is
(60)   each side of the square?

2. There are 365 days in a common year. How many full
(98)   weeks are there in 365 days?

3. Barbara passed out cookies to her 6 friends. Each of
(104) her friends received 3 cookies. There were 2 cookies
left for Barbara. How many cookies did Barbara have
when she began?

4. Three fifths of the 60 leprechauns were less than 2 feet
(105) tall. How many leprechauns were less than 2 feet tall?
Illustrate the problem.

5. (a) Find the length of this line segment in millimeters.
(112) (b) Find the length of the line segment in centimeters.
Write the answer as a decimal number.

```
┌─────────────────────────────────┐
│ mm  10   20   30   40   50       │
│ ┄┄┄┄┄┄┄┄┄┄┄┄┄┄┄┄┄┄┄┄┄┄┄┄┄┄┄┄     │
│                                  │
│ ┄┄┄┄┄┄┄┄┄┄┄┄┄┄┄┄┄┄┄┄┄┄┄┄┄┄┄┄     │
│ cm   1    2    3    4    5       │
└─────────────────────────────────┘
```

6. What fraction name for 1 is shown
(113) by this circle?

7. Use words to write 432.58.
(108)

8. Estimate the product of 87 and 71. Then find the
(103) actual product.

9. Change the improper fraction $\frac{5}{4}$ to a mixed number.
(114) Draw a picture to show that the fraction and the mixed
number are equal.

10. The chance of winning the game was 10%. What was
(65) the chance of not winning?

11. The cook used about 30 pounds of flour each day to
(59) cook pancakes and bread. How many pounds of flour
did the cook use in 73 days?

12. The cook found that 132 pounds of potatoes would
(106) last 6 days. On average, how many pounds of potatoes
were eaten each day?

13. $6.52 + $12 + $1.74 + 26¢
(53)

14. 43,217 + 367,490
(61)

15. $80 − ($63.72 + $2)
(55)

16. 37,614 − 29,148
(62)

17. 3^4
(72)

18. 24 × 1000
(95)

19. 79¢ × 6
(58)

20.   50
(96)   × 50

21.   51
(100)   × 49

22.   47
(100)   × 63

23. 4)2304
(86)

24. 5)4815
(86)

25.   7
(2)   2
          A
26. 6)3629   **27.** 1435 ÷ √49   6
(90)   (90,40)   5
                                                7
28. $18.56 ÷ 8   **29.** $\dfrac{234}{9}$ 3
(86)   (75)   + 2
                                               ___
                                                57

30. The area of this square is 9 square
(94,60) feet. Find the length of each side
        and the perimeter.

**LESSON
115**

Dividing by 10

Facts Practice: 100 Addition Facts (Test A in Test Masters)

Mental Math: Think of one cent more or less than quarters.

  a. 126 + 375   **b.** 651 − 225   **c.** $6.51 + $2.75

Review:

  d. 50 × 60   **e.** $20.00 − $16.25   **f.** 84 − 47

Patterns: This sequence has an alternating pattern. Copy this
sequence on your paper and continue the sequence to 18.

           0, 5, 3, 8, 6, 11, 9, 14, ...

We have used a four-step procedure to divide by one-digit
numbers. We will use the same four-step procedure to
divide by two-digit numbers. In this lesson we will learn
how to divide by 10.

Example $10\overline{)432}$

Solution   Ten will not divide into 4 but will divide into 43 four times. In Step 1, we are careful to write the 4 above the 3 in 432.

Step 1. We divide $10\overline{)43}$ and write "4."

Step 2. We multiply 4 × 10 and write "40."

Step 3. We subtract 43 − 40 and write "3."

Step 4. We bring down the 2, making 32.

$$\begin{array}{r} 43\ \text{r}\ 2 \\ 10\overline{)432} \\ -40 \\ \hline 32 \\ -30 \\ \hline 2 \end{array}$$

REPEAT:

Step 1. We divide $10\overline{)32}$ and write "3."

Step 2. We multiply 3 × 10 and write "30."

Step 3. We subtract 32 − 30 and write "2."

Step 4. There is no number to bring down. The answer is 43 with a remainder of 2.

Practice   **a.** $10\overline{)73}$ **b.** $10\overline{)342}$ **c.** $10\overline{)243}$

d. $10\overline{)720}$ **e.** $10\overline{)561}$ **f.** $10\overline{)380}$

Problem set 115

1. How many 6¢ mints can be bought with 2 quarters?
(98)

2. Two quarters is what percent of a dollar?
(65)

3. Jason has $8. David has $2 more than Jason. How much money do they have altogether?
(104)

4. Three eighths of the 32 elves packed toys on the sleigh. How many elves packed toys on the sleigh? Illustrate the problem.
(105)

5. What is the value of 6 hundred-dollar bills, 4 ten-dollar bills, 2 one-dollar bills, 1 dime, and 3 pennies?
(45)

6. Write a fraction equal to one that has a denominator of 10.
(113)

7. Use words to write 8674.3.
(108)

8. Estimate the difference when 496 is subtracted
(70) from 604.

9. Change each improper fraction to a whole number or a
(114) mixed number:

(a) $\frac{9}{5}$ (b) $\frac{9}{3}$ (c) $\frac{9}{2}$

10. Soon after James Marshall discovered gold at John
(104) Sutter's mill in California on January 24, 1848, the
"gold rush" began. If 2400 people came in 10 days,
about how many came each day? About how many
people came in 1 week?

11. The seasons spring, summer, winter, and fall are each
(98) one fourth of a year. A season lasts about how many
days?

12. One miner bought 6 bags of flour at $4.20 a bag and 8
(104) pounds of salt at 12¢ per pound. How much money
did the miner spend?

13. $26.47 + $8.52   **14.** 49,249 − 3,755
(53)   (62)

15. 30 × 30   **16.** 28 × 32   **17.**
(96)   (100)   (2)

19. 54 × 29
(100)

20. 10$\overline{)230}$
(115)

21. 7$\overline{)2383}$
(90)

22. 10$\overline{)372}$
(115)

23. $5.76 ÷ 8
(75)

24. 412 ÷ 10
(115)

17.	18.
5	1
1	6
6	3
8	5
4	K
3	7
7	2
2	1
4	8
5	6
+ N	+ 2
62	58

25. (61)	**26.** (51)	**27.** (21)

25.
(61)

$$\begin{array}{r} 351{,}426 \\ + 449{,}576 \\ \hline \end{array}$$

26.
(51)

$$\begin{array}{r} \$50.00 \\ - \$49.49 \\ \hline \end{array}$$

27.
(21)

$$\begin{array}{r} 12 \\ 26 \\ 13 \\ 35 \\ 110 \\ 8 \\ + \quad 15 \\ \hline \end{array}$$

28.
(86)

$$\begin{array}{r} \$12.49 \\ \times \qquad 8 \\ \hline \end{array}$$

29.
(100)

$$\begin{array}{r} 73 \\ \times 62 \\ \hline \end{array}$$

30. A field is 300 feet long and 200
(60) feet wide. How many feet of fenc-
ing would be needed to go around
the field?

300 ft

200 ft

LESSON
116

Adding Decimal Numbers

Facts Practice: 100 Addition Facts (Test A in Test Masters)

Mental Math: Find each fraction of 24.

   a. $\frac{1}{2}$ of 24   **b.** $\frac{1}{3}$ of 24   **c.** $\frac{1}{4}$ of 24

Review:

   d. 4×18 **e.** $\$3.75 + \$4.51$ **f.** $54 - 38$

Problem Solving: Two cups make a pint. Two pints make a
quart. Two quarts make a half gallon, and two
half gallons make a gallon. A pint of water
weighs about one pound. Find the approx-
imate weight of a cup, a quart, a half gallon,
and a gallon of water.

We remember that when we add money, we line up all the
decimal points.

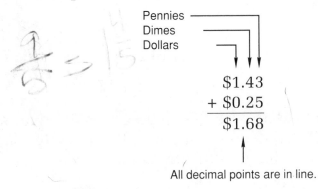

Pennies
Dimes
Dollars

$$\begin{array}{r} \$1.43 \\ + \$0.25 \\ \hline \$1.68 \end{array}$$

All decimal points are in line.

We also line up the decimal points when we add other decimal numbers. When we add decimal numbers, we must be careful to line up the decimal points so that we add digits with the same place value.

Example   Add: 3.47
                  0.36
               + 1.4

Solution   We add decimal numbers with all the
           decimal points in line. The decimal
           point in the answer is also in line. We
           think of empty places as zeros.

$$\begin{array}{r} 3.47 \\ 0.36 \\ +\ 1.4 \\ \hline 5.23 \end{array}$$

Practice   Add these decimal numbers. Put the decimal point in each answer in line with the other decimal points.

a.   2.37   b.   1.36   c.   3.65   d.   3.4
      4.6   0.47   12.4   6.75
   + 1.25   + 6.2   + 0.57   + 15.1

Problem set   Use the information given to answer questions 1–3:
116

Samantha has 6 cats. Each cat eats $\frac{1}{2}$ can of food each day. Cat food costs 47¢ per can.

1. How many cans of cat food are used each day?
(104)

2. How much does Samantha spend on cat food per day?
(104)

3. How much does Samantha spend on cat food in a week?
(104)

4. If the perimeter of a square is 240 inches, how long is each side?
(60)

5. Math was the favorite class of five sevenths of the 28 students. Math was the favorite class of how many students? Illustrate the problem.
(105)

6. Something is wrong with this sign. Draw two different signs to show two ways to correct this error.

Admission
★ .75¢ ★
each

(109)

7. (a) What is the radius of this circle?
(110) (b) What is the diameter of this circle?

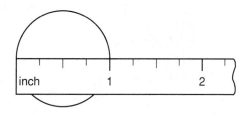

8. Use words to write 523.43.
(108)

9. Estimate the product of 61 and 397.
(103)

10. Change each improper fraction to a whole number or mixed number:
(114)

(a) $\frac{10}{10}$ (b) $\frac{10}{5}$ (c) $\frac{10}{3}$

11. Jewell went to the fair with $20. She paid $6.85 for a doll and $4.50 for lunch. Then she bought a soft drink for 75¢. How much money did she have left?
(53)

12. Mary Jane bought 2 dolls for $7.40 each. The tax was 98¢. She paid the clerk with a $20 bill. How much change did she get back?
(93)

13. The big truck that transported the ferris wheel could go only 140 miles in 5 hours. What was the truck's average speed in miles per hour?
(106)

14.   37.49
(116) + 6.35

15.   5.43
(116)   12.7
          + 3.2

16.   73.48
(116)   5.63
          + 17.9

17. $65.00
(51) − $29.87

18.   24,375
(62) − 8,416

19. $3.68
(68) ×   9

20. 90^2
(72)

21. 89×91
(100)

22.
(2)

$$
\begin{array}{r}
2 \\
5 \\
7 \\
4 \\
N \\
2 \\
5 \\
8 \\
1 \\
+ \ 6 \\
\hline
48
\end{array}
$$

23. $\dfrac{36}{\sqrt{36}}$
(57,40)

24. $3\overline{)763}$
(86)

25. $10\overline{)430}$
(115)

26. $6\overline{)\$57.24}$
(86)

27. $765 \div 9$
(75)

28. $563 \div 10$
(115)

LESSON 117

Subtracting Decimal Numbers

Facts Practice: 100 Subtraction Facts (Test B in Test Masters)

Mental Math: Find each fraction of 30.

a. $\frac{1}{2}$ of 30   **b.** $\frac{1}{3}$ of 30   **c.** $\frac{1}{5}$ of 30

Review:

d. 50×28 **e.** $\$5.00 - \$2.75$ **f.** $47 + 29$

Problem Solving: In parts of the country where "daylight savings time" is observed, we follow the rule, "Spring forward and fall back." This rule means we turn the clock forward one hour in the spring and back one hour in the fall. Officially, clocks are reset at 2 a.m. on Sunday. How many hours long are those particular Sundays?

When we subtract money, we put all the decimal points in line.

$$
\begin{array}{r}
\$6.57 \\
- \ \$1.30 \\
\hline
\$5.27
\end{array}
$$

Pennies
Dimes
Dollars

When we subtract other decimal numbers, we are careful to put all the decimal points in line. This way we subtract digits with the same place value. The decimal point in the answer is below the other decimal points.

Example Subtract: 6.57
  − 1.3

Solution All the decimal points are in line. We think of empty places as zeros. The decimal point in the answer is directly below the other decimal points.

Practice Subtract:

a. 26.45   **b.** 5.46   **c.** 42.7   **d.** 15.31
  − 12.14   − 2.3   − 6.4   − 8.5

Problem set 117

1. Wendy bought 5 tickets for $2.75 each. She paid for
(93) them with a $20 bill. How much money did she get back?

2. If fifty cents is divided equally among 3 friends, there
(98) will be some cents left. How many cents will be left?

3. What is the result we get when four hundred nine is
(37) subtracted from nine hundred four?

4. Two ninths of the 45 stamps were from Brazil. How
(105) many of the stamps were from Brazil? Illustrate the problem.

5. (a) Find the length of this line
(112)   segment in millimeters.
    (b) Find the length of the segment in centimeters.

6. The pizza was cut into 10 equal
(113) slices. The entire sliced pizza
shows what fraction name for 1?

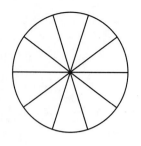

7. One slice of the pizza in problem
(65) 6 is what percent of the whole
pizza?

8. Use words to write 3722.91.
(108)

9. Round 5167 to the nearest thousand.
(91)

10. Change the improper fraction $\frac{9}{4}$ to a mixed number.
(114)

11. Which of these fractions is **not** equal to 1?
(113)
    A. $\frac{12}{12}$ B. $\frac{11}{11}$ C. $\frac{11}{10}$ D. $\frac{10}{10}$

12. In the summer of 1926, there were only 17 stores in
(82) the town. Today there are 8 times as many stores in
the town. How many stores are there in the town
today?

13. The wagon train took 9 days to make the 243-mile
(106) journey. What was the average number of miles
traveled per day?

14.   36.27   **15.**   3.62   **16.**   26.14
(116)   + 14.7   (116)   12.8   (116)   8.9
                         + 17.42   + 13.7

17.   36.31   **18.**   8.41   **19.**   23.73
(117)   − 7.4   (117)   − 3.26   (117)   − 9.8

20. 27 × 32   **21.** 62 × 15   **22.** $7^2 \times \sqrt{49}$
(100)   (100)   (72,40)

23. $10\overline{)460}$ **24.** $9\overline{)\$27.36}$ **25.**
(115)   (90)   (2)

```
        9
        8
        7
        2
        4
        6
        5
        4
        3
      + N
      ———
       55
```

26. $6\overline{)2316}$ **27.** $1543 \div 7$
(86)   (90)

28. $532 \div 10$ **29.** $\dfrac{256}{8}$
(115)   (75)

30. How many square feet of shingles
(94)   are needed to cover a roof that is
       40 feet wide and 60 feet long?

LESSON
118

Setting Up Decimal
Addition Problems

Facts Practice: 100 Subtraction Facts (Test B in Test Masters)

Mental Math: Find each fraction of 36.

    a. $\frac{1}{2}$ of 36   **b.** $\frac{1}{3}$ of 36   **c.** $\frac{1}{4}$ of 36

Review:

    d. 36×100 **e.** $\$8.50 + \$3.75$ **f.** $83 - 68$

Patterns: In this sequence, each term is the sum of the two preceding terms. Copy this sequence and find the next four terms.

$$1, 1, 2, 3, 5, 8, \_\_, \_\_, \_\_, \_\_, \ldots$$

When we add numbers, we add digits that have the same place values. To be sure we add digits with the same place values when we add decimal numbers, we line up the decimal points.

Example Add: 36.4 + 4.26 + 3.1

Solution We begin by writing the numbers in a
column with the decimal points in
line. This lines up digits with the
same place values. Next, we put the
decimal point of the answer in line
with the other decimal points. Then
we add.

$$
\begin{array}{r}
36.4 \\
4.26 \\
+\ 3.1 \\
\hline
\end{array}
$$
← decimal point

$$
\begin{array}{r}
36.4 \\
4.26 \\
+\ 3.1 \\
\hline
\mathbf{43.76}
\end{array}
$$

Practice Add these decimal numbers:

a. 4.6 + 12.57

b. 2.36 + 42.8

c. 3.6 + 0.27 + 1.29

d. 14.6 + 36.4 + 16.35

Problem set 118

1. Nelson bought 8 pounds of oranges. He gave the
storekeeper a $5 bill and received $1.96 back in
change. What did 1 pound of oranges cost? (First find
how much *all* the oranges cost.)

2. Mark had a dozen cookies. He ate two cookies and
then gave half of the rest to a friend. How many
cookies did he have left?

3. What number is six less than the product of five and
four?

4. Two thirds of the 12 guitar strings were out of tune.
How many of the guitar strings were out of tune?
Illustrate the problem.

5. What is the value of 7 ten-dollar bills, 4 one-dollar
bills, 3 dimes, and 2 pennies?

6. Write a fraction equal to 1 that has a denominator of 5.

7. Use words to write $397\frac{3}{4}$.

8. Estimate the sum of 4178 and 6899.
(70)

9. Change these improper fractions to whole numbers or
(114) mixed numbers:

(a) $\frac{7}{3}$ (b) $\frac{8}{4}$ (c) $\frac{9}{5}$

10. The hiking club went on hikes of 8 miles, 15 miles, 11
(106) miles, and 18 miles, respectively. What was the average length of the four hikes?

11. For the first 3 hours the hikers hiked at 3 miles per
(104,67) hour. For the next 2 hours they hiked at 4 miles per hour. If the total trip was 25 miles, how far did they still have to go?

12. What percent of a quart is a pint?
(83,65)

13. 41.6 + 13.17 + 9.2   **14.** 45.32 + 4.39 + 16.2
(118)   (118)

15. 23.4 + 17.8 + 3.27   **16.** 43.17 + 2.86 + 17.4
(118)   (118)

17. $0.35   **18.**   54   **19.**   67
(58) $\times$ 8   (100) $\times$ 12   (77) $\times$ 30

20. 80 × 80   **21.** 78 × 82   **22.** $\sqrt{25} \times \sqrt{25}$
(96)   (100)   (40,34)

23. $4\overline{)\$6.36}$ **24.** $10\overline{)520}$ **25.**   6
(86)   (115)   (2)   2

26. $7\overline{)4345}$ **27.** 24 ÷ 1   5
(90)   (74)   9

28. 5448 ÷ 6   **29.** $\frac{175}{5}$ 3
(90)   (75)   7

30. What is the perimeter and area of   8
(94,60) this square?   2

                                                                 3
        10 m   4
                                                              $+ N$
                                                              ―――
                                                               57

LESSON
119

Setting Up Decimal
Subtraction Problems

Facts Practice: 100 Subtraction Facts (Test B in Test Masters)

Mental Math: Find each fraction of 40.

  a. $\frac{1}{2}$ of 40   **b.** $\frac{1}{4}$ of 40   **c.** $\frac{1}{10}$ of 40

Review:

  d. 120 × 20   **e.** $10.00 − $1.95   **f.** 145 + 65

Problem Solving: Jimmy was born on a Monday in April of 1990. On what day of the week was his first birthday?

When we subtract numbers, we subtract digits that have the same place values. To be sure we subtract digits with the same place values, we line up the decimal points.

Example 1   Subtract: 36.45 − 4.2

Solution   We write the first number on top. We write the second number underneath **so that the decimal points are lined up. Then we write the decimal point in the answer so that this decimal point is lined up with the other two decimal points.** Then we subtract. We think of empty places as zeros.

$$\begin{array}{r} 36.45 \\ -\ \ 4.2 \\ \hline . \end{array}$$ ← decimal point

$$\begin{array}{r} 36.45 \\ -\ \ 4.2 \\ \hline \mathbf{32.25} \end{array}$$

Example 2   Subtract: $\begin{array}{r} 4.5 \\ -\ 3.27 \end{array}$

Solution   We subtract the bottom digits from the top digits. We see that we need a digit above the 7, so we write a zero in the empty place. Then we subtract.

$$\begin{array}{r} 4.5^{4}{}^{1}0 \\ -\ 3.27 \\ \hline \mathbf{1.23} \end{array}$$ ← We write a zero here.

Practice Subtract:

a.   3.63
    − 1.4

b.   26.2
    − 12.56

c.   8.7
    − 6.54

d.   1.9
    − 0.19

e. 3.45 − 2.1   f. 36.47 − 3.6   g. 34.6 − 3.46

Problem set 119

Use the information given to answer questions 1 and 2:

Mark kept a tally of the number of vehicles that drove by his house during 1 hour.

Number of Vehicles

Cars	卌 卌 卌 卌 IIII
Trucks	卌 卌
Motorcycles	II
Bicycles	卌 II

1. How many more cars than trucks drove by Mark's
(85) house?

2. Altogether, how many vehicles drove by Mark's
(85) house?

3. What number is six less than the sum of seven and
(104) eight?

4. Beth read three tenths of 180 pages in one day. How
(105) many pages did she read in one day? Illustrate the
problem.

5. What percent of the pages in problem 4 did Beth read
(80,65) in one day?

6. (a) What is the diameter of the
(110)   dime?

(b) What is the radius of the
    dime?

7. The candy bar was broken into 4 equal pieces. The
⁽¹¹³⁾ broken candy bar is what fraction name for 1?

8. Estimate the product of 78 and 32. Then find the
⁽¹⁰³⁾ actual product.

9. Change the improper fraction $\frac{5}{2}$ to a mixed number.
⁽¹¹⁴⁾ Draw a picture that shows that the fraction and the
mixed number are equal.

Use the information in this story to answer questions 10
and 11:

*The camel walked 12 miles the first day. Each of
the next 4 days it walked 2 more miles than it
walked the day before.*

10. How far did the camel walk in 5 days?
⁽¹⁰⁴⁾

11. What was the average number of miles the camel
⁽¹⁰⁶⁾ walked in each of the 5 days?

12. Solve this problem by guessing and then checking
⁽¹¹⁹⁾ your guess: There were red checkers and black
checkers on the checkerboard. There were 8 more red
checkers than black checkers. Altogether, there were
20 checkers. How many were red and how many were
black?†

13. 86.34 + 7.96 + 3.1   **14.** 29.15 + 4.6 + 16.2
⁽¹¹⁸⁾   ⁽¹¹⁸⁾

---

†*Guess and check* (also called *trial and error*) is a strategy for solving some
kinds of problems. In this problem there are two conditions that need to be
met:

    1. The total number of checkers needs to be 20 checkers.
    2. There needs to be 8 more red checkers than black checkers.

We begin by guessing an answer like 15 red checkers and 5 black checkers.
This guess meets the condition of totaling 20 checkers. However, the guess is
wrong because there are not 8 more red checkers than black checkers. So we
use what we have learned from our first guess and guess again.

15. $24.34 - 8.5$
(119)

16. $26.4 - 15.18$
(119)

17. $4 \times 3 \times 2 \times 1$
(72)

18. 26×30
(77)

19. 46×12
(100)

20. 20×20
(96)

21. 18×22
(100)

22. $\sqrt{36} \times \sqrt{64}$
(40,34)

23. $8\overline{)\$16.48}$
(90)

24. $6\overline{)3744}$
(86)

25.
(2)

26. $\dfrac{360}{10}$
(115)

27. $\dfrac{3000}{5}$
(90)

28. $423 \div 10$
(115)

29. $\dfrac{138}{6}$
(75)

$$
\begin{array}{r}
8 \\
4 \\
7 \\
6 \\
8 \\
4 \\
7 \\
6 \\
2 \\
+ K \\
\hline
55
\end{array}
$$

30. How many square feet of paper
(94) are needed to cover a bulletin
board that is 3 feet high and 6 feet
wide?

LESSON
120

Dividing by Multiples of 10, Part 1

Facts Practice: 100 Subtraction Facts (Test B in Test Masters)

Mental Math: Find each fraction of 100.

   a. $\frac{1}{2}$ of 100   **b.** $\frac{1}{4}$ of 100   **c.** $\frac{1}{10}$ of 100

Review:

   d. 5×46 **e.** $\$4.37 + \$2.98$ **f.** $86 - 68$

Problem Solving: Using at least one of each coin, which nine coins would be needed to make 99¢, but not more than 99¢?

We have practiced dividing by 10. In this lesson we will begin dividing by multiples of 10. Multiples of 10 are 20, 30, 40, 50, 60, and so on. Dividing by multiples of 10 is a little harder than dividing by one-digit numbers because we have not memorized the division facts for two-digit numbers. To help us divide by a two-digit number, we may think of dividing by the first digit only.

To help us divide this,   → $20\overline{)72}$

we may think this: → $2\overline{)7}$

We use the answer to the easier division to estimate the answer to the more difficult division. Since there are three 2s in 7, we estimate that there are also three 20s in 72. We write "3" above the 72 and finish by doing the multiplication and subtraction steps.

$$
\begin{array}{r}
3 \text{ r } 12 \\
20\overline{)72} \\
60 \\
\hline
12
\end{array}
$$

← We write the answer this way.

Since we divided 72 by 20, we put the 3 above the 2 in 72.

$$
\begin{array}{r}
3 \\
20\overline{)72}
\end{array}
$$

This is not correct!

Do not write the 3 above the 7.

This means there are three 20s in 7, which is not true.

$$
\begin{array}{r}
3 \\
20\overline{)72}
\end{array}
$$

This is the correct way.

The 3 above the 2 means there are three 20s in 72.

It is important to place the digits in the answer correctly!

Example $30\overline{)127}$

Solution   To help us divide this, we may mentally block out the last digit of each number.

We see $30\overline{)127}$, but we think $3\overline{)12}$.

Since there are four 3s in 12, we estimate that there are also four 30s in 127. We write "4" above the 7 of 127. Next, we multiply 4×30 and write "120." Then we subtract 120 from 127 and write "7." This is the remainder. The answer is **4 r 7.**

$$
\begin{array}{r}
4\ \text{r}\ 7 \\
30\overline{)127} \\
120 \\
\hline
7
\end{array}
$$

Practice   **a.** $30\overline{)72}$ **b.** $20\overline{)87}$ **c.** $40\overline{)95}$

d. $20\overline{)127}$ **e.** $40\overline{)127}$ **f.** $30\overline{)217}$

Problem set   **1.** Eighty students were divided among three classrooms
120 $^{(98)}$ as equally as possible. For your answer, write three numbers to show how many students were in each classroom.

2. If the sum of three and four is subtracted from the
$^{(104)}$ product of three and four, what is the difference?

3. Irma is twice as old as her sister and three years
$^{(104)}$ younger than her brother. Irma's sister is six years old. How old is Irma's brother? (First find Irma's age.)

4. Four ninths of 513 fans cheered when the touchdown
$^{(105)}$ was scored. How many fans cheered? Draw a diagram to illustrate the problem.

5. Something is wrong with this
$^{(109)}$ sign. Draw two different signs to show ways to correct this error.

Cash
for cans
.85¢ per
pound

6. This circle shows what fraction
$^{(113)}$ name for 1?

7. The chance of winning the jackpot is 1%. Which is
$^{(65)}$ more likely, winning or not winning?

8. Estimate the sum of 589 and 398.
(70)

9. Change the improper fraction $\frac{5}{2}$ to a mixed number.
(114)

10. Jim ran 7 miles in 42 minutes. What was the average
(106) number of minutes it took Jim to run one mile?

11. Salamona bought 3 scarves for $2.75 each. Tax was
(93) 58¢. She paid with a $10 bill. How much change did
she receive?

12. Two tickets for the play cost $26. How much would
(104) twenty tickets cost?

13. 7.43 + 6.25 + 12.7   **14.** 13.24 + 12.5 + 1.37
(118)   *(118)*

15. 14.36 − 7.5   **16.** 28.6 − 2.86
(119)   *(119)*

17. 90 × 800   **18.** 8 × 73¢
(96)   *(58)*

19. 7 × 6 × 5 × 0   **20.** 24 × 30
(72)   *(77)*

21. 60 × 25   **22.** $\sqrt{49} \times \sqrt{49}$
(77)   *(40,34)*

23. $5\overline{)\$37.15}$ **24.** 423 ÷ 7   **25.**
(86)   *(81)*   *(2)*

26. $\dfrac{1240}{10}$ **27.** $60\overline{)240}$
(115)   *(120)*

28. $30\overline{)95}$ **29.** $40\overline{)88}$
(120)   *(120)*

$$\begin{array}{r} 1 \\ 2 \\ 5 \\ 3 \\ 6 \\ 5 \\ 4 \\ 7 \\ 9 \\ 2 \\ + N \\ \hline 48 \end{array}$$

30. This square has a perimeter of
(94,60) 8 cm. Find the length of each side
and the area.

LESSON 121

Adding Fractions with Like Denominators

Facts Practice: 100 Subtraction Facts (Test B in Test Masters)

Mental Math: Find each fraction of 20.

    a. $\frac{1}{4}$ of 20   **b.** $\frac{2}{4}$ of 20   **c.** $\frac{3}{4}$ of 20

Review:

    d. 60×30 **e.** $\$20.00 - \$7.50$ **f.** $48 + 47$

Problem Solving: There was a tall stack and a short stack of books on the shelf. There were 8 books in the short stack. Nathan moved some books from the tall stack to the short stack so that both stacks had 15 books. How many books did Nathan move? How many books were in the tall stack before Nathan began moving the books?

Adding fractions is something like adding apples.

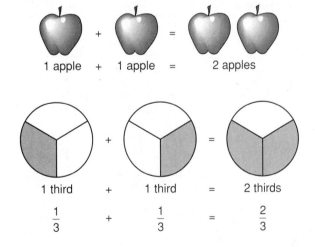

$$\begin{array}{ccccc} \text{1 apple} & + & \text{1 apple} & = & \text{2 apples} \end{array}$$

$$\begin{array}{ccccc} \text{1 third} & + & \text{1 third} & = & \text{2 thirds} \\ \frac{1}{3} & + & \frac{1}{3} & = & \frac{2}{3} \end{array}$$

When we add fractions, we add the top numbers (numerators). We do not add the bottom numbers (denominators).

Example Add: $\dfrac{3}{5} + \dfrac{1}{5}$

Solution Three fifths plus one fifth is four fifths. **We add the top numbers only.** $\dfrac{3}{5} + \dfrac{1}{5} = \dfrac{4}{5}$

Practice Add these fractions:

a. $\dfrac{1}{3} + \dfrac{1}{3}$ **b.** $\dfrac{1}{4} + \dfrac{2}{4}$ **c.** $\dfrac{1}{5} + \dfrac{2}{5}$

d. $\dfrac{3}{10} + \dfrac{4}{10}$ **e.** $\dfrac{5}{12} + \dfrac{6}{12}$ **f.** $\dfrac{8}{25} + \dfrac{9}{25}$

g. How much is three eighths plus four eighths?

Problem set 121 The table below shows how much is charged to ship a package to different parts of the country. Use the information given to answer questions 1–3:

WEIGHT	SHIPPING CHARGES		
	ZONE 1	ZONE 2	ZONE 3
Up to 4 pounds	$1.75	$1.93	$2.36
4 pounds, 1 ounce to 7 pounds	$1.91	$2.15	$2.68
7 pounds, 1 ounce to 10 pounds	$2.07	$2.38	$3.02
Over 10 pounds	$2.48	$2.71	$3.38

1. How much does it cost to ship an 8-pound package to Zone 2?
(89)

2. How much more does it cost to ship a 12-pound package to Zone 3 than to Zone 2?
(89)

3. What is the total cost to ship two 5-pound packages to Zone 1 and five 2-pound packages to Zone 3?
(89)

4. If 2 apples cost 30¢, how much will 4 apples cost?
(104)

5. Two fifths of the 70 polliwogs already had back legs.
(105) How many of the polliwogs had back legs?

6. What percent of the polliwogs already had back legs?
(80,65)

7. (a) Find the length of this line segment in millimeters.
(112) (b) Find the length of this segment in centimeters.

8. The apple was cut into 8 equal slices. The sliced apple
(113) is what fraction name for 1?

9. One third of the students earned an A. One third of the
(121) students earned a B. What fraction of the students
earned an A or a B?

10. Change each improper fraction to a whole number or a
(114) mixed number:

(a) $\frac{11}{2}$ (b) $\frac{11}{3}$ (c) $\frac{11}{4}$

11. Michelle took 6 strokes on the first hole, 7 strokes on
(106) the second hole, and 5 strokes on the third hole. What
was the average number of strokes Michelle took on
each of the first three holes?

12. Solve this problem by guessing and checking your
(119) guess: Mike and Carl played the first hole on the golf
course. Together, they hit the ball a total of 13 times.
Carl hit the ball 3 more times than Mike did. How
many times did Carl hit the ball?

13. 9.7 + 14.6 + 0.83
(118)

14. 8.79 + 16.4 + 7.3
(118)

15. 86.34 − 19.2
(119)

16. 13.6 − 4.21
(119)

17. $\dfrac{5}{9} + \dfrac{2}{9}$
(121)

18. $\dfrac{2}{10} + \dfrac{3}{10}$
(121)

19. One fifth plus two fifths equals what fraction?
(121)

20. 27×60
(77)

21. 36×35
(100)

22. 30×200
(96)

23. $1\overline{)54}$
(74)

24. $\$23.80 \div 10$
(115)

25. $8^2 \div \sqrt{16}$
(72,40)

26. $30\overline{)153}$
(120)

27. $20\overline{)84}$
(120)

28. $40\overline{)367}$
(120)

29. Draw a rectangle that is 8 cm long and 3 cm wide.
(24)

30. Find the perimeter and area of the rectangle in
(94,60) problem 29.

LESSON 122

Subtracting Fractions with Like Denominators

Facts Practice: 64 Multiplication Facts (Test G in Test Masters)

Mental Math: Find each fraction of 30.

  a. $\frac{1}{5}$ of 30   **b.** $\frac{2}{5}$ of 30   **c.** $\frac{3}{5}$ of 30

Review:

  d. 4×120 **e.** $\$7.50 + \$3.74$ **f.** $93 - 55$

Problem Solving: Copy this subtraction problem on your paper and fill in the missing digits.

$$\begin{array}{r} 4\_6 \\ -\ 13\_ \\ \hline \_87 \end{array}$$

We remember that when we add fractions, we add only the top numbers (numerators). We do not add the bottom numbers (denominators).

$$\frac{3}{7} + \frac{2}{7} = \frac{5}{7}$$

When we subtract fractions, we subtract only the top numbers. The bottom number does not change. Five sevenths minus two sevenths is three sevenths.

$$\frac{5}{7} - \frac{2}{7} = \frac{3}{7}$$

Example 1 Subtract: $\frac{3}{5} - \frac{1}{5}$

Solution **We subtract only the numerators.** Three fifths minus one fifth is two fifths. $\quad \frac{3}{5} - \frac{1}{5} = \frac{2}{5}$

Example 2 Subtract: $\frac{8}{23} - \frac{5}{23}$

Solution When we subtract fractions, we subtract the top numbers (numerators). We do not change the bottom numbers. $\quad \frac{8}{23} - \frac{5}{23} = \frac{3}{23}$

Practice Subtract these fractions:

a. $\frac{2}{3} - \frac{1}{3}$

b. $\frac{3}{4} - \frac{2}{4}$

c. $\frac{4}{5} - \frac{2}{5}$

d. $\frac{9}{10} - \frac{6}{10}$

e. $\frac{8}{12} - \frac{3}{12}$

f. $\frac{5}{6} - \frac{5}{6}$

Problem set 122   Use the information given in the graph to answer questions 1–3:

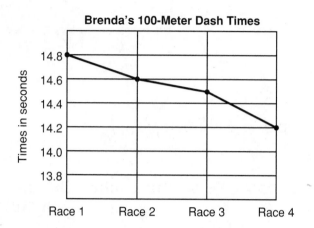

Brenda's 100-Meter Dash Times

1. What was Brenda's time for the 100-meter dash in Race 3?
(92)

2. Are Brenda's times getting faster or slower?
(92)

3. Tania ran one second slower in Race 3 than Brenda. What was Tania's time in Race 3?
(92)

4. Johnny planted two thousand apple seeds. Five hundred twenty grew to be trees. How many seeds did not grow to be trees?
(17)

5. Write each decimal number as a mixed number:
(107)
    (a) 12.41   (b) 24.1   (c) 2.03

6. Seven tenths of the 300 students bought their lunch. How many of the students bought their lunch? Draw a diagram to illustrate the problem.
(105)

7. What percent of the students in problem 6 bought their lunch?
(65)

8. Estimate the product of 41 and 39. Then find the actual product.
(103)

9. Change the improper fraction $\frac{8}{3}$ to a mixed number.
(114)

10. In Greek mythology, Jason sailed the ship *Argo* in
(106,67) search of the Golden Fleece. His shipmates were
called *Argonauts*. They sailed 33 miles in 3 days.
(a) What was the average number of miles they sailed
each day?
(b) At the same rate, how far could they sail in 7 days?

11. Jason found five eighths of a pie in the refrigerator. He
(122) ate two eighths of the pie. What fraction of the pie was
left?

12. Solve this problem by guessing and checking your
(119) guess: For dessert they had ambrosia. Altogether,
Jason and Castor ate 33 spoonfuls of ambrosia. Jason
ate 5 more spoonfuls than Castor did. How many
spoonfuls did each man eat?

13. 3.6 + 4.25 + 16.7   **14.** 5.34 + 1.9 + 16.18
(118)   *(118)*

15. 43.27 − 12.6   **16.** 16.4 − 1.64
(119)   *(119)*

17. $\frac{4}{10} + \frac{5}{10}$ **18.** $\frac{5}{11} + \frac{3}{11}$
(121)   *(121)*

19. $\frac{3}{5} + \frac{2}{5}$ **20.** $\frac{8}{9} - \frac{4}{9}$ **21.** $\frac{5}{7} - \frac{4}{7}$
(121)   *(122)*   *(122)*

22.   3   **23.**   54   **24.** $\frac{1}{3} - \frac{1}{3}$
(2)   7   *(21)*   17   *(122)*
     6   14
     4   68
  + N   + 20
   30

25. $4.39   **26.**   49   **27.** $\frac{120}{40}$
(68)   ×   8   *(100)* × 73   *(120)*

28. $60\overline{)480}$
(120)

29. $30\overline{)271}$
(120)

30. How many square feet of sod are
(94)   needed to cover a yard that is 60
feet long and 40 feet wide?

60 ft

40 ft

LESSON
123

Equivalent Fractions

Facts Practice: 64 Multiplication Facts (Test G in Test Masters)

Mental Math: Find each fraction of 40.

  a. $\frac{1}{8}$ of 40   **b.** $\frac{3}{8}$ of 40   **c.** $\frac{5}{8}$ of 40

Review:

  d. 20×14 **e.** $\$5.00 - \$1.98$ **f.** $126 + 375$

Patterns: Find the next five numbers in this sequence.

       0.2, 0.4, 0.6, 0.8, 1.0, 1.2, __, __, __, __, __, ...

The same fraction of each circle below has been shaded.
We see that different fractions are used to name the
shaded parts.

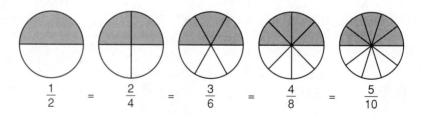

$$\frac{1}{2} \quad = \quad \frac{2}{4} \quad = \quad \frac{3}{6} \quad = \quad \frac{4}{8} \quad = \quad \frac{5}{10}$$

These fractions all name the same amount. Different
fractions that name the same amount are called **equivalent
fractions.**

Example 1 The rectangle on the left has three equal parts. We see that two parts are shaded. Two thirds of the figure is shaded.

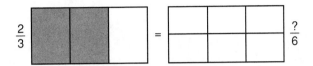

The rectangle on the right has six equal parts. How many parts must be shaded so that the same fraction of this rectangle is shaded?

Solution We see that **four** of the six parts must be shaded. Two thirds is the same as four sixths.

$\frac{2}{3}$ and $\frac{4}{6}$ are equivalent fractions

Example 2 What equivalent fractions are shown?

Solution The same fraction of each rectangle is shaded. The rectangles show that

$$\frac{2}{8} = \frac{1}{4}$$

Practice Name the equivalent fractions shown:

a.   b.

Draw pictures to show that the following pairs of fractions are equivalent:

c. $\frac{2}{4} = \frac{1}{2}$ d. $\frac{4}{6} = \frac{2}{3}$ e. $\frac{2}{8} = \frac{1}{4}$

**Problem set
123**

1. A pie was cut into 8 equal slices. Half the pie was
(123) eaten. What fraction of the pie was left? Write two
equivalent fractions for the answer.

2. A can of soup serves 3 people. How many cans of soup
(98) are needed to serve 14 people?

3. Mark was 9 years old when his brother was 12. How
(82) old will Mark be when his brother is 21 years old?

4. Three tenths of the 2000 trees in the forest were pine
(105) trees. How many pine trees were in the forest?
Illustrate the problem.

5. What percent of the trees in problem 4 were pine
(65) trees?

6. Change each improper fraction to a mixed number:
(114)
(a) $\frac{19}{3}$ (b) $\frac{19}{4}$ (c) $\frac{19}{5}$

7. Use words to write 4.56.
(108)

8. What equivalent fractions are
(123) shown?

9. Draw a picture to show that $\frac{2}{4}$ and
(123) $\frac{1}{2}$ are equivalent fractions.

10. Jamie drove 135 miles in 3 hours. What was her
(106,67) average speed in miles per hour? At the same rate,
how far could she drive in 9 hours?

11. There were 30 seats in each room. There were 15
(59) rooms. How many students could sit in all the rooms?

12. 16.24 − 5.7
(119)

13. 32.4 − 1.26
(119)

14. 3.4
(116)

                   2.7

                   1.52

                   3.6

             + 1.47

15. $\dfrac{7}{10} + \dfrac{2}{10}$
(121)

16. $\dfrac{1}{4} + \dfrac{1}{4} + \dfrac{1}{4}$
(121)

17. $\dfrac{3}{7} - \dfrac{1}{7}$
(122)

18. $\dfrac{5}{12} - \dfrac{4}{12}$
(122)

19. $\dfrac{3}{4} - \dfrac{3}{4}$
(122)

20. $4.53
(68)   ×   7

21.   78
(100)   × 36

22.   64
(77)   ×   80

23. $56.40 ÷ 6
(90)

24. 27 ÷ 1
(74)

25.   24
(21)   36

            25

            43

            19

             7

            66

            43

            50

        + 93

26. $9\overline{)545}$
(81)

27. 260 ÷ 10
(115)

28. 275 ÷ 30
(120)

29. 350 ÷ 50
(120)

30. A sheet of plywood is 8 feet long
(94)   and 4 feet wide. What is the area of
one side of a sheet of plywood?

LESSON
124

Estimating Area

Facts Practice: 64 Multiplication Facts (Test G in Test Masters)

Mental Math: Find each fraction of 60.

  a. $\frac{1}{3}$ of 60   **b.** $\frac{2}{3}$ of 60   **c.** $\frac{3}{3}$ of 60

Review:

  d. 50×46 **e.** $6.59 + $2.95   **f.** $62 - 25$

Problem Solving: On Gabriella's first nine tests she earned these scores:

        90, 95, 80, 85, 100, 95, 75, 95, 90

List these scores in order from highest to lowest. Which score is the middle score in the ordered list? Which score did Gabriella earn the most number of times?

Remember that a square unit is a square with a side of a certain length. Here we show a **square centimeter** and a **square inch** in actual size.

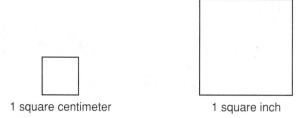

1 square centimeter   1 square inch

To measure the areas of shapes that are not rectangles, we may use a grid to estimate the area. Here we show a triangle drawn on grid paper. What is the area of this triangle? We will describe two strategies that can be used to estimate its area.

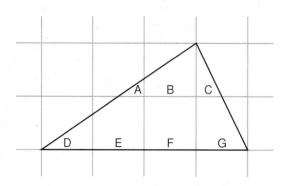

First strategy:

Look within the outline of the figure. Count all of the entire squares. Then estimate the number of entire squares that could be formed with the remaining partial squares.

Using this strategy, we see that F is an entire square. C and G could be fit together like a puzzle to make another square. D and B could make a third square. A and E would make a fourth square. Using this strategy, we estimate that the area of the triangle is about four square units.

Second strategy:

Look within the outline of the figure. Count all the entire squares as in the first strategy. Then count all the squares that seem to have at least half their area within the outline of the figure. Do not count the squares that have less than half their area within the figure.

Using this strategy, we again count F as an entire square. Then we count E, B, and G because at least half the area of each square is within the outline of the triangle. We do not count A, C, or D. Using this strategy, we again estimate the area of the triangle is about four square units.

Both strategies help us to estimate areas. An estimate is an approximation. Estimates may differ slightly from person to person. The purpose is to make each estimate carefully.

Activity   Materials needed:

- a sheet of square-inch grid paper for each student[†]
- Optionally, a square-inch grid transparency may be used as an overlay to measure areas of figures, much as a ruler is used to measure lengths.

Have each student outline a shoe or a hand on the grid paper. Then use the strategies described to estimate the area of the shoe print or handprint.

[†]Master available in *Math 54 Test Masters*.

Practice   Estimate the area of each figure on these grids:

a.

b.

c. On the floor of the classroom, mark off 1 square foot, 1 square yard, and 1 square meter. Estimate the number of each kind of square it would take to cover the whole floor.

Problem set 124

1. Three hundred seconds is how many minutes? (There are 60 seconds in each minute.)
   (62)

2. David, Ann, and Chad were playing marbles. Ann had twice as many marbles as David had, and Chad had 5 more marbles than Ann had. David had 9 marbles. How many marbles did Chad have? (First find how many marbles Ann had.)
   (104)

3. On each of 5 bookshelves there are 44 books. How many books are on all 5 shelves?
   (59)

4. Nine tenths of the 30 students remembered their homework. How many students remembered their homework?
   (105)

5. What percent of the students in problem 5 did not remember their homework?
   (65)

6. What fraction name for 1 has a denominator of 3?
   (113)

7. What equivalent fractions are shown?
(123)

8. Draw a picture to show that $\frac{6}{8}$ and $\frac{3}{4}$ are equivalent fractions.
(123)

9. This is a golf card for 9 holes of golf. What was Michelle's average score on each hole?
(106)

Putt 'N' Putt

PLAYER	1	2	3	4	5	6	7	8	9	TOTAL
Michelle	6	7	5	2	4	1	3	5	3	36
Mathea	5	4	4	3	4	3	2	5	3	33

10. Sarah had to hurry. The laboratory had to be cleaned by 4:20 p.m. It was already 11:00 a.m. How much time did she have to clean the lab?
(33)

11. Sixty minutes is how many seconds?
(59)

12. 4.3 + 12.6 + 3.75
(118)

13. 0.24 + 6.7 + 83.49
(118)

14. 2126.47 − 183.5
(119)

15. 364.1 − 16.41
(119)

16. $\frac{5}{8} + \frac{2}{8}$
(121)

17. $\frac{3}{5} + \frac{1}{5}$
(121)

18. $\frac{9}{10} - \frac{2}{10}$
(122)

19. 60 × 800
(96)

20. 73 × 48
(100)

21. 9 × 78¢
(58)

22. 10^3
(72)

23. $35.00 ÷ 4
(86)

24. $\frac{4824}{8}$
(90)

25. $60\overline{)540}$
(120)

26.
(2)
$$\begin{array}{r} 9 \\ 4 \\ 3 \\ 6 \\ N \\ 2 \\ 5 \\ 7 \\ + \ 3 \\ \hline 43 \end{array}$$

27. Estimate the area of this figure.
(124)

28. 10)463
(115)

29. 70)295
(120)

30. Draw a rectangle that is 4 cm long and 1 cm wide and
(65) shade 25% of it.

LESSON 125

Reducing Fractions

Facts Practice: 64 Multiplication Facts (Test G in Test Masters)

Mental Math: Find each fraction of 60.

   a. $\frac{1}{4}$ of 60   **b.** $\frac{2}{4}$ of 60   **c.** $\frac{3}{4}$ of 60

Review:

   d. 30 × 12   **e.** $10.00 − $5.63   **f.** 37 + 45

Patterns: Find the next five terms in this sequence.

$$\frac{1}{2}, \frac{2}{4}, \frac{3}{6}, \frac{4}{8}, \underline{\quad}, \underline{\quad}, \underline{\quad}, \underline{\quad}, \underline{\quad}, \ldots$$

When we **reduce** a fraction, we find an equivalent fraction written with **smaller** numbers. The picture below shows $\frac{4}{6}$ reduced to $\frac{2}{3}$.

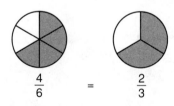

$$\frac{4}{6} = \frac{2}{3}$$

Not all fractions can be reduced. Only a fraction whose top and bottom numbers can be divided by the same number can be reduced. Since the top and bottom numbers of $\frac{4}{6}$ can both be divided by 2, we can reduce the fraction $\frac{4}{6}$.

To reduce a fraction, we divide the fraction by a name for 1. We reduce $\frac{4}{6}$ by dividing 4 by 2 and dividing 6 by 2.

$$\frac{4}{6} \div \frac{2}{2}\mathbf{1} = \frac{2}{3} \quad \begin{array}{l}(4 \div 2 = 2)\\(6 \div 2 = 3)\end{array}$$

When deciding if a fraction can be reduced, it is helpful to look at three numbers. The three numbers are the numerator, the denominator, and the difference between the numerator and the denominator.

numerator ⟶ ④ $6 - 4 = ②$ ⟵ difference
denominator ⟶ ⑥

The three circled numbers are the numerator, the denominator, and the difference. A reducing name for 1 must be able to divide all three numbers.

Example Write the reduced form of each fraction:

(a) $\frac{6}{8}$ (b) $\frac{6}{9}$ (c) $\frac{6}{7}$

Solution (a) The numerator and denominator of $\frac{6}{8}$ are 6 and 8. The difference of 8 and 6 is 2. All three of these numbers can be divided by 2. That means we can reduce the fraction by dividing by $\frac{2}{2}$.

$$\frac{6}{8} \div \frac{2}{2}\mathbf{1} = \frac{3}{4}$$

Illustration:

$$\frac{6}{8} \quad = \quad \frac{3}{4}$$

(b) The numerator and denominator of $\frac{6}{9}$ are 6 and 9. Their difference $(9 - 6)$ is 3. Each of these numbers can be divided by 3. So we reduce $\frac{6}{9}$ by dividing by $\frac{3}{3}$.

$$\frac{6}{9} \div \mathbf{1}\frac{3}{3} = \frac{2}{3}$$

Illustration:

$$\frac{6}{9} \qquad = \qquad \frac{2}{3}$$

(c) The numerator, denominator, and difference of $\frac{6}{7}$ are 6, 7, and 1 $(7 - 6)$, respectively. The only number that divides all three of these numbers is 1. Dividing a fraction by $\frac{1}{1}$ does not reduce the fraction.

$$\frac{6}{7} \div \mathbf{1}\frac{1}{1} = \frac{6}{7}$$

This fraction cannot be reduced. Any fraction whose numerator and denominator have a difference of 1 cannot be reduced.

Practice   Write the reduced form of each fraction:

    a. $\frac{2}{4}$ **b.** $\frac{2}{6}$ **c.** $\frac{3}{9}$ **d.** $\frac{3}{8}$

    e. $\frac{2}{10}$ **f.** $\frac{6}{10}$ **g.** $\frac{9}{12}$ **h.** $\frac{9}{10}$

**Problem set
125**

Use the information below to answer questions 1 and 2:

> *One fence board costs 90¢. It takes 10 boards to build 5 feet of fence.*

1. How many boards are needed to build 50 feet of fence?
(104)

2. What will the boards in problem 1 cost?
(104)

3. Find the perimeter and area of this rectangle.
(76)

4. (a) Find the length of this line segment in millimeters.
(112)
(b) Find the length of the segment in centimeters.

5. Five ninths of the 36 burros were gray. How many of the burros were gray? Illustrate the problem.
(105)

6. Change each improper fraction to a whole number or to a mixed number:
(114)

(a) $\frac{15}{2}$ (b) $\frac{15}{3}$ (c) $\frac{15}{4}$

7. What equivalent fractions are shown?
(123)

8. What percent of each rectangle in problem 7 is shaded?
(65)

9. Write the reduced form of each fraction:
(125)

(a) $\frac{3}{6}$ (b) $\frac{4}{6}$ (c) $\frac{5}{6}$

10. In three tries Rodney bounced the ball on his head 23 times, 36 times, and 34 times. What was the average number of bounces in each try?
(106)

11. T-shirts cost $5 each. Mark had $27. He bought 5 T-shirts. Tax was $1.50. How much money did he have left?
(93)

12. 25.42 − 24.8   **13.** 36.2 − 4.27   **14.**   37.2
(119)   (119)   (116)   135.7
                                                           10.62
                                                            2.47
15. $\frac{3}{9} + \frac{4}{9}$ **16.** $\frac{1}{7} + \frac{2}{7} + \frac{3}{7}$ + 14.0
(121)   (121)   ‾‾‾‾‾‾

17. $\frac{5}{8} - \frac{5}{8}$ **18.** $\frac{11}{12} - \frac{10}{12}$ **19.** $\frac{8}{10} - \frac{5}{10}$
(122)   (122)   (122)

20.   48   **21.**   72   **22.** $4.08
(100)   × 36   (100)   × 58   (68)   ×   7
        ‾‾‾‾   ‾‾‾‾   ‾‾‾‾‾‾‾‾

23. $\frac{4716}{6}$ **24.** $7\overline{)2549}$ **25.** $19.40 ÷ 5
(86)   (86)   (86)

26. 490 ÷ 10   **27.** 90 ÷ 20   **28.** 171 ÷ 40
(115)   (120)   (120)

29. Estimate the area of this footprint. Each small square is one square inch.
(124)

LESSON
126

Dividing by Multiples of 10, Part 2

Facts Practice: 64 Multiplication Facts (Test G in Test Masters)

Mental Math: We find half of a number by dividing the number by 2. We can often divide by 2 mentally. Find half of each number.

   a. $\frac{1}{2}$ of 36   **b.** $\frac{1}{2}$ of 52   **c.** $\frac{1}{2}$ of 76

Review:

   d. 50 × 46   **e.** \$4.63 + \$1.98   **f.** 54 − 35

Problem Solving: There were three stacks of books on the shelf. There were six books in the first stack and eleven books in the second stack. Teresa rearranged the books so that there were nine books in each of the three stacks. How many books were in the third stack before the books were rearranged?

When we divide by multiples of 10, we continue to follow the four-step division method. We divide, multiply, subtract, and bring down. We have practiced division problems with one-digit answers. In this lesson, we will practice division problems with two-digit answers.

Example 1 $30\overline{)963}$

Solution   **Step 1.** We begin by breaking the problem into the smaller division problem, $30\overline{)96}$, and write "3."

$$\begin{array}{r} 32 \text{ r } 3 \\ 30\overline{)963} \\ \underline{90} \\ 63 \\ \underline{60} \\ 3 \end{array}$$

Step 2. We multiply 3 × 30 and write "90."

Step 3. We subtract 96 − 90 and write "6."

Step 4. We bring down the 3, making 63.

REPEAT:

Step 1. We divide $30\overline{)63}$ and write "2."

Step 2. We multiply 2 × 30 and write "60."

Step 3. We subtract 63 − 60 and write "3."

Step 4. There are no more numbers to bring down. The answer is 32 with a remainder of 3.

Example 2 $40\overline{)2531}$

Solution **Step 1.** We begin by breaking the problem into a smaller division problem. Since $40\overline{)25}$ does not give an answer of 1 or more, we start with the division $40\overline{)253}$ and write "6" above the 3.

$$\begin{array}{r} 63\text{ r }11 \\ 40\overline{)2531} \\ \underline{240} \\ 131 \\ \underline{120} \\ 11 \end{array}$$

Step 2. We multiply 6 × 40 and write "240."

Step 3. We subtract 253 − 240 and write "13."

Step 4. We bring down the 1, making 131.

REPEAT:

Step 1. We divide $40\overline{)131}$ and write "3."

Step 2. We multiply 3 × 40 and write "120."

Step 3. We subtract 131 − 120 and write "11."

Step 4. There are no more numbers to bring down. The answer is 63 with a remainder of 11.

Practice Divide:

a. $20\overline{)862}$ **b.** $30\overline{)870}$ **c.** $40\overline{)888}$

d. $50\overline{)2300}$ **e.** $60\overline{)2400}$ **f.** $70\overline{)2453}$

Problem set 126

1. Admission to the zoo was $3.25 for adults and $1.50 [82] for children. Gary bought tickets for 2 adults and 3 children. Altogether, how much did the tickets cost?

2. Find the perimeter and area of
(76) this square.

3 ft

3 ft

3. Ten quarters is the same as how
(104) many nickels?

4. Something is wrong with this
(109) sign. Draw two different signs to
show ways to correct the error.

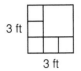

5. What fraction of the letters in
(84) AARDVARK are A's?

6. What fraction name for 1 has a
(113) denominator of 4?

7. Use words to write 7.8.
(108)

8. Draw a picture to show that $\frac{1}{3}$ and $\frac{2}{6}$ are equivalent
(123) fractions.

9. The champion bike rider could ride 58 miles in 2
(104) hours. At the same speed, how far could the champion
ride in 10 hours?

10. The bikers bought 11 caps at $5.40 each and 7 straps at
(93) $1.20 each. Tax was $3.55. They paid for the items
with a $100 bill. How much change did they receive?

11. There were three piles of books on the shelf. Maria
(106) rearranged the three piles so that there were the same
number of books in each pile. Then how many books
were in each pile?

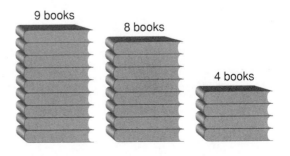

9 books

8 books

4 books

12. 38.42 + 5.71 + 14.3
(118)

13. $6 + 6¢ + $3.45
(53)

14. 43.0 − 7.49
(119)

15. 125.46 − 24.9
(119)

16. $\dfrac{1}{9} + \dfrac{1}{9}$
(121)

17. $\dfrac{4}{11} + \dfrac{5}{11}$
(121)

18. $\dfrac{8}{9} - \dfrac{1}{9}$
(122)

19. $\dfrac{8}{12} - \dfrac{1}{12}$
(122)

20. $9^2 \times 10^2$
(72)

21. 8 × $3.75
(68)

22. 47 × 36
(100)

23. $36.28 ÷ 4
(90)

26. $9\overline{)4321}$
(90)

27. $\dfrac{456}{6}$
(75)

28. $30\overline{)480}$
(126)

24.
(2)

```
   4
   3
   8
   5
   2
   7
   9
   9
   4
+ N
  73
```

25.
(21)

```
   17
   22
   33
   42
   17
   85
   21
   37
   46
   13
+ 20
```

29. $20\overline{)1240}$
(126)

30. Write the reduced form of each fraction:
(125)

(a) $\dfrac{8}{10}$ (b) $\dfrac{8}{9}$ (c) $\dfrac{6}{8}$

LESSON
127

Multiplying a Three-Digit Number by a Two-Digit Number

Facts Practice: 90 Division Facts (Test I in Test Masters)

Mental Math: An odd number may be written as an even number plus 1. For example, 9 is 8 + 1. Half of 9 is half of 8 plus half of 1. Since half of 8 is 4 and half of 1 is $\frac{1}{2}$, half of 9 is $4\frac{1}{2}$. Find half of each of these odd numbers.

 a. 3   **b.** 7   **c.** 11   **d.** 21   **e.** 33

Patterns: Notice that $1 \times 1 \times 1 = 1$, $2 \times 2 \times 2 = 8$, and $3 \times 3 \times 3 = 27$. The products 1, 8, and 27 begin this sequence. Find the next three numbers in the sequence.

$$1, 8, 27, \_\_, \_\_, \_\_, \dots$$

We have learned to multiply a two-digit number by another two-digit number. In this lesson we will learn to multiply a three-digit number by a two-digit number.

Example 1   Multiply: 364 × 24

Solution   We write the three-digit number on top. We write the two-digit number underneath so that the last digits are lined up. We multiply 364 by 4. Next we multiply 364 by 2. Since this 2 is actually 20, we write the last digit of this product in the tens' place, which is under the 2 in 24. Then we add and find that the product is **8736.**

$$
\begin{array}{r}
\scriptstyle 1 \\
\scriptstyle 2\,1 \\
364 \\
\times\ \ 24 \\
\hline
1456 \\
728\ \ \\
\hline
8736
\end{array}
$$

Example 2   Multiply:
$$
\begin{array}{r}
\$4.07 \\
\times\ \ \ \ 38 \\
\hline
\end{array}
$$

Solution   We will ignore the dollar sign and decimal point until we are finished multiplying. First we multiply 407 by 8. Then we multiply 407 by 3, which is actually 30. We write the last digit of this product in the tens' place. We add and find the product is 15466. Now we place the dollar sign and decimal point. The answer is **$154.66.**

$$
\begin{array}{r}
\overset{2}{\underset{5}{}} \\
\$4.07 \\
\times \quad 38 \\
\hline
32\ 56 \\
122\ 1 \\
\hline
\$154.66
\end{array}
$$

Practice   Multiply:

a. 235 × 24   **b.** 14 × 430   **c.** $1.25 × 24

d.   406   **e.** $6.20   **f.**   562
     × 32   ×   31   × 47

Problem set 127

1. Carrie's cousin lives 3000 miles away. If Carrie drove 638 miles the first day, 456 miles the second day, and 589 miles the third day, how much farther does she need to drive to get to her cousin's house?
(17)

2. Find the perimeter and area of this square.
(94,60)

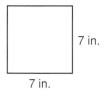

7 in.

7 in.

3. If the perimeter of a square is 2 meters, each side is how many centimeters long?
(27)

4. Gracie found 35 pinecones. Four sevenths of the pinecones still had seeds. How many of the pinecones still had seeds? Illustrate the problem.
(105)

5. Round 6843 to the nearest thousand.
(91)

6. Write the reduced form of each fraction:
(125)   (a) $\frac{4}{5}$ (b) $\frac{5}{10}$ (c) $\frac{4}{10}$

7. Use words to write 374.25.
(108)

8. Draw a picture to show that $\frac{1}{2}$ and $\frac{4}{8}$ are equivalent
(123) fractions.

9. A decade is what percent of a century?
(64)

10. Daniel Boone furnished the settlers with 750 pounds
(106) of meat in 5 days. What was the average amount of
meat he furnished each day?

11. The explorer Zebulon Pike estimated that the
(12) mountain was eight thousand, seven hundred forty-
two feet high. His estimate was five thousand, three
hundred sixty-eight feet less than the actual height.
Today, we call this mountain *Pike's Peak*. How high is
Pike's Peak?

12. $30.07 - 3.7$ **13.** $46.0 - 12.46$ **14.** 37.15
(119)   (119)   (116) 6.84

15. $\dfrac{8}{15} + \dfrac{6}{15}$ 1.29
(121) 29.1
                                                                      $+\ \ 3.6$

16. $\dfrac{3}{10} + \dfrac{3}{10} + \dfrac{3}{10}$
(121)

17. $\dfrac{5}{15} - \dfrac{3}{15}$ **18.** $\dfrac{7}{8} - \dfrac{7}{8}$ **19.** $\dfrac{5}{6} - \dfrac{4}{6}$
(122)   (122)   (122)

20. $\$3.20$ **21.** N **22.** 25
(127) $\times\quad 46$ (2) 4 (21) 31
                                           3 42
                                           2 22
                                           2 $+\ 13$
23. 142 $+\ \ 1$
(77) $\times\quad 30$ $\overline{15}$

24. 307 **25.** $6\overline{)4837}$ **26.** $\dfrac{1372}{\sqrt{16}}$
(127) $\times\quad 25$ (90)   (86,40)

27. $30.00 ÷ 8   **28.** 40$\overline{)960}$ **29.** 20$\overline{)1360}$
(86)   (126)   (126)

30. Estimate the area of this triangle.
(124) Each small square is one square
centimeter.

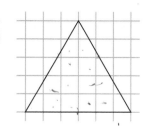

LESSON
128

Finding Equivalent Fractions by Multiplying

Facts Practice: 90 Division Facts (Test I in Test Masters)

Mental Math: Find $\frac{1}{2}$ of each odd number.

  a. $\frac{1}{2}$ of 5   **b.** $\frac{1}{2}$ of 15   **c.** $\frac{1}{2}$ of 25

Review:

  d. 3 × 140   **e.** $20.00 − $18.25   **f.** 474 + 475

Problem Solving: Find the missing digits in each of these
multiplication facts.

$$\begin{array}{r} 7 \\ \times\ \underline{} \\ \hline \underline{}4 \end{array} \qquad \begin{array}{r} \underline{} \\ \times\ 3 \\ \hline \underline{}4 \end{array} \qquad \begin{array}{r} 9 \\ \times\ \underline{} \\ \hline \underline{}4 \end{array}$$

We remember that when we multiply a number by 1, the
answer equals the number we multiplied.

$$2 \times 1 = 2 \qquad 2000 \times 1 = 2000 \qquad \frac{1}{2} \times 1 = \frac{1}{2}$$

We also remember that there are many ways to write "1."

$$1 = \frac{2}{2} = \frac{3}{3} = \frac{4}{4} = \frac{5}{5} = \frac{6}{6} = \ldots$$

We can use these two facts to find equivalent fractions. If we multiply a fraction by a fraction name for 1, the result is an equivalent fraction.

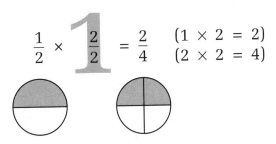

$$\frac{1}{2} \times \frac{2}{2} = \frac{2}{4} \qquad \begin{matrix} (1 \times 2 = 2) \\ (2 \times 2 = 4) \end{matrix}$$

We found that $\frac{1}{2}$ is equivalent to $\frac{2}{4}$ by multiplying $\frac{1}{2}$ by $\frac{2}{2}$, which is a fraction name for 1. We can find other fractions equivalent to $\frac{1}{2}$ by multiplying by other fraction names for 1.

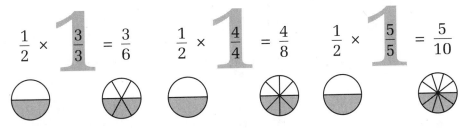

$$\frac{1}{2} \times \frac{3}{3} = \frac{3}{6} \qquad \frac{1}{2} \times \frac{4}{4} = \frac{4}{8} \qquad \frac{1}{2} \times \frac{5}{5} = \frac{5}{10}$$

Example Find four fractions equivalent to $\frac{1}{3}$ by multiplying $\frac{1}{3}$ by $\frac{2}{2}$, $\frac{3}{3}$, $\frac{4}{4}$, and $\frac{5}{5}$.

Solution

$$\frac{1}{3} \times \frac{2}{2} = \frac{2}{6} \qquad\qquad \frac{1}{3} \times \frac{3}{3} = \frac{3}{9}$$

$$\frac{1}{3} \times \frac{4}{4} = \frac{4}{12} \qquad\qquad \frac{1}{3} \times \frac{5}{5} = \frac{5}{15}$$

We find that four fractions equivalent to $\frac{1}{3}$ are

$$\frac{2}{6}, \frac{3}{9}, \frac{4}{12}, \text{ and } \frac{5}{15}$$

Practice Find four equivalent fractions for each of these fractions by multiplying each fraction by $\frac{2}{2}$, $\frac{3}{3}$, $\frac{4}{4}$, and $\frac{5}{5}$:

a. $\frac{1}{4}$ 　　　　　　　　　　b. $\frac{5}{6}$

c. $\frac{2}{5}$ 　　　　　　　　　　d. $\frac{1}{10}$

Problem set 128 Use the information in the table to answer questions 1 and 2:

Lengths of Rivers

RIVER	MILES	KILOMETERS
Nile	4145	6671
Amazon	3915	6300
Yangtze	3900	6276
Congo	2718	4374
Mississippi	2348	3778

1. The Nile is how many kilometers longer than the Yangtze?
(89)

2. The Amazon is how many miles longer than the Congo?
(89)

3. How many feet are in 10 yards?
(49)

4. The squirrel found 1236 acorns during the summer. It saved two thirds of the acorns for winter. How many acorns did the squirrel save for winter?
(105)

5. Find the perimeter and area of this rectangle.
(94,60)

2 cm

3 cm

6. Estimate the sum of 627 and 288.
(70)

7. Use words to name $3578\frac{2}{3}$.
(44)

8. Find three fractions equivalent to $\frac{1}{2}$ by multiplying by $\frac{3}{3}$, $\frac{6}{6}$, and $\frac{10}{10}$.
(128)

9. Write the reduced form of each fraction:
(125)
(a) $\frac{9}{10}$ (b) $\frac{9}{12}$ (c) $\frac{10}{12}$

10. Solve this problem by guessing and checking your answer: In one week Balboa saw 77 buffalo and deer. He saw 13 more buffalo than deer. How many deer did he see?
(119)

11. Only 1% of those who enter the contest win. What
(65) percent of those who enter the contest do not win?

12. 4.63 + 26.7 + 0.34   **13.** 8.4 + 23.57 + 16.9
(118)   (118)

14. 23.91 − 9.3   **15.** 60.4 − 0.64
(119)   (119)

16. $\dfrac{8}{12} + \dfrac{3}{12}$ **17.** $\dfrac{2}{7} + \dfrac{3}{7}$
(121)   (121)

18. $\dfrac{15}{16} - \dfrac{6}{16}$ **19.** $\dfrac{3}{8} - \dfrac{2}{8}$
(122)   (122)

20. 234 × 42   **21.** 36 × 47
(127)   (100)

22.   7   **23.**   42   **24.** 408 × 29
(2)   4   (21)   23   (127)

       2   35

       1   47   **25.** $9\overline{)981}$

       4   74   (90)

       N   53

       2   32   **26.** $25.00 ÷ 4

       7   24   (86)

       4   21

    + 8   5   **27.** $\dfrac{\sqrt{64}}{\sqrt{4}}$

      68   + 7   (56,40)

28. $50\overline{)750}$ **29.** $40\overline{)1280}$ **30.** $30\overline{)843}$
(126)   (126)   (126)

LESSON
129

Chance and Probability

Facts Practice: 90 Division Facts (Test I in Test Masters)

Mental Math: The percent form of $\frac{1}{2}$ is 50%. Find 50% of each
number.

  a. 50% of 28   **b.** 50% of 38   **c.** 50% of 9

Review:

  d. 20 × 44   **e.** $6.47 + $1.95   **f.** 82 − 28

Patterns: Write five different fractions equal to $\frac{1}{2}$.

When a meteorologist states that the chance of rain is 80%,
then the prediction is that it will probably rain. If the chance
of rain is 20%, then the meteorologist means that it might
rain, but it probably will not rain. Meteorologists use
percentages to describe the chance, or the likelihood, of rain.

We can also use a fraction to describe the likelihood of
an event. When we use a fraction, we refer to the
likelihood of an event as *probability*. For instance, if a coin
is flipped, the probability that it will land "heads up" is $\frac{1}{2}$.

$$\frac{1}{2} \leftarrow \text{Only 1 of the 2 possibilities is heads up.}$$

There are 2 possibilities: $\rightarrow$ heads up and tails up.

Since 50% is equivalent to $\frac{1}{2}$, we may also say that the
chance that the coin will land heads up is 50%. Events
that are more likely than not to happen have probabilities
greater than $\frac{1}{2}$ and chances greater than 50%. Events
which are more likely not to happen have probabilities
less than $\frac{1}{2}$ and chances less than 50%.

Example   A number cube is rolled. What is the probability that the
number rolled will be an even number?

Solution   When we write a probability, the bottom number is the
total of all possible outcomes, while the top number is the
number of described outcomes.

$$\frac{\Box}{\Box} \begin{array}{l} \leftarrow \text{described outcomes} \\ \leftarrow \text{possible outcomes} \end{array}$$

With a number cube there are 6 possible outcomes, so 6 is the bottom number. Three of the 6 numbers on the cube are even, so there are 3 ways to roll an even number.

$$\frac{3}{6}$$ ← described outcomes
← possible outcomes

The probability of rolling an even number is $\frac{3}{6}$. We usually reduce fractions, so the probability is also $\frac{1}{2}$.

Practice   **a.** What is the probability of a flipped coin landing tails up?

b. What is the probability of rolling a square number with one roll of a number cube?

c. What is the probability of this spinner stopping on 4?

d. The meteorologist said that the chance of rain is 50%. What does that forecast mean?

Problem set   **1.** A stagecoach was pulled by a 4-horse team, and a
129 $^{(82)}$ covered wagon was pulled by a 6-horse team. Altogether, how many horses were needed to pull 3 stagecoaches and 7 covered wagons?

2. Find the perimeter and area of
$^{(94,60)}$ this rectangle.

8 cm

5 cm

3. Sixteen quarters equals how many
$^{(104)}$ dimes?

4. Gilbert watched TV for 60 minutes. He found that
(105) commercials were on for two tenths of the time.
Commercials were on for how many minutes? Draw a
diagram to illustrate the problem.

5. The commercials in problem 4 were on for what
(80,65) percent of the hour the TV was watched?

6. (a) What is the radius of this circle?
(110) (b) What is the diameter of the circle?

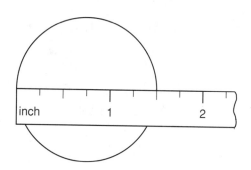

7. Write the reduced form of each fraction:
(125)
(a) $\frac{4}{6}$ (b) $\frac{5}{10}$ (c) $\frac{6}{7}$

8. Draw a picture to show that $\frac{4}{6}$ and $\frac{2}{3}$ are equivalent
(123) fractions.

9. Find three fractions equivalent to $\frac{2}{3}$ by multiplying by
(128) $\frac{2}{2}$, $\frac{3}{3}$, and $\frac{4}{4}$.

10. In three batches of cookies there were 20, 28, and 30
(106) cookies, respectively. What was the average number of
cookies in each batch?

11. James bought 15 apples at 23¢ each, 13 oranges at 41¢
(82) each, and 3 cans of juice at 63¢ each. How much
money did he spend?

12. What is the probability that the spinner in practice
(129) problem (c) will stop on an odd number?

13. 7.6 − 0.76   **14.** 26.04 − 25.7
(119)   *(119)*

15. $\dfrac{1}{10} + \dfrac{2}{10}$
(121)

16. $\dfrac{5}{13} + \dfrac{4}{13} + \dfrac{3}{13}$
(121)

17. $\dfrac{4}{9} - \dfrac{3}{9}$
(122)

18. $\dfrac{6}{7} - \dfrac{3}{7}$
(122)

19. $\dfrac{4}{33} - \dfrac{4}{33}$
(122)

20. $\begin{array}{r} 502 \\ \times\ \ 52 \\ \hline \end{array}$
(127)

21. $\begin{array}{r} 327 \\ \times\ \ 26 \\ \hline \end{array}$
(127)

22. $\begin{array}{r} 490 \\ \times\ \ \ 70 \\ \hline \end{array}$
(77)

23. $1000 \div 5$
(90)

24. $\$42.72 \div 6$
(86)

25. $\dfrac{3627}{3^2}$
(90,72)

26. $60\overline{)1320}$
(126)

27. $30\overline{)2220}$
(126)

28. $40\overline{)963}$
(126)

Change each improper fraction to a mixed number:

29. $\dfrac{35}{8}$
(114)

30. $\dfrac{35}{9}$
(114)

LESSON 130

Dividing by Two-Digit Numbers, Part 1

Facts Practice: 90 Division Facts (Test I in Test Masters)

Mental Math: Find the stated percent of each number.
   a. 50% of 34   **b.** 50% of 25   **c.** 100% of 25

Review:
   d. 5×66 **e.** $\$10.00 - \$9.13$ **f.** $67 + 29 + 200$

Problem Solving: The weather forecast stated that the chance of rain was 30%. What was the chance that it would not rain? Was it more likely to rain or not to rain? If it were as likely to rain as not to rain, what would be the chance of rain?

We have divided by two-digit numbers that are multiples of 10. In this lesson we will begin dividing by other two-digit numbers. When we divide by two-digit numbers, sometimes we accidentally choose an answer to a division problem that is too large. If this happens, we start over and try a smaller number for the answer.

Example 1   31$\overline{)95}$

Solution   **Step 1.**   To help us divide 31$\overline{)95}$, we
think 3$\overline{)9}$ and try that answer.
We write "3."

$$\begin{array}{r} 3\ r\ 2 \\ 31\overline{)95} \\ 93 \\ \hline 2 \end{array}$$

Step 2.   We multiply 3 × 31 and write "93."

Step 3.   We subtract 93 from 95 and write "2."

Step 4.   There are no digits to bring down. The answer is **3 with a remainder of 2.**

Example 2   43$\overline{)246}$

Solution   **Step 1.**   To help us divide 43$\overline{)246}$, we
may think 4$\overline{)24}$ and try that
answer. We write "6."

$$\begin{array}{r} 6 \\ 43\overline{)246} \\ 258 \end{array}$$ ← too large

Step 2.   We multiply 6 × 43 and write "258." We see that 258 is greater than 246. We tried 6, but 6 was too large.

START OVER:

Step 1.   This time we try 5 as the division answer.

$$\begin{array}{r} 5\ r\ 31 \\ 43\overline{)246} \\ 215 \\ \hline 31 \end{array}$$

Step 2.   We multiply 5 × 43 and write "215."

Step 3.   We subtract and write "31."

Step 4.   There are no digits to bring down. The answer is **5 with a remainder of 31.**

Practice Divide:

    a. $32\overline{)128}$ **b.** $21\overline{)90}$ **c.** $25\overline{)68}$

    d. $42\overline{)250}$ **e.** $46\overline{)164}$ **f.** $31\overline{)225}$

Problem set 130

1. There are 60 minutes in 1 hour and 24 hours in 1 day.
(67) How many minutes are in 1 day?

2. Davey had 56 baseball cards. He gave half of them to
(104) Janeen. Janeen gave half of those to Jason. How many
cards did Jason get?

3. How many 1 square foot floor tiles are needed to cover
(76) the floor of a room that is 12 feet long and 8 feet wide?

4. If 2 apples cost 60¢, how much money would 6 apples
(104) cost?

5. (a) What is the diameter of the
(110)   quarter?

    (b) What is the radius of the
         quarter?

6. A number cube is rolled. What is the probability that
(129) the number rolled will be more than four?

7. Write the reduced form of each fraction:
(125)
    (a) $\frac{3}{6}$ (b) $\frac{3}{12}$ (c) $\frac{8}{10}$

8. Find three fractions equivalent to $\frac{3}{4}$ by multiplying $\frac{3}{4}$
(128) by $\frac{2}{2}$, $\frac{3}{3}$, and $\frac{4}{4}$.

9. Guess and check your guess to solve this problem:
(119) There were 14 rocks and bricks in all. There were 2
more rocks than bricks. How many rocks were there?

Use the information in this description to answer questions 10 and 11:

Able, Baker, and Charlie carried weights. Able could carry twice as much as Baker. Baker could carry ten pounds. Charlie could carry one pound more than Able.

10. Together, how many pounds could all three boys carry?
(104)

11. What was the average weight each of the three boys could carry?
(106)

12. 39.42 + 9.5 + 16.1   **13.** 6.34 + 0.17 + 19.8
(118)   (118)

14. 37.1 − 9.46   **15.** 4.91 − 4.91
(119)   (119)

16. $\dfrac{3}{10} + \dfrac{6}{10}$ **17.** $\dfrac{1}{8} + \dfrac{4}{8}$
(121)   (121)

18. $\dfrac{5}{7} - \dfrac{1}{7}$ **19.** $\dfrac{15}{16} - \dfrac{8}{16}$
(122)   (122)

20. 476 × 14   **21.** 240 × 68   **22.** 34 × 904
(127)   (127)   (127)

23. 8$\overline{)4325}$ **24.** $47.16 ÷ 9   **25.** $\dfrac{1221}{3}$
(90)   (86)   (90)

26. 40$\overline{)3210}$ **27.** 32$\overline{)98}$ **28.** 34$\overline{)184}$
(126)   (130)   (130)

29. Estimate the area of this fish pond. Each small square is one square foot.
(124)

LESSON
131

Adding Mixed Numbers • Subtracting Mixed Numbers

Facts Practice: 90 Division Facts (Test I in Test Masters)

Mental Math: The percent form of $\frac{1}{4}$ is 25%. Find the stated percent of each number.

   a. 25% of 80   **b.** 25% of 20   **c.** 50% of 5

Review:

   d. 4×25 **e.** $1.00 - 63¢   **f.** 280 + 630

Problem Solving: Robert used toy blocks to build these steps. How many blocks did he use? How many more blocks would he need to add another step?

Adding mixed numbers
We remember that a mixed number is a number with a whole number part and a fraction part. To add mixed numbers, we add the fraction parts together. Then we add the whole number parts together.

Example 1 Add: $2\frac{3}{5} + 3\frac{1}{5}$

Solution We may write the numbers one above the other. We add the fractions and get $\frac{4}{5}$. We add the whole numbers and get 5. The sum of the mixed numbers is $5\frac{4}{5}$.

$$\begin{array}{r} 2\frac{3}{5} \\ + 3\frac{1}{5} \\ \hline 5\frac{4}{5} \end{array}$$

Example 2 Add: $3 + 1\frac{1}{3}$

Solution The number 3 is a whole number, not a mixed number. Therefore, there is no fraction to add to $\frac{1}{3}$. We add the whole numbers and get $4\frac{1}{3}$.

$$\begin{array}{r} 3 \\ + 1\frac{1}{3} \\ \hline 4\frac{1}{3} \end{array}$$

Subtracting mixed numbers To subtract mixed numbers, we subtract the fractions. Then we subtract the whole numbers.

Example 3 Subtract: $5\frac{2}{3} - 1\frac{1}{3}$

Solution We must subtract the second number from the first number. To do this, it is helpful to write the first number above the second number. Then we subtract the fractions and get $\frac{1}{3}$. Then we subtract the whole numbers and get 4. The difference is $4\frac{1}{3}$.

$$\begin{array}{r} 5\frac{2}{3} \\ -\ 1\frac{1}{3} \\ \hline 4\frac{1}{3} \end{array}$$

Practice

a. $2\frac{1}{4} + 4\frac{2}{4}$ **b.** $5\frac{3}{8} + 1\frac{2}{8}$ **c.** $8 + 1\frac{2}{5}$

d. $4\frac{3}{5} - 1\frac{1}{5}$ **e.** $9\frac{3}{4} - 4\frac{2}{4}$ **f.** $12\frac{8}{9} - 3\frac{3}{9}$

g. $3\frac{1}{3} - 2\frac{1}{3}$ **h.** $6\frac{1}{2} - 3$ **i.** $2\frac{3}{4} - 2\frac{2}{4}$

Problem set 131

1. If Thorton can do 1 problem in 3 seconds, how many **minutes** will it take him to do 100 problems?
(104)

2. (a) What is the area of this rectangle?
(94,60) (b) What is the perimeter of this rectangle?

9 in.

4 in.   4 in.

9 in.

3. Gilbert earned $40. He saved $\frac{5}{8}$ of what he earned. How much money did he save?
(105)

4. After spending $2.50 on a ticket and $1.25 on popcorn, Jill still had 75¢. How much money did she start with?
(82)

5. Tim's shoes weigh $2\frac{1}{4}$ pounds. The rest of his clothes
(131) weigh $3\frac{2}{4}$ pounds. What is the total weight of Tim's shoes and clothes?

6. Draw a circle and shade 75% of it.
(65,32)

7. Write the reduced form of each fraction:
(125) (a) $\frac{2}{8}$ (b) $\frac{4}{10}$ (c) $\frac{4}{9}$

8. Draw a picture to show that $\frac{5}{10}$ and $\frac{1}{2}$ are equivalent
(123) fractions.

9. The first weight was twice the second weight. The
(82) third weight was three times the second weight. The second weight was 20 pounds. What was the sum of the three weights?

10. Allison kept track of the number
(106,89) of laps she swam each day on a table like this. What was the average number of laps she swam on the days shown?

Swimming Chart	
DAY	LAPS
Monday	15
Tuesday	18
Wednesday	16
Thursday	20
Friday	21

11. What is the probability that the
(129) number on a rolled number cube will be less than six?

12. $36.4 + 6.75 + 7.3$
(118)

13. $6.3 - (4.21 - 3.6)$
(55)

14. $3 + 1\frac{1}{4}$
(131)

15. $3\frac{2}{5} + 1\frac{1}{5}$
(131)

16. $12\frac{1}{3} + 1\frac{1}{3}$
(131)

17. $5\frac{4}{5} - 3\frac{1}{5}$
(131)

18. $3\frac{1}{2} - 1\frac{1}{2}$
(131)

19. $6\frac{2}{3} - 4$
(131)

20. $\begin{array}{r} 473 \\ \times\ 62 \\ \hline \end{array}$
(127)

21. $\begin{array}{r} 590 \\ \times\ 37 \\ \hline \end{array}$
(127)

22. $\begin{array}{r} \$12.57 \\ \times\ \ \ \ \ 6 \\ \hline \end{array}$
(68)

23. $\$2.92 \div 4$
(75)

24.
(2)

$$
\begin{array}{r}
4 \\
7 \\
N \\
3 \\
2 \\
1 \\
6 \\
4 \\
+\ 2 \\
\hline
33
\end{array}
$$

25.
(21)

$$
\begin{array}{r}
14 \\
21 \\
43 \\
88 \\
77 \\
66 \\
31 \\
25 \\
+\ 43 \\
\hline
\end{array}
$$

26. $7\overline{)3565}$
(90)

27. $\dfrac{6876}{9}$
(86)

28. $60\overline{)4900}$
(126)

29. $21\overline{)89}$
(130)

30. $42\overline{)244}$
(130)

LESSON 132

Simplifying Fraction Answers

Facts Practice: 100 Multiplication Facts (Test H in Test Masters)

Mental Math: The percent form of $\frac{3}{4}$ is 75%. Find the stated percent of 24.

  a. 25% of 24   **b.** 50% of 24   **c.** 75% of 24

Review:

  d. 20×250 **e.** $\$3.67 + \$2.99$ **f.** $56 - 38$

Problem Solving: Copy this division problem on your paper and fill in the missing digits.

$$
\begin{array}{r}
8\_ \\
\_\ )\overline{\_\ \_\ 7} \\
2\ 4 \\
\hline
2\ \_ \\
\hline
0
\end{array}
$$

It is customary to write math answers in the simplest form possible. If an answer contains a fraction, there are two procedures that we usually follow.

1. Improper fractions are written as mixed numbers (or whole numbers).
2. Fractions are reduced when possible.

Example 1 Add: $\dfrac{2}{3} + \dfrac{2}{3}$

Solution We add to get the sum $\frac{4}{3}$. We notice that $\frac{4}{3}$ is an improper fraction. We take an extra step and change $\frac{4}{3}$ to the mixed number $1\frac{1}{3}$.

$$\dfrac{2}{3} + \dfrac{2}{3} = \dfrac{4}{3}$$

$$\dfrac{4}{3} = \mathbf{1\dfrac{1}{3}}$$

Example 2 Subtract: $\dfrac{3}{4} - \dfrac{1}{4}$

Solution We subtract and get the difference $\frac{2}{4}$. We notice that $\frac{2}{4}$ can be reduced. We take an extra step and reduce $\frac{2}{4}$ to $\frac{1}{2}$.

$$\dfrac{3}{4} - \dfrac{1}{4} = \dfrac{2}{4}$$

$$\dfrac{2}{4} = \mathbf{\dfrac{1}{2}}$$

Example 3 Add: $3\dfrac{1}{3} + 4\dfrac{2}{3}$

Solution We add and get the sum $7\frac{3}{3}$. We notice that $\frac{3}{3}$ is an improper fraction that equals 1. So $7\frac{3}{3} = 7 + 1$, which is 8.

$$3\dfrac{1}{3} + 4\dfrac{2}{3} = 7\dfrac{3}{3}$$

$$7\dfrac{3}{3} = \mathbf{8}$$

Example 4 Add: $5\dfrac{3}{5} + 6\dfrac{4}{5}$

Solution We add and get $11\frac{7}{5}$. We notice that $\frac{7}{5}$ is an improper fraction which can be changed to $1\frac{2}{5}$. So $11\frac{7}{5}$ equals $11 + 1\frac{2}{5}$, which is $12\frac{2}{5}$.

$$5\dfrac{3}{5} + 6\dfrac{4}{5} = 11\dfrac{7}{5}$$

$$11\dfrac{7}{5} = \mathbf{12\dfrac{2}{5}}$$

Example 5 Subtract: $6\dfrac{5}{8} - 1\dfrac{3}{8}$

Solution We subtract and get $5\frac{2}{8}$. We notice that $\frac{2}{8}$ can be reduced. We reduce $\frac{2}{8}$ to $\frac{1}{4}$. So $5\frac{2}{8}$ equals $5\frac{1}{4}$.

$$6\dfrac{5}{8} - 1\dfrac{3}{8} = 5\dfrac{2}{8}$$

$$5\dfrac{2}{8} = \mathbf{5\dfrac{1}{4}}$$

Practice   Simplify each answer:

    a. $\dfrac{4}{5} + \dfrac{4}{5}$ **b.** $\dfrac{5}{6} - \dfrac{1}{6}$ **c.** $3\dfrac{2}{3} + 1\dfrac{2}{3}$

    d. $5\dfrac{1}{4} + 6\dfrac{3}{4}$ **e.** $7\dfrac{7}{8} - 1\dfrac{1}{8}$ **f.** $5\dfrac{3}{5} + 1\dfrac{3}{5}$

Problem set 132

1. Sharon made 70 photocopies. If she paid 6¢ per copy
(93) and the total tax was 25¢, how much change did she
get back from a $5 bill?

2. (a) What is the area of this
(94,60)   square?
    (b) What is the perimeter of this
    square?

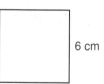

6 cm

Use the information in this description to answer
questions 3 and 4:

*Danny has $9. David has twice as much money as
Danny. Chris has $6 more than David.*

3. How much money does Chris have?
(104)

4. What is the average amount of money each boy has?
(106)

5. There are 40 quarters in a roll of quarters. What is the
(104) value of 2 rolls of quarters?

6. Estimate the product of 29 and 312. Then find the
(103) actual product.

7. Write the reduced form of each fraction:
(125)   (a) $\frac{2}{12}$ (b) $\frac{6}{8}$ (c) $\frac{3}{9}$

8. Find three fractions equivalent to $\frac{1}{6}$ by multiplying by
(128) $\frac{2}{2}, \frac{3}{3}$, and $\frac{4}{4}$.

9. Draw diagrams to help work this problem: Their
(82) noses were black, red, and green. Green came just
before black, and red was not last. Who came first?

10. If an event cannot happen, its probability is 0. If an
(129) event is certain to happen, its probability is 1. What is
the probability of rolling a 7 with one roll of a number
cube?

11. Dresses were on sale for 50% off. If the regular price
(80) was $40, what was the sale price?

12. 4.62 + 16.7 + 9.8   **13.** 14.62 − (6.3 − 2.37)
(118)   (55)

14. $\dfrac{3}{5} + \dfrac{4}{5}$ **15.** $16 + 3\dfrac{3}{4}$ **16.** $1\dfrac{2}{3} + 3\dfrac{1}{3}$
(132)   (131)   (132)

17. $\dfrac{2}{5} + \dfrac{3}{5}$ **18.** $7\dfrac{4}{5} + 7\dfrac{1}{5}$ **19.** $6\dfrac{2}{3} + 3\dfrac{2}{3}$
(132)   (132)   (132)

20. 372 × 39   **21.** 47 × 142   **22.** $360 \times \sqrt{36}$
(127)   (127)   (68,40)

23. Estimate the area of this circle.
(124) Each small square is one square
centimeter.

24. $8\overline{)4834}$ **25.**   2
(90)   (2)   5
                                     1
26. $\dfrac{2840}{2^3}$ 3
(86,72)   2
                                     3
                                     7
27. $36.00 ÷ 5$ 8
(90)   2
                                  $+ N$
28. $30\overline{)963}$ ─────
(126)   48

29. $51\overline{)310}$
(130)

30. $24\overline{)124}$
(130)

LESSON
133

Renaming Fractions

Facts Practice: 100 Multiplication Facts (Test H in Test Masters)

Mental Math: Find the stated percent of 36.

  a. 25% of 36   **b.** 75% of 36   **c.** 100% of 36

Review:

  d. 4 × 250   **e.** $5.00 − $4.25   **f.** 156 + 29

Patterns: What are the next three terms in this sequence?

$1000.00, $100.00, $10.00, __, __, __, ...

We remember that if we multiply a fraction by a fraction that equals 1, the result is an equivalent fraction. If we multiply $\frac{1}{2}$ by $\frac{2}{2}$, we get $\frac{2}{4}$. The fractions $\frac{1}{2}$ and $\frac{2}{4}$ are equivalent fractions because they have the same value.

$$\frac{1}{2} \times \mathbf{1}\frac{2}{2} = \frac{2}{4}$$

Sometimes we must choose a particular multiplier that is equal to 1.

Example 1 Find the equivalent fraction for $\frac{1}{4}$ whose denominator is 12.

Solution To change 4 to 12, we must multiply by 3. So we multiply $\frac{1}{4}$ by $\frac{3}{3}$.

$$\frac{1}{4} \times \mathbf{1}\frac{3}{3} = \frac{3}{12}$$

The fraction $\frac{1}{4}$ is equivalent to $\frac{3}{12}$.

Example 2 Complete the equivalent fraction: $\frac{2}{3} = \frac{?}{15}$

Solution The bottom number changed from 3 to 15. The bottom number was multiplied by 5. The correct multiplier is $\frac{5}{5}$.

$$\frac{2}{3} \times \frac{5}{5} = \frac{10}{15}$$

The fraction $\frac{2}{3}$ and the fraction $\frac{10}{15}$ are equivalent fractions.

Practice Find the top numbers so the pairs of fractions will be equivalent fractions:

a. $\frac{1}{4} = \frac{?}{12}$ b. $\frac{2}{3} = \frac{?}{12}$ c. $\frac{5}{6} = \frac{?}{12}$

d. $\frac{3}{5} = \frac{?}{10}$ e. $\frac{2}{3} = \frac{?}{9}$ f. $\frac{3}{4} = \frac{?}{8}$

Problem set 133

1. (104) If a can of soup costs $1.50 and serves 3 people, how much would it cost to serve soup to 12 people?

2. (94,60) (a) What is the perimeter of this rectangle?
(b) What is the area of this rectangle?

5 ft   5 ft

7 ft

3. (104) What number is eight less than the product of nine and ten?

4. (105) The woodpecker found 3069 bugs in the tree and ate $\frac{2}{3}$ of them. How many bugs were left in the tree? Illustrate the problem.

5. (112) (a) Find the length of the line segment in centimeters.
(b) Find the length of the segment in millimeters.

mm 10 20 30 40

cm 1 2 3 4

6. Use words to write 356,420.
(42)

7. Complete each equivalent fraction:
(133)
(a) $\frac{1}{2} = \frac{?}{6}$ (b) $\frac{1}{3} = \frac{?}{6}$ (c) $\frac{2}{3} = \frac{?}{6}$

8. Write the reduced form of each fraction:
(125)
(a) $\frac{2}{6}$ (b) $\frac{6}{9}$ (c) $\frac{9}{16}$

9. There were 40 workers on the job. Of those workers,
(125) 10 had worked overtime. What fraction of the workers had worked overtime? (Remember to reduce the fraction.)

10. What percent of the workers in problem 9 had worked
(65) overtime?

11. Bill received $10 for his tenth birthday. Each year after
(104) that he received $1 more than he did on his previous birthday. He saved all his birthday money. Altogether, how much birthday money did he have on his fifteenth birthday?

12. $9.36 - (4.37 + 3.8)$ **13.** $24.32 - (8.61 + 12.5)$
(55)   (55)

14. $\frac{4}{5} + \frac{4}{5}$ **15.** $5\frac{5}{8} + 3\frac{3}{8}$ **16.** $6\frac{3}{10} + \frac{2}{10}$
(132)   (132)   (132)

17. $8\frac{2}{3} - 5\frac{1}{3}$ **18.** $4\frac{3}{4} - 2\frac{1}{4}$ **19.** $7\frac{1}{2} - 5$
(131)   (132)   (131)

20. 60×400 **21.** 536×3^3 **22.** $12 \times \$1.50$
(96)   (127,72)   (127)

23. $6\overline{)3642}$ **24.** $\$125 \div 5$ **25.**   26
(90)   (75)   (21)   9
                                                                   14
26. $40\overline{)645}$ **27.** $41\overline{)165}$ 11
(126)   (130)   2
                                                              + 34
28. $\dfrac{4380}{10}$
(115)

29. Estimate the area of this piece of
(124) land. Each small square is one
square mile.

30. What is the probability that the
(129) spinner will stop on a number
greater than 5?

LESSON
134

Naming Geometric Solids

Facts Practice: 100 Multiplication Facts (Test H in Test Masters)

Mental Math: The percent form of $\frac{1}{10}$ is 10%. Find the stated
percent of 40.

  a. 25% of 40   **b.** 75% of 40   **c.** 10% of 40

Review:

  d. 50 × 48   **e.** $8.75 + $4.50   **f.** 71 − 25

Problem Solving: The probability of a flipped coin landing
heads up is 1 out of 2. The probability of
rolling a 1 with a number cube is 1 out of 6.
What is the probability of a coin landing tails
up? What is the probability of rolling a six
with one number cube? What is the
probability of rolling an even number with
one number cube?

We have practiced naming shapes such as triangles,
rectangles, and circles. These are flat shapes. They do not
take up **space.** Objects that take up space are things like
cars, basketballs, desks, houses, and people.

Geometric shapes that take up space are called **geometric solids.** The chart below shows the names of some geometric solids.

SHAPE				NAME
				Cube
				Rectangular solid
				Pyramid
				Cylinder
				Sphere
				Cone

Example 1 Name each shape:

(a)   (b)   (c)

Solution If we check each shape with the chart, we see that (a) is a **sphere,** (b) is a **cube,** and (c) is a **cone.**

Example 2 What is the shape of a soup can?

Solution A soup can has the shape of a **cylinder.**

Example 3 This rectangular solid is made of how many small cubes?

Solution We see that the rectangular solid is made of 2 layers of cubes with 6 cubes on each layer (2 × 6 = 12). The rectangular solid is made of **12 small cubes.**

Practice Name the shape of each object listed:

a. Basketball

b. Shoebox

c. Ice-cream cone

d. What is the shape of this Egyptian landmark?

e. This rectangular solid is made of how many small cubes?

Problem set Use the information given in the graph to answer
134 questions 1–3:

Test Grades of Class
(32 Students)

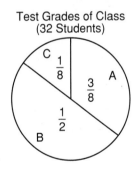

1. Of the 32 students in the class, how many earned a C
(111) on the test?

2. How many students earned an A?
(111)

3. Altogether, how many students earned an A or a B?
(111)

4. If the perimeter of a square is 3 feet, each side is how
(60) many inches long?

5. This rectangular solid is made of
(134) how many small cubes?

6. Name each shape:
(134)

(a)   (b) ▲   (c) ⬤

7. Complete each equivalent fraction:
(133)

(a) $\frac{1}{2} = \frac{?}{8}$ (b) $\frac{1}{4} = \frac{?}{8}$ (c) $\frac{3}{4} = \frac{?}{8}$

8. Write the reduced form of each fraction:
(125)

(a) $\frac{9}{10}$ (b) $\frac{10}{15}$ (c) $\frac{4}{8}$

9. Draw diagrams to help solve this problem: Wilbur
(82) was not first. Roger came just before Sarah. Sarah was not last. Who was in the middle?

10. The first five square numbers are 1, 4, 9, 16, and 25.
(39) What are the next five square numbers?

11. There were 5 containers for 37 items. The items were
(98) divided as evenly as possible between the containers. List the number of items in each container.

12. $9.43 - (6.43 + 1.7)$
(55)

13. $16.1 - (1.23 + 12.3)$
(55)

14. $\frac{2}{3} + \frac{2}{3} + \frac{2}{3}$
(132)

15. $3\frac{1}{2} + 4\frac{1}{2}$
(132)

16. $5\frac{1}{6} + 1\frac{1}{6}$
(132)

17. $3\frac{1}{3} - 1\frac{1}{3}$
(131)

18. $4\frac{3}{8} - 1\frac{1}{8}$
(132)

19. $4\frac{1}{4} - 2$
(131)

20. Four is what percent of 4^2?
(65)

21. $25 \times \$6.40$
(127)

22. 68×47
(100)

23. $6\overline{)4564}$
(90)

24. $\$12.40 \div 10$
(115)

25. $\frac{4624}{8}$
(86)

26. $30\overline{)246}$
(120)

27. $41\overline{)246}$
(130)

28. $32\overline{)246}$
(130)

29. Brad's drawer contains only white socks and blue
(129) socks. There are 12 white socks and 8 blue socks. If
Brad takes one sock from his drawer without looking,
what is the probability that the sock will be blue?

LESSON
135

Roman Numerals Through 39

Facts Practice: 100 Multiplication Facts (Test H in Test Masters)

Mental Math: The percent form of $\frac{2}{10}$ is 20%. Find the stated
percent of 50.

  a. 50% of 50   **b.** 10% of 50   **c.** 20% of 50

Review:

  d. 20 × 30 × 40   **e.** \$10.00 − \$1.95   **f.** 147 + 63

Problem Solving: There were only 9 coins in the cash register,
but it was enough to make change for any
purchase of less than one dollar. What coins
were in the cash register? (*Hint*: It should be
possible to make any amount of money from
1¢ to 99¢ with the coins.)

Roman numerals are letters used by the ancient Romans to
write numbers. Roman numerals are still used today on
clocks and buildings and are used to number such things
as book chapters and Super Bowl games.

    Some Roman numerals and their values are

           I   which equals 1

           V   which equals 5

           X   which equals 10

Roman numerals do not use place value. Instead, the
values of the digits are added or sometimes subtracted.

        II   means   2 ones, which is 2, not 11

The Roman numerals for the numbers 1–20 are listed below. Study the patterns.

I = 1	XI = 11
II = 2	XII = 12
III = 3	XIII = 13
IV = 4	XIV = 14
V = 5	XV = 15
VI = 6	XVI = 16
VII = 7	XVII = 17
VIII = 8	XVIII = 18
IX = 9	XIX = 19
X = 10	XX = 20

The multiples of 5 include 5, 10, 15, and 20. The numbers that are one less than these (4, 9, 14, and 19) have Roman numerals that involve subtraction.

4 = IV	(one less than five)
9 = IX	(one less than ten)
14 = XIV	(ten and one less than five)
19 = XIX	(ten and one less than ten)

In each of these cases, a smaller Roman numeral (I) precedes a larger Roman numeral (V or X).

Example (a) Write XXVII in our number system.[†]

(b) Write 34 in Roman numerals.

Solution (a) We add 2 tens plus 5 ones plus 2 ones and get 27.

XX   V   II
20 + 5 + 2 = **27**

[†]The modern world has adopted the Hindu-Arabic number system with the digits 0, 1, 2, 3, 4, 5, 6, 7, 8, 9, and base 10 place value. For simplicity, we refer to the Hindu-Arabic system as "our number system."

(b) We think of 34 as 30 plus 4.

30 + 4

XXX   IV

So 34 is written **XXXIV**.

Practice   Write the Roman numerals in order from 1–39.

Problem set 135

1. Grampa bought meat for $4.70, potatoes for $1.59,
(93) bananas for $1.65, and lettuce for 87¢. He gave the grocer $10. How much did he get back?

2. What is the area of this rectangle?
(94)

15 mm

10 mm   10 mm

3. Bill can blow up 1 balloon in 1 minute. At that rate,
(104) how many balloons can Bill blow up in ten hours?

4. This rectangular solid is made of
(134) how many small cubes?

5. The number V is what percent of X?
(135)

6. Draw a diagram to help with this problem: You have
(50) to drive south through Dalton to get to Calhoun from Chattanooga. It is 21 miles from Chattanooga to Dalton. It is 39 miles from Chattanooga to Calhoun. How far is it from Dalton to Calhoun?

7. Wilba's lunch cost $4.85. Norton's lunch cost $3.94.
(106) Danielle's lunch was $5.22. What was the average price of the three lunches?

8. (a) Write XXIV in our number system.
(135)
(b) Write 36 in Roman numerals.

9. Name the shape of each object:
(134)
(a) Marble   (b) Cereal box

10. Complete each equivalent fraction:
(133)
(a) $\frac{1}{2} = \frac{?}{10}$ (b) $\frac{1}{5} = \frac{?}{10}$ (c) $\frac{4}{5} = \frac{?}{10}$

11. Write the reduced form of each fraction:
(125)
(a) $\frac{2}{10}$ (b) $\frac{4}{6}$ (c) $\frac{4}{12}$

12. $4.76 + 12.8 + 6.7$ **13.** $24.3 - (12.14 - 3.2)$
(118)   (55)

14. $\frac{5}{8} + \frac{6}{8}$ **15.** $4\frac{1}{4} + 2\frac{3}{4}$ **16.** $3 + 4\frac{5}{6}$
(132)   (132)   (131)

17. $5\frac{3}{5} + 3\frac{1}{5}$ **18.** $8\frac{1}{4} + 3\frac{1}{4}$ **19.** $\frac{7}{8} + \frac{1}{8}$
(131)   (132)   (132)

20. What is the probability that the
(129) spinner will stop on a number
less than 7?

21. $24 \times 15¢$ **22.**
(100)   (2)

$$\begin{array}{r} 1 \\ 6 \\ 3 \\ N \\ 4 \\ 8 \\ 9 \\ 7 \\ + \ 6 \\ \hline 63 \end{array}$$

23. 472×60
(77)

24. 54×23
(100)

25. $\$6.72 \div 8$
(75)

26. $10\overline{)737}$
(115)

27. $\dfrac{4935}{7}$
(90)

28. $60\overline{)4270}$ **29.** $41\overline{)210}$ **30.** $31\overline{)210}$
(126)   (130)   (130)

LESSON
136

Common Denominators

Facts Practice: 100 Multiplication Facts (Test H in Test Masters)

Mental Math: The percent form of $\frac{3}{10}$ is 30%. Find the stated percent of 60.

   a. 10% of 60   **b.** 20% of 60   **c.** 30% of 60

Review:

   d. 8 × 25   **e.** \$4.63 + \$3.98   **f.** 84 − 45

Problem Solving: Samantha keeps video tapes in a box that is 16 inches long, 8 inches wide, and 4 inches tall. The tapes are 4 inches long, 1 inch wide, and $7\frac{1}{2}$ inches tall. How many tapes can she fit into the box?

Tape   Box

Two fractions have common denominators if the denominators are equal.

$$\frac{3}{8} \qquad \frac{5}{8} \qquad\qquad\qquad \frac{3}{8} \qquad \frac{5}{9}$$

    These two fractions   These two fractions do
    have common   **not** have common
    denominators.   denominators.

Fractions that do not have common denominators can be renamed so that they do have common denominators.

Example 1   Rename $\frac{2}{3}$ and $\frac{3}{4}$ so that they have a common denominator of twelve.

Solution   To rename a fraction, we multiply the fraction by a name for one. To change the denominator of $\frac{2}{3}$ to twelve, we multiply by $\frac{4}{4}$. To change the denominator of $\frac{3}{4}$ to twelve, we multiply by $\frac{3}{3}$.

RENAME $\frac{2}{3}$ RENAME $\frac{3}{4}$

$$\frac{2}{3} \times \mathbf{1}\frac{4}{4} = \frac{8}{12} \qquad\qquad \frac{3}{4} \times \mathbf{1}\frac{3}{3} = \frac{9}{12}$$

$$\frac{2}{3} = \frac{8}{12} \qquad\qquad\qquad \frac{3}{4} = \frac{9}{12}$$

Example 2 Rename $\frac{1}{2}$ and $\frac{1}{3}$ so that they have a common denominator.

Solution This time we need to figure out a common denominator before we can rename the fractions. The denominators are 2 and 3. We will list some multiples of 2 and of 3 to find multiples they have in common.

Multiples of 2: 2, 4, ⑥, 8, 10, ⑫, ...

Multiples of 3: 3, ⑥, 9, ⑫, 15, 18, ...

We see that 6 and 12 are both multiples of 2 and 3. Since 6 is less than 12, we will use 6 as the common denominator and multiply by $\frac{3}{3}$ and $\frac{2}{2}$, respectively.

RENAME $\frac{1}{2}$ RENAME $\frac{1}{3}$

$$\frac{1}{2} \times \mathbf{1}\frac{3}{3} = \frac{3}{6} \qquad\qquad \frac{1}{3} \times \mathbf{1}\frac{2}{2} = \frac{2}{6}$$

$$\frac{1}{2} = \frac{3}{6} \qquad\qquad\qquad \frac{1}{3} = \frac{2}{6}$$

Note: If we had used 12 as the common denominator, the fractions would have been $\frac{6}{12}$ and $\frac{4}{12}$. Usually, we try to write fractions with the **lowest** common denominators.

Practice

a. Rename $\frac{1}{2}$ and $\frac{1}{5}$ so that they have a common denominator of 10.

b. Rename $\frac{3}{4}$ and $\frac{5}{6}$ so that they have a common denominator of 12.

Rename each pair of fractions so that they have the lowest common denominators:

c. $\frac{1}{2}$ and $\frac{2}{3}$ **d.** $\frac{1}{3}$ and $\frac{1}{4}$

e. $\frac{1}{2}$ and $\frac{3}{5}$ **f.** $\frac{2}{3}$ and $\frac{2}{5}$

Problem set 136

1. Tim caught 24 polliwogs. If he let one fourth of them go, how many did he keep? Illustrate the problem.
$^{(80)}$

2. Rectangular Park was 2 miles long and 1 mile wide. Gordon ran around the park twice. How many miles did he run?
$^{(60)}$

2 mi

1 mi

3. If 2 oranges cost 42¢, how much would 8 oranges cost?
$^{(104)}$

4. Three fourths of the 64 baseball cards showed players from the American League. How many of the baseball cards showed American League players? Illustrate the problem.
$^{(105)}$

5. What percent of the baseball cards in problem 4 showed players from the American League?
$^{(80,65)}$

6. (a) Write XIX in our number system.
$^{(135)}$ (b) Write 28 in Roman numerals.

7. Complete each equivalent fraction:
$^{(133)}$

(a) $\frac{1}{2} = \frac{?}{12}$ (b) $\frac{1}{3} = \frac{?}{12}$ (c) $\frac{1}{4} = \frac{?}{12}$

8. Write the reduced form of each fraction:
$^{(125)}$

(a) $\frac{5}{10}$ (b) $\frac{8}{15}$ (c) $\frac{6}{12}$

9. Randy paid 42¢ for 6 clips and 64¢ for 8 erasers. Find
(104) the cost for 1 clip and for 1 eraser. What would be the cost of 10 clips and 20 erasers?

10. There were 14 volunteers the first year, 16 volunteers
(82) the second year, and 18 volunteers the third year. If they continued to increase at 2 volunteers per year, how many volunteers would there be in the tenth year?

11. (a) Rename $\frac{1}{4}$ and $\frac{2}{3}$ so that they have a common
(136)   denominator of 12.

(b) Rename $\frac{1}{3}$ and $\frac{3}{4}$ so that they have the lowest common denominator.

12. A number cube is rolled. What is the probability that
(129) the number rolled will be less than seven?

13. $47.14 - (3.63 + 36.3)$ **14.** $50.1 + (6.4 - 1.46)$
(55)   (55)

15. $\frac{3}{4} + \frac{3}{4} + \frac{3}{4}$ **16.** $4\frac{1}{6} + 1\frac{1}{6}$ **17.** $5\frac{3}{5} + 1\frac{2}{5}$
(132)   (132)   (132)

18. $\frac{5}{6} + \frac{1}{6}$ **19.** $12\frac{3}{4} + 3\frac{1}{4}$ **20.** $6\frac{1}{5} + 1\frac{1}{5}$
(132)   (132)   (131)

21. 340×15 **22.** 26×307 **23.** 70×250
(127)   (127)   (127)

24. $\dfrac{3550}{5}$ **25.** $\$20.00 \div 8$ **26.** $9\overline{)5784}$
(90)   (90)   (86)

27. $432 \div 30$ **28.** $342 \div 42$ **29.** $243 \div 43$
(126)   (130)   (130)

30. Estimate the area of this pentagon.
(124) Each small square is one square inch.

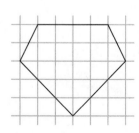

LESSON
137

Naming Numbers Through Hundred Millions

Facts Practice: 90 Division Facts (Test J in Test Masters)

Mental Math: The percent forms of $\frac{4}{10}$, $\frac{5}{10}$, and $\frac{6}{10}$ are 40%, 50%, and 60%, respectively. Find the stated percent of 70.

  a. 10% of 70   **b.** 20% of 70   **c.** 30% of 70

  d. 40% of 70   **e.** 60% of 70   **f.** 100% of 70

Patterns: These fractions all equal one fourth. Write four more fractions equal to one fourth that continue this sequence.

$$\frac{1}{4}, \frac{2}{8}, \frac{3}{12}, \underline{\quad}, \underline{\quad}, \underline{\quad}, \underline{\quad}, \cdots$$

The table below names the values of the first nine whole number places.

hundred-millions' ten-millions' millions' comma hundred-thousands' ten-thousands' thousands' comma hundreds' tens' ones' decimal point

— — — , — — — , — — — .

Example 1 Which digit is in the ten-millions' place in 156,374,289?

Solution We see that the ten-millions' place is eight places from the right. We count eight places in 156,374,289 and find that the digit in the ten-millions' place is **5.**

Example 2 The 3 is in what place in 23,485,179?

Solution The 3 is seven places from the right. We see that seven places from the right is the **millions' place.**

To read whole numbers of more than six digits, we use two commas. To read the number

496874235

we place the thousands' comma three places from the right-hand end. Then we place the millions' comma three places to the left of the thousands' comma.

496 , 874 , 235

millions' comma   thousands' comma

To write this number in words, we read the number to the left of the millions' comma.

Four hundred ninety-six

Now we read the millions' comma by saying "million," and we put a comma after the word *million*.

Four hundred ninety-six million,

Then we read the rest of the number.

Four hundred ninety-six million,
eight hundred seventy-four thousand,
two hundred thirty-five

We remembered to write a comma after the word *thousand* just as we did after the word *million*.

Example 3   Use words to write the number 374196285.

Solution   We use commas to separate the number into three sections, which we read one section at a time. When we get to the first comma, we write "million." When we get to the second comma, we write "thousand."

374   ,   196   ,   285
million   thousand

**Three hundred seventy-four million,
one hundred ninety-six thousand,
two hundred eighty-five**

Practice Use words to name each of these numbers. Insert commas as necessary.

 a. 27196384

 b. 176245398

 c. 3541286

Problem set **1.** Robin separated his 45 merry men as equally as
137 $^{(98)}$ possible into 4 groups. How many merry men were in the largest group?

 2. (a) What is the area of this rectangle?
$^{(94,60)}$ (b) What is the perimeter of this rectangle?

12 cm

8 cm

 3. Tom answered $\frac{5}{6}$ of the 90 questions correctly. How
$^{(105)}$ many questions did Tom answer correctly? Illustrate the problem.

 4. Name the shape of each object:
$^{(134)}$ (a) Roll of paper towels   (b) Baseball

 5. Write the reduced form of each fraction:
$^{(125)}$ (a) $\frac{3}{6}$ (b) $\frac{5}{15}$ (c) $\frac{8}{12}$

 6. Rename $\frac{3}{4}$ and $\frac{5}{6}$ so that they have a common
$^{(136)}$ denominator.

 7. Which digit is in the ten-millions' place in
$^{(137)}$ 328,496,175?

 8. Draw a picture to help you solve this problem:
$^{(50)}$ Winder is on the road from Atlanta to Athens. It is 60 miles from Athens to Atlanta. It is 18 miles from Winder to Athens. How far is it from Winder to Atlanta?

9. The chance of rain is 80%. What is the chance that it
(65) will not rain?

10. A nickel is what percent of a dime?
(65)

11. 4.36 + 12.7 + 10.72   **12.** 8.54 − (4.2 − 2.17)
(118)   (118)

13. $\dfrac{5}{9} + \dfrac{5}{9}$ **14.** $3\dfrac{2}{3} + 1\dfrac{2}{3}$ **15.** $4\dfrac{5}{8} + 1$
(132)   (132)   (131)

16. $7\dfrac{2}{3} + 1\dfrac{2}{3}$ **17.** $4\dfrac{4}{9} + 1\dfrac{1}{9}$ **18.** $\dfrac{11}{12} + \dfrac{1}{12}$
(132)   (131)   (132)

19. 570 × 64   **20.** 382 × 31   **21.** 54 × 18
(127)   (127)   (100)

22. $\dfrac{3731}{7}$ **23.** $9\overline{)5432}$ **24.** $20.80 ÷ 8
(86)   (90)   (90)

25. $60\overline{)548}$ **26.** $13\overline{)50}$ **27.** $72\overline{)297}$
(120)   (130)   (130)

28. If the perimeter of a square is 6 centimeters, each side
(79,60) is how many millimeters long?

29. This cube is made of how many
(134) smaller cubes?

30. Write   the   Roman   numerals
(135) between XX and XXX.

Dividing by Two-Digit Numbers, Part 2

Facts Practice: 90 Division Facts (Test J in Test Masters)

Mental Math: Find the stated percent of 80.

  a. 25% of 80   **b.** 75% of 80   **c.** 30% of 80

Review:

  d. 50 × 32   **e.** $5.00 − $0.74   **f.** 47 + 39

Problem Solving: Copy this division problem on your paper and fill in the missing digits.

$$
\begin{array}{r}
5\,\_ \\
\_\,)\overline{\_\,\_\,\_} \\
3\,5 \\
\overline{1\,\_} \\
\overline{1}
\end{array}
$$

We have used four steps to do two-digit division problems that have one-digit answers. In this lesson we will practice two-digit division problems that have two-digit answers.

    We will continue to follow the four steps: divide, multiply, subtract, and bring down.

Example $21\overline{)487}$

Solution   **Step 1.** We break the problem into a smaller division problem, $21\overline{)48}$, and write "2."

$$
\begin{array}{r}
2 \\
21\overline{)487} \\
\underline{42} \\
67
\end{array}
$$

    Step 2. We multiply 2×21 and write "42."

    Step 3. We subtract 42 from 48 and write "6."

    Step 4. We bring down the 7, making 67.

REPEAT:

Step 1. We divide 21)67 and write "3."

Step 2. We multiply 3 × 21 and write "63."

Step 3. We subtract 63 from 67 and write "4."

$$\begin{array}{r} 23 \text{ r } 4 \\ 21\overline{)487} \\ 42 \\ \overline{67} \\ 63 \\ \overline{4} \end{array}$$

Step 4. There are no digits to bring down. The answer is **23 with a remainder of 4.**

Practice
a. 21)672 **b.** 12)384 **c.** 32)675

d. 23)510 **e.** 41)880 **f.** 11)555

Problem set 138

Use the information in the graph to answer questions 1–3:

Temperatures During Week

1. On what day was the temperature the highest?
(92)

2. What was the temperature on Tuesday?
(92)

3. From Monday to Wednesday, the high temperature went up how many degrees?
(92)

4. (a) What is the perimeter of this rectangle?
(94,60)
(b) What is the area of this rectangle?

15 m

24 m

5. The first five square numbers are 1, 4, 9, 16, and 25,
(106) and their average is 11. What is the average of the next five square numbers?

6. What percent of the months of the year begin with the
(84,65) letter J?

7. What is the probability of drawing an ace from a full
(129) deck of cards? (There are 52 cards in a deck, and 4 of
these cards are aces.)

8. Name each shape:
(134)

(a)   (b) ◀   (c) ●

9. Write the reduced form of each fraction:
(125)

(a) $\frac{6}{8}$ (b) $\frac{4}{9}$ (c) $\frac{4}{16}$

10. Rename $\frac{2}{3}$ and $\frac{3}{4}$ so that they have common
(136) denominators.

11. Use words to name 27386415.
(137)

12. 4.75 + 16.14 + 10.9   **13.** 18.4 − (4.32 − 2.6)
(118)   (55)

14. $4\frac{4}{5} + 3\frac{3}{5}$ **15.** $5\frac{1}{6} + 1\frac{2}{6}$ **16.** $7\frac{3}{4} + \frac{1}{4}$
(132)   (132)   (132)

17. $5\frac{3}{8} + 5\frac{1}{8}$ **18.**   5   **19.**   28
(132)   (2)   2   (21)   47
4   74
7   36
3   91

20. $4\frac{1}{6} + 2\frac{1}{6}$ 5   87
(132)   3   21

21. 720 × 36   6   12
(127)   5   + 14

22. 147 × 54   N
(127)   + 4

23. $8\overline{)5766}$ 55
(90)

24. $36.30 ÷ 10
(115)

25. $\frac{4735}{5}$ **26.** $21\overline{)441}$
(86)   (138)

27. 32)960
(138)

28. 12)518
(138)

29. Estimate the area of this figure.
(124) Each small square is one square
inch.

LESSON
139

Adding and Subtracting Fractions with Unlike Denominators

Facts Practice: 90 Division Facts (Test J in Test Masters)

Mental Math: Find the stated percent of 90.
  a. 50% of 90   **b.** 10% of 90   **c.** 90% of 90
Review:
  d. 5 × 84   **e.** $2.75 + $3.76   **f.** 66 − 48

Problem Solving: The wall is four cubits tall. A cubit is about 18
inches. So the wall is about how many feet tall?

We have practiced adding and subtracting fractions that
have the same denominators. In this lesson, we will begin
adding and subtracting fractions that have different
denominators.

SAME DENOMINATORS   **DIFFERENT DENOMINATORS**

$\dfrac{1}{5} \longleftrightarrow \dfrac{3}{5}$ $\dfrac{1}{2} \longleftrightarrow \dfrac{3}{4}$

> **To add or subtract fractions that have
> different denominators, we must first change
> the name of the fractions so that they will
> have the same denominators.**

Recall that we change the name of a fraction by
multiplying the fraction by a fraction name for 1.

Example 1 Add: $\dfrac{1}{4} + \dfrac{3}{8}$

Solution The denominators are not the same. We multiply $\frac{1}{4}$ by $\frac{2}{2}$ and get $\frac{2}{8}$. Now we can add.

$$
\begin{array}{r}
\overset{\text{Rename}}{\longrightarrow} \\[4pt]
\dfrac{1}{4} \times \dfrac{2}{2} = \dfrac{2}{8} \\[8pt]
+\;\dfrac{3}{8} \qquad\;\; = \dfrac{3}{8} \;\Big|\; \text{Add} \\[8pt]
\hline
\dfrac{5}{8}
\end{array}
$$

Example 2 Subtract: $\dfrac{5}{6} - \dfrac{1}{2}$

Solution The denominators are not the same. We change $\frac{1}{2}$ to a fraction whose denominator is 6. Then we subtract. We reduce the answer.

$$
\begin{array}{r}
\overset{\text{Rename}}{\longrightarrow} \\[4pt]
\dfrac{5}{6} \qquad\;\; = \dfrac{5}{6} \\[8pt]
-\;\dfrac{1}{2} \times \dfrac{3}{3} = \dfrac{3}{6} \;\Big|\; \text{Subtract} \\[8pt]
\hline
\dfrac{2}{6} = \dfrac{1}{3} \\[4pt]
\underset{\text{Reduce}}{\longrightarrow}
\end{array}
$$

Practice Add or subtract. Reduce when possible.

a. $\dfrac{1}{2} + \dfrac{2}{6}$ **b.** $\dfrac{1}{3} + \dfrac{1}{9}$ **c.** $\dfrac{1}{8} + \dfrac{1}{2}$

d. $\dfrac{3}{8} - \dfrac{1}{4}$ **e.** $\dfrac{2}{3} - \dfrac{2}{9}$ **f.** $\dfrac{7}{8} - \dfrac{1}{2}$

Problem set
139

1. Clotilda laid 1-foot-square floor tiles in a room 15 feet
(94) long and 12 feet wide. How many floor tiles did she
use?

2. What is the perimeter of this
(60) triangle?

1.2 cm   1.9 cm
2.2 cm

3. Tim found that $\frac{3}{8}$ of the 32 pencils
(105) in the room had no erasers. How
many pencils had no erasers?
Illustrate the problem.

4. Seventy-two eggs is how many dozen eggs?
(50)

5. How many eggs is 50% of one dozen eggs?
(65)

6. This cube is made of how many
(134) smaller cubes?

7. Farmica bought 10 tapes at $4.23
(93) each and 2 compact disks at
$10.95 each. The tax was $3.80.
What was the total price?

8. Roger drove 285 miles in 5 hours. What was his
(106) average speed in miles per hour?

9. (a) Write XXIX in our number system.
(135) (b) Write 24 in Roman numerals.

10. Write the reduced form of each fraction:
(125)
(a) $\frac{8}{10}$ (b) $\frac{6}{15}$ (c) $\frac{8}{16}$

11. Use words to name the number 123415720.
(137)

12. 8.3 + 4.72 + 0.6 + 12.1
(118)

13. 17.42 − (6.7 − 1.23)
(55)

14. $3\frac{3}{8} + 3\frac{3}{8}$
(132)

15. $\frac{1}{4} + \frac{1}{8}$
(139)

16. $\frac{1}{2} + \frac{1}{6}$
(139)

17. $5\frac{5}{6} - 1\frac{1}{6}$
(132)

18. $\frac{1}{4} - \frac{1}{8}$
(139)

19. $\frac{1}{2} - \frac{1}{6}$
(139)

20. 87×16
(100)

21. 49×340
(127)

22. 504×30
(127)

23. $\$35.40 \div 6$
(90)

24. $\frac{5784}{4}$
(86)

25. $7\overline{)2385}$
(90)

26. $30\overline{)450}$
(126)

27. $32\overline{)450}$
(138)

28. $15\overline{)450}$
(138)

29. What is the probability of drawing a heart from a full
(129) deck of cards? (There are 13 hearts in a deck.)

30. Draw a rectangle that is 5 cm long and 2 cm wide.
(65) Draw lines to divide the rectangle into square centimeters. Then shade 30% of the rectangle.

LESSON
140

Writing Numbers Through Hundred Millions

Facts Practice: 90 Division Facts (Test J in Test Masters)

Mental Math: Find the stated percent of 100.
  a. 75% of 100   **b.** 70% of 100   **c.** 100% of 100
Review:
  d. 20×23 **e.** $\$20.00 - \$12.75$ **f.** $127 + 35$

Patterns: Find the next eight numbers in this sequence.
$\frac{1}{8}, \frac{1}{4}, \frac{3}{8}, \frac{1}{2}, \frac{5}{8}, \frac{3}{4}, \frac{7}{8}, 1,$ ___, ___, ___, ___, ___, ___, ___, ___, ...

For a few lessons, we have practiced naming numbers through hundred millions. In this lesson we will begin writing these numbers.

Example   Use digits to write forty-six million, eight hundred ninety-five thousand, two hundred seventy.

Solution   It is a good idea to read the entire number before we begin writing it. We see *millions* and *thousands*, so we know the number will have this form:

___, ___, ___

We go back and read "forty-six million" and write "46" and a comma. We read "eight hundred ninety-five thousand" and write "895" and a comma. We read "two hundred seventy" and write "270."

46,895,270

Practice   Use digits to write each number:

a. Nine million, two hundred sixty-three thousand, five hundred twelve

b. Eleven million, one hundred twenty-three thousand, four hundred

c. Nine hundred eighty-seven million, six hundred fifty-four thousand, three hundred twenty-one

d. Sixteen million, five hundred forty-three thousand

e. Ninety-three million

f. Seven hundred fifty-three million, eight hundred seventy-two thousand, one hundred ninety

Problem set
140

1. The Martins drank 11 gallons of milk each week. How many quarts of milk did they drink each week?
(83)

2. Sixty fleas leaped on Rover as he ran through the field. If one fourth of them perished from flea powder, how many survived? Illustrate the problem.
(80)

3. (a) What is the area of this
(94,60)   square?

□ 10 mm

   (b) What is the perimeter of this
     square?

4. Mark is 8 inches taller than Jim. Jim is 5 inches taller
(104) than Jan. Mark is 61 inches tall. How many inches tall
is Jan?

5. What is the average height of the three children in
(106) problem 4?

6. Mayville is on the road from Altoona to Watson. It is
(50) 47 miles from Mayville to Altoona. It is 24 miles from
Mayville to Watson. How far is it from Altoona to
Watson?

7. What is the probability of this
(129) spinner stopping on a number
greater than 4?

8. (a) Write XXXIII in our number system.
(135) (b) Write 39 in Roman numerals.

9. Name each shape:
(134) (a)   (b)   (c)

10. Write the reduced form of each fraction:
(125) (a) $\frac{9}{15}$ (b) $\frac{10}{12}$ (c) $\frac{12}{16}$

11. Use digits to write one hundred nineteen million, two
(140) hundred forty-seven thousand, nine hundred eighty-
four.

12. 14.94 − (3.6 + 4.7)   **13.** 6.8 − (1.37 + 2.2)
(55)   (55)

14. $3\frac{2}{5} + 1\frac{4}{5}$
(132)

15. $\frac{5}{8} + \frac{1}{4}$
(139)

16. $\frac{1}{3} + \frac{1}{6}$
(139)

17. $5\frac{9}{10} - 1\frac{1}{10}$
(132)

18. $\frac{5}{8} - \frac{1}{4}$
(139)

19. $\frac{1}{3} - \frac{1}{6}$
(139)

20. 38×217
(127)

21. 173×60
(127)

22. 90×500
(96)

23. $\dfrac{6752}{4}$
(86)

24.
(2)

```
  7
  5
  8
  6
  9
  N
  8
  7
  6
+ 4
────
 75
```

25.
(21)

```
   27
   99
   77
   86
   68
   54
   45
   74
   85
 + 27
─────
```

26. $7\overline{)2942}$
(90)

27. $\$80.01 \div 9$
(86)

28. $10\overline{)453}$
(115)

29. $11\overline{)453}$
(138)

30. $22\overline{)453}$
(138)

LESSON 141

Reading Roman Numerals Through Thousands

Facts Practice: 90 Division Facts (Test J in Test Masters)

Mental Math: Find the stated percent of 200.

  a. 75% of 200   **b.** 70% of 200   **c.** 100% of 200

Review:

  d. 20×24 **e.** $\$20.00 - \$7.75$ **f.** $136 + 25$

Patterns: Find the next eight numbers in this sequence.

$$\frac{1}{8}, \frac{1}{4}, \frac{3}{8}, \frac{1}{2}, \underline{\quad}, \underline{\quad}, \underline{\quad}, \underline{\quad}, \underline{\quad}, \underline{\quad}, \underline{\quad}, \underline{\quad}, \ldots$$

We have practiced using these Roman numerals.

I   V   X

In this lesson, we will practice using more Roman numerals. These are listed in the table.

NUMERAL	VALUE
I	1
V	5
X	10
L	50
C	100
D	500
M	1000

Example Write each Roman numeral in our number system.

(a) LXX   (b) DCCL   (c) XLIV   (d) MMI

Solution (a) LXX is 50 + 10 + 10, which is **70.**

(b) DCCL is 500 + 100 + 100 + 50, which is **750.**

(c) XLIV is 10 less than 50 and 1 less than 5. That is, 40 + 4 = **44.**

(d) MMI is 1000 + 1000 + 1, which is **2001.**

Practice Write each Roman numeral in our number system:

a. CCCLXII   **b.** CCLXXXV   **c.** CD

d. XLVII   **e.** MMMCCLVI   **f.** MCMXCIX

Problem set 141

1. Beth is reading a 210-page book. If she has read one
(80) third of the book, how many pages does she still have to read? Illustrate the problem.

2. Iceland covers an area of 39,768 square miles. The
(38) area of Virginia is 40,767 square miles. How much greater is the area of Virginia than the area of Iceland?

3. Molly Pitcher carried 21 buckets of water to the thirsty
(104) troops. If each bucket held 3 gallons, how many **quarts** of water did she deliver?

4. What is the perimeter of this
(132) triangle?

$\frac{3}{4}$ inch $\frac{3}{4}$ inch

$\frac{3}{4}$ inch

5. Write each Roman numeral in our number system:
(140) (a) MDCLXVI   (b) CCXXIV   (c) XCIX

6. Write the reduced form of each fraction:
(125) (a) $\frac{9}{12}$ (b) $\frac{12}{15}$ (c) $\frac{10}{20}$

7. This cube is made of how many
(134) smaller cubes?

8. Use digits to write ninety-three
(140) million, one hundred seventy-five
thousand, two hundred twelve.

9. Rita flipped a coin 21 times. It came up heads 17
(84) times. What fraction tells the number of times it did
not come up heads?

10. Five red shirts cost $100. Six green jackets cost $480.
(104) What did each red shirt and each green jacket cost?
What would be the cost of 6 red shirts and 5 green
jackets?

11. The number C is what percent of the number M?
(65)

12. $59.34 - (12.6 + 7.5)$ **13.** $47.6 - (3.7 + 12.23)$
(55)   *(55)*

14. $8\frac{1}{4} + 1\frac{3}{4}$ **15.** $\frac{1}{2} + \frac{3}{10}$ **16.** $\frac{2}{3} + \frac{1}{6}$
(132)   *(139)*   *(139)*

17. $7\frac{3}{8} - 1\frac{1}{8}$ **18.** $\frac{1}{2} - \frac{3}{10}$ **19.** $\frac{2}{3} - \frac{1}{6}$
(132)   *(139)*   *(139)*

20. 47 × 31
(100)

23. 430 × 26
(127)

24. 48 × 250
(127)

25. 9)$\overline{7227}$
(90)

26. $37.00 ÷ 4
(86)

27. $\dfrac{810}{6}$
(86)

21.
(2)

```
    4
    7
    3
    2
    5
    8
    6
    N
+   5
_____
   54
```

22.
(21)

```
   27
   32
   11
   22
   33
   41
   14
   26
+  48
_____
```

28. 70)$\overline{6440}$
(126)

29. The front cover of this book has an area of about how
(94,48) many square inches? (Measure each side to the nearest inch.)

30. If there is one correct answer, and the choices are A, B,
(129) C, and D, then what is the probability of guessing the correct answer?

Appendix A

Multiplication by 10's, 11's, and 12's

We know that when we multiply by 10 the answer has a zero at the end.

1 × 10 = 10	5 × 10 = 50	9 × 10 = 90
2 × 10 = 20	6 × 10 = 60	10 × 10 = 100
3 × 10 = 30	7 × 10 = 70	11 × 10 = 110
4 × 10 = 40	8 × 10 = 80	12 × 10 = 120

Multiplying by 11 is easy also because every answer listed below except the last three has double digits that are the same.

1 × 11 = 11	5 × 11 = 55	9 × 11 = 99
2 × 11 = 22	6 × 11 = 66	10 × 11 = 110
3 × 11 = 33	7 × 11 = 77	11 × 11 = 121
4 × 11 = 44	8 × 11 = 88	12 × 11 = 132

Multiplying by 12 is important because many items are sold in sets of 12. A set of 12 things is called a **dozen.** Memorizing the 12's table requires practice in saying the table aloud.

1 × 12 = 12	5 × 12 = 60	9 × 12 = 108
2 × 12 = 24	6 × 12 = 72	10 × 12 = 120
3 × 12 = 36	7 × 12 = 84	11 × 12 = 132
4 × 12 = 48	8 × 12 = 96	12 × 12 = 144

Appendix B

Supplemental Practice Problems for Selected Lessons

This appendix contains additional practice problems for concepts presented in selected lessons. It is very important that no problems in the regular problem sets be omitted to make room for these problems. This book is designed to produce long-term retention of concepts, and long-term practice of all the concepts is necessary. The practice problems in the problem sets provide enough initial exposure to concepts for most students. If a student continues to have difficulty with certain concepts, some of these problems can be assigned as remedial exercises.

Supplemental Practice for Lesson 19

1.
```
   42
 − 23
```

2.
```
   30
 − 16
```

3.
```
   24
 − 17
```

4.
```
   54
 − 27
```

5.
```
   31
 − 24
```

6.
```
   60
 − 36
```

7.
```
   23
 − B
    6
```

8.
```
    D
 − 19
   21
```

9.
```
   57
 − F
   29
```

10.
```
    H
 − 36
   34
```

11.
```
   42
 − J
    5
```

12.
```
    L
 − 47
   27
```

13. $36 - 18$

14. $24 - 17$

15. $40 - 23$

16. $60 - R = 33$

17. $P - 39 = 18$

18. $72 - 64$

19. $T - 46 = 28$

20. $35 - W = 7$

Supplemental Practice for Lesson 21

1.
```
   12
    8
   15
 +  7
```

2.
```
   36
    8
   24
 + 16
```

3.
```
   12
   23
   24
 + 20
```

4.
```
   16
   36
   54
 + 32
```

5.
```
   74
   37
   60
 + 46
```

6.
```
   57
   24
   38
 + 83
```

7.
```
   95
    9
   78
 + 35
```

8.
```
   47
   58
   62
 + 55
```

9.
```
   34
   27
    8
 + 27
```

10.
```
   67
   15
  436
 + 25
```

11.
```
  314
   28
  116
 + 42
```

12.
```
    9
   32
  154
 + 97
```

13.
```
  374
  257
   38
 + 146
```

14.
```
   66
  207
   84
 + 259
```

15.
```
  360
   45
  179
 + 78
```

16.
```
   40
   95
  379
 + 86
```

17.	18.	19.	20.
36	436	363	273
275	39	247	54
175	147	152	106
+ 384	+ 88	+ 148	+ 50

Supplemental Practice for Lesson 37

1.	2.	3.	4.
263	432	520	287
– 147	– 141	– 336	– 179

5.	6.	7.	8.
196	479	360	424
– 57	– 286	– 134	– 254

9.	10.	11.
316	260	415
– 79	– 146	– 387

12. 247 – 79   **13.** 163 – 127   **14.** 459 – 367

15. 770 – 287   **16.** 612 – 78   **17.** 340 – 149

18. 210 – 86   **19.** 436 – 156   **20.** 520 – 417

Supplemental Practice for Lesson 43

Use words to write each of these numbers:

1. 363

2. 1,246

3. 12,280

4. 25,362

5. 123,570

6. 253,500

7. 112,060

8. 220,405

9. 204,050

10. 546,325

Use digits to write each of these numbers:

11. One thousand, two hundred seventy-eight

12. Eleven thousand, five hundred forty-four

13. Twenty-two thousand, four hundred thirty

14. Fifty-seven thousand, nine hundred

15. One hundred seventy-one thousand, two hundred thirty

16. Two hundred ten thousand, nine hundred

17. Five hundred sixty-three thousand, fifty-eight

18. Nine hundred eighty-seven thousand, six hundred fifty-four

19. One hundred five thousand, seventy

20. Six hundred fifty thousand, four hundred three

Supplemental Practice for Lesson 46

Use a fraction or mixed number to name every point marked with an arrow on these number lines:

Supplemental Practice for Lesson 51

1.	2.	3.	4.
300 − 136	403 − 257	200 − 143	306 − 157

5.	6.	7.	8.
600 − 249	201 − 165	100 − 36	405 − 229

9.	10.	11.	12.
400 − 349	101 − 94	700 − 436	501 − 127

13.	14.	15.	16.
100 − 79	907 − 65	500 − 249	804 − 756

17.	18.	19.	20.
800 − 48	602 − 575	900 − 617	107 − 28

Supplemental Practice for Lesson 53

1. $6.35 + $4   2. $4.84 − $3

3. 48¢ + 67¢   4. $0.49 − 15¢

5. $0.36 + 85¢

6. $1.25 − 8¢

7. $2.45 + 6¢

8. 75¢ − $0.67

9. 98¢ + $12

10. $1.00 − 95¢

11. $3.46 + $2 + 49¢

12. 50¢ − $0.07

13. 36¢ + $0.12 + $2.14

14. $2 − $1.37

15. $15 + $1.50 + 15¢

16. $1 − 37¢

17. 36¢ + 24¢ + 78¢

18. $5 − $4.63

19. $5 + $0.36 + 9¢

20. 87¢ − 78¢

Supplemental Practice for Lesson 58

1. 36×2	2. 43×5	3. 57×3	4. 24×6

5. 38×4	6. 52×7	7. 27×5	8. 19×8

9. 28 × 6   10. 9 × 56   11. 47 × 7

12. 4 × 89   13. 64 × 8   14. 5 × 75

15. 63 × 9   16. 4 × 76   17. 97 × 6

18. 2 × 68   19. 54 × 7   20. 3 × 45

Supplemental Practice for Lesson 62

1. $3486 - 1687$	2. $2175 - 1346$	3. $3747 - 1654$
4. $4403 - 1475$	5. $6300 - 3149$	6. $2048 - 1951$
7. $3000 - 1346$	8. $4005 - 2418$	9. $3040 - 1535$

10. 6000 − 2164	**11.** 8010 − 7825	**12.** 5007 − 1838
13. 36,247 − 1,456	**14.** 30,148 − 23,109	**15.** 40,015 − 16,438
16. 30,000 − 256	**17.** 30,604 − 1,915	**18.** 90,040 − 37,478
19. 376,142 − 36,174	**20.** 403,700 − 394,672	

Supplemental Practice for Lesson 63

1. $2\overline{)15}$ 2. $5\overline{)23}$ 3. $3\overline{)25}$ 4. $26 \div 6$

5. $31 \div 4$ 6. $50 \div 7$ 7. $5\overline{)37}$ 8. $8\overline{)35}$

9. $6\overline{)43}$ 10. $30 \div 9$ 11. $45 \div 7$ 12. $17 \div 2$

13. $8\overline{)49}$ 14. $3\overline{)25}$ 15. $9\overline{)60}$ 16. $27 \div 4$

17. $15 \div 8$ 18. $32 \div 5$ 19. $3\overline{)20}$ 20. $6\overline{)34}$

Supplemental Practice for Lesson 68

1. 136 × 2	**2.** 235 × 5	**3.** 430 × 3
4. 216 × 6	**5.** 450 × 4	**6.** 7 × 642
7. 307 × 5	**8.** 458 × 8	**9.** 740 × 6
10. 368 × 7	**11.** 9 × 403	**12.** 490 × 8
13. 609 × 2	**14.** 470 × 9	**15.** 518 × 3
16. 2 × 296	**17.** 708 × 4	**18.** 3 × 430
19. 275 × 5	**20.** 4 × 308	

Supplemental Practice for Lesson 74

1. $3\overline{)48}$ 2. $2\overline{)56}$ 3. $4\overline{)72}$ 4. $7\overline{)98}$

5. $5\overline{)80}$ 6. $8\overline{)96}$ 7. $6\overline{)90}$ 8. $3\overline{)81}$

9. $7\overline{)91}$ 10. $4\overline{)68}$ 11. $2\overline{)76}$ 12. $5\overline{)90}$

13. $3\overline{)54}$ 14. $6\overline{)84}$ 15. $3\overline{)78}$ 16. $7\overline{)84}$

17. $4\overline{)84}$ 18. $5\overline{)85}$ 19. $6\overline{)72}$ 20. $5\overline{)65}$

Supplemental Practice for Lesson 75

1. $2\overline{)110}$ 2. $9\overline{)126}$ 3. $3\overline{)222}$ 4. $8\overline{)432}$

5. $4\overline{)256}$ 6. $7\overline{)455}$ 7. $5\overline{)320}$ 8. $2\overline{)192}$

9. $6\overline{)342}$ 10. $3\overline{)204}$ 11. $7\overline{)266}$ 12. $4\overline{)100}$

13. $8\overline{)456}$ 14. $5\overline{)365}$ 15. $9\overline{)468}$ 16. $6\overline{)162}$

17. $4\overline{)252}$ 18. $7\overline{)665}$ 19. $8\overline{)600}$ 20. $5\overline{)245}$

Supplemental Practice for Lesson 76

1. $4\overline{)93}$ 2. $2\overline{)115}$ 3. $5\overline{)182}$ 4. $3\overline{)173}$

5. $6\overline{)289}$ 6. $4\overline{)181}$ 7. $7\overline{)164}$ 8. $5\overline{)319}$

9. $8\overline{)218}$ 10. $6\overline{)235}$ 11. $9\overline{)220}$ 12. $7\overline{)442}$

13. $2\overline{)189}$ 14. $8\overline{)595}$ 15. $3\overline{)109}$ 16. $9\overline{)892}$

17. $4\overline{)218}$ 18. $2\overline{)55}$ 19. $5\overline{)232}$ 20. $3\overline{)220}$

Supplemental Practice for Lesson 77

1. $\begin{array}{r} 32 \\ \times\ 20 \\ \hline \end{array}$ 2. $\begin{array}{r} 43¢ \\ \times\ 30 \\ \hline \end{array}$ 3. $\begin{array}{r} 56 \\ \times\ 40 \\ \hline \end{array}$

4. $\begin{array}{r} \$0.68 \\ \times\ 20 \\ \hline \end{array}$ 5. $\begin{array}{r} 47 \\ \times\ 60 \\ \hline \end{array}$ 6. $\begin{array}{r} \$1.68 \\ \times\ 20 \\ \hline \end{array}$

7. 20×75 8. $30 \times 49¢$ 9. 40×87

10. $\$0.97 \times 50$ 11. $70 \times \$1.49$ 12. 60×38

13. 80 × 76   **14.** 48¢ × 90   **15.** 20 × 89

16. $2.25 × 50   **17.** $0.39 × 60   **18.** 30 × 78

19. 40 × 67¢   **20.** 84 × 70

Supplemental Practice for Lesson 86

1. 3)‾700‾   **2.** 6)‾738‾   **3.** 4)‾892‾   **4.** 7)‾868‾

5. 5)‾1606‾   **6.** 8)‾915‾   **7.** 6)‾1275‾   **8.** 9)‾1926‾

9. 7)‾2415‾   **10.** 3)‾1603‾   **11.** 8)‾1161‾   **12.** 4)‾1111‾

13. 9)‾3000‾   **14.** 5)‾625‾   **15.** 3)‾1333‾   **16.** 6)‾1518‾

17. 4)‾2250‾   **18.** 7)‾1162‾   **19.** 8)‾1000‾   **20.** 5)‾3743‾

Supplemental Practice for Lesson 90

1. 4)‾960‾   **2.** 5)‾1600‾   **3.** 3)‾1206‾   **4.** 9)‾936‾

5. 4)‾2082‾   **6.** 6)‾1820‾   **7.** 7)‾2801‾   **8.** 2)‾1819‾

9. 5)‾3404‾   **10.** 3)‾2712‾   **11.** 6)‾3000‾   **12.** 4)‾2681‾

13. 7)‾5650‾   **14.** 8)‾3275‾   **15.** 3)‾450‾   **16.** 5)‾2001‾

17. 2)‾381‾   **18.** 8)‾6080‾   **19.** 9)‾3686‾   **20.** 6)‾4202‾

Supplemental Practice for Lesson 100

1. 12 × 36   **2.** 46 × 15   **3.** 31 × 27

4.   74   **5.**   36   **6.**   35
      × 16   × 63   × 35

7. 14 × 63   **8.** 78 × 22   **9.** 25 × 37

10.   74   **11.**   63   **12.**   18
       × 58   × 49   × 65

13. 96 × 32   **14.** 51 × 76   **15.** 38 × 24

16.   38   **17.**   49   **18.**   29
       × 47   × 86   × 31

19. 33 × 79   **20.** 57 × 42

Supplemental Practice for Lesson 114

Change each improper fraction to a mixed number or a whole number:

1. $\dfrac{3}{2}$ 2. $\dfrac{9}{3}$ 3. $\dfrac{4}{3}$ 4. $\dfrac{7}{4}$

5. $\dfrac{12}{5}$ 6. $\dfrac{4}{2}$ 7. $\dfrac{5}{4}$ 8. $\dfrac{7}{5}$

9. $\dfrac{3}{3}$ 10. $\dfrac{9}{5}$ 11. $\dfrac{5}{2}$ 12. $\dfrac{8}{4}$

13. $\dfrac{15}{15}$ 14. $\dfrac{5}{3}$ 15. $\dfrac{9}{4}$ 16. $\dfrac{6}{2}$

17. $\dfrac{6}{3}$ 18. $\dfrac{10}{3}$ 19. $\dfrac{7}{2}$ 20. $\dfrac{7}{3}$

Supplemental Practice for Lesson 118

1. 3.6 + 2.17 2. 5.28 + 12.4

3. 15.4 + 23.56 4. 6.7 + 15.8

5. 16.36 + 14.7 6. 45.3 + 2.91

7. 0.4 + 45.91 8. 3.71 + 6.3

9. 103.7 + 7.41 10. 9.09 + 90.9

11. 1.3 + 4.26 + 2.7 12. 12.4 + 1.5 + 3.3

13. 2.1 + 1.91 + 12.12 14. 6.58 + 3.7 + 0.4

15. 29.6 + 2.96 + 29.62 16. 3.4 + 4.56 + 1.41

17. 36.4 + 6.4 + 0.64

18. 1.2 + 0.21 + 12.1 + 10.21

19. 3.5 + 0.35 + 5.03 + 35.53 + 35.0

20. 2.4 + 4.12 + 20.4 + 42.21 + 1.2

Supplemental Practice for Lesson 119

1. $3.45 - 1.2$

2. $23.1 - 2.2$

3. $14.25 - 1.6$

4. $15.3 - 4.4$

5. $7.59 - 1.8$

6. $25.34 - 1.21$

7. $16.25 - 1.9$

8. $8.19 - 0.4$

9. $13.26 - 12.2$

10.
$$\begin{array}{r} 3.4 \\ -1.26 \\ \hline \end{array}$$

11.
$$\begin{array}{r} 4.0 \\ -2.14 \\ \hline \end{array}$$

12.
$$\begin{array}{r} 12.4 \\ -1.24 \\ \hline \end{array}$$

13. $7.4 - 1.22$

14. $3.68 - 1.7$

15. $12.1 - 1.21$

16. $30.1 - 3.01$

17. $34.05 - 6.4$

18. $58.0 - 2.14$

19. $3.09 - 1.8$

20. $20.1 - 3.19$

Supplemental Practice for Lesson 126

1. $20\overline{)460}$

2. $30\overline{)630}$

3. $40\overline{)520}$

4. $50\overline{)1600}$

5. $60\overline{)720}$

6. $70\overline{)1470}$

7. $80\overline{)1700}$

8. $90\overline{)1200}$

9. $20\overline{)680}$

10. $40\overline{)1325}$

11. $60\overline{)1450}$

12. $70\overline{)2177}$

13. $80\overline{)2001}$

14. $90\overline{)1359}$

15. $20\overline{)920}$

16. $40\overline{)2088}$

17. $60\overline{)2640}$

18. $70\overline{)1624}$

19. $30\overline{)1680}$

20. $50\overline{)2710}$

Supplemental Practice for Lesson 127

1. 320 × 12

2. 132 × 21

3. 143 × 23

4. 150
× 32

5. 304
× 13

6. 315
× 24

7. 42 × 163

8. 230 × 15

9. 25 × 402

10. 357
× 34

11. 780
× 56

12. 406
× 17

13. 28 × 196

14. 460 × 39

15. 43 × 179

16. 108
× 39

17. 349
× 74

18. 470
× 68

19. 29 × 357

20. 186 × 37

Supplemental Practice for Lesson 129

Reduce each fraction:

1. $\frac{5}{10}$
2. $\frac{2}{4}$
3. $\frac{6}{8}$
4. $\frac{2}{6}$

5. $\frac{3}{9}$
6. $\frac{4}{10}$
7. $\frac{3}{6}$
8. $\frac{2}{12}$

9. $\frac{9}{12}$
10. $\frac{4}{6}$
11. $\frac{6}{9}$
12. $\frac{8}{10}$

13. $\frac{2}{8}$
14. $\frac{3}{12}$
15. $\frac{2}{10}$
16. $\frac{4}{8}$

17. $\frac{8}{12}$
18. $\frac{6}{10}$
19. $\frac{4}{12}$
20. $\frac{6}{12}$

Supplemental Practice for Lesson 130

1. 12)72
2. 31)124
3. 11)100
4. 41)125

5. 13)91
6. 21)107
7. 52)212
8. 25)130

9. 32)130
10. 22)135
11. 51)310
12. 14)80

13. $42\overline{)180}$ **14.** $23\overline{)161}$ **15.** $34\overline{)175}$ **16.** $15\overline{)105}$

17. $43\overline{)150}$ **18.** $24\overline{)200}$ **19.** $33\overline{)300}$ **20.** $19\overline{)100}$

Supplemental Practice for Lesson 131

1. $3\frac{1}{2} + 1$ **2.** $3\frac{1}{3} + 1\frac{1}{3}$

3. $1\frac{1}{5} + \frac{3}{5}$ **4.** $4 + \frac{1}{2}$

5. $6\frac{3}{5} + 1\frac{1}{5}$ **6.** $5\frac{5}{8} + 6$

7. $3\frac{3}{7} + 2\frac{2}{7}$ **8.** $6 + 7\frac{1}{2}$

9. $\frac{5}{9} + 3\frac{2}{9}$ **10.** $3\frac{3}{10} + 6\frac{6}{10}$

11. $5\frac{2}{3} - 1\frac{1}{3}$ **12.** $3\frac{3}{4} - 2$

13. $6\frac{1}{2} - \frac{1}{2}$ **14.** $8\frac{3}{4} - 1\frac{3}{4}$

15. $2\frac{5}{8} - 2\frac{2}{8}$ **16.** $4\frac{4}{5} - \frac{1}{5}$

17. $4\frac{4}{9} - 3$ **18.** $1\frac{4}{5} - \frac{4}{5}$

19. $3\frac{1}{2} - 1\frac{1}{2}$ **20.** $4\frac{5}{7} - 1\frac{3}{7}$

Supplemental Practice for Lesson 132

Simplify each fraction answer:

1. $\frac{1}{2} + \frac{1}{2}$ **2.** $\frac{1}{3} - \frac{1}{3}$

3. $\dfrac{1}{4} + \dfrac{1}{4}$ **4.** $\dfrac{3}{8} - \dfrac{1}{8}$

5. $\dfrac{1}{6} + \dfrac{2}{6}$ **6.** $\dfrac{5}{6} - \dfrac{1}{6}$

7. $\dfrac{2}{3} + \dfrac{2}{3}$ **8.** $\dfrac{7}{8} - \dfrac{1}{8}$

9. $\dfrac{4}{5} + \dfrac{3}{5}$ **10.** $3\dfrac{1}{2} - 1\dfrac{1}{2}$

11. $2\dfrac{2}{3} + 1\dfrac{1}{3}$ **12.** $3\dfrac{3}{4} - 1\dfrac{1}{4}$

13. $4\dfrac{2}{3} + 5\dfrac{2}{3}$ **14.** $3\dfrac{4}{9} - 1\dfrac{1}{9}$

15. $1\dfrac{1}{6} + 1\dfrac{1}{6}$ **16.** $6\dfrac{7}{10} - 4\dfrac{1}{10}$

17. $4\dfrac{5}{12} - 1\dfrac{1}{12}$ **18.** $5\dfrac{3}{4} + 4\dfrac{1}{4}$

19. $7\dfrac{4}{5} + 4\dfrac{4}{5}$ **20.** $7\dfrac{7}{8} - 3\dfrac{3}{8}$

Supplemental Practice for Lesson 133

In problems 1–8, find the fraction name for 1 used to make the equivalent fraction:

1. $\dfrac{1}{2} \times M = \dfrac{3}{6}$ **2.** $\dfrac{1}{2} \times Z = \dfrac{5}{10}$

3. $\dfrac{1}{2} \times R = \dfrac{6}{12}$ **4.** $\dfrac{1}{3} \times Q = \dfrac{3}{9}$

5. $\dfrac{1}{6} \times G = \dfrac{2}{12}$ **6.** $\dfrac{3}{4} \times B = \dfrac{9}{12}$

7. $\dfrac{2}{5} \times P = \dfrac{4}{10}$ **8.** $\dfrac{2}{3} \times K = \dfrac{8}{12}$

In problems 9–20, complete the equivalent fraction:

9. $\dfrac{1}{4} = \dfrac{?}{8}$ **10.** $\dfrac{1}{3} = \dfrac{?}{6}$

11. $\dfrac{1}{2} = \dfrac{?}{4}$ **12.** $\dfrac{1}{2} = \dfrac{?}{8}$

13. $\dfrac{3}{4} = \dfrac{?}{8}$ **14.** $\dfrac{2}{3} = \dfrac{?}{9}$

15. $\dfrac{2}{5} = \dfrac{?}{10}$ **16.** $\dfrac{1}{2} = \dfrac{?}{12}$

17. $\dfrac{5}{6} = \dfrac{?}{12}$ **18.** $\dfrac{1}{2} = \dfrac{?}{4}$

19. $\dfrac{3}{4} = \dfrac{?}{12}$ **20.** $\dfrac{2}{3} = \dfrac{?}{12}$

Supplemental Practice for Lesson 138

1. $11\overline{)253}$ **2.** $21\overline{)672}$ **3.** $31\overline{)682}$ **4.** $12\overline{)504}$

5. $32\overline{)992}$ **6.** $21\overline{)483}$ **7.** $11\overline{)165}$ **8.** $22\overline{)924}$

9. $12\overline{)181}$ **10.** $31\overline{)963}$ **11.** $23\overline{)760}$ **12.** $41\overline{)945}$

13. $15\overline{)375}$ **14.** $25\overline{)555}$ **15.** $11\overline{)375}$ **16.** $21\overline{)924}$

17. $22\overline{)489}$ **18.** $12\overline{)600}$ **19.** $33\overline{)1000}$ **20.** $25\overline{)800}$

Supplemental Practice for Lesson 139

1. $\dfrac{1}{4} + \dfrac{1}{2}$ **2.** $\dfrac{1}{4} + \dfrac{1}{8}$ **3.** $\dfrac{1}{2} + \dfrac{1}{8}$

4. $\dfrac{1}{4} - \dfrac{1}{8}$ **5.** $\dfrac{1}{2} - \dfrac{1}{8}$ **6.** $\dfrac{1}{3} - \dfrac{1}{6}$

7. $\dfrac{2}{3} + \dfrac{1}{6}$ **8.** $\dfrac{3}{4} + \dfrac{1}{8}$ **9.** $\dfrac{1}{3} + \dfrac{2}{9}$

10. $\dfrac{5}{6} - \dfrac{2}{3}$ **11.** $\dfrac{7}{8} - \dfrac{3}{4}$ **12.** $\dfrac{9}{10} - \dfrac{4}{5}$

13. $\dfrac{5}{6} + \dfrac{1}{12}$ **14.** $\dfrac{3}{10} + \dfrac{2}{5}$ **15.** $\dfrac{1}{3} + \dfrac{1}{12}$

16. $\dfrac{4}{5} - \dfrac{1}{10}$ **17.** $\dfrac{8}{9} - \dfrac{2}{3}$ **18.** $\dfrac{7}{8} - \dfrac{1}{4}$

19. $\dfrac{3}{5} + \dfrac{3}{10}$ **20.** $\dfrac{2}{3} - \dfrac{7}{12}$

Glossary

addend   Any one of the numbers added in an addition problem.

  2 + 3 = 5   *The **addends** in this problem are 2 and 3.*

angle   The opening between two lines or segments that intersect.

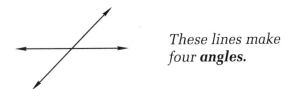

*These lines make
four **angles.***

area   The size of the inside of a flat shape.

*The **area** of this rectangle
is 10 square inches.*

average   The number that would be in each group if the groups were made equal.

*If we make equal groups with
the boxes on the left, we find
the **average** number of boxes
in a group is 5.*

bar graph   A graph that uses rectangles (bars) to show numbers or measurements.

century   One hundred years.

*The twentieth **century** began on January 1, 1901, and
ended on December 31, 2000.*

chance   How likely it is that something will happen. (We will write chance as a percent.)

*The **chance** of rain is 20%. It is not likely to rain.*

*There is a 90% **chance** of snow. It is likely to snow.*

circle graph   A graph made of a circle divided into sections. Sometimes called a *pie graph*.

Hair Colors of Students

circumference   The distance around a circle; the perimeter of a circle.

*If the distance from point A around to point A is 3 inches, then the **circumference** of the circle is 3 inches.*

common denominators   Denominators that are the same.

*The fractions $\frac{2}{5}$ and $\frac{3}{5}$ have **common denominators.***

common years   Years with 365 days; not leap years.

*The year 2000 is a leap year, but 2001 is a **common year.***

*In a **common year,** February has 28 days. In a leap year, it has 29 days.*

congruent   Having the same size and shape.

*These polygons are **congruent.** They are both squares, and they are the same size.*

counting numbers   All the numbers in this sequence: 1, 2, 3, 4, 5, 6, 7, 8, 9, ...

*The numbers 12 and 37 are **counting numbers,** but 0.98 and $\frac{1}{2}$ are not.*

decade   Ten years.

*January 1, 2001, through December 31, 2010, is one **decade.***

decimal point   The dot in a decimal number.

denominator   The bottom number in a fraction. It tells how many parts are in a whole.

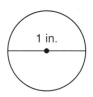

*The **denominator** of the fraction is 4. There are 4 parts in the whole circle.*

diameter   The distance across a circle through its center.

*The **diameter** of this circle is 1 inch.*

difference   The answer in a subtraction problem.

$12 - 8 = 4$ *The **difference** in this problem is 4.*

digit   Any of these symbols: 0, 1, 2, 3, 4, 5, 6, 7, 8, 9. Digits are used to write numbers.

*The last **digit** in the number 2587 is 7.*

division bar   A line between two numbers that shows division.

$\frac{4}{2}$ ◀— **division bar** $\frac{4}{2}$ *means "four divided by two."*

equals   Has the same value as.

*Twelve inches **equals** 1 foot.*

equivalent fractions   Different fractions that name the same amount.

$\frac{1}{2}$ *and* $\frac{2}{4}$ *are **equivalent fractions.***

estimate   To carefully guess how much something is.

*I **estimate** that the sum of 203 and 304 is about 500.*

even numbers   Numbers that can be divided by 2 without a remainder. Even numbers have 0, 2, 4, 6, or 8 in the ones' place.

*398 is an **even number,** but 399 is not.*

expanded form   A way to show a number by writing the value of each digit.

*The **expanded form** of 234 is 200 + 30 + 4.*

exponent   A number that shows how many times another number is a factor.

5^3 ◂— 3 is the **exponent.** 5^3 *means 5 × 5 × 5.*

fact family   Three numbers that can make four facts.

*The numbers 3, 4, and 7 are a **fact family.** They make these four facts:*

   3 + 4 = 7   4 + 3 = 7   7 − 3 = 4   7 − 4 = 3

factor   A number that is multiplied.

   2 × 3 = 6   *The **factors** in this problem are 2 and 3.*

fraction   A number that names part of a whole.

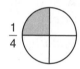

fraction bar   A line between the numerator and denominator in a fraction.

$\dfrac{3}{4}$ ◂— **fraction bar**

geometric solid   A shape that takes up space.

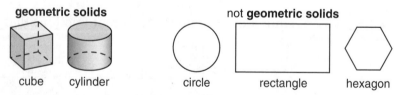

geometric solids   not **geometric solids**

   cube   cylinder   circle   rectangle   hexagon

graph   A diagram that shows counts or measures. *See also* **bar graph, circle graph, line graph,** and **pictograph.**

greater than   Larger than.

*Five is **greater than** three (5 > 3).*

hexagon   A polygon with six sides.

hexagon

improper fraction   A fraction with a numerator greater than or equal to the denominator; a fraction that is greater than or equal to 1.

$\dfrac{4}{3}$ $\dfrac{2}{2}$ *These fractions are **improper fractions.***

intersecting lines   Lines that cross.

intersecting lines

leap years   Years with 366 days; not common years.

*In a **leap year**, February has 29 days.*

less than   Smaller than.

*Three is **less than** five (3 < 5).*

line graph   A graph that uses segments and points to show information.

line segment   Part of a line.

$\overline{AB}$ *is a **line segment**.*

mixed number   A number made of a whole number and a fraction.

*The **mixed number** $5\frac{3}{4}$ means "five and three fourths."*

multiple   The product of one whole number and another whole number greater than zero.

$4 \times 1 = 4$
$4 \times 2 = 8$
$4 \times 3 = 12$ *The **multiples** of 4 are 4, 8, 12, 16, ...*
$4 \times 4 = 16$

$9 \times 3 = 27$ *The number 27 is a **multiple** of both 9 and 3.*

number line A line that has marks labeled with numbers in order.

number line

number sentence A complete sentence that uses numbers and symbols, not words.

> *The **number sentence** 4 + 5 = 9 means "four plus five equals nine."*

numerator The top number in a fraction. It tells how many parts of a whole are counted.

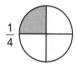

> *The **numerator** of the fraction is 1. One part of the whole circle is shaded.*

octagon A polygon with eight sides.

octagon

odd numbers Numbers that have a remainder of 1 when divided by 2. Odd numbers have 1, 3, 5, 7, or 9 in the ones' place.

> *467 is an **odd number,** but 468 is not.*

ordinal numbers Numbers that tell position or order.

> *"First," "second," and "third" are **ordinal numbers.** Their abbreviations are "1st," "2nd," and "3rd."*

parallel lines Lines that stay the same distance apart; lines that do not cross.

parallel lines

pentagon A polygon with five sides.

pentagon

perimeter   The distance around a closed, flat shape.

*The **perimeter** of this rectangle (from point A around to point A) is 32 inches.*

perpendicular lines   Lines that intersect and make square corners (right angles).

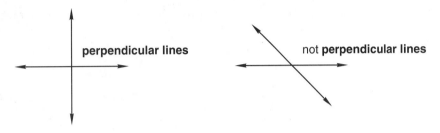

pictograph   A graph with pictures of things being counted.

*This is a **pictograph.** It shows how many stars each person saw.*

pie graph   *See* **circle graph.**

polygon   A flat, closed shape with straight sides.

probability   How likely it is that something will happen. (We will write probability as a fraction.)

*The **probability** of spinning C is $\frac{1}{4}$. There are four letters. You will spin one of them.*

product   The answer in a multiplication problem.

$5 \times 3 = 15$ *The **product** of 5 and 3 is 15.*

quadrilateral   A polygon with four sides.

quadrilaterals

radius   The distance from the center of a circle to a point on the circle.

*The **radius** of this circle is 1 centimeter.*

reduced fraction   An equivalent fraction written with a smaller numerator and denominator.

$\dfrac{10}{100} = \dfrac{1}{10}$ *The fraction $\dfrac{1}{10}$ is a **reduced fraction.***

regular polygon   A polygon with all sides the same length and all angles the same size.

regular polygons   not **regular polygons**

right angle   A square angle (corner).

right angle   not **right angles**

Roman numerals   Symbols used by the ancient Romans to write numbers.

*The **Roman numeral** for 3 is III.*

*The **Roman numeral** for 13 is XIII.*

scale   A type of number line used to measure things. Rulers, clocks, thermometers, and many other things have scales.

The distance between each mark on this ruler's scale is 1 centimeter.

segment   *See* **line segment.**

sequence   A list of numbers that follows a rule.

The numbers 5, 10, 15, 20, ... form a sequence. The rule is "count up by fives."

solid   *See* **geometric solid.**

square unit   A square with sides of designated length. Square units are used to measure area.

 The shaded part is 1 square unit. The area of the large rectangle is 8 square units.

sum   The answer in an addition problem.

   2 + 3 = 5   *The sum of 2 and 3 is 5.*

table   Information written in columns and rows.

Our Team's Grades

NAME	GRADE
Juan	98
Tim	72
Laura	85
Min	96

This table shows the grades of four students.

tally mark   A small mark used to help keep track of a count.

   卌   *I used tally marks to count cars. I counted five cars.*

triangle   A polygon with three sides and three angles.

triangles

whole numbers   All the numbers in this sequence: 0, 1, 2, 3, 4, 5, 6, 7, 8, 9, ... Whole numbers are the counting numbers and zero.

The number 35 is a whole number, but $35\frac{1}{2}$ and 3.2 are not.

Index

Abbreviations

U.S. CUSTOMARY		METRIC	
UNIT	ABBREVIATION	UNIT	ABBREVIATION
inch	in.	meter	m
foot	ft	centimeter	cm
yard	yd	millimeter	mm
mile	mi	kilometer	km
ounce	oz	gram	g
pound	lb	kilogram	kg
degree Fahrenheit	°F	degree Celsius	°C
pint	pt	liter	L
quart, gallon	qt, gal	milliliter	mL

OTHER ABBREVIATIONS	
square	sq.
square mile	sq. mi
square centimeter	sq. cm

Equivalence Table for Units

LENGTH	
U.S. CUSTOMARY	METRIC
12 in. = 1 ft	10 mm = 1 cm
3 ft = 1 yd	1000 mm = 1 m
5280 ft = 1 mi	100 cm = 1 m
1760 yd = 1 mi	1000 m = 1 km

WEIGHT	MASS
U.S. CUSTOMARY	METRIC
16 oz = 1 lb	1000 g = 1 kg
2000 lb = 1 ton	

LIQUID MEASURE	
U.S. CUSTOMARY	METRIC
16 oz = 1 pt	1000 mL = 1 L
2 pt = 1 qt	
4 qt = 1 gal	

Time

60 seconds	= 1 minute
60 minutes	= 1 hour
24 hours	= 1 day
7 days	= 1 week
365 days	= 1 common year
366 days	= 1 leap year
10 years	= 1 decade
100 years	= 1 century

Place Value Chart

hundred millions	ten millions	millions	,	hundred thousands	ten thousands	thousands	,	hundreds	tens	ones	.	tenths	hundredths	thousandths

Geometric Solids

SHAPE	NAME
	Cube
	Rectangular solid
	Pyramid
	Cylinder
	Sphere
	Cone

Common Polygons

SHAPE	NUMBER OF SIDES	NAME
	3	Triangle
	4	Quadrilateral
	5	Pentagon
	6	Hexagon
	8	Octagon

Measures of a Circle

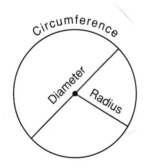

Roman Numerals

NUMERAL	VALUE
I	1
V	5
X	10
L	50
C	100
D	500
M	1000